JUDAH P. BENJAMIN

Photograph by U. S. Army Signal Corps

Judah P. Benjamin

CONFEDERATE STATESMAN

ROBERT DOUTHAT MEADE

WITH A NEW FOREWORD BY
WILLIAM C. DAVIS

LOUISIANA STATE UNIVERSITY PRESS
BATON ROUGE

Louisiana Paperback Edition, 2001
10 09 08 07 06 05 04 03 02 01
5 4 3 2 1

Library of Congress Cataloging-in-Publication Data

Meade, Robert Douthat, 1903–1974.
Judah P. Benjamin : Confederate statesman / Robert Douthat Meade ; with a new foreword by
William C. Davis
p. cm.
Originally published : New York : Oxford University Press, 1943.
Includes bibliographical references (p.) and index.
ISBN 0-8071-2744-2 (pbk. : alk. paper)
1. Benjamin, J. P. (Judah Philip), 1811–1884. 2. Statesmen—Confederate States of America—
Biography. 3. Jewish statesmen—Confederate States of America—Biography. 4. Confederate
States of America—History. 5. Legislators—United States—Biography. 6. United States.
Congress. Senate—Biography. 7. Lawyers—Southern States—Biography. 8. Lawyers—Great
Britain—Biography. I. Title.

E467.1.B4 M4 2001
973.7'13'092—dc21
[B]   2001038185

TO
LUCY BURWELL BOYD MEADE

Contents

Foreword by William C. Davis · xi

Preface · xv

I. EARLY INFLUENCES · 3

II. THE ABBREVIATED COLLEGE YEARS · 20

III. THE EARLY NEW ORLEANS YEARS · 31

IV. POLITICIAN AND SUGAR PLANTER · 46

V. MAN OF AFFAIRS · 64

VI. BENJAMIN REPRESENTS LOUISIANA IN THE SENATE · 86

VII. HIGH TIDE UNDER THE OLD GOVERNMENT · 107

VIII. SECESSION · 139

IX. CONFEDERATE ATTORNEY-GENERAL · 159

X. ACTING SECRETARY OF WAR · 179

XI. MOUNTING DIFFICULTIES · 208

XII. CENSURED BUT PROMOTED · 233

XIII. SECRETARY OF STATE · 244

XIV. SOUTHERN DIPLOMACY · 257

XV. LIFE IN RICHMOND · 272

XVI. THE LOST CAUSE · 288

XVII. ESCAPE FROM THE SOUTH · 311

XVIII. BRITISH BARRISTER · 326

XIX. A LEADER OF THE BRITISH BAR · 346

XX. FULL OF YEARS AND HONORS · 366

Notes · 381

Select Bibliography · 415

Index · 419

List of Illustrations

JUDAH P. BENJAMIN about 1860   *Frontispiece*

I. JUDAH, NATALIE, AND NINETTE BENJAMIN, probably about 1845   *facing* 57

II. SOME BENJAMIN HOMES   *facing* 191

     A. His probable home at 8 B and C Company Street, Christiansted, St. Croix

     B. 327 Bourbon Street, New Orleans (in center) where he lived about 1835-45

     C. Bellechasse, his plantation mansion near New Orleans

     D. The Decatur House on Lafayette Circle, his residence in 1860

     E. 9 Main Street, Richmond. His home as a Confederate cabinet minister

III. BENJAMIN AS A BRITISH BARRISTER   *facing* 332

Foreword

HE WAS CALLED MANY THINGS—wizard, sycophant, jack-of-all-trades, Shylock of the Confederacy, and a "jolly rotundity." But no one called Judah P. Benjamin dull. Of all of the statesmen of the Confederacy, and certainly among Jefferson Davis's cabinet members, he has always stood out in memory. In part it is because he held three different cabinet portfolios. In part it is because he was Davis's favorite and, some believed, a power behind the throne. In part it may be because Benjamin was an unusual thing in the Old South—a Sephardic Jew, though essentially nonpracticing. He has been described as "the brains of the Confederacy," though his actual contributions and influence diminish considerably on hard scrutiny. Davis saw him as his closest friend and confidant in the government, while others saw him merely as the president's lapdog. Davis never questioned his loyalty, though others would maintain that Benjamin's only true loyalty was to himself, and there was ample enough testimony that even with Davis his friendship was calculated. No wonder that more than 140 years after Benjamin first appeared on the Confederate scene, historians still debate his place in the history of the Lost Cause.

Even the raw outline of his life seems improbable. Born in unusual circumstances on Saint Croix in the Virgin Islands, a cloud over his education, he began his professional life as an impecunious lawyer and notary in New Orleans. Perhaps it was only in the wide open society of south Louisiana that a Jew could actually prosper in the Old South. Benjamin gradually acquired professional prestige and private fortune. Along the way he also acquired a wife who was nearly a child, then spent the rest of his life separated from her. Meanwhile he purchased a sugar plantation at Belle Chase and established himself in the lifestyle of the local grandees, then went into politics. By the 1850s he had won election to the United States Senate and had become one of the spokesmen for his state in the secession controversy. He also became acquainted with Senator Jefferson Davis of Mississippi, though unfortunately at first as the two nearly fought a duel. But then came disunion. Though not involved with the founding of the Confederacy itself, Benjamin's legal attainments were on Davis's mind as he assembled his first cabinet in February 1861, and he tapped Benjamin, now a friend, as his attorney general. As even Benjamin would attest, it was largely a meaningless position, especially in a new nation that intended to leave judicial matters to the states and would never even convene its mandated supreme court. As a result, Benjamin's duties consisted of such mundanities as adjudicating on the import duty for hoopskirts and oranges.

No wonder he spent much of his time in the early months at the more congenial pursuits of socializing. He could always be counted on for a smile and pleasant conversation, punctuated by puffs from an ever-present cigar, and the hint of a smile that seemingly never left his lips. But before long Davis would tap Benjamin to move to a vacancy in the office of secretary of war, and suddenly Benjamin found himself fully involved in the thick of the war itself, as well as in the growing controversies between Davis and his generals. Indeed, Benjamin would become such a magnet for discontent and criticism that Davis was all but forced to replace him in a few months, but rather than send the Louisianian back to his plantation, Davis—who by now had come to rely personally on Benjamin as confidant and advisor—simply handed him another portfolio as secretary of state. There Benjamin remained for the rest of the war, down to the moment the government evacuated Richmond and began its long and futile flight. It is most of all on his tenure in the foreign office that Benjamin's reputation rests, yet the story of Confederate diplomacy is one of consistent underachievement or failure.

In a fate somehow emblematic of a man who many thought obeyed no true loyalty but to himself, Benjamin, though regarded as the least likely to make good his escape, was in fact one of only two members of the Davis regime to elude capture. After a dramatic escape, he began a new life in England as a barrister, and eventually became a queen's counsel. He published important legal treatises and became a distinguished member of the British bar, but he never wrote a word, and spoke hardly more, about his Confederate career. The ultimate pragmatist, Benjamin seemed never to look back after the cause was lost. He stayed completely out of the feuds and controversies of the postwar years as Davis and his generals waged a battle of memoirs over who was responsible for Confederate defeat, and after 1868 there is scant evidence of Benjamin even communicating with his old Confederate comrades, Davis included. In his own massive two-volume history of the Confederacy, Davis himself scarcely mentioned his onetime right-hand man.

That disinclination to ruminate on the past did not make the task of would-be Benjamin biographers an easy one. They could have used a memoir, or even a few articles of recollections, but there are none. Benjamin actively contributed to the difficulty of fully appreciating and assessing his life when he burned much of the archives of his State Department at the fall of Richmond, and apparently either did not retain, or else destroyed, his own personal papers prior to his death. The result was that little seemed to be left behind. Nevertheless, he would be not only the first of Davis's cabinet secretaries to be the subject of a biography but for many years the only one. Pierce Butler's *Judah P. Benjamin* appeared in 1906 and had much to recommend it, most of all the papers Butler had obtained from Francis Lawley, the London *Times* war correspondent who had known Benjamin well in Richmond, and who himself earlier intended a biography but never completed the task. It provided a good outline of Benjamin's life, included some primary materials nowhere else available, and remained the standard life for the next thirty years.

Then in 1943 came *Judah P. Benjamin, Confederate Statesman*, by Robert Douthat Meade. This was altogether biography on a higher plain. Not only was it the best work yet—or ever—on Benjamin, but at the time it appeared it was arguably the finest biography yet done of any Confederate statesman. Even Jefferson Davis himself had not received anything like this kind of thorough treatment, and only Douglas Southall Freeman's 1934–36 four-volume *R. E. Lee* surpassed it in the field of Confederate biography, though Freeman had the advantage of voluminous surviving primary sources, and a subject so popular and revered that a mountain of personal reminiscences of him was left behind. Meade's own research was voluminous, adding substantially to the corpus of newly discovered Benjamin sources, and utilizing materials ranging from the Carribean to England.

The author was born Robert Douthat Meade in 1903, a native of Danville, Virginia, who would spend virtually all his life in the Old Dominion. He attended the Virginia Military Institute, then moved on to the University of Virginia for his master's degree before earning his doctorate at the University of Chicago. First joining the faculties of the University of Illinois, Vanderbilt, and then the University of North Carolina, he moved in 1936 to Randolph-Macon College, where he remained as head of the history department until his retirement in 1971. His biography of Benjamin was his first major publication, followed by a two-volume biography of Patrick Henry. He was an active member of the Southern Historical Association and a frequent contributor to scholarly journals and periodicals. Coincidentally, one of his last publications was a profile article on Benjamin that appeared in 1973, just months before his death on April 27, 1974.

Reviewers recognized the stature of *Judah P. Benjamin, Confederate Statesman* from the moment it first appeared, and historians have continued to regard it as the definitive work for almost sixty years despite the appearance of subsequent biographies that simply do not measure up. It won the Southern Author's Award for 1943, and thereafter its original publisher kept Meade's book in print for thirty years, through several printings, before finally letting it go out of print in the 1970s. Even the most recent works on Confederate politics, such as George Rable's *The Confederate Republic*, acknowledge the biography as the best available. Meade's judgments are thoughtful and well reasoned, balanced and mature. Certainly he finds his subject a valuable and influential member of the Confederate leadership, but his is not the Benjamin that more shallow chroniclers have unquestioningly accepted as the genius of the doomed nation. Benjamin was feared, hated, resented, and reviled for everything from his loyalty to Davis to his Judaism, and some offered cloaked suggestions that he was a homosexual, or at the least a failure as a man. Meade addresses much of this, and if he still finds Benjamin a greater influence in Confederate affairs than might some others, still his version of the Louisianian has warts that other biographers overlook.

With a growing interest in Confederate political history underway, it is fitting—indeed, essential—that *Judah P. Benjamin, Confederate Statesman* be once more available, and Louisiana State University Press has made a wise decision in putting one of the classics of Confederate biography back in print. Its subject may always be something of an enigma to us, even as he was to people of his own era, but his is an unfailingly interesting and arresting story against the backdrop of the Confederacy, as the debate continues on just which of the many masters he served held his true allegiance. Clement C. Clay of Alabama once referred to Jefferson Davis as the "Sphinx of the Confederacy," but the sobriquet was misapplied. Rather, it applied far more aptly to that perpetually half-smiling, unctuous, yet impenetrable "rotundity," who seemed ever at the periphery, and at the same time at the center, of the leadership of the Lost Cause.

William C. Davis

Preface

JUDAH P. BENJAMIN—one of the most secretive men who ever lived —did not decrease the troubles of a biographer. At times he seemed not to care what people thought about him; he would not even bother to defend himself from deliberate misrepresentation. Fortunately, when destroying some of his papers he could not reach those in other hands or remove what was on public record.

The most important source of unpublished Benjamin data is an obvious one: the United States and Confederate records now collected at the National Archives. Here are contained several thousand original or, usually, letter-book copies of Benjamin letters (some unpublished). Other important sources of unpublished Benjamin material are the Pickett Public and Private Papers at the Library of Congress (the latter containing a few valuable items which appear to have been in one of Benjamin's private trunks, lost at the end of the Civil War); the Pierce Butler Papers; and the Bradford family papers at Avery Island, Louisiana. The Butler Papers contain the manuscripts for the uncompleted Benjamin biography by Francis Lawley of London and considerable other material, some of which was not used in Professor Butler's valuable biography of Benjamin and was kindly contributed. The Benjamin letters at Avery Island were written to his former law partner, E. A. Bradford, and Mrs. Bradford, then living in Europe, and portray the close and devoted friendship of Benjamin to the Bradford family as well as other interesting phases of his life. These letters are the property of Mrs. Sidney Bradford of Avery Island, who has generously allowed me the privilege of copying the extracts. Mrs. Bradford retains the ownership of the letters and their rights in every respect.

The circularization of principal manuscript repositories in the United States, surviving relatives of Benjamin's contemporaries, and numerous other possible sources of information, also resulted in many small additions to the unpublished data. Altogether, the work required my available time for twelve years; several thousand original or letter-book copies of unpublished Benjamin letters were discovered as well as a large mass of material obtained from diaries, personal interviews, memoirs, contemporary publications, private and public records, as specifically mentioned in the Notes. A visit to every place importantly connected with Benjamin's life, whether in America, England, or France, gave an understanding of the milieu in which he lived as well as the more tangible evidence that served to re-create him as he moved in his stirring times.

In addition to the persons already mentioned, grateful acknowledgments are due to the Smith Fund of the University of North Carolina and the Rosenwald Foundation for research funds contributed, and to the following for data supplied or other valuable assistance:

Paxton Blair, Maxwell Aley, Henry S. Commager, and numerous members of the staff of the Oxford University Press, New York City; A. R. Newsome, Hugh Lefler, and J. G. de Roulhac Hamilton, Chapel Hill, N. C.; C. G. Rose and H. M. Pemberton, Fayetteville, N. C.; Andrew Howell, Wilmington, N. C.; C. C. Crittenden, Raleigh; Mrs. Judith Hyams Douglas, Archie M. Smith, Miss Mary Evelyn Kay, Edgar Grima, Miss Elsie Bing, R. J. Usher, and Edwin J. Putzell, Jr., New Orleans; Walter Prichard, Baton Rouge; and Frank Ellis, Covington, La.

Also, Edwin Embree, Avery Craven, Herbert Kellar and W. T. Hutchinson, Chicago; James G. Randall, Urbana, Ill.; the staffs of the National Archives and of the Manuscript Division, Library of Congress; Anson P. Stokes, David Cohn, Mrs. Wallace Neff, Senator Josiah W. Bailey, and Gen. T. J. J. Christian, in care of the War Department, all of Washington, D. C.; the staff of the Virginia State Library, Douglas Freeman, H. J. Eckenrode, the late Herbert Ezekiel and Edward N. Calisch, Richmond; F. D. G. Ribble, Charlottesville; Mrs. W. L. Heartwell, Jr., Norfolk; Mrs. William Prizer, Petersburg; Capt. Andrew J. Stewart, Fortress Monroe; Theodore Jack, Lynchburg; Mrs. Janie Hagan, and my mother, Mrs. E. B. Meade, Danville, Va.

Also, Lauriston Bullard and Raymond Wilkins, Boston; the late Barnett Elzas and J. H. Easterby, Charleston, S. C.; Miss Ann Pratt,

New Haven; Mrs. G. F. Trigg, Henderson, Ky.; Miss Anne Carroll, Morristown, Tenn.; A. J. Hanna, Winter Park, Fla.; Raymond Paty, Birmingham, Ala.; Peter A. Brannon, Montgomery, Ala.; Col. William Robinson, Augusta, Ga.; Mrs. N. L. Hilles, Wilmington, Del.; the Huntington Library, San Marino, Cal.; Duncan Campbell Lee, Philip Guedalla and the staff of Bevis Marks Synagogue, London; the Marquise de Courtivron and Pierre Caillé, Paris.

I also wish to express especial thanks to my wife for faithful and intelligent assistance over a long period, and to my brother, the late Julian R. Meade, for literary criticism of the earlier chapters and the inspiration of a high literary craftsmanship. It is regretted that space does not permit individual mention of hundreds of other persons who have contributed generously of their talents or historical material.

Thanks are also due the following for permission to use printed material: Mrs. Bettie V. Adams, Gurley, Ala., for Mrs. Virginia Clay-Clopton, *A Belle of the Fifties* (Doubleday, Doran & Company); G. P. Putnam's Sons for Benjamin speeches in their World Writers Series; Pierce Butler and the Macrae-Smith Company for Pierce Butler, *Judah P. Benjamin;* the Curtis Publishing Company for G. G. Vest, 'Judah P. Benjamin' in *Saturday Evening Post,* 3 October 1903; Charles Scribner's Sons for Hamilton Basso, *Beauregard, the Great Creole;* Harcourt, Brace and Company for Lloyd Lewis, *Sherman: Fighting Prophet;* Houghton Mifflin Company for John S. Wise, *The End of an Era;* and Harper and Brothers for C. C. Coffin, *Drum Beat of the Nation.*

R. D. M.

May 1943
Randolph-Macon Woman's College,
Lynchburg, Va.

JUDAH P. BENJAMIN

I. Early Influences

'A MASTER of law and the most accomplished statesman I have ever known.' This was the tribute Jefferson Davis paid Judah P. Benjamin some twenty years after the Civil War.[1] Davis had known Benjamin as a United States senator and a leader of the American bar; then, as the most influential member of the Confederate cabinet, his 'chief reliance . . . among men.' And later Davis felt that Benjamin's career in England 'confirmed' his opinion of him.[2]

For Benjamin's sun had not set at Appomattox. After his American life had crumbled beneath him, he had escaped to England where he rose to be a leader of the English bar. When he died in 1884 the London *Times* ran a two-column leader on 'one of the most remarkable of modern careers.' Benjamin's life, it declared, 'was as various as an Eastern tale, and he carved out for himself by his own unaided exertions not one, but three . . . histories of great and well-earned distinction.'[3]

* * *

An exotic and often mysterious figure in a Christian-Occidental milieu, Judah Philip Benjamin was of Spanish Jewish ancestry—of the same racial stock as Ibn Ezra, Baruch Spinoza, and Benjamin Disraeli.[4] The aristocrats of Jewry, the Sephardic Jews are today little known in the United States, to which they migrated chiefly in our early national period, in relatively small numbers; and their cultural traditions and contributions are little appreciated. But first settling on the Iberian peninsula during ancient times, the Sephardim were numbered for many centuries among its ablest and most energetic inhabitants. Under the flowering civilization of the Moorish caliphs and their earlier Christian successors, they enjoyed privileges

3

unknown to the less-favored Askenazic Jews of northern Europe. To a large extent they were the financial and commercial leaders, the scientists and teachers of Spain. As some intermarried with the native stock, distinguished Christian Spaniards had the blood of Abraham in their veins.[5]

But during the reign of Ferdinand of Aragon (he himself the great-grandson of the beautiful Jewess, Paloma of Toledo) [6] and Isabella of Castille, the infamous edict of expulsion was issued against the Jews. Several hundred thousand were forced to leave their native land, to become Christians, or to face torture and death. Among the thousands of intelligent and industrious Sephardim who fled to enrich the civilization of other countries were several ancestors of the Confederate statesman, both in the paternal and maternal lineage.

Of the earlier Benjamins little is known beyond the fact that they went from Spain to Holland and thence to the West Indies.[7] But the de Mendes or Mendes, Judah's maternal ancestors, are listed among thirty prominent Jewish families that escaped from Spain to Portugal under the leadership of an aged rabbi.[8] Doubtless impelled by the religious persecution that had long since spread into Portugal from Spain, Solomon de Mendes came to Holland and married Eva Levy, a Dutch Jewess of Askenazic ancestry.[9] A child of this union, Rebecca de Mendes, born about 1790 and, it seems, not long before her parents moved from Holland to England, was the mother of Judah Philip Benjamin.[10]

Whatever the facts of their earlier history, in oligarchic England of the eighteenth century Judah's ancestors were humble folk. 'Solomon de Mendes, Merchant' is listed in London directories for 1790-94. He lived at Goodman's Fields and at Bishopgate Within, a neighborhood in the old part of London where numerous Jews then lived and engaged in trade. Later he moved to Finsbury in the suburbs, where a more prosperous class of Jews resided.[11] When Solomon's daughter, Rebecca, was about eighteen years old, she was married to Philip Benjamin, a little dark-skinned man in his mid-twenties, born on the British island of Nevis.[12] Just how Philip met Rebecca is not clear, but there is a vague tradition that after their marriage they ran a small shop in one of the streets leading into Cheapside near Bow Church, where they sold dried fruit.[13]

A few records of Judah's mother's people were, before the Second World War, still preserved at historic Bevis Marks or Kaal Kadish Sh'ar Hashmayim, the Sephardic synagogue in the old Jewish quarter of London, along with the baptismal record of his distinguished English contemporary, Benjamin Disraeli.[14] Philip and Rebecca Benjamin were married about 1807, the time of the battles of Jena and Friedland, and of the Berlin and Milan decrees issued in the effort to crush British trade. Life was precarious enough for the Jews even in good times, and now with business disrupted it was a difficult period for the young couple to get started in life. They probably felt that they would find a better opportunity for trade in the New World. At any rate, by 1808 or soon thereafter, they were settled at Christiansted, on the island of Saint Croix in the Virgin Islands, a part of Philip's native West Indies.[15] Incidentally, they were still under the Union Jack, for the Danish islands had been seized the year before by the British, an episode in the wearisome Napoleonic wars.

The cosmopolitan spirit with which Judah Philip Benjamin was so early imbued came easily in the West Indies. In a day's sail among the close-lying islands, one might meet people of half a dozen races, representing a medley of colors, religions, and nationalities. At Nevis, a great cone rising out of the tropical sea, Philip Benjamin had been born about 1781, and it was from this place that he moved—probably after an interlude in London—to the larger and more thriving island of Saint Croix. There was then a little clan of the Benjamins living in the Virgin Islands. They and all the old Jewish families here were of Sephardic stock: their relatives, the Da Costas; the Sassos, de Castros, Benlissas, and Halmans; and all had come to the islands from Holland, whence they had fled from the Inquisition.[16]

At Saint Croix, the second largest of the Virgin Islands, there are two main towns, Fredricksted and Christiansted, known locally as West End and Bassin. In the early nineteenth century, Christiansted was a small port deriving its livelihood from the plantation and export trade. Large ships sailing from Saint Thomas or more distant ports had to anchor some distance offshore, and passengers were brought to the wharf in small boats. Landing, they saw the puncheons of sugar and rum piled up for shipment, the fort and the

more pretentious coral or sandstone residences perched on the hill-
sides sloping down to the water front, and perhaps some huts of
poor natives scattered among the palm trees. Of the larger houses a
number are still standing, picturesque, with brightly painted walls,
sidewalk arcades, and galleries from which one can catch the
breeze from the Caribbean and enjoy the leisurely tropical life.[17]

The surviving matriculs or lists of taxpayers for Saint Croix in
1810 mention P. Benjamin, his wife, daughter, and two slaves as
living at 28 Hospital Street, Christiansted. The daughter was Judah's
oldest sister, Rebecca. Two years later, in 1812, the matriculs list
Philip as living at 8 B and C Company Street with his family—two
boys, one girl and three 'Capable' slaves. One of these boys was
Judah's elder brother, Solomon. The other was Judah. He had been
born on 6 August 1811, and his birth is recorded as of this date or
the sixteenth of Ab, 5571 in the archives of the Hebrew congregation at the neighboring island of Saint Thomas.[18] The house in
which he is believed to have been born still stands on a hillside overlooking the waterfront—a two-story building with a flat roof and
wooden superstructure.[19] From it one can see across the out-lying
harbor and, on a clear day, even forty miles northward over the
blue Caribbean to Saint Thomas where Judah was soon taken en
route to the United States.[20]

* * *

Judah P. Benjamin was born during the period of Virgin Island
history which a Danish writer accurately terms *Urolige Aar*, or the
Troubled Years. The garrison of British Red Coats, which occupied
the islands in 1807, did not sail away until 1815—a long enough
period to affect Judah's life in two important ways. It brought hard
times to the islands, which must have influenced the decision of his
family to move to the United States; and it gave him an excuse—
a half century later—to claim British citizenship at a time when he
was in exile from the United States and wished to facilitate his admission to the British Bar.

The lot of the Benjamins was a hard one. Philip would never have
been a Rothschild under the best conditions, and at Saint Croix he
seems to have found it difficult to make a living for his growing

brood. When he chose the islands for his son's birthplace he had unconsciously placed him in illustrious company: Alexander Hamilton and the Empress Josephine were also born in the West Indies. But as the ambitious young Hamilton had so early realized, there was little opportunity there to become more than a rich planter or merchant. If Judah had remained in the Virgin Islands his name would be as obscure as that of many clever Sephardic Jews who have lived there since the days of the Conquistadors.

At Wilmington, North Carolina, Mrs. Benjamin had an uncle, Jacob Levy, established as a merchant in the town for several years. Probably from Uncle Jacob's letters, slowly forwarded by ships calling at the West Indian ports, Philip and Rebecca learned of the opportunity in Wilmington for members of their race. They decided to move to the Carolina port, where they could begin life in the new country under Jacob's protection, and about 1813 they sailed there from the Virgin Islands.[21]

In a contemporary Wilmington newspaper, a Jewish merchant of the town advertised a cargo of salt, sugar, coffee, castor oil, and similar commodities which had just arrived aboard the Haytian ship, *Saint Joseph*, Captain Pierret.[22] Ships like the *Saint Joseph* called at Saint Thomas for cargoes of sugar and rum, and for water and provisions, and also handled goods brought over in smaller boats from Saint Croix. A few poor passengers like the Benjamins might sometimes be accommodated; they could make the best of the available quarters. On such a vessel, smelling of its semi-tropical cargo and manned by sweating, roughly clad seamen, the future Confederate cabinet minister must have made his entrance into the United States.

In the little town near the mouth of the Cape Fear River, life for a family like the Benjamins was largely a matter of working at the store, waiting on customers, and attending to the demands of growing children. Philip probably worked for Jacob Levy at his Wilmington store, and Judah found some of his earliest incentives to a business career in Levy and Gomez's auction sales of 'Turks Island salt,' 'prime green coffee,' West Indian and New England rum, sugar, crockery, glassware, padlocks, 'Negro cloths,' 'callicoes,' and assorted articles.[23]

Wilmington was then a prosperous port and merchants came

from long distances to lay in their stocks of goods. Although Judah lived here only a few years, it was long enough for him to store up some of his earliest childhood memories. In later years, as a busy lawyer in New Orleans, he probably gave little thought to the town. But when he was Confederate Secretary of State and George Davis of Wilmington was Attorney-General—when Wilmington was the last remaining port on the Atlantic through which the blockade runners could enter the beleaguered Confederacy—his thoughts must have reverted to that childhood period. He perhaps recalled a few impressions of his home near the waterfront: Uncle Jacob's store; the boats moving up the Cape Fear from the near-by ocean; the foreign sailors, so fascinating to a small boy; the chattering slaves in their scanty cotton garments; the near-by rice plantations, and, beyond, the pine forests.

Among the Wilmington Negroes, the family slaves must have left the deepest impression upon him. There are no available records of slaves then owned by Judah's father, but Uncle Jacob owned the mulatto woman, Margaret, and her son Jacob, and in 1817 he bought for $600 a certain Negro boy named Isaac, 'about the age of Twenty-Six years.' [24] Margaret probably served at times as Judah's nurse, and Isaac must have been one of his earliest companions. A surviving record in the Wilmington Courthouse is of interest:

On March 28, 1817 Jacob Levy in pursuance of an order of the County Court and . . . in consideration of the Meritorious Services of a Certain mulattoe Woman Slave named Margaret Allan & her child named Jacob & in consideration of the Sum of one dollar to me in hand paid have manumitted, emancipated and set free the Said mulattoe woman slave . . . & her child named Jacob.[25]

When the Benjamins settled at Wilmington, scarcely a generation had elapsed since Cornwallis's surrender at Yorktown. Some of the men, now middle-aged, whom the small boy passed on the street had fought with Washington or Greene. But the war itself had now faded into the background. While Judah was a little boy in Wilmington, his elders were talking of Andrew Jackson and New Orleans, and of the Treaty of Ghent. In the *Cape Fear Recorder* [26] they were reading that the grass was growing over Marshal Ney's grave—a reminder of the end of the Napoleonic Wars—and that there were 'upwards of 79,000' signatures in Bolton, Chowbeat, Leigh, and neighboring English communities on a petition to his Royal Highness, George, Prince Regent, seeking relief from the new economic changes. The Industrial Revolution, which had already changed the whole civilization of England, was spreading across the Atlantic. The American nation, now freed from the burden of war, was ready to turn her face inward to meet her own rising problems of industrialism—and of expansion and conflict. Even the poor family of Philip Benjamin felt the impact of the new movements.

The fortunes of the Benjamins were now definitely linked with Uncle Jacob. After Jacob bought a tract of land in or near Fayetteville, North Carolina, in 1817, he and the Benjamins moved to this town, Jacob giving Philip employment.[27] Philip's sister, Mrs. Harriet Wright, also lived here at this time.[28]

Fayetteville was a small town about a hundred miles up the Cape Fear River from Wilmington, its few streets sprawling away from the river and intersecting Cross Creek. Situated near the head of navigation on the Cape Fear, the place was, even before the appearance of the steamboat, an important river port as well as a station for two stage lines. During this period before the coming of railroads, it had a large commerce with the western part of the state and the upper counties of South Carolina. Great wagons, drawn by two to six horses, brought produce to Fayetteville from as far as two hundred miles. At night Judah could see the campfires of the wagoners, could hear their songs, their grumbling, and their laughter as they waited for morning and the opening of market.[29]

Nearly a century before, the first Scotch emigrants in the community had moved up the Cape Fear from Wilmington and settled where the river was joined by Cross Creek. Then, after 'The Forty-Five' or last Jacobite uprising, hundreds of the persecuted Highland clansmen—Macdonalds, McLeods, McPhersons, and the rest—had left their native glens and settled in the region of the upper Cape Fear. Seventy-first Township near Fayetteville derived its name from the large number of veterans of the Seventy-First Highland regiment at the battle of Culloden who had settled in the Carolina community.[30] Judah heard the strange Celtic tongue spoken on the street by some of the Fayetteville people and by farmers who came to market from their homes in the surrounding hills. Report had it that Gaelic had even crept into the vocabularies of some of the slaves.[31]

During the next few years Uncle Jacob bought large real-estate holdings in Fayetteville and also became a prominent merchant and auctioneer.[32] Among numerous articles which he offered for sale in a newspaper advertisement of early 1819 [33] was 'an Elegant and Melodious Toned PIANOFORTE,' which prospective purchasers 'could see and try' by calling at Mr. Benjamin's. But the brief good fortune of their uncle while in Fayetteville extended only indirectly to the Benjamin family. The generous Jacob paid the fees of Judah, his sister Hannah, and his brother, Solomon, which made it possible for them to attend the Fayetteville Academy.[34] At home, however, they lived quite simply and appear to have been of little social consequence in the town. There is a local tradition that they lived over their store and got water from a spring across the street.[35]

Today there are few Jews in Fayetteville, and in the early nineteenth century there were almost none with whom Judah could associate. A story of this early period indicates that he was already being weaned from the faith of his fathers. The elder members of his family were orthodox Jews for whom hog meat was banned by Mosaic law. But Solomon could not resist the lure of the forbidden delicacy.

'Often . . . did I take from my mother's table slices of ham for him and Judah,' wrote a Gentile schoolmate, R. C. Belden.[36]

Thus passed the brief period in the little river town. The Carolina Scotchmen perhaps influenced Judah in the direction of conservatism and industry; certainly, they helped him to get a good scholastic education. For in Fayetteville the transplanted Highlanders preserved many of their original characteristics. Cautious, economical, industrious, religious, and 'not a little stubborn in their prejudices,' they chose plain comfort and the education of their children in preference to 'feverish striving after display.' [37] As early as 1796 they had founded the Fayetteville Academy, and by the time the Benjamins moved there it was one of the best in the South, with a reputation for good scholastic standards. The trustees advertised that the students would not only be prepared to enter the junior year at college but would also have 'vigilant attention' given to their morals and manners.[38] Walking over the bridge on Cross Creek, down Green Street past the former home of the romantic Flora Macdonald, and crossing a stile, little Judah would enter the grounds of the Academy.[39] He studied under the Reverend Colin McIver, a native Scotch Presbyterian of considerable local reputation, under whose guidance he made marked progress and displayed a seriousness and quickness of mind which set him apart from his schoolmates. Reserved in his manner, he had no intimate playmates at the Academy, and while the other boys were at play during recess he would make preparations for his coming lessons. He stood at the head of his class and was undoubtedly the cleverest boy in the Academy. R. C. Belden, his old schoolmate, said that he never knew Benjamin to make an imperfect recitation.[40]

Little else need be said of the North Carolina years. Although before Judah died his immediate family was to be scattered in several countries, they were all together at Fayetteville. Still fast increasing, the family included Philip and his wife, and the children Rebecca, Solomon, Judah, Hannah, Judith, and Jacob Levy. The last named was a baby, born in Fayetteville on March 20, 1818; the next year Jacob Levy deeded 'the Mustee Girl Slave, Maria, and her future increase' to his namesake in consideration of natural love and affection and $10 paid by Philip Benjamin.[41]

The business failure of Jacob Levy seems to have been chiefly the result of the deflation attendant upon the panic of 1819. His estates in Fayetteville were mortgaged and by 1822 he had returned to Wilmington.[42] The Benjamins also left Fayetteville, and next tried their luck in Charleston, South Carolina. When he was a member of the United States Senate, Benjamin often discussed with a congressman from the Fayetteville district his childhood years there,[43] but during the crowded life that followed he must have given little more thought to the town and its sober-sided Scotchmen.

* * *

By 1822 the Benjamins were settled in Charleston, South Carolina. The city directory for that year listed 'Philip Benjamin, dry goods store, 165 King,' and, in addition, Mrs. Rebecca Benjamin was mentioned in a local newspaper among those having letters remaining in the post-office on 1 May.[44] The exact dates should be noted, for it was during the following summer that the city experienced the nightmare of an attempted slave insurrection—in many respects the worst which ever took place in the United States. Occurring when Judah was nearly eleven years old, it must have left a deep impression upon him. There is every reason to believe that the instinctive revulsion developing from that summer of fearsome rumors, protracted criminal trials, and public hangings definitely influenced his political career.

In Fayetteville and, particularly, in Wilmington Judah had lived in communities where slavery was strongly entrenched. But in neither of these towns was there such a preponderance of blacks over whites as in Charleston and the surrounding parishes, and, therefore, were the potential results of a slave insurrection so dangerous. Many of the South Carolina Negroes were not long removed from the jungle—indeed a considerable number had been born in Africa. Though sturdy and long suffering, they were highly superstitious and had a primitive concept of the value of human life.

It was in such a fertile field that the free Negro, Denmark or Télémaque Vesey, planned his slave conspiracy, working out the details with great cunning and ingenuity over a period of several years. Plans which can be at least partly credited called for Charleston to be set afire, the white men murdered, the women raped or killed, the banks robbed, and perhaps ships in the harbor seized to take the insurrectionists to the independent Negro state of Santo Domingo. Every detail was worked out, even to whiskers and wigs to be used by the conspirators in approaching the guards of the arsenal. If the well-laid plans had succeeded, Judah, his parents, and, in fact, all the white people of the city would have been killed or forced to submit to worse horrors.

The Benjamins appear to have arrived in Charleston before June 1822, and the insurrection was not set to start until the next month. In late May and early June, however, some information about the plot was betrayed to the white people, and for the next two months the citizens of the city were kept in a state of tremendous excitement by the flying rumors, investigations, trials, and punishments.

Altogether, several hundred of the conspirators were brought to justice. The first court to try them was held about the middle of June and remained in session until 20 July, while another, meeting soon thereafter, did not adjourn until 8 August. The Negroes were given fair trials—that is, according to the standards of the day—and there were the inevitable penalties. On 2 July six Negroes were hanged; then two on 12 July; twenty-two on Friday, 26 July; four on 30 July; and another on 9 August.

On 2 July when Denmark Vesey and five associates were given public hangings 'immense crowds of whites and blacks were present,' one of Judah's contemporaries vividly recalled over eighty years later. On 26 July he saw distinctly from the third-story window of his father's house in upper King Street, not far from the scene, a long gallows erected on 'The Lines,' and twenty-two Negroes hanging on it at one time. 'I might say that the whole city turned out on this occasion, a sight calculated to strike terror into the heart of every slave.' Nor was their terror decreased by the provision in certain cases—'and their bodies to be delivered to the surgeons for dissection, if requested.'

It may be added that few if any of the whites present doubted the wisdom of the sentence or felt there was any other way to deal with the slaves.

Further evidence of the white point of view was found in the proceedings of the trials published later in the year by the city of Charleston. Denmark Vesey, the chief author of the bloody plot, was acknowledged to have superior qualities of courage and intelligence. But his passions were 'ungovernable and savage'; he showed toward 'his numerous wives and children . . . the haughty and capricious cruelty of an Eastern bashaw.' One of his ringleaders was Jack Pritchard. Known as 'Gullah' or 'Couter' Jack ['Couter' was the Negro dialect words for a crab claw, which he used as a charm], he had been 'born a conjurer' in Angola. 'All his country born promised to join him [in the uprising] because he was a Doctor,' a witness stated. 'His charms and amulets would protect them from all harm unless it came through treachery of their own color.'

At his trial Couter Jack's wildness and vehemence, the malignant glances he cast at the opposing witnesses, all 'indicated the savage who had been caught but not tamed.' And apparently he was not

even tamed by the dread words of the magistrate who imposed
sentence:

Your boasted charms have not preserved yourself and of course
could not protect others. 'Your altars and your gods have sunk together in the dust.' The airy spectres, conjured by you have been
chased away by the special light of Truth, and you stand exposed,
the miserable and deluded victim of offended Justice. Your days
are literally numbered. You will shortly be consigned to the cold
and silent grave, and all the Powers of Darkness cannot rescue you
from your approaching Fate! Let me then, conjure you to devote
the remnant of your miserable existence, in fleeing from the 'wrath
to come . . .'

To Judah this terrible plot came close to home. Some of the arms
which the slaves planned to seize were deposited at Wharton's on
King Street. Mauidore, who was hanged on the Lines in July, belonged to a member of the synagogue, and, indeed, since 6,000
Negroes in the Charleston district were said to have been 'cor-
rupted,' Judah doubtless knew a number of the Negroes involved
in the conspiracy.[45]

Of such stuff are conservatives made. Prince Metternich, when
a youth at Strasbourg, witnessed the excesses of a mob incited by
some events of the French Revolution, and what he saw influenced
his future political philosophy. So may Judah have been affected
by the Denmark Vesey plot and related events of his formative
American years.

Denmark Vesey's attempted uprising occurred only a few years
after the bitter debates over the Missouri Compromise. The small
but growing number of Abolitionists were agitating for the freedom of all the slaves. In reality, the Negroes recently smuggled in
from Africa were in a state little less civilized than those Anglo-
Saxon ancestors of the Charlestonians who over a thousand years
before had harried and killed on the shores of Briton. But Judah
could hardly have appreciated that fact. Nor was his conservative
point of view to be changed by later residence in Louisiana among
Negroes, some of whom were just as primitive as those in South
Carolina, or by his marriage to a Creole girl whose father had
escaped from the horrors of the slave uprising in Santo Domingo.

Such an overpowering event as the Denmark Vesey plot must be given its full place among the events of Judah's early life. But there was much else at Charleston to influence the impressionable lad. Although more fluid than it is sometimes depicted by historical writers, Charleston society retained an aristocratic basis. The city then offered a fairly good chance for a young white man to rise in accordance with his merits. James L. Petigru, a member of a rather obscure back-country family, who came to Charleston in 1819, had three years later been chosen attorney-general of the state, and Christopher G. Memminger, Judah's future associate in the Confederate cabinet, had landed in the city a fatherless immigrant boy and lived for several years in an orphan asylum.[46] And yet in many respects Charleston adhered to the old English ideas of an ordered society. 'The politics of the immortal Jefferson! Pish!' wrote Hugh Legaré, whose attitude typified that of many Charleston gentlemen of the ruling class.[47]

Precocious though he was, young Judah hardly perceived the incongruities in the Charleston social order. 'To be Hired,' he could read in the *Courier*[48] one day in March 1822, 'The half of one of the best PEWS in St. Philip's Church . . . Also a remarkable smart stout young FELLOW . . . sober and uncommonly well disposed. Also, a handy GIRL, about 16 years of age.' It would not have occurred to the owner of the pew that there was any inconsistency in church-going and slaveholding, any more than it did to William Hasell Gibbes when, in offering thirty dollars' reward for the return of his servant Daniel, 'a smart, active intelligent lad,' he said, 'no cause can be assigned for his departure.' As if the desire for freedom was not a cause![49]

Scattered items in the contemporary newspapers give glimpses of many other phases—some often overlooked—of this culture that Judah was absorbing: notices of plantations for sale; of arrivals and departures of schooners and packets; long lists of theological books for sale at the booksellers; mention of a few deaths from the 'country fever'; numerous advertisements of pills and patent medicines; notices of the annual Charleston races to be held the following February; extracts from Irving's *Bracebridge Hall* quoted from the *Edinburgh Review*; and an announcement that the St. Cecilia Society would hold a general meeting on 15 August 1822 at 2 o'clock 'to transact business before Dinner, which will be on table precisely at half past 3 o'clock.'[50]

In their effect on Judah's career, few of the newspaper items were more important than those advertising the sale of plantations. For Charleston was losing in the economic competition with the virgin lands in the Black Belt. The total dues collected in the port from 1819 to 1826 were only half the total from 1815 to 1818; by 1828 a committee of the Chamber of Commerce reported that grass was growing on some of the chief business streets. Much of the best blood in the state was being drained to the newer states, and a South Carolina governor who sought vainly to check the tide was to die while visiting in Mississippi.[51]

In the Charleston society with its amenities and complexities the Jews had a separate and well-defined place. Many of the old Hebrew families of the city had no desire to be admitted to the Gentile society and formed a proud and distinct class. But a poor family like the Benjamins lived obscurely; the contemporary records show that they shared only to a limited degree in the privileges secured by the local Jews. And they also reveal that there were now further influences to alienate Judah from the orthodoxy if not the very religious faith of his ancestors.

During the first part of the century, before Charleston had entered fully upon its period of decline, the city had the largest Hebrew population of any city in the United States. The Jews were represented in every branch of commerce, the arts, and the professions.[52] But Philip Benjamin would hardly have availed himself of such opportunities. He now appears to have been chiefly absorbed in the struggle to eke out a living for himself and family. In 1823 he did pay a relatively large assessment to the synagogue[53] and give $3,000 cash for the house and lot at 165 King Street.[54] Yet the demands of his large family, combined probably with his usual impecuniousness and the effects of declining trade in the city, proved too much for him. In 1827 he lost the King Street home at a sheriff's sale.[55]

Little more is known of Philip's career. It was not until 1826 that he took out his naturalization papers, and by so doing made his minor son an American citizen.[56] There is no truth in the assertion, widely circulated within the past few years,[57] that Judah became a

United States senator without being a citizen of the country. In his later years Philip was a small shopkeeper in Charleston;[58] he was a failure as a businessman. He did, however, serve as a member of the Corresponding Society of Israelites along with several leaders of the Charleston Jews, and he joined in the local movement for reform of the Jewish Church—the first effort of its kind in the United States. A failure at the time, this movement bore rich fruit in the history of what is now one of the important American religious sects.

In Charleston the Benjamins worshipped at Beth Elohim Synagogue on Hasell Street, a 'remarkably neat' little building, crowned by a cupola and with grounds surrounded by an iron railing. At the east end of the single large room was the ark, containing the writings of Moses; over the ark were the Ten Commandments, inscribed on two marble tablets; in the center was the reader's desk. With the separate gallery for women, the interior was much like that of Bevis Marks in London—as were also the ritual and *Ascamot* or by-laws. It was the harsh nature of the *Ascamot* that contributed so largely to the separation of Isaac Disraeli and, indirectly, therefore, his son Benjamin, from Bevis Marks, and it was this too that contributed to the rebellion of Philip Benjamin and later his son Judah, against Jewish orthodoxy in America.

Philip joined with the members of Beth Elohim who rebelled against this tyrannical and, in their opinion, out-moded rule, and organized a new church with fewer doctrines and a simpler, more comprehensible service, chiefly in English. The Reformed Society of Israelites flourished for a few years but was dissolved in 1833. There were numerous reasons for its failure but chief among them was the fact that the reform movement was somewhat ahead of the times.

Philip Benjamin had been expelled before the Society was disbanded,[59] but this was probably not because of any serious moral failing, as he and Rebecca were said to be honest and industrious.[60] Philip's business failures and the sacrifices they entailed upon his family made Judah appreciate the hardships of life without financial security. They must have partly accounted for the strong if not exaggerated emphasis which he later placed upon financial success. And from Philip also he may have inherited his short stature and some of his mental characteristics—to say nothing of the influence of his father's opposition to Jewish orthodoxy.

As for Judah's mother, Rebecca de Mendes Benjamin, she was a superior woman, possessed of her full share of pride. Many years later her granddaughter recalled 'the stern and severe rule of the old lady, resolved to hold her head high in spite of poverty.' In one instance her prosperous sisters in the West Indies, suspecting the condition of the family budget, sent 'generous gifts of linen and other luxuries.' But Mrs. Benjamin returned the chests unopened; she appreciated the presents but her wants were provided for. And yet she did not let her pride stand in the way of her children's education. It was owing to the 'less offensive kindness and assistance of friends and relatives nearer at hand' that her children obtained their education.

Like her husband, Rebecca did not set for Judah an example of adherence to orthodox tenets. She was reported to be a strict Jewess, but a little shop which she ran in Charleston was kept open on Saturday and this at a time when rigid observance of the Jewish Sabbath was customary in the city. Her trading on the Sabbath was much resented by the old-time Jews of Charleston. During her last years she was separated from her husband, and lived for some time at Beaufort, South Carolina.[61] An elderly resident of Fayetteville recalled that her mother-in-law had boarded with Mrs. Benjamin and had become quite devoted to her—a 'very lovely lady' with an 'admirable character.'[62]

There was also the matter of Judah's preparatory school education in Charleston. Although the Charleston gentlemen seemed to have a special fondness for a good drink or a horse race (stores, offices, and even schools were closed for the February races), many of them were well educated in the best classical tradition. Instinctively conservative, these gentlemen were hostile to mass education. William Gilmore Simms, another poor Charleston boy who won distinction, testified from his own experience to the 'worthless' public school system in Charleston during that period.[63] But the Charlestonians did support a number of academies which gave a good preparatory training of the conventional type admired in the city, and Judah was fortunate in attending at least one of these schools. Already 'bright and studious' and 'giving evidence of an extraordinary character,' he attracted the attention of Moses Lopez, the president of the local Hebrew Orphan Society, who found the means to place him in a private school, where he was given a thorough English and classical course and made remarkable progress.

The Hebrew Orphan Society is also said to have paid Judah's tuition at a private academy conducted by Rufus Southworth, in St. Michael's Alley, where he and Solomon were members of a large class of boys. According to one report, Judah quoted Shakespeare even while playing marbles with his schoolmates, but such a parade of learning was more easily forgiven in that classical age. He was well liked by his schoolmates.

In the brick school house near aristocratic St. Michael's and its graveyard, where, as the saying goes, it was better to be dead than alive anywhere else, he studied under Rufus Southworth—a Yankee. At this time Southworth was only about twenty-four years old. In a surviving oil portrait we see the face of a keen, interesting young man. After he died a few years later, his pupils erected a monument to his memory; he was evidently a good teacher and Judah must have benefited from his instruction.[64]

In 1825, when only fourteen years old, Judah finished his preparatory education and was sent to Yale. Except for a brief period, he never again lived in Charleston. Denmark Vesey had proved that life was not as calm there as it appeared on the surface. Nor was it in accord with the spirit of the new age of industrialism, liberalism, and democracy. And yet, Charleston was a delightful place. It produced a few Grimkés burning with the zeal to reform and uproot. But in Judah apparently, as in most of its citizens, it chiefly bred a desire to enjoy and to emulate the traits of the prevailing civilization.

II. *The Abbreviated College Years*

D URING the last quarter of the nineteenth century, after Benjamin had won distinction in both America and England, several old Charlestonians tried to recall some facts about his obscure boyhood years in their city. One of several points about which they were uncertain was the circumstances leading to his matriculation at Yale. There was a tradition in Charleston that Benjamin's college expenses were paid by Moses Lopez, a wealthy Jewish merchant of the city, but his classmate, Samuel Porter, stated that they were defrayed by a lady from Massachusetts. The truth appears to be that they were provided partly by this or similar means and partly by Philip Benjamin.[1] In any case, the amount provided was inadequate and this may help to explain another and more important problem connected with his Yale career—the cause of his sudden departure.

Why did the boy go to college at distant New Haven rather than to a Southern institution? Perhaps he was influenced by his teacher, young Rufus Southworth, and by the Massachusetts lady aforementioned, but there is a more obvious explanation. As early as 1788 Yale had been known in Charleston and the Southeast as the Athens of America. By the first quarter of the nineteenth century it was one of the favorite Northern colleges for Southern students; they comprised a fifth of the class of 1820 and a few years after Judah matriculated the percentage rose to twenty-nine, the highest ever attained. And of these a large proportion were Charlestonians or South Carolinians. During the quarter century after John C. Calhoun's graduation in 1802, New York, New Haven, and Hartford were the only cities with a larger representation at Yale than Charleston.[2]

Judah is said to have made the long trip under the charge of Dyer Ball, a student at the Yale Theological Seminary.[3] Little did he dream of the shadow that Ball would later cast across his path!

Before matriculating at Yale, he was required to pass the entrance examinations and he satisfied the college requirements in Cicero's *Select Orations*, Clark's *Introduction to the Making of Latin*, Virgil, Sallust, the Greek Testament, Dalzel's *Graeca Minora*, Adam's *Latin Grammar*, Latin Prosody, and Arithmetic.[4] In June 1825 he entered the freshman class.[5]

Judah first roomed at the home of Professor Porter, where he found two students from Baltimore and several from the North.[6] He had entered Yale when the college was in a period of transition. For the authorities were initiating a number of progressive changes in the curriculum and methods of teaching, as well as other innovations of more or less value. Begun during the presidency of Reverend Timothy Dwight, this policy was being continued by his successor, the Reverend Jeremiah Day. A visible sign of the new order was impressed upon Judah soon after his admission, when he was required to bedeck himself in one of the recently prescribed student uniforms—thin black frock coat, black or white pantaloons and vest, cravat in one of the same sober shades; while, at the beginning of cold weather, he changed to the winter uniform: blue frock coat with standing cape, made of broadcloth or cassimere, blue or black vest, and cravat.[7]

A little fellow, much smaller than many of his college mates, Judah was the youngest boy in his class.[8] He was only fourteen years old when he entered upon what was largely a period of self-education. Not that there was a lack of able professors at Yale; Benjamin Silliman, for example, was a distinguished scientist who had been called to a full professorship at the age of twenty-three. But the students had little contact with their professors until the senior year,[9] and Judah left college while a junior. Such personal instruction as was provided him came chiefly from his tutor, Simeon North, later president of Hamilton College.[10]

The curriculum emphasized the classics, and Judah showed this influence until the end of his life. During his freshman year he first studied Livy, Adam's *Roman Antiquities*, and English grammar, reviewed some arithmetic, and began Day's *Algebra*. Then, later in the year, he had Xenophon, Herodotus, Thucydides, Lysias, and Isocrates, Morse's *Geography*, finished Day's *Algebra*, and studied five books of Euclid.[11]

There was enough Puritan spirit left at Yale to require compulsory chapel every morning and evening. Since morning prayers a few years later were at six in the winter and five in the summer, Judah also must have adhered to this 'rigid and often frigid rule.' We can picture him as he rose before daybreak on a New Haven winter morning and, drowsy and shivering from the cold, hurried to get into the chapel by the last stroke of the bell.[12]

As a sophomore, Judah lived at Mrs. Mills's. He now studied Horace, the Greek orators, Xenophon's *Memorabilia*, Cicero, and mathematics in the form of Plane Trigonometry, Logarithms, Mensuration of Superficies and Solids, Isoperimetry, Mensuration of Heights and Distances, and Navigation. This was later followed by more Cicero, more mathematics, Surveying, Dutton's *Conic Sections*, Spherical Geometry and Trigonometry, and Jameison's *Rhetoric*.

He moved again in his junior year and is listed as living at 11 South Building. This year his course included Cicero, *Graeca Majora*, Philosophy and Astronomy, Tacitus, Hedge's *Logic*, Lytler's *History*, Vince's *Fluxions*, Hebrew, and French or Spanish at his option. He also had to exhibit daily a specimen of English composition, to attend experimental lectures in Natural Philosophy, and, since the college laid special emphasis on forensic exercises for the juniors and seniors, to debate once or twice a week before his instructors and to obtain frequent practice in declamation before the professor of oratory, the faculty, and students in chapel.[13]

Even as a junior Judah was younger than the average college freshman of today. Yet his entire record at Yale compared favorably with that of almost any of his college mates. The Book of Averages for the period he was at Yale shows that he received the grade of 3.3 in May 1826; 3 in May 1827; and 3.3 in September 1827. The maximum grade was 4, and 2 was the lowest average a student could receive and graduate. His tutor, Simeon North, said that Judah stood at the head of his class. After he left college, North took charge of his furniture and other possessions, including a Hebrew Psalter and a Berkleian prizebook inscribed by President Day for excellence in scholarship.[14]

But Judah was no intellectual snob and was popular with his college mates. He entered heartily into the student escapades, and

North admitted to having closed his eyes to many of Judah's college pranks because of his brilliant scholarship and attractive manner.[15]

Whether Judah was a leader in any of the serious riots during that period at Yale is not certain. But among the lighter diversions which he probably enjoyed were breaking or purloining dishes in the dining hall (30 coffee pots and 600 tumblers were destroyed or carried away during a single term at Yale), and 'bleating and blattering' his weariness of ill-fed and poorly dressed lamb.[16]

And then there were the pranks connected with the final disposal of Euclid. After the students had completely mastered this text—'the terror of the dilatory and inapt'—they would have an elaborate celebration, which might take any of several forms. In one the boys first drove a red-hot poker through the obnoxious volume. Then, marshalled in line, they would 'see through' the book, 'understand it' as it was passed over their heads, and, having marched over it in solemn procession, truthfully assert that they 'had gone over it.' In other ceremonies Euclid was buried with a formal ceremony, celebrated by verse or prose, or was cremated, using a 'ponderous' jar of whiskey or turpentine as the fragrant incense.[17]

Although the surviving Puritanism at Yale had no great influence on Judah, he did join a temperance organization, the Philencratian Society. The preamble of its constitution called attention to the 'alarming extent' of intemperance in the United States and to its 'peculiarly ruinous and disgraceful effect in an institution like' Yale. Judah agreed not to drink to intoxication while a student in college and residing in New Haven, and not to use or influence others to use any kind of spirits in his room. He also undertook 'by all honorable means' to 'discountenance intemperance' in non-members of the Society.[18]

Aside from his academic training, probably no experience at Yale was more valuable to Judah than the debating and public speaking. A member of one of the student debating societies, the Brothers in Unity, on 7 June 1826 he was a disputant on the subject: 'Was the confinement of Bounparte [sic] on the island of St. Helena justifiable?'; and, two months later, he argued the question, 'Are the abilities of the sexes equal?' Of the latter meeting the minutes state that the discussion 'was taken up quite generally by the Soc., but became rather desultory toward the close. The students of 1826 proved themselves more gallant than those of 1818 . . . and coincided with the Vice-President in an affirmative decision.' On 22 February 1827 Benjamin received an honorable dismissal from the Brothers and recommendation to the Calliopean Society.[19]

When Judah entered Yale it was only a few years since the bitter debates over the Missouri Compromise. In 1819, the year they began, some Southern members of the Linonian Society had taken offense at the election of a Northern man as their president and organized the Calliopeans. And now about half of its members were from the South. They formed, with the other Southern students, 'a sort of class by themselves,' and had their own library and place of meeting. Judah was now associated on relatively equal terms with the scions of some aristocratic Southern families—Frederick Porcher, Nicholas Rutledge, John Lanneau, and Theodore Dubose, all of South Carolina; Archibald Henderson of North Carolina, and Benjamin F. Dabney of Virginia.

Musty minute books of the Calliopean Society show that in April 1827 Judah debated the proposition, 'Ought the United States to take possession of Cuba, if the British Government makes an attempt upon it?' and that a few months later he argued the question, 'Has the wealth accruing to Spain from her possessions in South America been beneficial to the Mother Country?'

It was also while he was a Calliopean that the Society defeated a motion to appoint a committee to confer with the committee of the Linonians and Brothers in Unity in regard to a communication from Transylvania College in Kentucky seeking assistance in the 'manumission of slaves.' Evidently the sectional beliefs which he and so many of the other Calliopeans had brought from their Southern homes were not easily upset by such missionary efforts.[20]

* * *

In the early part of his junior year Judah abruptly left Yale. Over thirty years later, after Louisiana had seceded from the Union, the story was circulated in several Northern newspapers that he had left college after being detected in thievery. Resented at that time as an alleged Northern fabrication, the facts of the episode have had a contemporary revival and aroused further doubts and suspicions.[21]

Although evidence regarding the alleged incident is derived from several sources, the chief accusations are contained in two letters, one addressed to the *New Haven Journal* and another to the *New York Independent*,[22] both in early 1861. The letter to the *Journal*, which was signed 'Veritas' and reinforced by a confirmatory statement from the editor, accused Benjamin on the authority of the Reverend Dyer Ball, who was his 'private' teacher, of stealing from his classmates while at Yale—stealing so that it seemed 'almost impossible to break him of it.' The letter to the *Independent*, written by D. Francis Bacon, added that after Benjamin's college mates had missed watches, pins, knives, and other articles, including even 'sundry sums of money,' they had set a trap and caught Benjamin. 'He begged pitifully not to be exposed' and they relented to the extent of letting him leave college, which he did with a certificate of honorable dismissal from President Day, who was not then informed of the episode.

Since the charge was published in the bitter days of early 1861, it might well be considered as unfounded Northern propaganda, the more so since the *Independent* was then an Abolitionist journal and a mouthpiece of Henry Ward Beecher, and D. Francis Bacon was an Abolitionist and a former missionary to Liberia.[23] Indeed, the *New Orleans Delta* asserted that 'the story was hatched by abolition malice, and the place and time of the incidents were selected with cunning regard to the difficulty of refutation.' [24] But, unhappily, the charge cannot be disposed of so easily. For even if 'Veritas' and Bacon were the same person, and his testimony was unreliable, there is the statement of the editor of the *Journal* and other evidence that must be considered in detail.

After learning of the attack upon his character, Benjamin employed two well-known Northern attorneys, Charles J. O'Connor and S. L. M. Barlow, as counsel to prosecute the parties responsible for the 'libel.' He said that he planned to bring suit, but the lawyers dissuaded him. The advice which he declared they gave him, and his final action are explained in two letters which he wrote his friends, James A. and Thomas Bayard.[25] The first, to James A. Bayard, is dated from the Confederate Department of Justice at Montgomery on 19 March 1861:

... I preferred a suit to an indictment for several reasons, principally because it gave the man a better chance to exhaust all possible means of proving the truth, and thereby render it out of his power to say that if he could take testimony under commission, he would have succeeded in establishing a justification of his infamous calumny. But O'Connor, instead of bringing suit, writes a letter to Barlow, of which I enclose a copy, the tone and temper of which are so manly and generous, and at the same time so apparently discreet and wise, that he has almost unsettled me. I shall advise with my friends about it in N. O. . . .

I am decided in one conviction; that it is not advisable to have any publication in any manner or form on the subject, whether from myself or friends. I feel fully your kind offer to make a communication to the editor of the Confederacy but of what use, with such infamous scoundrels as those who have evidently delighted in circulating this attack, would it be to establish the absolute impossibility by a comparison of dates? I left college in the fall of 1827, in consequence of my father's reverses rendering him unable to maintain me there any longer. I was studying law in N. Orleans in February 1828, and maintaining myself whilst so doing, by giving private instruction in two families in New Orleans. The statement in the libel is that the facts occurred in the *fall* of 1828, with one Dyer Ball, whose name I never heard before in my life. Suppose all this shown in a publication of the most conclusive proof. The next week the same men come out and say they were mistaken in the *year;* that it was not in 1828 but in 1827—and the whole affair again goes the round of all the newspapers at the North, with the most malignant comments that can be invented. If I get friends that were College mates to state that no such things ever occurred, the answer will be that only a few were engaged in the scheme for exposure of the culprit, and that they promised secrecy as is asserted in the libelous article itself. I am satisfied that *nothing* is advisable, unless it be a suit that will sift the whole story, so as to make it *impossible* to evade the result or verdict by cutting off all equivocations. Yet O'Connor who agrees that this is the only mode, advises so strongly against it, that I must mistrust my own judgment . . .

The second letter, to T. F. Bayard, is dated 5 April 1861:

I have your kind favor of the 30th ulto. and am exceedingly touched by the warm and genial sympathy which it expresses. When I look back a few weeks I am myself somewhat shamed that I would have allowed myself to be moved so deeply by such a cause, and yet there was something so inexpressibly loathsome and revolting at the bare idea of having one's name published in the newspapers in connection with so degrading a charge, that it is scarcely to be wondered at, that feeling would usurp the place of judgment. However I have determined to yield to the advice of my friends, and to let a life-long career of integrity and honor make silent and contemptuous answer to such an attack. If anything could compensate for the mortification necessary incident to such an abominable outrage, it is the constant receipt from valued friends of just such letters as that which I have been gratified in receiving from you. I however needed nothing from you nor from any one bearing your name to feel assured in advance of the light in which such a publication could be received.

Judah does not appear to have told the literal truth in his letter to James A. Bayard. He referred to the Reverend Dyer Ball, his alleged private teacher, as a person 'whose name I never heard before in my life.' But Dyer Ball was the Yale theological student whom Benjamin's classmate, the Reverend Samuel Porter, recalled as having conducted him from Charleston to New Haven. And the Yale catalogue shows that Ball roomed that year at Mrs. Mills's, near Judah's room in South Building. It seems highly improbable that Judah could have forgotten him, even if he was not his private tutor.

On the other hand, Judah is correct in stating that the alleged thievery could not have occurred in 1828. But in asserting that if he called attention to this error his detractors would declare that the correct date was 1827, he may have been anticipating what he knew was the proper correction.

Another fact which should be considered is that Judah decided not to press the suit. The reasons he gives for doing so are plausible, though not absolutely convincing. But only a few weeks after the accusations were made, the Southern Confederacy was formed, with Benjamin as a cabinet member; and within another two months Fort Sumter was fired upon. A libel suit at that period would have been entirely impractical.

While investigating the case in 1901, Francis Lawley got in touch with Reverend Porter, the only surviving member of Yale 1829. Porter wrote that not long after Judah entered college

he fell into association with a set of disorderly fellows who were addicted to card playing and gambling, and his abrupt withdrawal from college was understood to be occasioned by difficulties growing out of this practice . . . During the short time of his residence at Yale College his brilliant and attractive qualities showed themselves both in the classroom and elsewhere, and helped to create the temptation which he had not the moral force to resist.[26]

Porter's evidence is certainly not creditable to Judah. And he left college owing the Treasurer $64.34, which was later charged off as a bad debt.[27] On the other hand, since the facts of the alleged thievery were said to have been known to only a few people, Porter may have referred to some other incident.

There is still more evidence to be considered. In one of the contemporary minute books of the Calliopeans is this entry for a meeting in December 1827:

The society proceeded to investigate the charge of ungentlemanly conduct etc., brought against Mr. Benjamin, which terminated in a motion that he should be expelled, which passed. It was requested that the charge against Mr. Benjamin be kept secret.

After Benjamin's name in the Register of the Society is written 'expelled.' [28]

The words 'ungentlemanly conduct' were then sometimes used for offenses that would be condoned today. But the *etc.* mark after 'conduct' is somewhat suspicious, as—more important—is the fact that the Calliopeans agreed to keep the accusation secret. This would be in accord with the agreement for secrecy mentioned in the newspaper articles.

After leaving Yale Judah stopped in New York State; probably he did not wish to face his parents. In a letter from Canandaigua, New York, of 15 November 1827,[29] he wrote Samuel Stone, a travelling companion since leaving New Haven, that on the journey between Syracuse and Auburn he had lost his pocketbook. 'Being thus left,' as he said, 'without resource in a strange land' and having only a small sum of money that had been lent him, he was in a serious predicament—the more so since he went to Rochester, where he contracted more debts which he was unable to pay. He besought Stone, therefore, to procure for him 'some respectable employment' so that he 'could avoid a dependance on strangers.' His classmates at Yale, however, sent a representative to Rochester to 'induce him to go to Charleston,' and he then proceeded to his home.

The facts of the Rochester interlude are given in a letter written by Simeon North in January 1828, in which he also stated that Judah's parents had been unable to deposit money with him to defray their son's college expenses. This somewhat contradicts Judah's assertion in 1861 that he had left college because his father could no longer support him there. More to his credit was North's further statement that his departure from Yale was 'without the knowledge or the permission of his friends and instructors.' This may seem to indicate that Judah had not been guilty of thievery, but these Yale associates may not have known the real facts in the case. There is also North's comment that Judah left college 'in a manner which justly exposed him to sensure' [sic].[30]

From New York State Judah returned to what must have been a distressing meeting with his parents in Charleston. Here on 14 January 1828 he wrote the following letter [31] to President Day:

Rev. Jeremiah Day:
Highly Respected Sir:

It is with shame and diffidence that I now address you to solicit your forgiveness and interference with the Faculty in my behalf. And I beseech you, Sir, not to attribute my improper conduct to any design or intentional violation of the laws of college, nor to suppose that I would be guilty of any premeditated disrespect to yourself or any member of the Faculty. And I think, Sir, you will not consider it improper for me to express my hopes, that my previous conduct in college was such as will not render it too presumptious in me to hope that it will make a favorable impression upon yourself and the Faculty.

Allow me, Sir, here to express my gratitude to the Faculty for their kind indulgence to my father in regard to pecuniary affairs; and also to yourself and every individual member of the Faculty for their attention and paternal care of me, during the time I had the honor to be a member of the institution.

With hopes of yet completing my education under your auspices, I remain, Sir, your most respectful and obedient Servant,

J. P. BENJAMIN.

P.S.

May I solicit, Sir, (if not too troublesome to you,) the favor of a few lines in answer to this letter, that I may be able to judge of the possibility of my return to the University?

J. P. BENJAMIN.

A week before the date of this letter, John D. Boardman, Judah's roommate, sent the faculty an apology 'for whatever was done by me, contrary to their Laws or wishes, in the late affairs.' This may indicate that Boardman was implicated in student disorders that occurred shortly before; [32] Judah, who was a prominent student, may have left college because of his participation in them. There is nothing in the Yale records, however, to indicate that he was forced out of college by the authorities, and it seems most unlikely that the students would have asked him to leave because of his participation in their own pranks.

Another possible explanation of the Charleston letter is that Judah wrote President Day at the insistence of his father, to whom he had given a false account of his reason for leaving college. Furthermore, he appears to have set out for New Orleans to make his fortune before he had any reply from Day.

Altogether the unpleasant evidence against Judah is too strong not to be considered; at Yale there was a lingering tradition that he was guilty of the offense charged. [33] Those who feel constrained to adhere to this belief should remember that he was only sixteen years old when he left New Haven.

III. *The Early New Orleans Years*

BENJAMIN had been in Charleston only a few weeks when he set out for New Orleans to make his fortune. After his unfortunate experience at New Haven, he probably wanted to settle in a city where the Yale influence was not so strong as in Charleston. But he may also have been persuaded to make the venture by Henry M. Hyams, his older cousin and the future lieutenant-governor of Louisiana, who accompanied him on the journey.[1] Not that any arguments should have been needed to convince him of the opportunities for a youth in the thriving Mississippi River port. For although Charleston was not the 'place of tombs' that it was labelled by the father of William Gilmore Simms,[2] Judah was quitting a declining seaboard city with a somewhat stratified society for a great river port in a period of fluid development. In New Orleans a man with brains and ambition could make his mark.

When Benjamin arrived at New Orleans in 1828 the city was in a period of transition. Only a quarter of a century had passed since the Louisiana Purchase, and many of the natives had been born under a foreign flag. But during the past fifteen years New Orleans had enjoyed remarkable progress. In 1812 the first steamboat had come down the river; in 1815 Creole and American had fought side by side against the British on Chalmette battlefield, weakening their traditional enmity. And the previous year the Treaty of Ghent had been signed, releasing a vast amount of commercial energy. Now there were scores of steamboats loading and unloading at the wharves, besides swarms of flatboats and other river craft.

On 26 January 1828, for example, the bilingual New Orleans *Argus* advertised the sailing date of the *Jeane* [Jeune] *Pierre*, a 'French ship . . . having all her cargo engaged' (*Le Navire français . . . ayant toute sa cargaison engagée*), and eight other boats for Havre, eighteen for New York, six for Liverpool, seven for

Boston, and five for Havana. Nor was this to mention the brigs from St. Thomas or the Balize, the steamboats from Cincinnati and Louisville, or loading for Port Gibson, Bayou Sarah, and more distant points.[3] Trade was to provide the backbone for Benjamin's career in New Orleans—trade based on the great river, on land and slaves, cotton and sugar.

The little town laid out a hundred years before by Bienville was now the gateway to the Mississippi Valley and one of the busiest ports in the world. The planters opening up the new black lands of the Southwest were dependent upon New Orleans for a market. The Middlewest was still sending much of its produce down the river to the city, while there was also a large commerce with Europe and the eastern seaboard and a growing sale of goods to Mexico. From every American state and many foreign countries, immigrants like Benjamin swarmed to share in the golden prosperity. New Orleans, a French colonial town of less than 8,000 population at the time of the American occupation, had jumped to nearly 50,000 in 1830, and would pass 100,000 in 1840. It would double in a decade! [4]

There was then no railroad connection from Charleston to New Orleans, and Judah probably sailed on one of the brigs or schooners that plied regularly between the two ports. Approaching New Orleans, he observed that the countryside had many similarities to eastern Carolina: balmy climate, the endless swamps interspersed with straggling settlements, the cypress and live oak dripping with Spanish moss. But New Orleans itself was very different from any place he had ever known—it was not only larger and more cosmopolitan, but more light-hearted and irresponsible.

Here was a proud and charming society, chiefly old Creole families but gradually taking in some of the newer, pushing American element. But more evident now to a stranger like Judah was the gayer and more licentious side of New Orleans. In the 'City of Sin,' dens for gambling and prostitution abounded and did a roaring business. On Sundays guitars were played in the streets, and shops and theaters were open. The streets were thronged with slaves in bright costumes, debonair Creoles, foreign sailors, and American flatboatmen with their great appetite for rum, women, and brawls. No one seemed to have a care in the world.

The tradition is that when Judah came to New Orleans he had less than five dollars in his pocket.[5] Poor as he was, almost any kind of work was welcome, and he was glad to obtain employment in a mercantile house. Although he worked there only a short time, he told a friend that the experience was of the greatest value to him after he was called to the bar. He then secured a position with Greenbury R. Stringer, a local notary who had a large business and was highly respected; while working for Stringer, Judah greatly increased his small circle of acquaintances. He also found time to do private tutoring, in some cases receiving fees, in others availing himself of the opportunity to teach English and learn French.[6]

Within a few weeks after he came to New Orleans, Judah began to study law in his spare time.[7] This was necessarily a slow process but was made somewhat easier by the knowledge of legal forms and procedure which he gained in Stringer's office. Judah worked hard and fortune smiled upon him, for he not only found business opportunity but escaped death in the terrible yellow fever epidemics of the next few years.

Every year the mosquitoes rose from the stagnant swamps and pools in or near New Orleans to spread death in a loathsome and agonizing form. One of the worst of the epidemics was in '32, the year of Judah's admission to the bar. The usual yellow fever period was soon followed by a wave of Asiatic cholera. The mortality was as high as five hundred or more persons a day, and within twelve days a sixth of the population was dead and buried.

At one cemetery a minister found over a hundred bodies 'without coffins, brought during the night and piled up like cord wood.'[8] Later Judah said that the city was like 'one great charnel house' during the epidemic periods.[9] With such shadows hanging over them, no wonder New Orleanians seemed to live for the day.

Judah was fortunate in being inured to the Southern climate, for the death rate was particularly heavy among the newly arrived Irish, Germans, and Americans.[10] In December of that terrible epidemic year he was admitted to the bar, and two months later he was married.[11] His legal study and, apparently, his courtship were pursued despite the death and desolation.

Judah's consuming ambition spurred him to work after business hours. It also helped him to resist the temptations always present in

New Orleans to lure a young man. He was strong-minded enough to live moderately, and did not lose his incentive to succeed.

When Judah was about twenty years old he was employed to give English lessons to a young French girl, the daughter of Auguste St. Martin, an official of a local insurance company.[12] St. Martin, whose full name was Auguste Barthelmy St. Martin de la Caze, had been a French settler in Santo Domingo. Fleeing from that island during the slave insurrection of the seventeen-nineties, he had lived for a number of years in Charleston, where he helped to found the Societé Française de Bienfaisance, for the relief of destitute French refugees from the island. Later he moved to New Orleans.

Madame Françoise Peire St. Martin also was a Creole. Little else is known of her, however, beyond the fact that before her marriage she had once been the innocent cause of a bloody duel. Only 'rather pretty' and with a *nez retroussée,* she had become engaged to an army officer, Captain Izard, who proved reluctant to marry, thus provoking a challenge from her vengeful brother. After the duel, the captain 'was relieved from all further engagement of marriage in that quarter,' and Mademoiselle Peire later became the wife of Auguste St. Martin.[13]

Marie Augustine Natalie, their eldest child, was born in Charleston shortly before the St. Martins moved to New Orleans.[14] When she met Judah she was about sixteen years old and a belle of the Creole type, with dark hair and eyes and 'the voice of a prima donna.'[15] In February 1833, only two months after Benjamin had been admitted to the bar, the couple were married. He was only twenty-one, she five years younger.

Still on record at the New Orleans Courthouse in the heart of the Vieux Carré is a copy of the marriage contract made on 12 February 1833 between Judah Philip Benjamin and Natalie St. Martin, 'fille mineure et légitime de M[r]. Auguste S[t]. Martin, et de Françoise Peire, tous les deux assistant et autorisant leur fille.' Natalie's *dot* is listed: the mulatto girl Mary, about sixteen years old, 'Estimée dix Cents piastres'; the mulatto girl Martha, about twelve years old, 'Estimée quatre Cents piastres'; and three thousand piastres in money. Although the marriage was a love match, this dowry was not to be scorned by a fledgling lawyer.

When Judah was courting Natalie, the St. Martins lived at what was then 123 Condé [Chartres] Street, and the young couple remained here with them for the first three years of their marriage. Indeed, they probably spent their honeymoon in her parents' home, for wedding trips were not yet customary in New Orleans. Still standing today, the St. Martin house was then a one-story building with an attic and separate kitchen and slave quarters.[16]

In 1833 St. Martin moved to another house at 85 (now 327) Bourbon Street, in the French Quarter, and Judah and Natalie continued to live with her parents. This residence, locally known as the Judah P. Benjamin House, is also still standing: a three-story mansion marked by the attractive bow-and-arrow design decorating the cast iron of the second floor balcony, on which the gay Natalie must so often have stood, chatting with her friends or waving to Judah as he came home late from his law office.[17]

Friction between Judah and Natalie probably developed quickly, for they were fundamentally uncongenial. He was well educated and had intellectual interests. Although he became something of a bon-vivant and dearly loved to relax over a good dinner with wine and cigars, his tastes were on the whole relatively simple. Above all, he wanted a real home and a family. Natalie, on the other hand, was selfish and shallow. She had little education: Mrs. Jefferson Davis, who was to know her well, spoke of her 'unassisted human nature.' She was extravagant and Benjamin's hard-earned money slipped easily through her fingers; she cared 'far more for brilliant society than for domesticity.' We have a surviving fragment from one of Natalie's letters, written after Judah had urged her to be more careful of her expenditures. 'Oh, talk not to me of economy! It is so fatiguing,' she replied.[18]

There were also other matters. Natalie was a devout Catholic; Judah a Jew. Although his ancestral religion had no strong hold upon him, he had no intention of embracing another faith. Children might have helped to strengthen the bonds between them, but their only child to live beyond infancy was born ten years after their marriage. Natalie was then in Paris,[19] and Judah saw little of his daughter except on his visits to France.

Although there were said to be faults on both sides, we can only conjecture the extent of Judah's responsibility. Unlike Abraham

Lincoln, he does not seem to have been deficient in the little things that make up a woman's happiness. We have reliable testimony that Judah 'knew how, even when preoccupied with affairs in the great world, to give himself up to the little loving services that count so much in the daily lives of the family.' [20] Certainly this was true of him in his relations with his mother and sisters. And what is more remarkable, there is no evidence of any discord between him and his wife's family. Judah and Natalie lived for some ten years either with the St. Martins or in an adjoining house.[21] When she left him to reside in Paris he remained with her parents for several years, and was their agent in the sale of their New Orleans house after they also moved to France.[22]

Judah's fault, if fault it be, probably lay in another direction. After the arduous labor of his growing legal practice—'he worked as few men have before or since'—he must have sought quiet evenings at home and been loath to attend the endless balls and parties of the Vieux Carré, which were so dear to his pleasure-loving wife.

In any case, it would seem he was far less responsible than Natalie for the failure of their marriage. And he bore his cross with courage. He tried to hide his domestic troubles even from his family and intimate friends.[23]

*   *   *

If he was disillusioned in his hopes for domestic happiness, Benjamin could find consolation in his increasing success as a lawyer. He had been admitted to the bar in December 1832. Only three months later, in March 1833, he carried an appeal from the District Court to the Louisiana Supreme Court, the first of several hundred that he was to argue before that tribunal. *Florance* v. *Camp* [24] was the type of suit which comes to lawyers in their early struggling years. The decision—hardly momentous—turned upon a technical point: whether in two articles of the Code of Practice the words 'leave the state' and 'remove from the state' were synonymous, and, if so, whether an affidavit of arrest made in accordance with the terms of either was sufficient in law. Benjamin, the attorney for the plaintiff, did the necessary hair-splitting to prove that the affidavit was legal and binding. The next year, 1834, he also successfully appealed to the state supreme court the case of *Petit et al.* v. *Drane*, involving the legality of a petition and a citation of appeal; but he lost *Allen and Deblois* v. *Their Creditors.*[25]

Yet cases even of the 'desperate' type came somewhat slowly in those years. Benjamin had the opportunity to display the energy and initiative that distinguished him from so many of his contemporaries. While waiting for clients to come to the obscure office on Canal Street, he might have sat around cursing his ill fortune—not merely at New Orleans but at Yale; or spent his time at the gambling table or race track. Instead he set himself to the slow and tedious work of preparing a digest of Louisiana appeal cases. In 1834 he and his friend, Thomas Slidell (Yale, class of 1825), published the *Digest of the Reported Decisions of the Superior Court of the Late Territory of Orleans and the Supreme Court of the State of Louisiana.*

Begun by Benjamin for his own convenience, the *Digest* originally covered the last nine volumes of the Louisiana *Reports*, including all the jurisprudence under the new Louisiana codes. The manuscript proved so useful, however, and was borrowed by so many of Benjamin's legal colleagues that Slidell collaborated with him in the publication of a more pretentious work—a digest not only of the nine volumes mentioned, but also of the sixteen preceding ones. The book contained references to the Spanish law as well as to the French Civil Code and to the legislation since the cession of Louisiana to the United States, with citations for over 6,000 cases. And the young authors undertook to present a full statement of 'every point or principle' decided in the individual cases as well as to subdivide the various titles of subjects covered.

Written with a clarity and simplicity which gave evidence not only of Benjamin's painstaking industry but also of his legal ability, the *Digest* seems all the more remarkable when we recall that he was only twenty-three years old and his legal education had been brief and irregular. The *Digest* won immediate success and was for many years the standard work in the field. In 1840 Thomas Slidell alone issued a revised edition, for Benjamin, then fast becoming one of the leading lawyers of New Orleans, was too busy to give further time to the work.[26]

Publication of the *Digest* had helped to bring his name before the public, and in 1835 he won some local prominence in another matter. He was associated with some progressive New Orleanians in the effort to promote one of the first Louisiana railroads. At a time when there were only nine miles of railroad track in the state, they made definite plans for a line to begin at New Orleans and extend northward toward Jackson, Mississippi. An engineer was sent to England to purchase rails and to seek financial aid, and advertisements were published in Mississippi and Louisiana papers soliciting contractors' bids for the first fifty miles of track. But the enterprise, at first quite promising, was defeated through the short-sightedness of the Mississippi legislature, which refused a charter for the railroad.[27]

Little is known about Benjamin's increasing legal practice during the next few years except that he appears to have already specialized in the kind of commercial litigation characteristic of a great river port. Doubtless his practice suffered a setback as a result of the Panic of 1837, for New Orleans, a center of the speculative activity in the Southwest, was disastrously affected. On 13 May 1837 fourteen of the city banks suspended payment; there was a wave of bankruptcies, and business was paralyzed. By 1839, however, Benjamin's name began to appear frequently in the cases before the state supreme court—strong evidence of his increasing business.[28]

The great Louisiana port provided a large and profitable business for commercial lawyers; Benjamin sharpened his wits in tilts with some of the best legal brains in the country. In later years he was to argue frequently before the United States Supreme Court, the House of Lords, and the Privy Council. But not even at these tribunals was he to meet a more remarkable group of lawyers.

The short, stout Etienne Mazureau, with his great head much too big for his body, was the best of the so-called Creole lawyers. Actually a native of France, he had seen service with the French navy, and had been a member of a French legal mission to Spain, where he had acquired a knowledge of the Spanish law and language. After being imprisoned by Napoleon he had emigrated to New Orleans, and was now one of Benjamin's ablest competitors, especially in cases involving detailed knowledge of the Civil Code. Louis Janin, whom Benjamin had defeated in one difficult case, was also born in France. The descendant of a noble Portuguese family and of a general under Frederick the Great, he had been reared in

Germany, had travelled in western Europe and seen military service; he spoke German, English, French, Italian, and Spanish. Able and energetic, Janin was later credited with being one of the best land lawyers in the United States. John Randolph Grymes, a Virginian of high social position, was a brilliant lawyer but had stained his reputation by resigning his office of district attorney in order to defend the pirate Lafitte, for a fee of $20,000. And Christian Roselius, who had secured passage from his native Germany by the sale of his future services, was within some twenty-five years to become attorney-general of the state and have so great a legal reputation that he was offered a partnership by Daniel Webster. (He declined because he preferred to live in New Orleans!) [29]

A considerable number of the contemporary New Orleans lawyers later served in important cabinet or diplomatic posts, in the United States Senate, and in various positions demanding broad experience and outstanding ability.

Benjamin was now able to compete successfully with such men. In typical appeal cases of the period about 1840 he upheld the right of a legitimate daughter to some real property against the claim of an illegitimate son; [30] successfully defended a client being sued for the purchase price of a slave who the buyer alleged had been afflicted with incurable consumption prior to the sale; [31] and won an action which, according to the court report, involved 'minute and intricate accounts' and 'a mass of testimony.' [32]

In the May 1839 term of the state supreme court, Benjamin had appeared in nine cases, and his business was increasing to heavy proportions. During the April and June terms of 1841, in the appeal court he won nine of eleven cases; in the May and October terms of 1844, twenty-three of thirty-five. A record was attained in 1846-47, when he or his firm appeared in forty-nine of the appeal cases reported in the current volume of the Louisiana *Law Reports*. The cases continued to be civil suits and were frequently of a technical nature. Benjamin handled some jury cases and was not without skill as a cross examiner, but he preferred commercial cases before courts without juries, and had a particular fondness and aptitude for appeals. [33]

* * *

In 1842 Benjamin appeared in his first legal cases of national significance—the suits resulting from the mutiny of slaves being transported on the Brig *Creole*. On 17 February 1828, just about the time Benjamin first arrived in New Orleans, a local newspaper had carried a typical notice of the arrival of a brig from Norfolk, Virginia, with 186 slaves. Such cargoes continued to land at New Orleans in considerable numbers, for the Old Dominion then did a large and profitable business in selling slaves from her exhausted or overpopulated plantations to the fertile Black Lands of the Lower South. Many of the Negroes were sold only out of necessity, and relatively few planters would admit that they approved of deliberate breeding for sale. Yet the fact remained that there was a steady flow of surplus slaves from Virginia to the dreaded cotton and sugar plantations, where they were worked in gangs without the patriarchal care to which many of them had been accustomed.

While they were being shipped to New Orleans, nineteen of the slaves on the *Creole* mutinied, killed a passenger, badly wounded the master, and forced the mate and crew to take the ship to Nassau in the British Bahamas. Here the authorities arrested the Negroes actually involved in the mutiny, but nearly all the others went ashore in British territory and became free. The owners thereupon brought suit in New Orleans against various insurance companies involved. There were six suits for a total of about $150,000; Benjamin, Thomas Slidell, and F. D. Conrad appeared for the insurance companies. They won nearly all the cases in the lower courts, and the owners of the slaves then appealed to the Louisiana Supreme Court.

McCargo v. *New Orleans Insurance Company* may be treated as typical of the suits. One master, McCargo, sued the insurance company for $28,000, the purported value of 26 slaves. After the Commercial Court rendered a judgment against the company for $18,000, Benjamin wrote the brief on appeal to the state supreme court. It contained a summary of the status of slavery under international law and the United States domestic law, as well as a lengthy treatment of the facts and principles involved, and provides, therefore, an excellent insight into the working of his legal mind.

The insurance policy involved was on certain slaves 'at and from' Norfolk to New Orleans, and contained the following written clause: 'This policy covers all risks; and chiefly that of foreign interference. Warranted by the assured free from elopement, insurrection and natural death.'

Benjamin first made several technical arguments. He contended that the risk never commenced, since the slaves were put on board at or near Richmond instead of Norfolk; that the insurers were discharged because the vessel was unseaworthy; that as soon as the mutiny was consummated the destination was changed and there was an unjustified deviation, which destroyed all claims against the underwriters. Developing this last point, he stated that it depended upon another: Were the underwriters or the owners responsible for the insurrection by the slaves? Benjamin asserted that the general principle that the master was responsible for the wrong-doing of his slaves was universally recognized in civilized countries; in proof he cited passages in Justinian's *Institutes*, Marlin's *Repertoire de Jurisprudence*, and the Civil Code of Louisiana.

After further discussion of technical points, Benjamin took up the most important point of the case: Whether the slaves acquired their freedom in Nassau by 'foreign interference, the risk assumed by the underwriters, or by the effect of the law of nations on the parties, against which no insurance was or would legally be made.' 'The position, that slavery is a contravention of the law of nature, is established by the concurrent authority of writers on international law, and of adjudications of courts of justice, from the era of Justinian to the present day,' Benjamin said. And developing this point he quoted the same passage of the Roman Law which he was later to debate with Seward in the United States Senate: 'Servitus . . . est constitutio juris gentium, qua quis domino alieno contra naturam subjicitur.' (Slavery is a fixed law of the law of nations by which any one is subjected contrary to nature to the mastery of another.)

Concluding his argument in the case, Benjamin made a strong appeal:

View this matter as we may, it at last resolves itself into the simple question—does the law of nations make it the duty of Great Britain to refuse a refuge in her domains to fugitives from this country, whether white or black, free or slave? It would require great hardihood to maintain the affirmative as to whites; but the color of the fugitive can make no possible difference. It will scarcely be pretended that the presumption of our municipal law, that blacks are slaves, is to be made a rule of the law of nations; and, if not, in what manner are the British authorities to determine whether the blacks and whites reaching their ports on the same vessel, the former asserting their liberty, the latter denying the fact and claiming the blacks are slaves?

It is obvious that the only criterion by which they can be governed is that which is insisted on by the American government, viz: if the blacks reach there under the control of the whites and as their slaves, so consider them; but if the blacks reach there uncontrolled by any master and apparently released from any restraint on the part of the whites, to consider them as free. These are the principles on which by the law of nations Great Britain has the right to regulate her conduct.

The decision of the Louisiana Supreme Court was in favor of the insurance companies, and Benjamin won a notable triumph. The *Creole* cases became a *cause célèbre*. They were discussed in Congress and were the subject of international arbitration, while one was later cited as a leading case in insurance law.[34]

*   *   *

The story of Benjamin's early years in New Orleans—and indeed his entire life there—is chiefly written in terms of work. He did find some relaxation at home with his family, and Natalie must have taken him, willingly or unwillingly, to numerous social functions. But his usual routine was work, work, work, early and late, except for a period during the summer season.

For after his first decade or so in the city, when the hot New Orleans summers rolled around with their damp, oppressive heat and consequent slackening of business, Benjamin would prepare to make his customary visit to his mother and sisters at Beaufort, South Carolina. He would arrive with a large supply of gifts to add to their pleasure and comfort—including trunkloads of the latest books; he delighted in reading to his family the more exciting volumes of G. P. R. James and other current literary idols.[35]

A small river port, only fifteen miles from the ocean, Beaufort

was then a 'Little Charleston,' a center for the rice planting aristocracy. It was a beautiful old town, with some spacious mansions
surrounded by palmettos, yellow jassamine, and other native shrub-
bery. And on the surrounding sea islands lived many of the Gullah
Negroes, perhaps more nearly resembling native Africans than any
other single group of Negroes in the United States. Even today
they speak a distinct dialect, often unintelligible to the average
white person.[36]

For relaxation Beaufort was ideal; Benjamin particularly relished
the long hours devoted to the dangerous sport of devil fishing. The
little town was not far from Port Royal Sound, and Benjamin and
Hannibal, his stout Negro companion, would go out on the sound
in a small boat to watch for their game. The devil fish was from
fifteen to twenty feet long, with long, powerful fins and feelers or
horns projecting several feet beyond his mouth. Sometimes as many
as eight to ten at a time congregated in these Carolina waters to
feed on shrimp and other small crustacea that abounded along the
coast. When struck with a harpoon, the fish would dart off with
lightning-like speed, running out the forty fathoms of rope in a few
seconds and pulling the boat with him. An experienced fisherman,
such as Benjamin probably became, would let the fish exhaust himself with his struggles, then draw him gently to the surface and
drive another harpoon into his body. But even after that it might
be several hours before he would stop lashing the water and give
up the fight. It was no sport for the weak and timid. The harpooner
needed a quick eye, a steady arm, and a cool head, since he might
forfeit his life if he lost his presence of mind. Benjamin must not
have been disturbed by such a risk, for many years later, during
the hot summer days at Richmond, the correspondent of the London *Times* heard him sigh 'for a few hours with old Hannibal fishing in Port Royal Sound.' [37]

Refreshed by these visits to his family, Benjamin would return
with new zest to his work at New Orleans. In the early 'forties this
was further increased when he entered actively into Whig politics
and became part owner of a large sugar plantation. A contemporary
biographical sketch, however, although calling attention to his
political activity—'he is a Whig, and one of the lights of the party
in this city'—and also to literary work, in which he had been lightly

engaged, said that 'it is very evident that Mr. Benjamin seeks rather the distinction of being a thorough and accomplished lawyer, than that of a literary man or politician.'

In business he is ever ready, never for a moment at a loss. This readiness, this activity of mind, are the fruits of labor and of study; he has not been a close student for nothing . . . From his appearance, he would scarcely be taken for a student, though perhaps, as industrious a man as there is in the city, and to be found at his office early and late, never neglecting business for social enjoyments, or the calls of pleasure.

Benjamin was then only about thirty-five years old, but he was described as a man whose career could 'be studied with advantage by young practitioners who seek distinction.' He is 'emphatically the *Commercial* Lawyer of our city, and one of the most successful advocates at our bar.' [38]

Benjamin was growing with New Orleans and fitting himself to be her representative in national affairs. He had absorbed her point of view—cosmopolitan yet very Southern, commercially progressive yet politically conservative—and he had become enamored of her way of life. During the next two decades he was to emerge as the most prominent New Orleanian of his century; Louisiana would choose him to represent her in the United States Senate and Jefferson Davis would appoint him a member of the Confederate cabinet. What course would Benjamin follow during the intervening years? In 1846 how was his character forming?

At the Cabildo in New Orleans, where there are a number of pictures of Louisiana's great and near-great, is displayed one of the earlier portraits of Benjamin: black beard, keen black eyes, and vigorous mien; the artist was able to give a suggestion, at least, of the driving energy of the man. To his associates it was already becoming obvious that he had exceptional ability, prodigious industry, commercial if not political vision. He was notably generous and indulgent to his family, even to his wife. Above all, he was attractive, impressive, forceful—certainly a coming man.

But what of the other side of the ledger? Benjamin had a comfortable income and was adding to it with larger and still larger fees. A wealthy lawyer, would he represent only the point of view of the rich, the conservative? In politics, in which he was now beginning to take a prominent part, would he be a mere opportunist? Politically speaking, would he change with the changing times, or would he defend only the old and the outworn? In a period when such issues as slavery would be in the forefront, would he let his caution, his prejudices outweigh his humanitarianism?

In 1846 there were indeed signs that Benjamin had become too much absorbed with money-getting; that whatever his good traits he would not stray far from the path of expediency. He had the ability needed for leadership; would he have the character? The next two decades—leading up to the Civil War—would be among the most critical in American history. Would they bring forth in him the needed qualities of greatness, or would they remain undeveloped until after he had undergone the stress and strain of the war and its aftermath? Benjamin was now approaching a turning point in his career—approaching it with some of his best traits still obscured.

IV. *Politician and Sugar Planter*

DURING the decade beginning in the early eighteen-forties two Jews were simultaneously winning political distinction in England and America, among the first honors of this kind won by members of their race in the two countries. The coincidence can be only partly explained by the increasing opportunities flowing from the economic and political revolutions of the preceding century. In 1837 Benjamin Disraeli, a Sephardic Jew, had been elected to Parliament, and in 1848 his attack on Sir Robert Peel won him a position of leadership in the Tory Party.[1] In 1842 Judah Philip Benjamin, another of the Sephardim, was elected a Whig member of the Louisiana legislature and within the next decade he not only reached the front rank in state politics but was chosen a member of the United States Senate.

Not merely in their parallel dates, but in their racial background, their political ideas and achievements, and their successful fight against adversity were there many similarities between Benjamin and his brilliant English contemporary.

Like a skillful juggler, Benjamin began by the early 'forties to keep several balls in the air at the same time. After the hard digging during the 'thirties, he had emerged as one of the leading lawyers in New Orleans. With a large income and assured position, he now increased the scope of his activities to politics and sugar planting.

Considering his large business interests and natural inclinations, it is not surprising that Benjamin joined the conservative party of Clay and Webster. In fact, since the Whigs had been organized only within the past decade and had not won a national election until the previous fall, he might be considered one of the pioneer Louisiana Whigs. Apparently well entrenched already in both New Orleans and the state, and with congenial policies, the new party had a definite appeal to a dynamic young conservative.

46

The Whig success in Louisiana was largely the result of the restricted electorate under the Constitution of 1812, but there were also a number of other explanations. In view of the liberal suffrage provisions in America today, it may be hard to realize that under the constitution by which Louisiana was governed from 1812 to 1845 there were provisions that barred from the polls a majority even of the white men. A small property test was sufficient to keep the ballot in every state election chiefly in the hands of landholders and tradesmen, while legislative and executive positions were restricted to men with landed estates ranging in value from $500 to $5,000 or more.[2]

With the property qualifications and unequal apportionment of legislative seats favoring the Whig planters and businessmen, they had an influence far out of proportion to their numbers.

Other explanations for the Whig strength were that the powerful commercial interests in New Orleans supported the party plan for a national bank, while there was strong feeling in the state as a whole for its program of internal improvements—especially waterways. Nor should one overlook the powerful opposition among the sugar interests to the Democratic program for the annexation of Texas. For this adjoining republic had won her independence from Mexico a few years before, and it was feared that, if she should be admitted to the Union, she would open up a sugar industry which would compete with that of Louisiana. In cordial sympathy with these ideas, it appears, for reasons both of principle and self-interest, Benjamin now entered heartily into the local Whig politics.

After failing in 1841 to be elected to the Board of Aldermen, he ran the next year for a higher office—that of member of the lower house of the state legislature. And this time he was successful, his influence in the city politics having become in fact much greater than the importance of the position to which he was elected. His law office in Exchange Alley was often the meeting place of the New Orleans Whig executive committee and its headquarters on election day, while, if we may believe the Democratic papers, he was chiefly responsible for a sharp trick that had much to do with the Whig victory.

Since under the Constitution of 1812 voting was restricted to property holders, was not the owner of a cab or carriage a property holder within the meaning of the constitution? And if so, did not the possession of a license tax receipt provide sufficient evidence of ownership? The Whigs asserted that it did—allegedly at the suggestion of Benjamin—and their claim was upheld by the election officials. According to the Democrats, licenses were even issued for nonexistent cabs; and on election day hundreds of license holders flocked to the polls, where they obediently voted for the Whig candidate. Benjamin's personal responsibility for the so-called fraud was not positively established but, like Banquo's ghost, the cab votes were to rise again to plague him.[3]

At the age of thirty-one Benjamin was now launched upon his officeholding career in America, a career which would include within the next two decades one higher position after another until he became the Confederate Secretary of State and Jefferson Davis's right-hand man. Introduced to the more social as well as workaday phase of Southern *ante-bellum* politics, he doubtless attended on 31 January 1843 (even without Natalie's urging) the inauguration of the picturesque Alexander Mouton, 'the Acadian of the Acadians,' as governor of Louisiana.

The floor of the House was filled by the members of the senate and the house of representatives. And in the grandiloquent phrases of the *Picayune*,

These were flanked in a crescent line by the officers, in their gorgeous and gaudy uniforms, and the beauty of Louisiana—every one of whom is in herself a booty—crowded the gallery, their bright and sparkling eyes making it look like a coronet surmounting the scene, studded with diamonds.[4]

Benjamin was finding at least one black-eyed beauty to be only too elusive and unsatisfactory. Perhaps that was one reason why he appeared to be burying himself so much in his work, his legislative duties now in addition to his heavy law practice. Through the entire session of the Louisiana legislature, from January into April, he took a prominent part for a new member. He was chairman of a committee that reported a banking bill;[5] he made a long speech on the unconstitutionality of a bill imposing a tax on tobacco;[6] and he gave a report from the Committee on Conference on the bill to divide the state into congressional districts.[7]

Meantime, in a New Orleans mayoralty election the Whig candidate won by a majority of only 315 in a total of 2,263 votes.[8] The new party would have to work hard for further successes in the city—it needed able, energetic, young men like Benjamin.

Never an impractical reformer, was he influenced by the close election in his opposition to a current bill for more stringent anti-duelling legislation? [9] In any case, he probably felt that such laws were unenforceable in a state where so many personal difficulties were settled on the 'Field of Honor.' Soon afterwards, on 16 April, the *Picayune* was referring to a duel fought the previous day with small swords by two Creole gentlemen. And three years later, on 24 January 1846, it published a long editorial against duelling, inspired by the death of a promising young man of the city.

'The crimson shrine of honor has again been dabbled with the blood of a noble and promising youth,' the *Picayune* said. The controversy had originated in a misunderstanding amid the gaiety and rejoicing at a festival. Neither party knew the other, 'so there could have been no malice.' And, to make the case still sadder, the father of the dead youth had used 'the savings and painstakings' of years to educate his children.

'We know of no one upon the face of the earth better, happier, or in any way benefitted by the death of young Kane,' the *Picayune* concluded.

But however much Benjamin might sympathize with such sentiments, he believed that there were times when one could protect his character only by resort to sword or pistol. And in considering anti-duelling legislation, he could not forget that Exchange Alley in New Orleans, where he worked, was full of fencing masters with a large popular support; that many of the men whom he saw thrusting and parrying or, as onlookers, eagerly encouraging other potential duellists, were his constituents.[10]

It should be noted that during Benjamin's early political career in Louisiana he met with little opposition based on racial prejudice. With the rapid growth of New Orleans there had been a commensurate increase in the Jewish population; from 1828, when he came to the city, to 1843, it had grown from a few scattered individuals to about 125 families. Two years later the Sephardic Jews of New Orleans began to hold services in a private home; one E. J. Solomon, a captain in the army, read in the 'Holy tongue' and chanted the ritual according to the Portuguese Meinhag. Yet Benjamin does not appear to have attended any of these services, and he was not among the 'gentlemen prominent in social, commercial and civic affairs' who were signatories to the charter approved in 1847 for a Sephardic congregation, the *Nefutzoth Yehudah*. Indeed, the only time we definitely find him linked with the Jewish religious community during this period is when he was listed by the *Jewish Advocate* among those who had not returned the earlier numbers of the periodical and were, therefore, considered as subscribers.[11]

Like so many of Jewish blood today, Benjamin tended to become cosmopolitan. But although he gradually separated himself from Jewish affairs, he never renounced his ancestral faith.[12]

In the spring of 1844 Benjamin's name was offered as a Whig delegate to the Louisiana Constitutional Convention, called in response to the popular demand for the revision of the Constitution of 1812. Aware of the evils brought on the state by the 'wild-cat banking' of the Jackson era, Benjamin argued that the constitution should restrict the powers of the legislature to create certain types of corporations, and he promised to vote to make the incorporators of state banks individually liable for the debts of the bank 'up to the whole extent of their fortune.' He also favored a state judiciary appointed by the governor and perhaps to be retired at sixty, a proposal which he admitted would have deprived New York state of the most valuable services of Chancellor Kent and the United States of the most valuable services of Chief Justice Marshall. The difficulty might be avoided, he said, by permitting the reappointment for short terms of judges still in the prime of their usefulness.

Another measure which he advocated was 'a registry system to prevent the fraudulent usurpation of the electoral franchise by those not really entitled to it'—the result perhaps of his sensitiveness at the outcry against him because of the 'cab votes.'

Elected on the face of the returns, Benjamin and his Whig colleague from New Orleans, Charles M. Conrad, did not find smooth sailing. Cries of fraud in the city election were raised by both Democrats and Whigs, and after the convention met early in August at the little town of Jackson, north of Baton Rouge, the members consumed much time in wrangling over whether or not

Benjamin and Conrad were rightfully elected. Meantime, however, they were allowed to retain their seats, and Benjamin was appointed to several important committees. On 21 August, shortly before the convention adjourned to meet at New Orleans in January 1845, he and Conrad agreed to resign, and to run for re-election with the understanding that their opponents would accept the results. In the second election they were vindicated by receiving an increased majority.

Benjamin, 'the little member from New Orleans,' with his tact and courtesy, his ability to secure compromises, was credited with being chiefly responsible for the removal of the convention from Jackson. Once it had assembled at New Orleans, he and the other city members felt that they stood a far better chance of preventing the proceedings from going against their interest. The transfer was not effected, however, without allusions by a country member to the 'sumptuous repasts' and 'rich and costly wines' with which the city had on an earlier occasion plied the members of the legislature meeting there when a measure favorable to New Orleans was to be carried. Even a city member, Bernard de Marigny, vainly argued against the removal from Jackson, where there were no balls, no theaters, no distracting business interests and 'mania for speculation.'

Before the constitutional convention met again in January 1845, the election of 1844 was held, and James K. Polk, a Democrat, was chosen President of the United States. Benjamin was one of the political leaders who worked unavailingly to carry the state for Henry Clay. And small wonder, in view of the questionable tactics used by the New Orleans Democrats.

For, although the Americans had brought material progress to New Orleans, politically the cost had been heavy. The Creole political leaders were on the whole men with high ideals of private and public honor, and while they were in the saddle the city and state politics were conducted on a relatively high plane. It was John Slidell, an expatriated New Yorker with first-hand knowledge of Tammany methods, who was most responsible for bringing machine methods into New Orleans. The Whigs were not political lilies, but it was Slidell and his henchmen who, through the so-called Placquemines Frauds in this presidential election, introduced the new tactics on an extensive scale.

In Louisiana the Whigs and Democrats had fought a hard battle throughout the campaign, with the result in doubt until the last. Influenced by the promise of Henry Clay to restore the duty on sugar and by other considerations, Benjamin, ex-governors White and Roman, and Henry Johnson had led the fight in the state for the Whig candidate, while Slidell marshalled the Democratic forces: Mouton, Soulé, Grymes, Charles Gayarré, and smaller fry. The Democrats controlled the election machinery in the County of New Orleans, which then extended to the Gulf and had the political power of any three parishes. And, there being no registration law such as Benjamin had advocated in his last campaign for office, each of the city voters could cast his ballot in New Orleans proper or anywhere else in the county. The winning candidate was the one who carried the greatest number of precincts. It was a clear opening for Slidell and his lieutenants.

Not long after dawn on election day, steamboats chartered by Slidell men began moving up and down the river, and at each doubtful precinct in the county, outside of New Orleans, they dropped their load of good Democrats, who dutifully contributed their bit toward the victory for Polk and Dallas. Although Benjamin and the other Louisiana Whigs could howl with rage at these 'Placquemines Frauds,' the Democrats were within the letter of the law and the Whigs had to accept the results of the election.

Now their main problem in the state was how to curb the powers of the Democrats in the impending session of the constitutional convention. And all the New Orleans members from both parties had their common problem of defending the commercial interests of the city against the encroachments of the planters and small farmers of the country parishes.

The convention met for its second session on 14 January 1845 at the elegant St. Louis Hotel in New Orleans, a center for the local social life. Here the ballroom was given over to the deliberations of the delegates, except on a few stipulated days before Lent when they had to adjourn at an early hour so that there would be enough time to prepare for more important 'society balls.'

Although he was not slated to be the leader of the city delegation, Benjamin rapidly assumed this position through his ability and industry. A regular attendant at the meetings of the convention, he was one of the hardest workers among the delegates and the only one who was at the same time a member of two of the most important committees: 'the executive department' and 'general provisions.' He drew up articles and corrected those drawn up by others; as a member of the Committee on Contingent Expenses he audited various accounts and kept a record of the printing; and he was one of the most active members in all the proceedings on the floor. When he arose to speak, it was usually to make short, businesslike talks on the problems at hand. Sometimes impatient of delays, on one occasion he warned his colleagues that by further procrastination 'we shall make ourselves the laughing stock of the public.' And when unable to secure full justice for the city on a question of representation, he was ready to make compromises so that even General Solomon Downs, the leader of the country party, praised his 'spirit of conciliation and harmony.'

Making a short speech in the effort to win over the city delegation to a compromise with the country members, Benjamin gave a key to his political methods.

How can any one expect that he can induce those who differ with him to change their opinions, when he begins by telling them that he is impractically wedded to his own . . . ? It is a notorious fact that the Federal Constitution would never have been formed had there not been mutual concessions on the part of its illustrious framers. The delegates from the city must make concessions . . . or withdraw from the Convention.

When contending successfully for an appointive judiciary and secretary of state and a registration law for voters, Benjamin did not differentiate himself from many able politicians of conservative leanings. Furthermore, he was still somewhat immature, as was shown by a number of his remarks during the convention. He had not yet learned all those virtues of simplicity in address for which he was later to win such praise—particularly in the English appeal courts. In a speech favoring a constitutional provision that the governor must be a native citizen, he was not only too florid in his style but he expressed doubt of the loyalty of the Creoles if they had been called on to fight French instead of British invaders during the War of 1812. It is not surprising that his tactless accusation drew fire from the Creole members.

Some indications of Benjamin's increasing ability as a speaker are given, however, in the statement of the reporter for the debates, who, apologizing for his fragmentary reports, said, 'It was very difficult to report the remarks of gentlemen that spoke with the fluency and rapidity of the delegate from New Orleans.'

Although a slaveholder and a champion of Southern rights, Benjamin opposed the use of the 'federal ratio' under which five slaves would be counted as three white men in determining the basis of representation in Louisiana state elections. In a strong and ingenious argument on the floor of the convention he declared:

Slaves were, by our laws, nothing but property. But, says the delegate from Lafourche . . . we should allow them to form a part of the basis of representation because they are productive labor, and labor should be represented. If this argument holds good, then it might, with equal propriety, be argued that we should allow representation to oxen, horses, etc., which are attached to the glebes, and which are equally productive labor . . .

By the principle which they [his opponents] lay down would not a man owning five minor slaves have a representation equal to four votes, whilst a man having five minor children would have a representation of but one vote? If property is to be represented at all, why not all property? Why not houses and lands? . . . Or if at all, why not make it a qualification for voting?

In his reply General Solomon Downs, a Democratic leader, taunted Benjamin with the notoriety he would acquire in the North, but admitted the ability with which he handled the subject. The Negroes outnumbered the whites in the sugar and cotton parishes of lower Louisiana, and it might seem, therefore, that Benjamin's advocacy of the white basis for voting was really because he was inimical to the slave interests. A more plausible explanation is found, however, in the fact that New Orleans had a large majority of whites, although Benjamin denied that this influenced his stand.

In a few instances during the convention Benjamin showed his potential ability to rise above the level of a politician. One was his action in calling attention to the result of the widening rift between the North and the South, and another was his ardent advocacy of popular education.

After Polk had been elected on an expansionist platform, Congress in December 1844 authorized the annexation of Texas, which would entail a large increase in the slave territory, and there was a stream of petitions and memorials against the measure from the free states. Already during the past year the Methodist Church had split on the slave issue, while the Baptist Church was fast drifting into a similar division. In addition to the small but vociferous group of Abolitionists, there was now a growing body of Northerners who resolutely opposed any expansion whatsoever of slavery into the territories. They were stoutly resisted by the Democratic party, which had now become a party of privilege, ruled by the Southern slaveholders and their Northern allies.

Although a Whig, Benjamin held basically the same point of view toward slavery as did the Southern Democrats. While arguing in favor of the state constitutional provision requiring that the members of the legislature be citizens of the United States and residents of Louisiana for four years, he turned to a discussion of the political situation.

There is one subject that I approach with great reluctance. A question may arise in a few months that will obliterate all party distinctions, when there will be neither whigs nor democrats. When the whole South will coalesce and form a single party, and that party will be for the protection of our hearths, of our families, of our homes. That man must be indeed blind not to perceive from whence the danger comes. The signs are pregnant with evil. The speck upon the horizon that at first was no bigger than a man's head, overshadows us, and there is not a breeze that blows that does not sound the tocsin of alarm.

Benjamin proved to be an alarmist so far as the immediate situation was concerned, but it was true that the South would have to unite in good time to preserve slavery—that is, if it was worth preserving.

But probably Benjamin's most statesmanlike work that year, in or out of the convention, was on behalf of public education. While asserting on the convention floor that the United States was fast falling into the extremes of democracy, he added that 'with public education you may extend democratic principles without danger.' One of his last speeches in the constitutional convention was in behalf of the movement to secure the proposed state university for New Orleans, but he met with only limited success.[13]

Other evidence of his activity in this connection is found in an address he delivered on Washington's Birthday to the public school children of the First Municipality in New Orleans. Public schools had been opened in the city two years before, and they now had some fifteen hundred pupils and seventy-five teachers.[14] Since the convention had adjourned for the day, Benjamin was doubtless heard by a considerable crowd, composed of adults as well as children, and he used the occasion to make an eloquent plea for public education.

Speaking in a liberal vein not often found in the South of that period, Benjamin advocated free schools not only for boys but for girls. Although he believed that the restless energy which actuated the American people had led them to make tremendous material progress, he said that

the absence of some basis of primary education had caused their mind, in a great degree, to run riot, for want of proper direction . . . Let this basis be supplied, and instead of indulging in visionary schemes . . . instead of becoming the votary of a Mormon or a Miller—the freeman of America will seek other and nobler themes for the exercise of his intellect . . . The boundless field of the arts and sciences will be opened . . . Then shall we cease morally as well as physically to be tributaries of the old world.

Later in his speech Benjamin indicated that he did not feel that the public schools could prepare every pupil to be a statesman any more than a chemist or an astronomer. But he said the schools could give them such instruction in the main principles of government as would enable them 'to discriminate between the artful demagogue and the shallow pretender, and the man whose true merit should inspire their confidence and respect.'

Thus spoke Benjamin, who was destined to be the most prominent Louisianian of the *ante-bellum* era. Do his words ring as a prophecy to another Louisiana who would have her fill of 'artful

I. JUDAH, NATALIE, AND NINETTE BENJAMIN, probably about 1845

demagogues' and 'shallow pretenders,' kept in office by an ignorant or deluded electorate?

Benjamin's address, though now forgotten, was printed in a contemporary literary publication in Louisiana and later included in a standard collection of orations.[15] He was developing a local reputation as an orator; the laudatory sketch, previously quoted, stated that 'as a speaker, he is calm, collected, forcible, though sometimes a little too rapid in his elocution. His voice has a silvery, mellifluous sweetness, and seldom jars upon the ear by degenerating into shrill or harsh tones,' while 'his manner and gesture are graceful and finished.'[16] The Washington's Birthday address was hardly designed for school children; Benjamin doubtless made a special bid for the attention of the more mature members of his audience. And apparently they were much impressed, even though his style may be too florid for the modern reader.

* * *

But speech-making was never more than subsidiary to Benjamin's political or legal interests. Turning now to his third important activity during this period, we find that he had in the early 'forties become the part owner of Bellechasse, a large Louisiana sugar plantation. Although Theodore Packwood, the other owner, was the actual manager of the estate, Benjamin was by 1845 taking a more and more active hand. Bellechasse is on the bank of the Mississippi, six miles below New Orleans on the opposite side of the river. Reached today in only half an hour by ferry and automobile over a paved road, the plantation was in the 'forties much more inaccessible, despite the steamboat traffic. Benjamin brought Natalie and Ninette here to live, though for business reasons he kept his own residence in New Orleans. He supplied Natalie with what he considered ample means for her comfort and pleasure; she entertained her friends at the plantation, and he joined her as often as his business interests in New Orleans would permit.

But the arrangement was distasteful to his wife. She found life at Bellechasse 'triste' and in the summer of 1845 she left for France.

We crossed the Atlantic from New York to Havre in the sailing ship Louis Philippe with Mrs. Benjamin and her brother Jules de

St. Martin as fellow passengers [later wrote Gabriel Manigault, of Charleston, in his diary]. She had with her a little girl about two years old and a black nurse who like her mother was also born in Charleston. This negro woman spoke the corrupt French of the West India Islands which was as unintelligible to a stranger as the negro English of the South Carolina rice plantations.

It may be interesting here to state that at a public ball given by the Americans in Paris in 1859 on the 22d February, I observed Mrs. Benjamin among the company. I immediately approached her and told her who I was. She was very cordial in response, called to her brother who was near by, explaining who I was, and invited me to her apartment in the Rue St. Florentin on her regular reception day. I thereupon went and afterwards dined with her, meeting on both occasions her father who was then an old man, and who seemed much interested to converse with me about events that he remembered as having occurred in Charleston.[17]

So far as is known, Natalie never returned to America except on one unfortunate occasion after Benjamin was elected to the Senate. One explanation of her action was that she wanted to educate Ninette in France. Yet we may be sure that Natalie was also thinking of her own pleasure. Benjamin now saw his wife and daughter only on his 'almost annual' trips to France. As much as he loved Natalie, her selfishness may have eased the pain of separation.[18]

Although she became a permanent resident of Paris and thus almost ignored her wifely duties, Natalie apparently did not scruple to take a liberal allowance from her husband; in fact, there is later evidence that she complained because it was not still larger.[19]

Two years after Natalie's departure, Benjamin invited his mother, his widowed sister, Mrs. Rebecca Levy, and her young daughter to come to Louisiana and live at Bellechasse. They made the trip from Beaufort by sea. Arriving at New Orleans on a bright spring morning, the next day they took the steamboat down the river to the plantation. At last they had a real home. And yet 'J.P.,' as his mother and sisters called him, was already planning to tear down the old Bellechasse house and build a larger one. Afire with the grandiose ambitions of the 'forties, he would not be content until he had a great mansion with many rooms and columns, and accommodations for a whole flock of guests.

A square house surrounded by double balconies supported by

twenty-eight square cypress columns, the new Bellechasse was built in the style of the large Louisiana plantation mansions of that time. There were twenty rooms, and hallways sixteen feet wide running through the house from front to back. The first floor rooms had heavy cornices typical of the period, while high folding doors divided Benjamin's library from the drawing-room. Other features were the crystal chandeliers, the spiral mahogany stairway ascending to the bedrooms on the second and third floors, and the great double porch surrounding the entire house. We are not surprised at Benjamin's statement that the contract price of the mansion was $15,000, 'and it cost $28,000 when I got through.'

Nor did this include the brick smokehouse, the sugar house, the building where gas was manufactured to light the mansion, and the great plantation bell made for Benjamin by a New York foundry. He is said to have had two hundred or more silver dollars melted into the bell to give it its beautiful tone.[20]

During the autumn of 1847—perhaps before the new mansion was completed—Benjamin's mother died. It was a deep sorrow for her devoted son, but he could find some comfort in the fact that she had lived to see him attain success, and that he had contributed to her comfort and pleasure. His sister, Rebecca Levy, was installed as mistress of the mansion, and here came many guests, chiefly members of the family and New Orleans friends or associates. The years that Benjamin played the part of plantation manager and host at Bellechasse were among the happiest of his life—despite the separation from wife and daughter, and other personal sorrows.[21]

But the many activities in which he had been engaged during the past few years were a strain upon even his strong constitution. Just about the time he built the new mansion, Benjamin's eyesight became seriously affected. It was a hard blow to his ambitions; he was moody and despondent.

But after a short time he pulled himself together. He decided to give up his law practice and devote himself chiefly to sugar planting. For several years this had been but an interesting avocation; it was now a business to which he turned with all the enthusiasm and intelligence that had won him success at the bar. He studied the best methods of sugar culture, and with the help of his partner, Theodore Packwood, applied them at Bellechasse.

At the time their experiments were begun, the Louisiana sugar industry was still in a formative stage. Although sugar cane had been planted in Louisiana since the colonial period, it was only since Benjamin had moved to the state that new methods of cultivating and refining and a favorable tariff had caused a great increase in production. During the middle 'forties the sugar yield was larger there than ever before, the number of hogsheads produced annually increasing to over 200,000—four times as many as in the year Benjamin came to New Orleans. More than 400 of the new steam engines were now being employed, with some 50,000 slaves and a capital estimated at about $60,000,000. In lower Louisiana the sugar cane was beginning to supplant the less profitable cotton, cane breaks and virgin forests were being cleared for its cultivation, swamp lands drained and protected from overflows of the Mississippi, the lakes, and bayous.

Benjamin became a pioneer in the utilization of new methods of sugar production. On his visits to Mrs. Benjamin and Ninette he devoted part of his time to the study of French inventions and agricultural methods. He also made a thorough study of the American methods of producing the sugar crop. His somewhat theoretical knowledge and Packwood's practical experience proved such a valuable combination that in 1846 they won the first prize for sugar loaf at the state agricultural fair.

At their invitation an expert who was making a survey for the United States Government came to Bellechasse and, examining the new Rillieux apparatus which had been built for them by Philadelphia machinists, was highly complimentary of the Bellechasse methods. He analyzed a specimen of sugar from the plantation and found that its 'crystalline grain and snowy whiteness are also equal to those of the best double refined sugar of our northern refineries.'

Under the Rillieux process it was possible to make sugar not only purer but with far less waste than under the conventional methods. Invented by Norbert Rillieux, a New Orleans chemist, the process was based on the plan of evaporating the syrup from the sugar by the use of a series of similar boilers or vacuum pans. The first pan or boiler was heated by exhaust steam from the steam engine used for grinding cane and by the pumping engine, and the other pans or boilers were then heated by vapor from the first one. The 'dried up little Rillieux' made frequent and protracted visits to Bellechasse, and was the center of interest for groups of planters from the surrounding plantations as he explained various points about the chemistry of sugar and his own refining apparatus.

Fortunately, Benjamin and Packwood were able to provide the heavy capital outlay necessary to pay for labor and machinery—the Rillieux apparatus alone cost them $33,000—and they saw the prospect of large profits. In a series of articles for *De Bow's Review*, a leading Southern commercial publication, Benjamin described the improved methods of sugar production and explained some of his own ideas on the development of Southern agriculture. Growing expansive, he asserted that, if the steam plow could be used successfully, the alluvial plains of the South could supply half the globe with sugar, and millions of people with cotton clothing; describing an experiment that had recently been made in France with this plow, he declared that he felt assured of the ultimate success of such a machine. His discussion of technical points could easily lead the reader to believe that it was written by a chemist. Benjamin had obtained a remarkable theoretical knowledge of the methods of sugar refining, and he presented it in a style that appealed to even the layman.

It must not be assumed, however, that Benjamin was uniformly successful as a sugar planter. His optimistic temperament sometimes led him into ventures that were more amusing than profitable. He purchased a machine for the plantation 'which produced, or was supposed to produce, ice in long candles when you turned the crank,' and various other new contraptions that did not always prove their utility.

Yet it was this willingness to venture into untried fields which, if at times impractical, was to distinguish Benjamin from many Southerners of that time. It was a piece with the dynamic conservatism which would make him a pioneer railroad promoter and, near the end of the Civil War, an advocate of arming and finally of freeing the slaves.

By 1847 Benjamin had recovered the full use of his eyesight and had partially resumed his law practice. Since his work again required him to live in New Orleans, he went to Bellechasse only for weekends and occasionally longer stays. He had lived regularly on the plantation for only a brief period. The experience had been profitable and healthful, however, and it had further ripened his point of view toward Negro slavery—a problem with which he was to be vitally concerned throughout his remaining American years.[22]

During the course of his argument in one of the *Creole* appeals, Benjamin had advanced some ideas on slavery that seem radical for a Southerner of that age. Referring to the cruel manner in which the slaves had been crowded into the *Creole*, he asked, 'Will this court be disposed to recognize one standard of humanity for the white man and another for the Negro?' Slaves were human beings, and, therefore, entitled to the same standards of comfort on shipboard as the Federal law required for white passengers, he said.

The argument was then commonly advanced in the South that the slaves were resigned to their lot. But Benjamin boldly attacked this contention. The subject matter of the insurance suffered from an inherent defect—'vice propre de la chose.' What was this defect? The Negroes were human beings and, therefore, all the more anxious to be free.

What is a slave? [Benjamin continued]. He is a human being. He has feeling and passions and intellect. His heart, like the white man's, swells with love, burns with jealousy, aches with sorrow, pines under restraint and discomfort, boils with revenge and ever cherishes the desire for liberty. His passions and feelings in some respects may not be as fervid and as delicate as those of the white man, nor his intellect as acute; but passions and feelings he has, and in some respects they are more violent, and consequently more dangerous, from the very circumstances that his mind is comparatively weak, and unenlightened. Considering the character of the slave, and the peculiar passions which, generated by nature, are strengthened and stimulated by his condition, he is prone to revolt in the very nature of things, and ever ready to conquer his liberty where a probable chance presents itself.

In view of these facts, Benjamin said, police measures had to be used to keep the Negro in slavery.[23]

This is the kind of argument that provokes dispute about Benjamin's real character. Some of his enemies would doubtless have contended that Benjamin was merely defending his clients. On the other hand, he appeared to be speaking with genuine feeling. A member of a race that had known more than its share of oppression, did that make him sympathetic with the Negro?

In any event, Benjamin was opposed to any plans for immediate emancipation of the Negroes. He agreed heartily with the sentiments the *Picayune* [24] expressed a few years later after learning of the slave insurrection in Martinque:

Violent interference in the structure of society, sudden and radical disturbances of domestic relations . . . are not long of producing their inevitable and disastrous effects . . . The last accounts from that doomed island inform us that the cities were sacked and destroyed, the white people . . . murdered . . . Henceforth we must expect to see that beautiful island cursed with the barbarous strife which half a century of civil war has not sufficed to suppress in St. Domingo.

The Louisiana slaves were still ignorant and superstitious, and if released from surveillance they might easily be stirred to unreasoned violence. The city Negroes were more civilized than those of the plantation, it is true, but many of the former also were close to the jungle. Nearly a century after Benjamin argued the *Creole* case, Love Powder, War Powder, Dragon's Blood, Goofer Dust (from a grave), and other voodoo charms were still being illicitly sold to the Negro trade. [25]

There is no evidence that Benjamin ever joined those Southerners who were now arguing that the Negro was a creature of the lower order, and that slavery was foreordained by God. But he saw the Negro problem from the close perspective of the native white, a perspective that was not, in this sense, improved by his experiences as a large slave owner. As he invested a large capital in Bellechasse, he appreciated the ruinous losses which would have been suffered by emancipation without compensation to the owners. But Benjamin was a good master to his slaves. A few of the Bellechasse Negroes were still living in the first years of the twentieth century and they had 'none but kindly memories' of their old master, coupled with 'romantic legends of the days of glory on the old place.' [26]

V. Man of Affairs

As the middle of the nineteenth century approached, Benjamin not only continued to develop with New Orleans and Louisiana but was expanding his activities into a larger scene. He had now become a man of affairs, a Southerner but with interests that were national in scope. The next few years, which immediately preceded his election to the United States Senate, were to be the last in which he would make his full-time residence in New Orleans.

The Mexican War had broken out in 1846, and Benjamin, like other New Orleans businessmen, was particularly concerned over the effect of the war on trade. Vessels fitted out in the city were turned back at Mexican ports, and numerous legal controversies arose, involving complicated questions of international law with which the commercial world was no longer familiar. Spurred on by this situation, Benjamin published in *De Bow's Review*, soon after the outbreak of the war, an article on 'The Law of Blockade,' explaining some of the problems of commercial and international law that the war had brought to the forefront. With commendable frankness he pointed out that in New Orleans certain clauses inserted in the policies of most insurance companies contained 'very inadequate indemnity' against loss by blockade, and quoted from a printed policy form to show how 'completely illusory' in nine cases out of ten was the indemnity offered if the port was blockaded when the vessel arrived.[1]

About 1847 Benjamin was appointed counsel to the new California land commissioner, and made the long journey by steamboat to the Pacific Coast. When he arrived in California it was only about a year since the territory had been wrested from Mexico, but a vigorous and none too scrupulous American element was already working its leaven in the more placid native population. Among the difficulties that were arising were many disputes over land titles granted under the former Spanish law; because of his familiarity with the diverse legal systems, Benjamin was well fitted to advise the American commissioner.

Gold had not yet been discovered but Benjamin was deeply impressed with other features of the new territory and had many reasons to foresee its great future. As for his legal work there, it was valuable experience and probably contributed to his selection as counsel in the great New Almaden mining case during the next decade.[2]

Returning to Louisiana, Benjamin was chosen an elector on the Whig ticket of 1848, and apparently was a member of the delegation which accompanied Zachary Taylor on his triumphal trip to Washington to be inaugurated. As a member of Taylor's suite he was present at a state dinner given by James K. Polk, the retiring President, at the White House, where he met some of the outstanding political figures in the country.

In three days the conscientious Polk was to be relieved of the wearisome duties of his high position. To the dinner—a parting social gesture—he had invited a large number of prominent guests whom, for one reason or another, he wanted to entertain: General Taylor, the President-elect, and his suite, including Benjamin, Judge Winchester, Colonel Hodge of New Orleans, Dr. McCormick, and Brevet-Colonel Garnett of the United States Army; General Cass, the defeated Democratic candidate; Millard Fillmore, the vice-president elect; all the members of Polk's cabinet; Senators Davis of Mississippi, Bell of Tennessee, and Pierce of Maryland; Justice Catron of the Supreme Court; and 'Father' Ritchie, the editor of the *Washington Union;* to say nothing of some of their ladies. President Polk 'waited on' Mrs. Dallas to the table, and General Taylor on Mrs. Polk. The dinner, 'finely gotten up' by Julian, Polk's French cook, must have suited Benjamin's discriminating taste. At least for a newcomer in capital society, it was a highly satisfactory occasion; Benjamin's pleasure was hardly diminished by the fact that there was not the 'slightest allusion' to politics.[3]

In all likelihood Benjamin made good use of his opportunities to improve his acquaintance with the President-elect. Zachary Taylor, a resolute, matter-of-fact old soldier, is said to have been so impressed with Benjamin that he wanted to make him a member of his cabinet. But, so the story runs, tales about Mrs. Benjamin reached the General's ears, and, hearing that she would not be received by Washington society, he gave up his plan.⁴ The shadow of Peggy O'Neale still hung over the capital, and, little as the General feared a real battle, he wisely decided to avoid another petticoat war.

From 1849 to 1852 Benjamin's time was taken up with his law practice, plantation interests, and efforts to promote two new railroads—one from New Orleans to Jackson, Mississippi, and another across the Isthmus of Tehuantepec in Mexico. His eye trouble had been a warning that he could overtax himself; the need for a law partner was evident. William C. Micou of New Orleans had been associated with him in commercial suits for several years, and about 1849 he became a member of the Benjamin firm.

A Georgian of Virginia Huguenot ancestry and a graduate of his state university, Micou had, like Benjamin, come to New Orleans to seek his fortune. Here his strict integrity, his ability, and his hospitality had won for him the admiration and respect of his friends and a high place in society. A junior partner upon whom Benjamin could lean heavily, he took over jury trials and also office duties during Benjamin's frequent absences from the city.⁵

During the next few years the firm of Benjamin and Micou appeared in a large number of commercial cases in the state courts. Although financially profitable to the partners, these suits were usually of no special significance, involving such matters as liability on a bill of exchange,⁶ or technical points of marine insurance.⁷ One case that afforded a sort of comic relief after the usual run of commercial cases was *Emile D. Baron* v. *Thomas Placide*.⁸ In the words of Judge Pierre Rost, the future Confederate minister to Spain, it dealt with 'the grave question, whether the plaintiff was bound under her engagement as the *danseuse* and *mime* at the theatre of the Varieties, to dance the polka in the comedy entitled the *Serious Family*, when required to do so by the stage manager.'

One of the two important cases which Benjamin argued during these years was the Cuban filibuster trials. In 1850 New Orleans had been the center of a movement led by the daring revolutionist, Narcisco Lopez, to overthrow the Spanish Government in Cuba and to secure the annexation of the island to the United States. A considerable part of Lopez's funds and recruits was secured in the Crescent City, and it was with the blessing of nearly all her citizens that his little force slipped away to Cuba. But the expedition was a dismal failure. Lopez was garrotted by the Spanish authorities; Colonel Crittenden, a relative of the American attorney-general, was shot with a number of the soldiers, and others were condemned to imprisonment with hard labor. The news was greeted in New Orleans by a wave of indignation; a mob wrecked the Spanish consulate and abused the Spanish flag.

While public opinion was in this feverish state, Benjamin agreed to assist the United States District Attorney for New Orleans in the prosecution of some Americans accused of violating the neutrality laws in behalf of the filibusterers. The Government was faced with a formidable task, which was not diminished by the fact that the defendents included General John A. Quitman and former Senator John Henderson, and that the filibusterers and their friends had obtained expert legal advice on the methods of avoiding violations of the Federal laws.

Benjamin did the best he could in the circumstances. With what an opponent termed 'oily, plausible pertinacity,' he contended for the right of the Federal Marshal to select a jury under the advisement of the court, instead of drawing names in the usual manner; later, he demonstrated to the jury the violations of the neutrality laws and painted a glowing picture of the happy life of the people whom the filibusterers were trying to liberate.

But Benjamin's efforts were wasted. If we may judge from the bill of fare served the jurors—including 'Dinner for Twenty-four' and liquors including brandy, Madeira, hock, and whiskey 'for forty-eight'—they were more interested in filling their stomachs and elating their spirits than in fulfilling their duties. For this and other reasons disagreements were to be expected, and there was a mistrial. After several other efforts to obtain convictions, the Government gave up the cases, and the New Orleanians celebrated by firing thirty-one guns in Lafayette Square—one for each state and one for Cuba.

When Benjamin took these cases, he risked his popularity in the 'Filibuster City.' Although probably sincere in his condemnation of filibustering, he seems to have helped the prosecution chiefly because of the fee entailed. General Quitman was quoted as saying that the Spanish Government had employed Benjamin to prosecute the would-be liberators of Cuba for a fee of $25,000, but Benjamin, in one of his rare letters to the newspapers, branded the story as 'ridiculous.' Not long afterward, however, the United States Government allowed him $5,000 for his work.[9]

Benjamin's most important case during this period was the legal battle to break the will of the eccentric New Orleans multimillionaire, John McDonogh. *Murdoch et al.* v. *Executors of McDonogh et al.* probably brought Benjamin more prominence than any other case he ever argued in Louisiana. First tried in the Louisiana courts after McDonogh's death in October 1850, and not finally disposed of in the United States Supreme Court until early 1854, the suit was regarded in New Orleans as a *cause célèbre*. It ranked with the contempt proceedings instituted by Judge Hall against General Andrew Jackson, and the case in which Edward Livingston became embroiled with President Jefferson. As one of the leading attorneys in the case, Benjamin received considerable notice in the newspapers and for the first time his reputation as a lawyer spread throughout a number of states.

A hint of the character of McDonogh is given in a letter which Benjamin had written him as early as August 1838. In it Benjamin said that he had been instructed by Miss Mary Ann Rusha [?] to recover a lot in the suburb Saint Mary, which belonged to her father at his death and was inherited by Miss Rusha [?] as his sole heir. Then he continued:

Having understood that you are in possession of said lot and claim the ownership of it, I beg leave to inform you that unless the matter be amicably adjusted, I shall commence suit for the recovery of said property.

During the succeeding years the miserly old bachelor continued with great shrewdness and tenacity to add to his enormous estate. Not squeamish in his business methods, he was said to have derived income from brothels and 'drunkeries' on Girod Street, and to have disdained all requests for charity, not even answering 'piteous appeals' from his sisters. By such means he accumulated property holdings that after his death were reported to have been the largest of any individual in the United States.

It is not surprising that the hard-fisted old Croesus was hated by many of the New Orleanians. As late as 1850 they would point out the tall, stern-featured old man as he walked along the city streets, dressed in the fashion of a half century before, with his hair combed back and gathered in 'a sort of queue,' and carrying an old green umbrella. His last public appearance, according to local tradition, was on 24 October 1850, when, feeling too weak and weary to walk, he did an unprecedented thing. Departing from his life-long habit of miserly self-denial, he paid a dime for a ride on a court-house-bound omnibus!

When McDonogh's will with his instructions to his executors was examined, it was found to contain over 12,000 words, filling 30 closely printed pages. To the amazement of every one, the old skin-flint, after making provision for his sister Jane and her family, and certain other matters, left the great bulk of his estate to the corporations of New Orleans and Baltimore to establish schools for the poor of these cities, regardless of race or color. No part of his enormous real-estate holdings was to be sold, and they were to be managed by agents appointed by the respective cities. Furthermore, there was to be no alienation of the general estate under penalty of forfeiture, in which case Louisiana and Maryland were to become residuary devisees for the purpose of educating the poor in those states.

After an appraisement, it was found that the value of the estate in New Orleans parish alone was over two million dollars. It is not surprising that the McDonogh heirs, living in various states of the Union, attempted to break the will, and there was a great legal battle. After losing in the Louisiana district court, the heirs appealed to the state supreme court, employing Benjamin to represent them; and, when they were unsuccessful in this court, he filed suit in the United States Circuit Court for the Eastern District of Louisiana.

At the trial he argued, besides various technical points, that McDonogh did not want to lose control of the property even after his death and had used illegal methods to secure its subsequent control. With eloquent but not entirely convincing arguments he contended that McDonogh's object was 'transparent. His soul revolted more at severance from his wealth, than at its separation from his body.' Incapable of being completely generous, he 'could not bear to part entirely with the ownership of his estate. He sought to take that with him from the earth—to have it interred with his bones, and, true in death to the passion of his life, he left the mere management and usufruct of the "General Estate"—the posthumous embodiment of himself—the only true heir of his fortune.' The court, with Justice Theodore McCaleb presiding, declared the entire will null and void, and Benjamin and his clients rejoiced in their good fortune.

But there was still one more appeal—to the United States Supreme Court. The case was not tried until February 1854, after Benjamin had become a United States Senator. The attorneys for the appellants were Randall Hunt and two other lawyers; for the appellees, Benjamin and Reverdy Johnson of Maryland, while briefs were filed that had been prepared by two Louisiana lawyers and two French jurists. One of the ablest lawyers in the United States, Johnson figured with Benjamin in a considerable number of cases argued before the Supreme Court during that period. Now partly blind, he largely overcame the handicap by his tact and courtesy, his mental alertness, and his deep oratorical voice.

Although Maryland law was involved in the McDonogh case, most of the points at issue were in connection with the Louisiana code, and it was evident that the brief for the appellees was largely Benjamin's handiwork.

A newspaper reporter, present at the trial, said that 'whoever was not in the Supreme Courtroom this morning missed hearing one of the finest forensic speakers in the United States.' Benjamin's address was 'refined, his language pure, chaste and elegant; his learning and reading evidently great; his power of analysis and synthesis *very* great.' Significantly, however, the reporter added that Benjamin's argument was 'as logical as the nature of the case will admit.' For although Justice Campbell in his majority opinion praised the 'great power and ability' with which Benjamin and Johnson had presented their arguments, he clearly showed that the weight of the law was against them. The decision of the court was in favor of the beneficiaries of the will; New Orleans and Baltimore were given the right to receive the legacies for the schools.[10]

* * *

On 31 March 1858, a noteworthy day in the history of the Lower South, the final rail was laid in a railroad from New Orleans to Jackson, Mississippi. And at eight o'clock that evening the engine *James Robb* with a special train roared into Jackson, its wood-fired boiler throwing out great clouds of black pine smoke. The cotton planters, accustomed to making their trips to New Orleans on the leisurely river boats where there was plenty of time for conversation, drinking, and gambling, would now complain at times because they were 'too late to catch the infernal railroad' and were left at stations along the line. Perhaps they would even condemn the railroad, as did one irate planter, because the 'captains' were not congenial, and the trains would not wait at the stations long enough for him to visit the local bars. More typical were those Mississippians who gathered at a barbecue to celebrate the opening of the new railroad, and hail the driving of the 'golden spike,' which marked an epochal advance in the economic history of their section.

For no longer would the planters see 'the cotton factors shake their heads in disgust at bales of cotton caked with mud after having been rolled up and down the river banks'—cotton that often had to be hauled long distances over bad roads, even to reach the few navigable rivers. New Orleans could now be reached by rail at the 'top' speed of thirty miles an hour, and it would no longer be necessary to ship by the slow river boats. Furthermore, the railroad might later be extended into Tennessee and connected with the great Northwest.

Appropriately, the first engine to reach Jackson had been named for James Robb, a public-spirited financier of New Orleans who served as president of the railroad. But Benjamin had been one of the most influential promoters of the new line; he had been one of its original directors and its legal adviser until his duties in the Senate required him to relinquish the position.

With characteristic business acumen, Benjamin had perceived the important part which railroads would play in the development of commerce, and he sought to obtain for New Orleans and the Mississippi Valley the benefits to be derived from this new means of travel. After the Mississippi legislature had foiled in the middle 'thirties the plans, which he helped to promote, for a railroad from New Orleans to Cairo, the Crescent City had been satisfied with her river traffic; during the next few years she had lost some of her aggressive business spirit and become too absorbed in purely local matters. But she soon had a rude awakening—railroads and canals connecting the East and West began tapping her trade and threatened to ruin her commerce. In 1847 some 50,000 bales of cotton were shipped up the Ohio River from the New Orleans trading area, and the losses were increasing yearly.

Benjamin did not miss the implications of the situation. Entering again into the fight for railroad development, he worked zealously to secure the line from New Orleans to Jackson. He helped to promote a railroad convention at Monticello, Mississippi, in 1850, and was one of the original directors of the New Orleans, Jackson, and Great Northern Railroad Company, chartered by the Louisiana legislature in 1852. Among other activities in this connection, he made a notable speech on railroad development at the meeting of the Southwestern Railroad Convention in New Orleans on 7 January 1852.

Addressing the audience in response to a general demand from the floor, he declared, 'Let us ask ourselves how we can bind the South and the West, and the Southwest, in common bonds; how we can unite them indissolubly with the Northeastern and Atlantic States? Some great lines of intercommunication we all agree upon.' He advocated a railroad line northward from New Orleans through Jackson, later crossing the Ohio and meeting the Illinois Central, 'thus putting us and the Southwest in direct and speedy action with the North,' and concluded with some 'glowing remarks' on the efficient service railroads would render in spreading republican principles throughout the world.

In stating that a railroad connecting New Orleans with the Northwest would help to bring the various sections together and aid the growth of democracy, Benjamin displayed a statesmanlike vision. For the past half century or more the Northwest had been economically tied up with the South, but the Erie Canal and the railroads from the East to the West were fast drawing Illinois and the adjacent states into the orbit of the Eastern seaboard. This commercial relation would be largely responsible for the fact that the Middlewest would throw her great strength alongside that of the North in fighting the Southern Confederacy. Had the New Orleans, Jackson, and Great Northern Railroad been completed within a few years after it was chartered, the Northwest would have given much less help to the North during the war. In fact, the railroad might have tipped the scales in favor of the South during the hard-fought conflict.

Despite Benjamin's boast about the South's advantages in terrain for building railroads, the construction crews of the Jackson line had to lay rails across miles of swamp land and to brave alligators, snakes, and swarms of insects; the estimated cost of the railroad from New Orleans to Nashville was $30,000 a mile, or $12,300,000. Benjamin was later severely criticized for refusing to give the city council of New Orleans details regarding the bonding operations of the company, and in a partisan attack was declared to be always ready for 'a nefarious blow aimed at popular rights or public justice.'

After Benjamin became a member of the United States Senate he made several efforts to obtain government aid for the railroad. Next to James Robb, he deserves the most credit for the construction of the line which is now such an important part of the Illinois Central system.

But Benjamin, his vision widened by his recent visit to California, was thinking in terms not merely of national but of international trade. In his speech before the Southwestern Railroad Convention he had not only depicted the advantages of the New Orleans, Jackson, and Great Northern Railroad, but linked it with the proposed Tehuantepec line, across the Isthmus of Tehuantepec in Mexico.

This straight line of railroad [the Jackson, or present Illinois Central] will stop at New Orleans, but it will not cease there as a line of travel. That line carries us straight across the Gulf of Mexico to the narrow neck of land which divides the Pacific from the Atlantic, whereon Nature has bestowed every blessing of soil and climate, where she has even lowered the hills as if purposely to point out the way for a railroad; then when we cross this Isthmus, this Isthmus of Tehuantepec—what have we before us? The Eastern World! Its commerce makes empires of the countries to which it flows, and when they are deprived of it they are as empty bags, useless, valueless. That commerce belongs to New Orleans.

Although Benjamin did not originate the plan to build a railroad across the Isthmus of Tehuantepec, he had only to study the map of the territory to realize that here was a favorable route by which man could bridge the gap between the Atlantic and Pacific Oceans. The Panama route was shorter, to be sure, but the distance across the Isthmus of Tehuantepec at its narrowest point was only about 125 miles, and it was closer to the axis of international trade. And although engineers estimated that a canal across the Isthmus would be too costly, that did not preclude the possibility of a railroad.

Plans to build this railroad had been started in Mexico as early as 1842 but had made little progress in the midst of her frequent political upheavals. Then, in 1850 one of the early promoters, P. A. Hargous, came to New Orleans, where he soon enlisted the interest of some ten or twelve of the more wealthy and progressive citizens in the enterprise—including Benjamin. He served as attorney and spokesman for the company which was organized, and became the leading spirit in the promotion of the road.

Benjamin issued a prospectus containing an optimistic account of the project, with the proposed method of incorporating and financing. When it was discovered that the Louisiana constitution would not permit the promoters to get a suitable charter without a special act of the legislature, he headed a delegation to Baton Rouge to petition Governor Walker to call a special session of the assembly. The governor refusing, the promoters proceeded to form a temporary organization, with Benjamin as chairman and Bernard Fallon as secretary.

For a time the plans for the railroad appeared to be moving smoothly. The Tehuantepec Company sent a group of men to survey a route across the Isthmus. Hargous and Benjamin secured the help of Daniel Webster, Secretary of State under Fillmore, and a provisional treaty was drawn up and adopted by the Mexican Government. But then the hopes of the promoters were dashed to the ground. A new Mexican President, Arista, came into office and revoked the so-called Garay grant, on which the Tehuantepec Company was basing its operations. With public confidence at a low ebb, Benjamin went to Washington in July 1851 to obtain further aid from the United States Government.

After what he described as an encouraging interview with President Fillmore, he set out for Marshfield, Massachusetts, where he had a hopeful talk with Webster. To quote the account of the *Delta*, with its sly praise:

On the whole, the visit of Mr. Benjamin to Washington, has evidently had a most favorable effect on the interests of the Company in that quarter, as we anticipated it would. But not satisfied with all he had done in Washington, we perceive that our courteous and energetic friend paid a visit to the Secretary of State, at Marshfield. Of course, it would be a breach of official etiquette to introduce the subject to Mr. Webster, in his secluded family mansion, so far away from his bureau, but what objection could there be to the accomplished New Orleans lawyer going there to take a dish of Daniel's farfamed chowder, and incidentally broaching the Tehuantepec subject to him, just while he was waiting for his chowder to cool? We don't see any. In fact, when a thing is well done, we should not be too hypercritical as to the manner of doing it.

Whether or not at Benjamin's direct suggestion, Webster now played a card which the Mexicans could readily understand. He wrote to Letcher, the American minister to Mexico, suggesting that he might hint to the Mexican Government that all the money due under the Treaty of Guadeloupe Hidalgo had not been paid and the United States might feel justified in withholding the balance. Yet the Mexican Government still remained obdurate. Benjamin would not give up the fight, however, and we shall see that he carried it into the United States Senate and even international banking circles.[11]

* * *

Although Benjamin was unable to give as much attention as he wished to Bellechasse after he returned to active practice, he retained his interest in the plantation. Mrs. Rebecca Levy remained as mistress at Bellechasse, and he joined her there whenever he could spare the time. Two years younger than Rebecca, he had always regarded her as 'a sort of superior being.' A strong character, witty, intelligent, and charming, she was, in the absence of a wife to whom he could turn when he felt the need, 'the sharer of his perplexities, his triumphs, his troubles, as much as if she were part of himself.' Their deep affection and understanding remained unbroken until her death.

At Bellechasse Benjamin found rest and relaxation after his exhausting mental labor. With a sensitive appreciation of the beauties of nature, he found the green lawn, the moss-hung trees, the long vista of water and cultivated fields constant sources of delight. He and Rebecca were never happier than when acting as hosts at the plantation. He would often arrive at the wharf on the week-end with 'a boatload of guests, old and young.' Rebecca rarely knew how many 'J.P.' would have with him, and although he usually brought a generous supply of provisions, fruit, and delicacies from New Orleans, she was sometimes hard put to feed the company. One guest who came so frequently as to be almost a member of the household was Benjamin's father-in-law, Auguste St. Martin, a delightful old gentleman who entertained the young people with tales of the bloody slave insurrection in Santo Domingo.

Benjamin entered heartily into the life of the young people at Bellechasse and was a favorite with them. He particularly enjoyed the company of young girls. His niece, Leah Levy, made him her confidant, and, whatever her troubles, they seemed less critical after she talked them over with him during a stroll in the garden; to Leah 'Uncle Ben' seemed like 'one of her own age, only more wise and gentle.'

When the young people gathered about the table in the evening, he often joined them in the old-fashioned game of capping verses. Benjamin could recite 'a wonderful stock' of verses from memory, and he would reel forth line after line, challenging his companions to complete the quotations. Another way of amusing his young friends was to tell them ghost stories. His favorite time for this was 'when midnight approached in stormy season,' and he could work his listeners up to the proper pitch of hushed excitement.[12]

* * *

In the summer of 1851 Benjamin made his customary trip to France to visit Natalie and Ninette. After the Revolution of 1848, Louis Napoleon had been elected President of a new French republic and now he was plotting to increase his power. It would not be until 2 December 1851—the anniversary of Austerlitz—that he would accomplish the coup d'état by which he was to become the French emperor. But Benjamin now had an opportunity to study the character of the wily adventurer at close range—an experience that would be most useful to him as Confederate Secretary of State.

When the New Orleans Whig Convention met in October 1851, Benjamin still had not returned to the city. In his absence he and James Robb were nominated for the state senate. Benjamin's friends assured the voters that the chief issue upon which he would accept the nomination was the calling of a state convention to remodel the constitution of 1845. More specifically, they announced that he favored constitutional provisions for an elective judiciary and a well-regulated system of free banks and for empowering the legislature to enact liberal laws for railways and manufacturing establishments. The Democratic papers in particular were quick to call attention to his radical change since 1845, but although he did not deny the professions made in his name he was elected without great difficulty.

When the legislature met at Baton Rouge in January 1852, Governor Walker sought to stave off the movement for the constitutional convention, but the legislature chose to let the people decide whether the convention should be called, and they voted in the affirmative. It was summoned to meet on the following July.[13]

Meantime, the legislature continued its session through January and into February 1853, with Benjamin taking an important part in the deliberations. With several of the matters under consideration he was seriously concerned, and one—the election of a United States Senator—affected the whole course of his political career.

Benjamin had hardly been elected to the upper house of the legislature when it became clear to the discerning that he was the strongest candidate for the United States Senate. Before the meeting of the state senate, it is true, there had been some opposition even among influential newspapers in his own party. Two of them had argued that such an honor should go to a candidate who, in their opinion, was better qualified or, at least, had a longer record of party service. One newspaper preferred Randall Hunt; another, Duncan F. Kenner, a wealthy and influential sugar planter of Ascension Parish.

To this opposition was added that of the *Delta*. After acknowledging that Benjamin was 'very sagacious,' possessed 'great tact, and would make a very brilliant and effective Senator,' it continued in an ironic vein:

His appearance in that body would startle the gossips at Washington. His boyish figure and girlish face,—his gentle, innocent, ingenuous expression and manner, his sweet and beautifully modulated voice, would render him decidedly the most unsenatorial figure in that body of grey beards and full grown men. But when he should arise in the Senate, and in the most modest and graceful manner proceed to pour forth a strain of the most fluent and beautifully expressed ideas, of the most subtle and ingenious arguments, of the most compact and admirably arranged statements,—casting a flood of light over the dryest and most abstruse subjects, and carrying all minds and hearts with him by his resistless logic and insinuating elocution,—then would the old Senators stretch their eyes and mouths with wonder, whispering to one another, 'That's a devilish smart little fellow,'—then would all the ladies declare, 'What a love of a man!—what a perfect Admirable Crichton,—so beautiful, yet so wise,—so gentle, yet so terrible in sarcasm,—so soft-toned, and yet so vigorous in logic!'

The *Delta* added, however, that Benjamin, despite his talents, would hardly be elected to the Senate, because as the leader of several great enterprises he was too much needed within the state, and the Whig candidate would be Duncan F. Kenner.[14]

But Benjamin was elected to the Senate by a large majority. In the Whig caucus he obtained 37 votes to 19 for Kenner and 11 for Randall Hunt. And he later secured an easy victory on the floor of the state senate, receiving a majority of 12 over General Solomon W. Downs, his leading opponent in the constitutional convention of 1845.

Benjamin's easy defeat of Kenner and Hunt was a surprise to their supporters. But the *Delta* offered a likely explanation:

The country members rather preferred a gentleman . . . [who] was a sugar planter, and had, therefore, a common interest and sympathy with them. Another great advantage enjoyed by Mr. Benjamin was in the fact of being a prominent member of the legislature . . . Mr. Benjamin made good use of this advantage. He not only rendered himself very agreeable to the members of the legislature, but he manifested a zeal, industry and capacity in the preparation of business for the legislature,—digesting and framing bills, and drawing up reports, etc.,—which produced a most favorable impression as to his great practical talent and usefulness.

Now outdoing itself in praising Benjamin, the *Delta* said,

Though not yet forty, he has reached the topmost round of the ladder of distinction as an advocate and counselor in this state . . . He has a fine imagination, an exquisite taste, great power of discrimination, a keen, subtle logic, excellent memory, admirable talent of analysis . . . [While attending to a very heavy law practice, he had] had time to look after one of the largest sugar plantations in the state, to pay a yearly visit to Paris, to see to the interest of the Great Tehuantepec enterprise, to fulfill all of the duties of an active partisan, of a public-spirited citizen, of a liberal gentleman, with a taste for the elegance, the social pleasures and refinements of life.' [15]

To this strong praise was added a tribute from a Washington correspondent of a New Orleans newspaper, who wrote that the National Whigs in the capital were much gratified at Benjamin's election, since he possessed, among other qualifications for his new position, 'that practical business ability wherewith' the Senate is 'not now, and seldom has been, overstocked.' [16]

Credit must also be given the Democratic leader, John Slidell, for his part in Benjamin's election. It was even asserted that Benjamin was seated in the Senate by 'the strenuous efforts of Slidell and his followers in Baton Rouge.' Although this statement was open to question, since there was a Whig majority in the legislature, already there was some evidence of an understanding between Benjamin and the crafty politician then fighting Pierre Soulé for the control of the state Democratic machine.[17]

During the following months Benjamin devoted much of his time to political activities. He was nominated as a Whig senatorial representative from New Orleans to the constitutional convention, and elected despite the criticism because of his changed opinions since the constitutional convention of 1845. Now one of the most influential Louisiana Whigs, he spoke at a party rally in New Orleans on 1 July, praising General Winfield Scott, the Whig presidential nominee; later, although he was not overly enthusiastic about the general, he stumped the state in his behalf.[18]

Meantime, at the constitutional convention which met in July 1852 he had been made a member of the judiciary committee and chairman of the committee on style, and took the lead in writing new constitutional provisions in the interest of the New Orleans merchants and lawyers and their planter allies. On every important issue he followed the program he had outlined in the campaign. Reversing his position in 1845, he and the other Whig leaders carried through articles providing for elective judges of the Supreme Court and District Courts, removing many of the restrictions on citizenship and office-holding, and liberalizing the provisions about banks and corporations.

Benjamin's most glaring change of front since 1845, however, was in his advocacy of the total population basis of representation—a system which gave an even greater influence to the slave interests and, consequently, to the Whig planters then under the suffrage provision of the Federal Constitution. The so-called Federal basis provided that five Negroes should be counted as three white men, but under the total population basis each Negro was counted in determining the basis for voting, and the additional representative strength was given to the masters. Benjamin was accused of using his eloquence and sarcasm to drive the reluctant members to vote for the provision. After adjournment for the day, so it was said, he would mollify 'the subject of his sarcasm by his pleasant smile, his silvery laughter, or—greatest concession' allow his opponent 'to excel him in a game of tenpins.' The measure was passed without great difficulty, but ten of the city delegation voted against it and there was considerable opposition in the press.

How could Benjamin justify his complete reversal of his position in 1845? The truth seems to be that he was governed by mixed motives of principle and expediency. For his support of the banking and corporation provision there appears to have been a satisfactory explanation. It had now been fifteen years since the Panic of 1837;

there had been a business revival, and he believed it was safe to give a freer hand to the various commercial projects then being launched. He could heartily concur in the indignant exclamation of James Robb, the railroad promoter: 'What instance is there in the history of the Anglo-Saxon race of an inhibition to embark in an enterprise requiring over five hundred thousand dollars capital?'

But Benjamin's attitude toward the provisions for elective judges and the total population basis was undoubtedly influenced by practical politics. The people wanted to select the judges and certain other officials by direct vote, and he felt the Whigs had better throw them a sop. They would be safe in doing so—and here was the crux of the situation—so long as the slaves were counted as equal to the whites in determining the basis of representation.

At a meeting on September 8 in the ballroom of the Louisiana Hotel the Democrats of the First and Second Wards in New Orleans resolved that the adoption of the total population basis was a 'Whig proceeding intended to give the legislative control of the State to that party, by degrading the free white citizen to the level of a negro slave,' and declared that they agreed with the opinion on the question given by J. P. Benjamin in 1845. A local newspaper openly insinuated that his change of views was due to the fact that he was now interested in a plantation.

The new constitution was severely criticized for a number of its provisions in the interest of the propertied classes, particularly the total population basis of representation. The 'Negro-good-as-white-man Constitution' met with strong opposition in northern Louisiana, and in the state as a whole it was ratified by only a small majority. The large plantation owners and their city allies had indeed secured a representation far out of proportion to their numbers, and, since they were mostly Whigs, the measure was indeed to the advantage of this still powerful party. The census figures showed that 11,264 white residents of 7 parishes in the alluvial lands where there were 47,373 Negroes obtained as much political power as 35,681 white residents of 13 parishes—chiefly of the upland pine country.

'The one hundred Negro slaves of J. P. Benjamin of Plaquemines, are made just as good as one hundred citizens,' one opposition paper complained. And yet one must not infer that Benjamin's motives in voting for the total population basis were entirely selfish, for he was fearful of the radical and demagogic tendencies in the country and felt that Louisiana should be kept under the control of the Whig planters and businessmen. Apparently, he was not greatly concerned with the fact that the discrimination against the poorer whites, with few or no slaves, would help to make them, in a later period, a fertile field for that very demagoguery which he tried to curb. Huey Long, the antithesis of almost everything that Benjamin stood for, was to spring from a North Louisiana parish which had few slaves and correspondingly small political influence in *ante-bellum* days.[19]

* * *

For better or for worse, *ante-bellum* Louisiana was ruled by gentlemen, and the three leading Whig candidates for the United States Senate in 1852, Benjamin, Kenner, and Hunt, were all gentlemen—and all members then or soon afterwards of the exclusive Boston Club. This club derived its name from the game of cards then in vogue and had no connection with the Massachusetts Puritan stronghold. Men who could mix a good drink or play a good hand of cards, as well as direct the political and commercial destinies of the state, the members included the so-called 'big four'—Slidell, Benjamin, Soulé, and Randall Hunt—who largely dominated Louisiana politics during that decade. And then there were Benjamin's personal friends, gentlemen like 'Dick' Taylor, the son of Zachary Taylor and a future Confederate general; Edward Bradford, the president of the club for a number of years, who was soon to become Benjamin's law partner; and the Huntington brothers, 'Wash' (Washington), an attorney, and Walter, a cotton merchant.

It was Walter Huntington—so we learn from the historian of the Boston Club—who should be remembered not only because he was a friend of Benjamin's and prominent in club affairs, signing the notation in the minute book in connection with the closing of the club during the Civil War, but also because he had the distinction of introducing barbarous Waukesha, Wisconsin, into the mysteries of the mint julep.

In 1852 Benjamin was also chosen a member of the Union Club of New York City, where he came into contact with the same type of men and ideas as he did at the Boston Club. Founded in 1836, the Union Club had suffered from the editorial diatribes of James Gordon Bennett and his *New York Herald*, which asserted that 'club life only flourishes among a particular caste in England . . . Down with all clubs say we'; and, again, that 'No system of society, no reunion of genius can be refined or pure . . . that excluded women.' But the Union Club weathered the storm. When Benjamin was a member he associated with the élite of New York—merchants, bankers, physicians, politicians, educators, and 'gentlemen of leisure' —as well as some Southern members such as George Eustis, later Secretary of the Confederate legation in Paris, John Slidell, and Stephen Duncan, the wealthy and cultivated Mississippi planter.

Without the usual ties of a married man, Benjamin found relaxation and companionship at his clubs. They also helped to further his career and to set his mind in a conservative mold. Obviously, the members of the Boston Club had the most influence upon him. For reasons of conviction or expediency, they were defenders of the *status quo* and many possessed that pleasant ability (not confined to Southerners) to look at a social abuse and not see it. And yet it is easy to criticize those *ante-bellum* New Orleanians too severely, for they were a charming, and, on the whole, admirable lot of men. They were able and energetic and conducted a vast commerce upon the principle, which they extended to other professions, that 'the law of merchants is the law of honor.' [20]

* * *

During the decade from 1840 to 1850 the white population of Louisiana had increased from 158,457 to 225,491 of which about half were foreign born—chiefly Irish, German, and French—and natives of other American states. Benjamin, who fitted easily into this cosmopolitan picture and was one of the most prominent men in 'the greatest city in the South,' was in constant demand socially and as a speaker for public meetings and at 'those semi-social public gatherings where ladies were gently inducted into political mysteries.' [21] Before he left New Orleans to take his seat in the United States Senate he was given a banquet by his fellow members of the Boston Club, in which some of the 'most prominent and substantial gentlemen' in the city joined in the tribute to their distinguished fellow citizen.

The banquet, held in the ladies' dining-room of the St. Charles Hotel, was quite an elegant affair, with covers laid for about a hundred guests, including such men as James Robb and John R. Grymes. Edward A. Bradford presided over the ceremonies, with Benjamin sitting at his right. When the guests had finished the dinner, selected and served according to the best style of old New Orleans, the speechmaking began.

After some introductory remarks, Benjamin arose and thanked his hosts for the honor they had bestowed upon him; he 'adverted feelingly to the time when, a poor and friendless boy, he came to this city twenty-six years ago; and expressed with much emotion the gratitude he felt to his fellow citizens here for the uninterrupted kindness, encouragement and confidence with which they had ever treated him.' He also took the occasion to refer to the commercial development of the state, so dear to his heart, and 'dwelt with peculiar emphasis on the great results that must flow from the carrying out of the Tehuantepec Railroad project. These great measures, he urged, had only failed, or had not been as greatly promoted as they might have been, for lack of energetic application and persistence on the part of the Representatives of Louisiana in Congress,' a deficiency which it might be inferred he would do his part to remedy.

Speeches were also made by James Robb and Garnett Duncan, who expressed their full confidence in the senator-elect; and 'the evening closed with a quick and joyous succession of speech, anecdote, and song.'[22]

Moreover, Benjamin soon received a greater honor from a national source. During the late winter of 1852-3 President Fillmore nominated him as a justice of the United States Supreme Court to succeed the late Justice John McKinley. Fillmore had previously nominated Edward A. Bradford and George E. Badger of North Carolina, but neither was confirmed by the Senate. The President was determined to make one more effort, and, there being considerable sentiment in favor of nominating a candidate resident in Judge McKinley's circuit, named Benjamin—the first Jew ever to be offered an appointment to the Court. There was a strong likelihood that he would have been approved by the Senate, but he declined the offer because of his preference for an active political career and his desire to secure a larger remuneration for himself and his family than the position would provide.

Although Fillmore then nominated William C. Micou on 24 February 1853, the outgoing Democratic Senate would not confirm any Whig appointee at this late date in the session, and when Congress adjourned the position was still vacant. We do not know whether Benjamin suggested Micou's name. In any case the nomination was offered to Benjamin and his partner and also to Bradford, who became a member of the firm the next month. There is no other instance in American history of a nomination to the Supreme Court being offered to three men who were or were to become law partners.

It was a notable tribute not only to Benjamin and his two partners but also to the New Orleans bar. At the time the nominations were made, Bradford was only thirty-nine years old, Micou forty-seven, and Benjamin, the ranking member of the firm, forty-one.[23]

VI. *Benjamin Represents Louisiana in the Senate*

BENJAMIN entered the United States Senate at the special session beginning on Friday, 4 March 1853. This was the day of the inauguration of President Franklin Pierce and the ceremonies were attended by one of the largest crowds that had ever gathered in Washington. The visitors poured in by carriage and horse and on foot, until there were some seventy or eighty thousand people within the city limits. Although there was the customary inauguration weather, raw and wet, with a cold northeasterly wind 'wafting a pretty continuous, though fast-melting snow,' thousands of undaunted spectators lined Pennsylvania Avenue to see the President-elect, with his military escort, as he rode in an open barouche from Willard's to the Capitol. The large gates of the Capitol yard were closed to carriages so that as many people as possible could listen to the inaugural address.

Rarely in bad spirits, Benjamin must have derived both pleasure and satisfaction from the exercises of the day—not merely the presidential inauguration but, more particularly, his own induction into office. The Senate had met at noon, shortly before the arrival of Pierce at the Capitol. After an opening prayer, the meeting had been called to order and the names of the new Senators read in alphabetical order by the Secretary. First came 'Honorable C. G. Atherton of New Hampshire,' then 'Honorable Judah P. Benjamin of Louisiana,' followed by a dozen others, including the 'Little Giant,' Stephen A. Douglas of Illinois; Sam Houston of Texas; and R. M. T. Hunter of Virginia, whom Benjamin was to succeed as the Confederate Secretary of State.

As Benjamin's name was called he stepped forward and the oath of office was administered to him by Lewis Cass, the oldest member of the Senate. Thus he had realized another of his ambitions. He was not the first Jew to sit in that body. David Levy Yulee of Florida, also of Sephardic Jewish ancestry and a native of the Virgin Islands, had served in the Senate a few years before and was soon to be re-elected. But Benjamin was the only Jew in Congress at that time and he made a record there that has never been surpassed by any member of his race.

In his inaugural address President Pierce struck a happy note when he said, 'We have been carried in safety through a perilous crisis. Wise counsel, like those which gave us the Constitution, prevailed to uphold it.'[1] For the country was now in the so-called Finality Period, when the great majority of Americans wanted to accept as a finality the Compromise of 1850. During the preceding session of Congress there had been little debate about slavery except in connection with foreign affairs. Business was prospering; the people generally were satisfied and backed the reigning politicians in their efforts to bury the old animosities.[2]

And yet, under the apparent calm, new forces were working and would soon begin to reach the surface. Only a few months before, the *Picayune* had appeared with black streamers to commemorate the death of Daniel Webster; Clay and Calhoun also had died within the past three years. Political leadership was passing to new men, vigorous and radical, and they were to take the lead in the movements culminating in disunion and civil war. During the same year that Benjamin was elected to the Senate there appeared an epochal book—*Uncle Tom's Cabin*—written by the wife of a poor Ohio college professor. Familiar with its emotional indictment of Southern society, Benjamin was all the more fearful of the future.[3]

During the quiet session of Congress following the inauguration of President Pierce, Benjamin had the opportunity to study his colleagues in the Senate, and to form a tentative estimate of their character and ability. During the next eight years in Washington and also the four years of the Confederacy, he was to be associated not only with R. M. T. Hunter but with numerous other public men then in the city. Although the Senate had already lost a little of the importance it had in the days of Clay, Calhoun, and Webster, it was still referred to as 'the greatest deliberative body on earth,' the only representative assembly comparable to it being the House of Commons.

In the Commons, Disraeli had already won a position of leadership. To what extent would Benjamin rival his record?

President Pierce had been a general in the Mexican War, and when he planned to stop by New Orleans on his return to his native New Hampshire, Lieutenant P. G. T. Beauregard had given him a letter of introduction [4] to Benjamin—a man of the 'highest order of talent,' who could stand among the first of his profession 'even in the New England States which have furnished our country with such a long list of imperishable names.' Whether or not Benjamin had the opportunity, as Beauregard hoped, to show Pierce the hospitality for which 'New Orleans was famous,' soon after Pierce became President he invited Benjamin to dine at the White House; Mrs. Jefferson Davis was present, and doubtless also her husband, the Secretary of War. A tall, dignified, and rather austere man with an encyclopedic though somewhat routine mind, Jefferson Davis was then only about forty-five years old and at the height of his mental and physical powers. Not for several years, however, was there to be any evidence of a rapprochement between him and the man who was to become his most influential adviser during the Civil War.

Varina Howell, the second wife of Davis, was an attractive woman still in her twenties, with dark hair and eyes, and a graceful carriage. The granddaughter of a Revolutionary governor of New Jersey (and, therefore, in the opinion of some Southern extremists, with an ineradicable Yankee taint), Mrs. Davis was not only a former Natchez belle but a woman of unusual charm and ability.

'When she is in the mood, I do not know so pleasant a person. She is awfully clever always,' later wrote a member of her feminine circle.[5]

Now meeting Benjamin at this White House dinner, Mrs. Davis was at first distinctly disappointed in him. She did not consider his appearance prepossessing; he had 'rather the air of a witty bon vivant than that of a great Senator,' and he seemed to prefer 'the light society topics' to graver subjects of conversation. In fact, he appeared to her 'only an elegant young man of the world, and a past master of the art of witty repartee.' And yet Mrs. Davis was deeply affected by Benjamin's voice; she found it difficult to give an adequate idea of the impression it left upon her. 'It seemed a silver thread woven amidst the warp and woof of sounds which filled the drawing room; it was low, full and soft; yet the timbre of it penetrated every ear like a silver trumpet. From the first sentence he uttered, whatever he said attracted and chained the attention of his audience.'⁶ Benjamin's voice was already contributing to his rise in the legal and political world. It was, his friend Thomas Bayard stated, 'of singularly musical timbre, high pitched, but articulate, resonant and sweet.' Also, according to Bayard, 'He excelled in conversation, with an easy flow of diction, embellished by a singular mastery of languages at the base of which lay the Latin and its fibres of the French and Spanish.'⁷

The first brief session of the Thirty-third Congress was over by early April. Two months later, on 15 June 1852, Philip Benjamin died in Charleston of 'cholera morbus.' He was seventy-three years old and, since giving up his small business several years before, had been living on Nassau Street, an obscure neighborhood on the outskirts of the city. It must have distressed Judah to think how slender had been the ties between him and his father; the remittances he had sent appear to have been an expression of duty, not affection.⁸

Meantime, Benjamin returned to New Orleans. During the next year he made two important changes in his business affairs: he sold his half interest in Bellechasse, and became associated with two new law partners. From two visitors to Bellechasse about this time we get an impression of the life there and in the near-by countryside during those last years in which Benjamin had an interest in the plantation. Charles Fleischmann, who was making a survey for the United States Commissioner of Patents, mentioned Benjamin as among the Louisianians to whom he was indebted for 'that far-famed hospitable welcome peculiarly characteristic of the southern gentleman and planter,' and wrote rhapsodically of the steamboat trip on the lower river by Bellechasse.

I cannot describe the delight I felt when I first entered the State of Louisiana. Its river, the creator of this rich alluvial territory, after having tossed and rolled its mighty waters against the wild shores of the upper country . . . begins at once to slacken its current and keep its turbid stream within the bounds of fertile banks, gliding majestically through highly cultivated plains covered with the graceful sugar cane, the uniformity of which is continually diversified by beautiful dwellings, gardens, and towering chimneys of the sugar-houses, the handsome fronts of which stand forth in the picturesque background of the forest, forming an ever-changing scene.

The traveller who floats in one of the gigantic palaces of the southwest, can from the high deck behold with delight the enchanting scenery the whole day long, and look with regret on the setting sun, which, gradually withdrawing behind the dark outline of the cypress forest, leaves this lovely country reposing under the dark mantle of night.

Idyllic as was the life at Bellechasse, Benjamin was now unable to devote much time to the place. Solon Robinson, who visited it in 1849, found that the refinery was under the direction of Benjamin's brother, who was 'very successful in the business' and 'making as good an article as ever need be called for.' There were then a hundred and forty slaves on the plantation, including eighty field hands; and eight white men, most of them Germans, were employed in the refinery.

But sugar growing was subject to many risks, with consequent fluctuation in profits. It was not surprising that about 1852 a flood swept over the fields near Bellechasse and, though Benjamin's own front levees held firm, the backwater crept in through crevasses on neighboring places. Higher and higher the water rose until it reached the very steps of the mansion and threatened to come into the house. The yard was filled with cattle and deer from the swamps, which huddled in the high ground near the mansion. The flood caused Benjamin severe loss. Sugar cane dies quickly under water; his growing crop and even the seed cane were destroyed.

To add to his troubles, a friend failed to meet his financial obligations, so that Benjamin had to pay a $60,000 note which, in accordance with the custom of the day, he had generously, but unwisely, endorsed. After his election to the Senate he sold his interest in Bellechasse to Samuel Packwood for about $168,000. He had shown great vision and energy as a sugar planter and his ultimate failure was largely owing to circumstances beyond his control.[9]

For several years the health of Benjamin's partner, William C. Micou, had been bad, and now with Benjamin in the Senate the burden was more than Micou could bear, even though a young lawyer, John Finney, had been added to the firm. Early in 1854 Micou died from a disease of the brain, 'brought on by intense mental application.' His death was a warning to the hard-working Benjamin.

For the next six years the New Orleans firm continued under the name of Benjamin, Bradford, and Finney. John Finney was a capable lawyer and Benjamin had a high respect for his personal character. But Finney never attained as eminent a position at the bar as did Edward Bradford, the new partner, whom Benjamin was to regard as the most finished lawyer he had ever known. A member of an old New England family and a graduate of Yale and the Harvard Law School, Bradford was not only trained to habits of patient research but was able to resist the lure of politics. He was not an orator like Benjamin, not 'so ingenious, so fertile in suggesting plausible pleas,' but he had the same gift for clear analysis of legal problems. Bradford's cool and cautious temperament proved a valuable check on Benjamin's over-sanguine nature. The two partners became fast friends and remained so until Bradford's death.[10]

* * *

Assured that the New Orleans practice was in capable hands, Benjamin devoted himself to his political duties, his practice before the United States Supreme Court, and various business projects, appearing only occasionally in the Louisiana courts. His legal earnings alone during this period were estimated at some $40,000 to $50,000 annually, a very large sum for that period.[11]

Early in December 1853, Benjamin had to be in Washington for his first long session of the Senate, which met from then until 7 August 1854. He was assigned to the committee on commerce, and, later, that on private land claims. The land claims committee, in particular, benefited from his work, a considerable number of its manuscript reports at this time being under his signature.[12] As early as February 1854, Senator Butler of South Carolina complimented 'the honorable Senator from Louisiana, who perceives with so much cleverness everything his mind touches.'[13] He made numerous talks, short and businesslike, on the floor, and commended himself to his fellow-senators by his intelligent attention to his duties.

As the months of the long session of the Thirty-third Congress passed, however, it was the slavery question with which Benjamin was most occupied. This was the absorbing topic of discussion in the Senate of that decade, and it was in reference to it that Benjamin made nearly all of his notable speeches. He was, as we know, not a fanatical defender of slavery, but respect for Southern rights, the extreme arguments of some of his opponents, and considerations of expediency all led him to become a more and more outspoken champion of the slave interests.

During this session of Congress some of the more radical Southerners started an agitation to embroil the United States in a war with Spain in order to acquire Cuba as a slave territory. This was only a few months before the publication of the bellicose Ostend Manifesto. On 17 May 1854 Senator Mallory of Florida, the future Confederate Secretary of the Navy, introduced a resolution stating that there was 'a settled design to throw Cuba ultimately into the hands of its negro population, and to revive there . . . the scenes of the San Domingo revolution.' [14]

That afternoon a severe thunder-storm, accompanied by heavy rain, swept over Washington and in the House of Representatives the roaring of the storm, as it beat upon the dome of the House, hushed 'the eloquence of a member into silence.' In the Senate, however, 'the artillery of the elements' was little heard, owing, the *National Intelligencer* [15] presumed, to its leeward position in the Capitol. But could this have been partly because the vocal artillery of the members was louder than that of the storm? In any event, Benjamin met with no such competition a week later when he presented to the Senate resolutions somewhat similar to Mallory's, which had been passed by the Louisiana legislature. The alarmist reports were, however, denied by both the Cuban Captain-General and the British Foreign Secretary, and Senator J. M. Clayton of Delaware, a recent Secretary of State, challenged Benjamin unavailingly to bring an expression of belief in the story from the incumbent Secretary or from any other man who had ever held the office.[16]

Far transcending in importance the discussion of the Cuban question was the debate during this session of Congress on the so-called Nebraska Bill. Late in 1853 the audacious young Senator Stephen A. Douglas of Illinois had returned, rested and refreshed, from a foreign tour made after the death of his wife. Plunging with new zest into his work, he brought out in January 1854, from the Senate Committee on Territories, a bill providing for popular sovereignty on the slavery question in the Kansas-Nebraska territory.

The quiet following the Compromise of 1850 now rudely disturbed, the Senate was plunged into a long and acrimonious debate during which Benjamin delivered several speeches that helped to increase his reputation as an orator and Southern protagonist. The plan to destroy the line separating the slave and free territory west of Missouri he defended as a return to 'the traditions of the fathers,' since it announced as a matter of principle that the Federal Government was not to legislate upon the question of slavery. He also reiterated the familiar contention of his political group that the South merely asked to be let alone, an argument that was now countered in the North with the assertion that it was Douglas, a Democrat, who had again opened up the slavery question in Congress.[17]

The Kansas-Nebraska Bill was passed in late May 1854, but the Senate continued to meet for another tumultuous three months. During June [18] Benjamin became involved in a debate with Senator Charles Sumner of Massachusetts over the constitutionality of the fugitive slave law. Sumner, one of the boldest and most scholarly members of the Senate,[19] was generally acknowledged to be the intellectual leader of the anti-slavery party in Congress. Six feet four inches tall, with an impressive figure, powerful voice, and deep convictions, Sumner was a formidable opponent in debate. The tilt between him and the nimble-witted Benjamin, with his musical voice and foreign appearance, was a treat for the spectators; it was also a real test of Benjamin's learning and forensic ability, the first debate of any national significance in which he participated.

Courteously, yet clearly and inexorably, Benjamin reviewed the chief provisions of the Constitution, including the fourth article, which required that full faith be given in each state to the public acts, records, and judicial proceedings of the other states; and also that fugitive slaves escaping from one state to another shall not be discharged from their 'service or labor, but shall be delivered up on claim of the party to whom such service or labor may be due.' Then Benjamin asked Sumner whether he acknowledged 'any obligation imposed by the Constitution of the United States for the return of fugitive slaves from the free states to those by whom they are held to service of labor in the slave states.'

Sumner was in a quandary. It was obvious that Benjamin was, outmaneuvering him. Instead of answering directly, Sumner attempted to slip out of the difficulty by asking Benjamin an awkward question.

'And before I answer that question,' Sumner said, 'I desire to ask the Senator from Louisiana, whether, under the clause of the Constitution of the United States, which secures to the citizens of every state the privileges and immunities of citizens of the United States, a colored citizen of Massachusetts can, without any crime, in South Carolina or Louisiana be so seized and thrown into prison, and then afterwards, on failure to pay certain alleged jail fees, be sold absolutely into slavery?'

Benjamin answered that he thought this was entirely unconstitutional.

Sumner then said that he was 'very glad that the Senator says it is entirely unconstitutional. I will then ask the Senator if he is ready in his place to introduce an act of Congress to carry out that provision of the Constitution to secure to the colored citizens of the North their rights in South Carolina and Louisiana.'

Sumner may have thought that he had Benjamin driven into a corner. But Benjamin cleverly eluded him.

'This is a very extraordinary method of answering a question,' he said. 'I have heard of the Yankee method of answering one question by asking another; but this is answering one by asking two. [Laughter] It is not my desire to enter into any polemical controversy upon this subject with the honorable Senator from Massachusetts, but, as I stated before, I put my question with a sincere and earnest desire to ascertain whether he and the gentlemen with whom he acts, or whose organ he is upon the floor, really recognized any constitutional obligation on the part of the free states, or on the part of Congress, to provide for the return of a fugitive slave from the free to the slave states? Whether that obligation exists any-where under the Constitution? Or, in other words, whether this article of the Constitution was intended to apply to slaves?'

'Before answering the question of the Senator [laughter],' Sumner countered, 'I should like to have him deal by me as he desired me to deal by him. I should like to have him tell me whether it is in the power of Congress, under the clause of the Constitution to which I have referred, and which is side by side with the other clause on fugitives from labor, to pass an act to secure to colored citizens of the North, their rights in South Carolina and Louisiana? The Senator must answer that question before he can confront this discussion.'

'My object is answered, sir,' was Benjamin's reply.

Senator Clay interpolated, 'Exactly; do not say another word.'

But Benjamin added, 'I imagine sir, that there is not a man in the country who will not now thoroughly understand the object for which I put the question. That object is entirely answered. To a plain, respectful inquiry put to the Senator from Massachusetts, in relation to his understanding of the provision of the Constitution, about which he declared his sentiments upon this floor, and in rela-tion to which he has always said that his sentiments have been mis-construed, he has answered by submitting to me a series of in-quiries. I answered the first, supposing that upon my answering that, he would then be willing to answer my question. Instead of that I find myself upon the stand. I shall therefore, decline further discussion.'

With all the debates on the slavery issue, this was one of the most trying sessions in the history of the Senate. On one occasion a member did not finish his speech until daybreak, and there was often great excitement.[20] Of the night session on 25-26 May, when the Nebraska Bill was passed, the *National Intelligencer* [21] had to admit that 'some of the closing scenes . . . were personal and not strictly within parliamentary bounds.' Certainly it would seem that the session would have been disturbing and exhausting for Benjamin. And yet in June he intimated that he found it pleasant and even diverting.

Writing to A. H. H. Stuart, the late Secretary of the Interior and a prominent Virginia Whig,[22] Benjamin said,

I have not been here long enough to feel as you suppose any inclination to abandon public life, and perhaps one great reason is that my whole previous life has been so *very* busy and laborious, that I feel with more sensitive pleasure than others the exquisite charm of comparative leisure, and freedom from the constant irksome demands on the time and patience of a lawyer practising in a large city. I suppose, however, that the novelty will wear off, and as is generally the case with poor human nature, I shall feel a longing for that very busy excitement from which I now feel happy in having escaped.

But he added:

I am sorry, my dear Sir, that I cannot take quite so hopeful a view of the future as you seem to anticipate. I fully agree with you that the present administration is already broken down, and that the democratic party properly so called is as much distracted by divisions and split into fragments as when it received so signal a defeat in 1840. But where is the Whig party? *Every northern Whig in both branches voted against the Nebraska bill.* Nay—more— In a recent visit to New York I became satisfied from all that I could see and hear from men whom I had formerly regarded as perfectly sound on Southern questions, that a gulf wide, deep, and I fear, impassable is already opened between the northern and southern Whigs. They will unquestionably form at the North for the next presidential election a grand coalition based *exclusively* on what they call opposition to the slave power, and when this coalition is formed, believe me, you will find that three-fourths of the Northern Whigs will join it. If I be right in this prediction God knows what awaits us. The future looks full of gloom to me. In the language of Mr. Webster, 'Where are we Southern Whigs to go?' I see but one salvation for us. I say it to you *confidentially*, but my honest conviction is that we shall be driven to forming one grand Union party to be made up of the entire South acting unanimously and joining the National wing of the Northern democracy. If this is not done, the North will carry out all the measures of the free-soil Whigs and democrats—and then what becomes of the Union?

* * *

In the fall of 1854 the New Orleans newspapers reported that Benjamin had left for the Pacific coast of South America. Actually, his trip, which consumed several months, took him to Ecuador and the Galapagos Islands, six hundred miles due westward in the Pacific Ocean. His client, the purported owner of the Galapagos—General José Villamil, a native of New Orleans—had been granted them by Ecuador in return for his proposed plan to colonize them. On one or more of the islands—World's End, they have been fittingly called—guano deposits had been reported and Benjamin hoped, therefore, to get valuable concessions from Ecuador for General Villamil, and perhaps for the United States Government. Guano, which was sorely needed to replete the worn-out farm lands of the United States, was brought from Peru at monopoly prices and often in inadequate quantity. If he succeeded in his project, the boon of cheaper fertilizer would be given the American farmer; General Villamil would be enriched; and Benjamin's own pockets would be filled with a sum rumored in New Orleans to be as high as $200,000. One of Villamil's agents, a New Orleanian named de Brissot, had displayed some samples of guano which he had allegedly brought back from the Galapagos. On the strength of this and other representations, Benjamin made the long trip to Ecuador to press the Villamil claim.

In Quito Benjamin ingratiated himself with Philo White, the American chargé d'affaires, and prominent Ecuadorians, and he successfully defended the guano claim in the local courts where he had to argue in Spanish under the Roman law. But after he had made a highly favorable treaty with the Ecuador Government, doubt arose about the existence of the guano, and Benjamin made a personal investigation on Albemarle Island, the largest of the Galapagos. It was on this island that Charles Darwin twenty years earlier had made observations of the local species which influenced his ideas on evolution; here Benjamin could find any number of strange animals, birds, and reptiles: there were turtles large enough to carry a human being, cormorants, sea lions, and the like, all amazingly unafraid of man. But of guano there was none. The long trip was fruitless.

Benjamin could only give a wry smile and hope his political opponents in Louisiana would not learn too many particulars of the episode. After all, the affair was not entirely to his discredit, for without such 'visionary' schemes, some failing, some succeeding, the

American continents would not have been opened up for commercial development. There was no excuse, however, for his apparent failure to offer due apologies to White and the Ecuadorian authorities. President Urbina of Ecuador was much embarrassed by 'sarcasms' and 'calumnies' to the effect that he had been 'duped by the crafty policy of the "Yankees."' [23]

The collapse of the guano project, however, had little effect on Benjamin's reputation. For several months afterwards he was occupied with other business in Washington, and in early April 1855 he went to Petersburg, Virginia, to deliver a lecture before the local Library Association. Advance notices in the Petersburg newspapers paid a high tribute to his learning and ability, one even stating that he possessed 'every talent that can render him popular as a speaker.' The subject of Benjamin's address was 'The Roman Lawyer, in the Age of Cicero,' a classical topic calculated to please the ladies and gentlemen of the cultured and conservative Virginia town. He enlivened the address with frequent anecdotes and classical citations, and concluded with a florid peroration, which one local newspaper described as 'an eloquent and most beautiful tribute to Washington' and another as a tribute 'as truthful as it was splendid' to Chief-Justice Marshall. [24]

* * *

The first session of the Thirty-fourth Congress was begun in December 1855, but Benjamin was not in his seat until the next month. [25] During the period since the adjournment of the Thirty-third Congress, which enacted the Kansas-Nebraska Act, the Republican party had been organized on the basis of opposition to all further extension of slavery in the territories, and in the recent congressional election had administered a severe defeat to the Democrats in the Northern states. Although the Democrats had had a majority of eighty-four in the previous House of Representatives, Benjamin found that they were now outnumbered by the Republicans; but the Democrats still had a majority in the Senate.

Although Benjamin had now been a member of the Senate for three years, he was handicapped by the fact that he was a member of the fast-dwindling Whig party. As a Whig he did not receive the most important committee assignments or have any voice in the councils of the dominant Democrats. Yet the Senate could not fail to be impressed by his ability and industry; likewise, to some extent, by the proof he was now beginning to offer that he could rise above the level of petty politics. During a debate in early January 1856 he took occasion to attack the spoils system of officeholding, condemning the policy that 'to the victor belongs the spoils' as 'the vilest revolutionary doctrine that was ever published throughout this country.'[26] Furthermore, in the same month he took a leading part in the effort of Congress to increase the efficiency of the Navy. The American Navy was then burdened with a considerable number of incompetent officers who should have been retired from active service; but when a duly authorized board of naval officers sought to remove some of the unfit there was strong opposition from the men affected and their champions in the Senate. Defending the action of the Naval Board, Benjamin argued that because they could not attain 'perfection,' because they could not strike out from the list of officers 'exactly such men as ought to be stricken out,' did not make it any less their duty 'as public, faithful servants' to remedy the wrong.[27]

And, expressing views that may seem quaint if not archaic to some latter-day Americans, he continued to advocate economy in the public administration. Thus in opposing an appropriation for marine hospitals, he declared that for the past two or three years he had been struggling in the Committee on Commerce to stop such grants for marine hospitals all over the country at points where there 'is no earthly necessity for them, when the appropriation is merely made for the sake of placing a pretty building in a town, and giving a salary to one or two officers.' A few such hospitals might be needed in the large ports, but to spread them about elsewhere would be a 'perfect waste of the public money.' Again he offered a resolution against another practice which has since become a fruitful source of argument against the waste of government funds—that of excessive printing of government publications.[28]

* * *

Ever since the introduction of the Nebraska bill, the Kansas issue had aroused animosities throughout the country. The popular sovereignty provided for by the act had, instead of settling the slavery question, only led to violent struggles between the pro-slavery and anti-slavery factions in Kansas. The local Free-Soilers protested against election frauds, and even refused to submit to the territorial government. The disputes were of course aired in the Senate; the Republicans had an opportunity to define their position and were answered by their pro-slavery opponents.

On 2 May 1856 Benjamin delivered his most notable speech on the Kansas question, a speech in which he also took occasion to announce publicly his transfer of allegiance to the Democratic party, and the reasons for his action. The *National Intelligencer* so far departed from its usually dry and concise account of the Senate debates as to say that Benjamin made 'an unusually eloquent address' and discussed the Kansas question 'at length and with great ability.' This speech was less flowery than many of his earlier efforts in the Senate; the argument, if not entirely candid and convincing, was in most instances clear and logical. During the ensuing debate he matched wits with Senator William H. Seward of New York, one of the leading anti-slavery champions, and won further recognition for his forensic talents.

Benjamin declared that the South had now at last realized its mistake in offering or accepting any compromises on the slave question which were not contained in the Constitution. This document—'compact,' he termed it, using the word adopted by the States' Rights school—was based on the principle of the equality of the states. 'Take away this league of love; convert it into a bond of distrust; of suspicion, or of hate; and the entire fabric which is held together by that cement will crumble to the earth, and rest scattered in dishonest fragments upon the ground.' Now apply these principles to the question of division of the common territory. The South was 'insulted and mocked' by an offer to give her portions of the common territory under such conditions that she could not use them. Yet when the South uttered 'some faint complaint' she was answered by 'shrieks for freedom'; the prejudices of the Northern people were aroused against the 'usurpations of the Southern slave power.'

As for the question of constitutionality of the Kansas-Nebraska Act, the South was willing to submit that to the proper tribunal, the Supreme Court. But the North did not wish to do so. Benjamin asserted it was 'strange, strange, sir,' that the section of the Union that bore the reputation of being 'so excited, so passionate, so violent' was always ready to submit her claims to the courts, while the 'calm, cold, quiet, calculating North, always obeying the law, always subservient to the behests of the Constitution, whenever this question of slavery arises—and this alone—appeals to Sharpe's rifles instead of courts of justice. What man, confident of his title, ever hesitated to submit those pretensions' to the Supreme Court? But Benjamin did not add that many Northern people had good reason to believe that the majority of the Court was in agreement with the legal argument of the pro-slavery party, as was definitely proved the next year by the Dred Scott decision.

Benjamin's next proposition was one which, he declared, 'emanated from the distinguished author of almost every heresy that appears on this subject'—the assertion of Senator Seward that slavery is an outlaw under the law of nations. In referring to Seward, Benjamin departed from the calm, friendly manner he customarily used in his Senate speeches. For the New Yorker he was already showing one of the few deep hatreds he ever revealed in public. One possible explanation is that Seward was a former Whig leader who had joined the new Republican party; another, that Benjamin thought that Seward was lacking in moral principle. In a letter to Thomas Bayard a few years later, Benjamin wrote,

A generous mind will repel with scorn any imputation of dishonor against a person of tried integrity, yet if to-morrow a newspaper should publish a charge of bribery against the Chief Justice, some one would be found to believe it, at all events to suspect that it might be true. Now Seward acts on this principle and I charged him with it in a speech made four years ago on the Kansas question. You speak of shame on his part—why, I had scarcely finished my speech when he said to me, 'Come, Benjamin, give me a segar & I won't be mad with you.'

Benjamin offered a contrary opinion by John Quincy Adams, who in his last years had been a leader of the anti-slavery forces, and another by Chief Justice Marshall in the *Antelope* case to show that slavery was not outlawed by international law. The real motive of the North was to secure political power so that she could subvert the equality of the states. When the North had secured the preponderant political power and reduced the South to a feeble minority, then would she reveal her real Abolitionist sentiments and 'ruin and desolation' would be spread over fifteen states of the Union—states in which the slave property was worth $2,000,000,000 by a low evaluation.

After some further comments on the slavery situation, Benjamin stopped his speech to say that he observed 'his friend from New York' was studying the law of nations. Benjamin would, therefore, give him another little passage from Cooper's *Justinian:*

'Slavery is where one man is subjected to the dominion of another according to the law of nations.'

This prompted the following tilt between Benjamin and Seward:

MR. SEWARD: 'Have you no more ancient authority?'

MR. BENJAMIN: 'I give you the earliest and the latest.'

MR. SEWARD: 'I beg to correct the honorable Senator. He did not read the whole of the passage. He ought to be candid and read the whole sentence.'

MR. BENJAMIN: ' "Slavery is where one man is subjected to the dominion of another according to the law of nations, though contrary to natural rights." '

MR. SEWARD: ' "Though contrary to natural rights." '

MR. BENJAMIN: 'The proposition of the Senator from New York did not touch natural rights. He spoke of the law of nations.'

Referring to the opinion of Northerners regarding the treatment of the Southern slave, Benjamin said that they were misled by the Black Republican leaders, and offered some controversial figures to show that the Negroes were actually well treated. In any case, Benjamin said, the Black Republican would not consider such statistics. 'He has read in a novel the authentic fact that Mr. Legree whipped Uncle Tom to death, and that is a thousand times more satisfactory than any such foolish things as official documents.'

Continuing with this argument, Benjamin advanced what may seem a strange contention to present-day readers—that it was more humane to whip and brand a Negro than to imprison or transport him. The cases of whipping and branding slaves pictured 'in such horrible colors' to the people of the North were really the exercise of a police magistracy, he said.

If a slave in the South broke open the cabin of another slave and stole his petty treasure he would be whipped and there the criminal procedure would end. But if the same event occurred in the North between white persons the offender would be given a term of years in the penitentiary. If it occurred in philanthropic England, the man . . . I believe, formerly would have been hung . . . but now he will simply be torn from wife, children, country, home and friends, manacled, and transported to a penal colony of Great Britain in the southern seas . . .

Benjamin had already spoken at considerable length. But before taking his seat he said that he would trespass on the attention of the Senate for a few moments in order to explain his change of party. After the disruption of the Whig party, he had on returning to Louisiana found four-fifths of the Whigs enrolled in the ranks of the Native American party. But he had been told by reliable persons 'that the true parents of the new birth were New England prejudices against Catholicism and against slavery. I did not like the parent; I did not believe in the brood.' And then in their Philadelphia convention, the Know-Nothings had displayed their 'hideous features' in 'all their naked deformity.' The entire Louisiana delegation had been expelled because they professed the Catholic religion; later the so-called National party after a long and violent debate voted a meager recognition of Southern rights. No sooner, therefore, had the real purpose of the American party been displayed at the Philadelphia Convention than his path of duty was clear. In an address to his constituents Benjamin told them what he had heard in Washington: the machinery of the party would be used to elevate to power the worst enemies of the South; 'the Northern Know-Nothings would coalesce with the Northern Abolitionists, and by their united action they would force on a crisis, on the result of which would depend the destiny of this country.'

The struggle had narrowed down to a contest between the Democrats and the Republicans, and Benjamin would be recreant to his 'trust—to every principle of duty and patriotism'—if he let himself be influenced by past party ties, past party prejudices. The Democratic platform was identical with that of the old Whig party and he declared his adhesion to the former; he changed 'name, not principle.'

After Senator Cass, an old-time Democrat, had made a few complimentary remarks about Benjamin's speech, Seward spoke in reply. Of Seward's ability there could be no question, nor should we let his frequent political wiles lead us to doubt his courage and sincerity. He said that Benjamin's very eloquent speech had given him provocation to follow with 'spirit excited to heat,' but that he would refrain from doing so. He did in fact indulge little in personalities, though he indirectly rebuked Benjamin for taking up the time of the Senate to explain his change in political party. His main efforts he devoted to controverting the proposition held by Benjamin that slavery was not contrary to the law of nations. After Seward had finished his legal argument, Benjamin rose again and delivered a reply in which, on the technical legal issue, he worsted the Republican Senator, leaving him without an effective reply. Morally Seward could feel that he was on sure ground in arguing against slavery, but in this and a number of other instances he could not fit the existing law to his purpose.

The next speaker, Hale of New Hampshire, stated that he had listened to Benjamin 'with great pleasure, as I always do, on account of his acknowledged ability, his great eloquence, his very persuasive powers, his mellifluous voice, his winning and graceful manner. All this only makes me regret that he is in a wrong position.' But Hale said that Benjamin had made one admission for which he thanked him: he had told the Senate that in changing from the Whigs to the Democrats he had changed his party but not his principles. 'I believe he is the first gentleman here, whom I have ever heard, that has had the candor to admit it. It inaugurates a new era, it gives a new starting point.'

It was hardly surprising that the *Louisiana Courier* not only printed a long report of Benjamin's speech but accompanied it with a laudatory editorial. 'This gentleman whose career in the Senate has already been so brilliant, has just gathered fresh laurels.' The *Courier* quoted from the *Washington Union*, which had extravagantly asserted that the address was one of the most powerful ever delivered on any subject, and warmly welcomed the new convert. 'He ought to have been a Democrat long years ago.' [29]

The next month—June 1856—the Democratic National Convention met at Cincinnati. Although Benjamin had not publicly announced his change of party until May, he was one of the politicians at the convention who were influential in defeating Franklin Pierce for renomination and nominating James Buchanan of Pennsylvania. Benjamin's motives for this action were not fully revealed but it seems clear that he took his cue from John Slidell and now favored Buchanan as more amenable than Pierce to their point of view on the Southern question and more likely of election.

Two weeks before the meeting of the convention, candidates' headquarters had been opened in Cincinnati. Slidell, Senator Bright, and W. W. Corcoran secured a large suite at the Burnet House and entertained 'lavishly' in Buchanan's behalf. Benjamin also was at his best on such occasions when opponents were won over by the charming address and flowing bowl.

During the crisis in the pre-convention maneuvering when the bad news was received that the forces of the chief rival candidates, Pierce and Douglas, were in agreement, Slidell made up a party of some of Pierce's worst political enemies, including Benjamin, his friend Senator Bayard of Delaware, and Senator Bright. They settled at the home of S. L. M. Barlow, a New York politician temporarily in Cincinnati, and under Slidell's leadership began working to overcome the Pierce-Douglas coalition.

Their success—if nominating James Buchanan may be so termed—is a matter of history. The convention was to meet on Monday, 2 June, and on the previous Friday night the Pierce forces met their Waterloo. They still had some hopes of the actual balloting but were doomed to disappointment. The 'Buchaneers' succeeded in getting control of the visitors' tickets and packed the galleries with their supporters; by Wednesday night pressure for Buchanan was becoming too strong to withstand. He was nominated by a large majority. Much credit went to Henry A. Wise, who had swung the Virginia delegation to Pierce in 1852 and now opposed him for renomination, but the politician most responsible for the actual nomination of Buchanan was John Slidell.[30]

If Buchanan were elected, no man in the country would be in a better position than Slidell to ask and receive the White House favors. And since Benjamin now became affiliated with the Slidell wing of the Louisiana Democrats and was the chief lieutenant in the party there, he also would be in a strategic position. He made a stump-speaking tour to help defeat Frémont, the Republican candidate, and even delivered one thumping campaign speech in Portland, Maine.[31]

VII. *High Tide Under the Old Government*

SKEPTICAL as he was of the future of the Union, Benjamin did not let his gloomy forebodings prevent him from enjoying himself. In Washington, where a Senator can always find much to ease the burden of statesmanship, one of his favorite amusements was card playing.

Indeed, the tale was that his love for the game made him 'a prey to older and cooler hands, who waited till the sponge was full at the end' of the Senate session, 'then squeezed it to the last drop.'

This tale belies somewhat the consummate skill as a whist player with which Benjamin was credited. Nor is it complimentary to the experience in the art which he doubtless received at the Boston Club. Benjamin himself denied the story, saying that he understood William T. Russell, the English newspaper correspondent who published it, had learned it from Charles Sumner. In any event, Benjamin said, Russell showed bad taste in repeating it after he had partaken of his (Benjamin's) hospitality.[1]

With the entire District of Columbia boasting of only about 52,000 people by the last census, the important Government office-holders lived much like a large family. Only those dignitaries were not accepted in the family circle who were too irregular in their conduct or—even worse—too radical in their opinions. In this society Benjamin found a ready welcome. For a time he lived at a private home, 258 F Street, on the north side between 13th and 14th; Senator Platt of Maryland also was listed at this address. Whether or not the house provided both room and board, we do not know, but in 1857 Benjamin was eating at a 'mess' here or near by, along with Senator Butler of South Carolina and Senator Mason and Representative Goode, both of Virginia. It was a fashionable neighborhood, much frequented by the Southerners who then set the tone for the capital society. Mrs. Clement Clay, the clever wife of the contemporary Senator from Alabama, has left us a vivid impression of the milieu. She wrote:

We are located in a delightful part of the city, on F Street, near the Treasury Buildings, the Court end as well as the convenient end; for all the Departments as well as the White House are in a stone's throw. Old Guthrie's is opposite, and we have, within two blocks, some true-line Senators, among them Bell, Slidell, Weller, Brodhead, Thomson, of New Jersey, who are married and housekeeping, to say naught of Butler, Benjamin, Mason and Goode in a 'mess' near us. Our 'mess' is a very pleasant one. Orr, Shorter, Dowdell, Sandidge and Taylor, of Louisiana, with the young Senator Pugh and his bride, Governor Fitzpatrick and wife, and ourselves compose the party. Taylor is a true Democrat, and Pugh is as strongly Anti-Free-soil as we.

And then Mrs. Clay added candidly, 'We keep Free-soilers, Black Republicans and Bloomers on the other side of the street. They are afraid even to inquire for board at this house.' [2]

In the 'fifties Washington was nothing if not a Southern city. Even after the outbreak of the Civil War, Benjamin was to have little difficulty securing recruits there for the Confederate secret service.

Among Benjamin's many friends in the capital was Senator Mason of Virginia, while he continued his close political liaison with the astute John Slidell. The only people in Washington, however, with whom he is known to have been intimate were the Bayards and David L. Yulee. James A. Bayard, an aristocratic Senator from the family borough of Delaware, was a strong States' Rights Democrat, with a long record of public service. His son, Thomas Bayard, who first met Benjamin at their Washington home, was not impressed with his personal appearance, but was struck with his conversational ability. According to Bayard, he 'shone in social life as a refined, genial, and charming companion.' As a 'consummate' whist player, he was companionable to Senator Bayard, and he was welcomed to the tea table by Mrs. Bayard and her young daughters, the charming girls who helped to introduce in Washington about that time the fashion of lifting up the long hoop skirts high enough to show the 'ravishing' new petticoats.

As for Yulee, the Democratic Senator from Florida, he and

Benjamin were drawn together by several congenial ties. Yulee was born in Saint Thomas the same year that Benjamin was born in neighboring Saint Croix. In both men flowed the proud blood of the Portuguese Jews, both had entered law and politics, and both had married Gentile wives, Yulee the pretty daughter of 'Duke' Wickliffe, Postmaster-General under Tyler. Benjamin was very fond of Yulee, and it was to Yulee that he was to turn later in the emotional crisis that nearly disrupted his career.[3]

* * *

During his residence in Washington Benjamin devoted a good deal of time to study and recreational reading. Some idea of his intellectual interests is shown by the list of books he borrowed from the Library of Congress. Although the list may appear to be a hodge-podge, it does show the wide range of an inquisitive mind. It includes several books on legal and constitutional subjects; several volumes on American history and diplomacy and Louisiana history; a few *Parliamentary Papers*; Boswell's *Johnson*; Paxton's *Magazine of Botany*; several numbers of *De Bow's Review*; Quevedo's *Autores Espagnoles*; Campbell's *Negro Mania*; *Duties of Human Life*; two of Bulwer-Lytton's novels; *Westminster* [Review], April 1853; Mopras's *Exploration de L'Oregon*; *British Essayists*; Marshall's *Washington*; Defoe's *History of the Union*; a book on Jamaica and another on the West Indies.

It is significant to note Benjamin's fondness for classical subjects. During 1858-60 when the country was fast drifting into civil war he was diverting himself with Landor's *Imaginary Conversations of Greeks and Romans*, and *Pericles and Aspasia*. A participant himself in one of the high dramas in history, he could enjoy to the full the imaginary conversations of such historical figures as Achilles and Helen, Hannibal and the dying Marcellus.

But most important, perhaps, in the list were two different editions of Horace. Benjamin read the great Latin poet in the original and, even though he apparently did not have a personal copy of Horace's works in Washington, there was no doubt that Horace was one of his literary idols.[4] Although Benjamin met with enough misfortune to disillusion most men, he still managed to find much happiness in life. Did he derive spiritual sustenance from the great pagan poet? For Horace, the first step in the enjoyment of this world was acquiescence. The second, to take wise advantage of life's opportunities:

'Mid all thy hopes and all thy cares, 'mid all thy wraths and fears, Think every shining day that dawns, the period of thy years.

Enjoy the solace of literature, of friends, of nature. Be moderate. Wine is to gratify the taste, but not to the point of causing trouble. So with the other pleasures. No doubt the point can be overemphasized, but Benjamin and Horace do appear to have had the same general attitude toward life.[5]

While Benjamin had become an influential member of the Southern party in the Senate, moving in the best circles of Washington society, he was also winning national distinction as a lawyer. Since he had become a member of the Senate he had appeared in an increasing number of cases before the Supreme Court. An efficient worker, he found considerable time for his private practice. A Senator then had much less governmental business to attend to than he does at the present day. And with the Supreme Court conveniently housed in a room in the Capitol, instead of its present imposing building, Benjamin could quickly slip back into the Senate chamber when his presence was needed.

Besides a number of dull though remunerative suits, Benjamin appeared during the next few years in an interesting case caused by a collision on the Mississippi River. A flatboat, which had been fastened to the bank of the Mississippi at night but not at a landing place, was run down and sunk by the steamer *Gipsey*. The lower court, sitting in admiralty, gave damages to the owners of the flatboat, and the owners of the steamer appealed. Benjamin, who represented the owners of the flatboat, declared the appellants pretended that the night was too dark to run and at the same time it was quite light enough for them to pursue their voyage with safety. 'The testimony is somewhat conflicting on this point; but on their own evidence they are in a fatal dilemma. By the evidence of her own officers, the *Gipsey* would have run directly into the bank of the river, if the flatboat had not intervened,' he said.

Now, if it was light enough to navigate with safety, the fact proves the grossest carelessness and negligence, sufficient to make the steamer responsible. If, on the contrary, it was not light enough to navigate with safety, there was criminal imprudence in continuing the voyage, instead of lying up till the darkness was dissipated. The district judge puts the dilemma very clearly in his opinion, and there is no escape from it . . .

It never has been even pretended, before, that a vessel of any kind, tied to the bank of a river, not in any port or harbor, or usual place of landing, is bound to show a light, still less when, as in the present case, the vessel was lying in a nook or recess of the bank, entirely out of the usual course of ascending or descending vessels.

With these and other arguments Benjamin satisfied the judges. The decision was rendered in favor of his clients.[6]

During the same term (December 1856) Benjamin also appeared in a case about the sale of some mortgaged property, and in a suit involving rival land claimants. Altogether during this term of the court he figured in eight cases, and in six was on the winning side; in the December 1857 term he appeared in ten—for him a record number. The fact that he won only five does not indicate that he was losing reputation but rather that some of the cases were of such a nature that even he could not convince the judges; he was usually willing to take risky suits if the fees were sufficiently alluring.[7]

The cases Benjamin won included an appeal from Texas,[8] a bankruptcy case in which he was associated with his friend Bayard;[9] and several in which he figured with Reverdy Johnson. Benjamin and Johnson were attorneys for the plaintiff in one of these cases, involving some disputed customs duties, and the Attorney-General, Jeremiah Black, was one of the defending counsel.[10] In another suit, an appeal from Indiana in 1859, the lawyers for the defendants—Benjamin, Vinton, and Samuel Judah, a leading Indiana lawyer and member of an old American Jewish family—defeated the opposing lawyers, Johnson and his associates.[11]

Benjamin continued to specialize in commercial cases and, particularly, commercial appeals before the Supreme Court. His fame as a lawyer continued to come chiefly as a result of his broad knowledge, his intelligence and industry. Despite his keen legal brain he was not tempted into relying too much on his wits, his past study and experience, but could always be counted on for solid work. Furthermore, he continued to impress his hearers at the pleadings by his rare ability to state his cases. Benjamin had the same gift as did Abraham Lincoln for resolving abstract questions into a few simple terms, as the reports of a number of his appeal cases demonstrate. During one of his suits before the Supreme Court Benjamin was opposed by Jeremiah Black. When the Court took its recess after Benjamin had stated his case, one of the justices is reported to have said to Black as he passed him, 'You had better look to your laurels, for that little Jew from New Orleans has stated your case out of court.' [12]

* * *

Benjamin was engaged in so many activities that it is sometimes bewildering to attempt to keep up with them. Even his opponents could not but admit that he did them well. In December 1856, the month after Buchanan's election, he was back in Washington for the meeting of the new Congress, glad to be done with stump-speaking for the elderly and none-too-inspiring Democratic nominee. Comparing himself with the schoolboy who, after a long term spent studying the classics, had declared, 'Thank God, I have got rid of the Greeks and Romans,' Benjamin said that he felt, 'Thank God, I have got rid of presidential stump-speaking.' [13]

During the next two years after the election of 1856, John Slidell was, except for Buchanan, the most influential man in the Democratic party. Buchanan offered Slidell the post of Minister to France, but he declined largely because of his 'preoccupation with Louisiana affairs.' [14] Here he and his lieutenant, Benjamin, had the patronage for the asking, and did not hesitate to press their advantage, as is shown by a typical letter they wrote from Washington, on 18 March 1857, to Isaac Toucey, the new Secretary of the Navy. Seeking a vacant pursership for one J. W. Nixon, they reminded Toucey that Louisiana had had no pursership on the Navy list for many years, enumerated Nixon's special qualifications, and ended on this familiar political note—'he had always been a consistent and active democrat. We feel a warm interest in his welfare and will be gratified by your conferring the appointment on him.' [15]

During the remainder of 1857, while Benjamin was much occupied with the affairs of the Tehuantepec Railroad and other activities, the political cliques in Louisiana began to turn their thoughts to the next senatorial election. Although their rivalry was largely the result of differences on state and national issues, the opposition factions could hardly have been satisfied with Slidellians filling 'almost every office, at least all the chief offices.' Louisianians in general were proud of Benjamin's national distinction. But there were several groups that were scheming to prevent his re-election, and they watched closely the attitude of Slidell.

As early as 30 April 1857, the *True Delta* had expressed its pleasure at the report that Slidell was 'setting the traps' to elect Representative J. W. Sandidge on the expiration 'of Colonel Benjamin's term of office, or on the appointment of this gentleman to a special mission to Mexico, of which there is some talk.' [16] The report about the Mexican mission may have been idle rumor. But early in 1858 the newspaper reported that John Slidell was scheming for the presidency, and for this reason was seeking the mission to Madrid for his wealthy Jewish relative, August Belmont, the New York representative of the Rothschilds, and for Benjamin the appointment to Mexico or France; Benjamin was 'anxious to obtain the greater distinction in order to be near his family.' [17]

Part at least of the newspaper story about Benjamin was true. Slidell wrote Buchanan from Atlantic City on 22 August 1858 that unless Belmont would accept the Madrid post he felt impelled to recommend Benjamin whose selection 'will not only be satisfactory but gratifying to me in every way.' [18] Buchanan did offer Benjamin the position, as is shown by the following letter from the President, of 31 August 1858:

I write for the purpose of tendering you the appointment of Minister to Spain & expressing a strong desire that you may accept it. I feel satisfied that the Country will unite with me in opinion that this is an appointment eminently fit to be made. Indeed I am not acquainted with any gentleman who possesses superior, if equal, qualifications to yourself for this important mission. Such being the case I think your Country has a right to the benefit of your services.

I told our friend Slidell yesterday that he might inform you I had determined to offer you the Spanish mission & his letter may probably reach you before this can arrive.

Repeating my ardent wish that you may accept the mission & assuring you that I shall do all in my power to make it agreeable to yourself, useful to your Country & promotive to your own fame . . .[19]

Buchanan's offer was made public, and was received with especial pleasure in Jewish circles.[20] But Benjamin declined to accept the Spanish post, probably because of the financial sacrifice involved, and a fear of being unduly diverted from his main professional and commercial interests.

A few months later Benjamin was in Washington for another session of the Senate. It was an important one for him not only on account of national affairs but because his legislative activities would be scanned closely by his opponents in Louisiana, eager to secure ammunition for use against him in his approaching campaign for re-election. Shortly after the adjournment of the previous Congress, the Supreme Court had issued its momentous opinion in *Dred Scott* v. *Sanford*, and during a discussion on 8 February 1858 of the Kansas question, Benjamin said that it was now settled 'from the origin' that all the 'agitation of the slavery question has been directed against the constitutional rights of the South; and both Wilmot provisos and Missouri compromise lines were unconstitutional.' [21]

In stating that Congress had no power to exclude slaves from a territory, the Supreme Court had outlawed the most important political principle of the Republican party and was violently attacked by its supporters on both legal and moral grounds. As a member of the Senate Judiciary Committee, Benjamin said that he felt it was his duty to defend the Court against the 'reckless' and 'untruthful' attacks that were being made upon it. He praised Chief Justice Taney in particular for his 'vast legal learning' and the 'conscientious, earnest, almost painful sense of responsibility with which he holds the scale of justice in even and impartial hand.' In fact, he paid such a high-flown tribute to Taney that Senator Wade declared that he had sent 'the old man to heaven even before he died.' But Benjamin's defense of the aged chief justice meets with the approval of many modern historians, for although the main decision in the Dred Scott case may well have been *obiter dicta*, Taney's motives were pure.[22]

Despite the highly controversial issues in which he was involved, Benjamin managed to retain his popularity in Washington. One reason for this was his ingratiating personality. He was usually considerate of his political opponents and, unlike some of his Southern colleagues, he kept on good terms with nearly all of the Northern Senators. But Benjamin's manner did not mean that he lacked firmness. There are numerous incidents to prove his physical courage—indeed on one occasion in 1858 he narrowly missed fighting a duel with Jefferson Davis. The incident was one of the most remarkable in Benjamin's career and it is surprising that it has not attracted greater attention.

It was Tuesday, 8 June 1858. There were few important matters on the calendar for the day and the Senate settled down to an afternoon of routine business. The journal of the previous day was read and approved. The credentials of R. M. T. Hunter and Clement Clay, newly re-elected as Senators for six years beginning 4 March 1859, were read and ordered to be filed. Various executive communications, petitions, and memorials were droned off by the clerk, the members listening idly. Benjamin, from the Committee on Private Land Claims, offered their report on some minor matters: a Missouri land claim, another from California, and so on. The Senate wisely rejected a bill by that Southern extremist, James M. Mason, authorizing use of force against Mexico and certain Central American republics, accused of indignities against Americans. The pension bill for the surviving widow (twenty-seven years his junior) of the elderly Major-General Gaines came up for final disposition: 'Bob' Toombs had an opportunity to refer to 'personal solicitations to old Senators' by 'a fascinating lady . . . I am told that attachment to the ladies, when it gets in the head, is worse than anywhere else.' (Laughter) And the battle-scarred Sam Houston, ever a valiant champion of the fair sex, had gone to the defense of the charming widow—perhaps none the less willingly since he was now married to a young girl.

Then the Senate took up the Army Appropriation Bill. A discussion arose between Benjamin and Jefferson Davis over a minor point relating to breech-loading arms. Davis, suffering already from the ill-health which so racked him as the Confederate President, was sickly and peevish this afternoon and, piqued to have Benjamin question his vaunted military knowledge, he let his temper get the best of him.

'I do not understand that the Secretary of War has asked for any part of this $100,000 here appropriated in the House bill, to purchase the breech-loading arms. If he has, I am very much mistaken,' Benjamin said.

'Oh, I will state the very simple fact that he asks money to buy breech-loading guns. Whether it is in this $100,000, or out of the Treasury, I do not know,' Davis declared.

'It is very easy for the Senator from Mississippi to give a sneering reply to what was certainly a very respectful inquiry,' Benjamin countered.

The tempers of both men were now rising.

'I consider it is an attempt to misrepresent a very plain remark,' Davis bluntly stated.

'The Senator is mistaken, and has no right to state any such thing. His manner is not agreeable at all,' Benjamin answered.

'If the Senator happens to find it disagreeable, I hope he will keep it to himself,' Davis said.

'When directed to me, I will not keep it to myself; I will repel it instanter,' Benjamin replied.

'You have got it, sir,' Davis snapped.

'That is enough, sir,' Benjamin responded, and finished his remarks on the subject of the muskets.

It was reported that Davis also stated he had 'no idea that he was to be met with the arguments of a paid attorney in the Senate chamber,' and when Benjamin asked him if he had rightly heard the words 'paid attorney' Davis replied with asperity, 'Yes, those were the very words.'

Benjamin felt that Davis had insulted him. He wrote a note to Davis which, according to James A. Bayard, contained a direct challenge to a duel 'without asking for a withdrawal or explanation.' When Bayard presented the note, Davis read it, then at once tore it up.

'I will make this all right at once. I have been wholly wrong,' he said.

The next day Davis offered adequate apologies in the Senate and, after Benjamin replied handsomely, the incident was closed. If blood had been shed, it is interesting to speculate what would have been the effect on history. As it was, the affair increased the mutual respect of Davis and Benjamin, and probably contributed to Benjamin's appointment to the Confederate cabinet.[23]

But the acquaintance of the two men did not yet ripen into intimacy. According to Mrs. Davis, they were too much alike to have been good friends at the outset. They both had the same 'quick perception,' 'tireless mental energy,' and 'nervously excitable tempers.' 'Sometimes when they did not agree on a measure, hot words in glacial polite phrases passed between them, and they had up to the year of secession little social intercourse; an occasional invitation to dinner was accepted and exchanged, and nothing more.'

Mrs. Davis also revealed one reason why a number of other people became irritated with Benjamin. Whenever Benjamin had an 'angry contest' with one of his colleagues, someone would say, 'How can anyone get provoked with Mr. Benjamin? he is so gentle and courteous.' But the truth was that his courtesy in argument was 'like the salute of the duellist to the antagonist' whom he hoped to kill. 'He was master of the art of inductive reasoning, and when he had smilingly established his point he dealt the coup de grâce with a fierce joy which his antagonist fully appreciated and resented.'

Mrs. Davis added that she never knew Benjamin to be very much in earnest in those days without infuriating his opponent. He could even annoy John Slidell, 'who loved him like a brother.'

'When I do not agree with Benjamin I will not let him talk to me; he irritates me so by his debonnaire ways,' Slidell told Davis.

On one occasion after Benjamin and Mrs. Davis had disagreed on a purely social matter, she playfully remarked, 'If I let you set one stone, you will build a cathedral before I know it.'

Benjamin laughed and replied, 'If it should prove to be the shrine of truth you will worship there with me, I am sure.'[24]

* * *

In January 1859 the Louisiana legislature was to elect a United States Senator. As the time for the balloting approached, Benjamin's opponents made a final effort to prevent his re-election. The Soulé faction in particular now engaged in 'a last death grapple' with him and Slidell. In a letter to the *True Delta*, 'Cosmos,' a political opponent, praised Benjamin's ability in strong terms but was severely critical in other respects. Benjamin was a 'capital' lawyer (surely 'Cosmos' was not punning!) who gave the best part of his time and talents while in Washington to the law. And, he asserted, Benjamin lacked 'the breadth and boldness' to be a statesman. Elsewhere the *True Delta* spoke of him as one of the 'subservient creatures' of Slidell and said, 'we do not want a Senator to say ditto' whenever requested by him.[25]

Such criticisms may have had their effect upon the Louisiana electorate. But the main issue that Benjamin's opponents used in their effort to defeat him was his somewhat questionable connection with the Houmas land claims. John Slidell was the chief butt for the scandalous charges in this connection, but Benjamin did not escape bitter criticism. At an 'indignant' meeting in Ascension Parish late in January 1859, protest was made against a bill recently introduced by Benjamin in the Senate 'to provide for the location of certain private land claims in the state of Missouri and for other purposes.' It was asserted that Benjamin and Slidell got this bill passed so they could secure 20,000 acres in the Houmas tract and evict several hundred persons who had lived on the land and claimed they possessed incontrovertible titles to their holdings. Resolutions were passed at the meeting to protest Benjamin's action before the Louisiana legislature, and to work against his re-election.

The tract of land that was the subject of this dispute had originally embraced several hundred thousand acres on the east side of the Mississippi, about fifty miles above New Orleans. It had been bought from the Houmas Indians in 1774 and had since been claimed by various settlers and speculators, disputes over the titles being particularly difficult to settle because of the vagueness of the land grants. Part of the tract, however, was purchased in 1835 by John Slidell and some business associates; the land was still a wilderness, and seems to have been acquired in good faith, although the purchasers relied on titles dating back to 1777.

Now Benjamin had apparently been convinced by personal examination that the Slidell group had a good title, and his judgment was confirmed by a decision of the Louisiana Supreme Court.

But there were further disputes over the tract, and he slipped a provision to aid Slidell's claim into the bill aforementioned. Slidell and his associates would not get absolute titles under this bill, but they would stand unless rival claimants instituted suit within two years and proved better ones. The result was that Slidell appeared likely to gain a large sum of money and several hundred settlers would be dispossessed from their holdings. Already Slidell's enemies delighted in calling him 'Houmas John,' while Benjamin was finding his own connection with the affair a political liability—none the less so since he served on the Private Land Claims Committee while it was investigating the case.[26]

When the legislature met in January 1859 Benjamin was re-elected to the Senate, but only after a protracted session. As late as the forty-second ballot in the Democratic caucus the vote stood Benjamin, 25; Representative Sandidge, 23; General Henry Gray, 19; Parham, 1. Under these circumstances it did not appear likely that Benjamin could secure the 57 votes in the legislature necessary for the actual election. But when the final voting took place, the first ballot gave Benjamin, 57; Gray, 50; and Randall Hunt, the Know-Nothing candidate, only 5.

Benjamin had received one more than a majority. His re-election was largely owing to a Know-Nothing member from New Orleans who failed to support the party candidate. As for the friends of Sandidge, they went home 'with long faces, most of them swearing that North Louisiana should have the senator to be elected two years hence, in place of John Slidell.'

Benjamin had kept his record of never being defeated in a major election, but he had had a close call. The *Picayune* spoke of the election as the most exciting contest for senator ever held in Louisiana. The *Delta* (again not to be confused with the *True Delta*), now favorable to Benjamin, wrote:

Without designing to be invidious, we cannot refrain from congratulating the people of this state at the result . . . As a profound lawyer, Mr. Benjamin has stood for years at the head of a bar that has no superior in the Union; as an orator, his reputation is as wide as the country itself, while as a man his life has been singularly pure.[27]

* * *

On 2 March 1859, next to the last day of Congress, Slidell sub-mitted Benjamin's credentials as Senator for a new term of six years.[28] He was to serve only two years of this term, and not long after it normally would have expired he would be a hunted fugitive. By the middle of April he was back in New Orleans and in a talk there with H. W. Conner of South Carolina had expressed himself rather freely on current political affairs. Conner found him now a 'thorough Democrat . . . for the party right or wrong.' He sup-ported Buchanan because he was made the President, but he said the President's foreign policy had been 'timid and weak, and his execution feeble, indecisive, and resultless.'

In fact, Benjamin criticized not only Buchanan's foreign policy but also his management of the party. The President had made fatal errors, he intimated, and, with the power to make the party omnip-otent, he had let it fall to pieces. Yet, dissatisfied as Benjamin was with the man he had helped to put in the White House, he pre-dicted that the Democrats would unite before the next election and elect their nominee.[29]

Since Benjamin was now so often in Washington he did not find it practical to maintain an elaborate establishment in Louisiana, and kept bachelor quarters in New Orleans with the Huntington brothers. After the sale of Bellechasse, his family there had moved for a short time to a plantation above New Orleans, and later settled in a residence which he purchased for them in the suburbs. Mrs. Levy always presided over the household, and his maiden sister, Harriet, lived with her also, as did a third sister, Mrs. Sessions, and her two sons for a brief time.

Benjamin doubtless paid the expenses of this establishment. Furthermore, he seems to have contributed most, if not all, the funds to support Mrs. Sessions's boys at the University of North Carolina. By 1860 Benjamin's youngest brother, Joseph, and three nephews had graduated at Chapel Hill—all, it appears, with his generous financial assistance. Without sons of his own, Benjamin could take double pride in the fact that Coleman Sessions was an editor of the university magazine and that both he and Lionel Levy graduated with distinction.[30]

* * *

Among the many business trips Benjamin took during the late 'fifties was a voyage on the steamer *Texas* to Mexico. Within a little over a decade he made his frequent journeys between Washington and New Orleans, the wild-goose chase to Ecuador and the Galapagos Islands, two long boat trips to California, and the almost annual voyages to France, not to mention numerous other trips. All of them were undertaken despite the often cheerless travel arrangements of the period.

The Mexican voyage, made in August 1857, was in the interest of a new Tehuantepec railroad which Benjamin had helped to organize. After the Mexican Government had blocked for several years his effort to promote the railroad across the Isthmus, Benjamin, P. A. Hargous, and Emile La Sère, pooling their resources, formed another company—the Louisiana Tehuantepec Company. Stockholders of the two old Tehuantepec companies were to be paid in stock of the new company, and liabilities were assumed of over three million dollars.

It was a risky project but promised large profits. Benjamin enlisted the help of his friend President Buchanan and Secretary of State Cass. Indeed, a dispatch that Cass wrote to John Forsyth, the American minister to Mexico, requesting that he support the project had all the earmarks of being written from memoranda supplied by Benjamin. Then he and La Sère set out to secure the Mexican Government's confirmation of the company charter.

Arriving in the cool Mexican Capital, they ran into many difficulties, not the least of which was a bitter quarrel with Forsyth. But Benjamin played all the cards in his hand, including, it appears, broad claims of his influence with Buchanan. The *True Delta* commented sarcastically:

We all know how . . . little Benjamin ran from one saloon to another in Mexico, pulling out from his breeches pocket in each, the well-thumbed autograph of the Sage of Wheatland [Buchanan] which, like Mahomet's signet, the little babbler fancied would be gazed upon and obeyed by his astounded acquaintance in the Halls of Montezuma.

In spite of the opposition stirred up by Forsyth and other opponents, Benjamin and La Sère secured a right of transit across the

Isthmus for sixty years. Although some stipulations of their agreement with the Mexican Government were more onerous than they had bargained for, preparatory work for the railroad was continued under hopeful conditions. On 26 January 1859, the *Picayune* reported that the engineering corps was on the ground and, because of the excellent navigation of several rivers, the view was 'very generally prevalent' on the Isthmus that the railroad would not have to be constructed north of the headwaters of the Atlantic slope. This would save three or four million dollars! Benjamin raised funds with which a vehicular road was built across the Isthmus, and he persuaded a 'reluctant' postmaster-general to send the California mail via Tehuantepec—a shorter route—for a year starting 1 November 1858.

Benjamin was further encouraged when President Juarez granted amendments to the company concession which greatly enhanced its value. He added an additional term of twenty-five years to the grant, abandoned the right to confiscate the charter if he felt its terms were violated, and granted the company half a million acres of land on the right of way and banks of the river. This agreement, Benjamin wrote Buchanan in April 1859, had 'infused new spirit into our people.' He would leave for England early the next month to buy the iron for the railroad.

But once again the Tehuantepec Company was overcome by ill-fortune. In May, Hargous Brothers of New York failed. Loaded with personal letters not only from Buchanan but the Barings and Slidell, Benjamin made a futile effort in Europe to get further financial backing. As a last resort negotiations were begun between the American and Mexican Governments, and McLane, the co-operative minister who had replaced Forsyth, had an encouraging talk with Juarez. But soon the Civil War ruined this and many other hopeful projects.

In a black box belonging to Benjamin, which after being confiscated by General B. F. Butler and subsequent adventures has now come to rest at the National Archives in Washington, are twenty-nine bonds of the Tehuantepec Company for $1,000 each, payable in ten years from 20 March 1857; certificates of company stock in his name for $94,100; and a record showing that he was to receive $45,000 in bonds as commission upon the issuance of $900,000 in bonds of the new company. Undoubtedly, his pockets would have been filled if the railroad connecting the two oceans had been put into successful operation.[31]

* * *

To return to the Washington scene, by 1859 Benjamin had been promoted to the chairmanship of the Committee on Private Land Claims and was a high-ranking member of the Judiciary Committee. Recognized as one of the ablest members of the Senate and a leading Southern lawyer, he had wealth and position. All that he lacked was marital happiness, and he now decided to make another bid for that. He determined to lease a house in Washington and bring Natalie back to America to be its mistress.

The mansion he rented was in keeping with his dignity—the famous Decatur House, now the Truxtun Beale residence. Located on Lafayette Circle near the White House, it is an elegant three-story brick mansion with perhaps as distinguished a history as any in the city except the White House. The house had been built for Stephen Decatur about 1819 by Latrobe, the most famous architect of his day. Decatur wanted it to be of simple design and 'sturdy as a ship,' as is attested by its condition today. Among its notable features are the wrought-iron porch rails and lamp standards, the vaulted entrance hall, the beautiful staircase and doors, and the suite of drawing-rooms on the second floor.

It was in this house that Stephen Decatur died after his duel with James Barron. And here later lived Baron de Neuville, the French minister; Baron Tuyl, the Russian minister; Henry Clay, while Secretary of State under John Quincy Adams; Martin Van Buren and Edward Livingston, while successive Secretaries of State under Jackson; Sir Charles Vaughn, the British minister; George M. Dallas, while vice-president under Polk; and Howell Cobb, while Secretary of the Treasury under Buchanan.

Many stories have been handed down of life in the historic mansion. Few if any of these anecdotes, however, contained more human interest than that to which Washington gossips were now treated after Benjamin had brought his wife back from Paris.

The trouble lay with Natalie. Judah must have had misgivings even before her arrival in Washington. In the first place, there was doubt whether his wife would be satisfied anywhere in America. Then he may have heard some of the tales about her which were being repeated in Washington. For curious gossip about Natalie had reached the city, and there was doubt how she would be received by Capital society.

Would Natalie meet the fate of Peggy O'Neale? Did Judah know that Van Buren had once entertained that lively lass at the Decatur House? All the influence of Old Hickory had not been sufficient to prevent the virtuous Washington matrons from giving her the cold shoulder. Would the house now prove unlucky for Judah and Natalie?

Whether or not he was influenced by this danger, Judah filled the Decatur House for her homecoming with 'hitherto undreamed-of magnificence'; *objets d'art* and other furnishings, 'the envy of local connoisseurs,' were imported regardless of cost. These preparations completed, Natalie arrived to be the mistress of the elegant establishment. Then about forty-five years old, she was still beautiful and 'very, very gay,' but 'very unhappy.' Although Judah idolized her and gave her everything she wanted, she left the impression that she resented being married to a Jew.

As Senator Benjamin's wife, Natalie enjoyed a certain prestige. Despite her 'rumored delinquencies,' society decided to call. Mrs. Clement Clay, a leader of the congressional set 'and one of the brightest ornaments' of Washington society, has described how the decision was reached at her 'mess.' The feminine members held a conclave to decide whether to make the visit. There was great difference of opinion and, agreement seeming impossible, they decided to refer the question to their husbands for settlement.

Mrs. Clay asked the opinion of her husband and his advice was generally accepted.

'By all means, call,' urged the politic Alabama Senator. 'You have nothing to do with the lady's private life, and, as a mark of esteem to a statesman of her husband's prominence, it will be better to call.'

What followed is vividly narrated in Mrs. Clay's own words; she did not mention Judah's and Natalie's names but they can be identified.

Upon a certain day, therefore, it was agreed that we should pay a 'mess' call, going in a body. We drove accordingly, in dignity and in state, and, truth to tell, in soberness and ceremony, to the mansion aforenamed. It was the lady's reception day. We entered the drawing-room with great circumspection, tempering our usually cordial manner with a fine prudence; we paid our devoirs to the hostess and retired. But now a curious retribution overtook us, social faint-hearts that we were; for, though we heard much gossip of the regality and originality of one or more dinners given to the several diplomatic corps (the lady especially affected the French Legation), I never heard of a gathering of Washingtonians at her home, nor of invitations extended to them, nor, indeed, anything more of her until two months had flown.

And then came the denouement:

Arab-like, the lady rose in the night, 'silently folded her tent and stole away' (to meet a handsome German officer, it was said), leaving our calls unanswered, save by the sending of her card, and her silver and china and crystal, her paintings, and hangings, and furniture to be auctioned off to the highest bidder!

Everyone in Washington now thronged to see the beautiful things, and many purchased specimens from among them, among others Mrs. Davis. By a curious turn of fate, the majority of these treasures were acquired by Mrs. Senator Yulee, who was so devoutly religious that her piety caused her friends to speak of her as the 'Madonna of the Wickliffe sisters!'

Some beautiful pieces of furniture in the gilded style of the time are still in the possession of the Yulee family. They also have a large and very beautiful tray and several candlesticks of Sheffield plate; a pair of hand-made candelabra of French bronze; some beautiful tea cups of eggshell china; a handsome epergne, which adorned one of Benjamin's tables; and other relics of the tragedy.

We can imagine the effect of the tragedy upon Benjamin. In his extremity he turned to his friend, Senator Yulee. He even talked of leaving Washington, but Yulee urged him to remain; he should stay and stick it out. Benjamin replied that it was impossible; his life was wrecked. He left the city, and the auction was afterwards held.[32]

Benjamin did bring himself to return to Washington, but there was little hope left for him of domestic happiness. Natalie went back to Paris and he continued to support her. There is no record of his ever seeking a divorce. A member of his family believes that this was because of the child, Ninette.[33] The young girl, now about eighteen years old, lived with her mother in France.

* * *

Natalie's infidelity left a wound that could never be completely healed. But gradually Benjamin regained his philosophical point of view. Life still offered many compensations. He could find peace by burying himself in his work, and satisfaction in the wealth and honors he was winning thereby.

During this period he became involved in an important mining suit, *United States* v. *Castillero*, the last significant case he was to argue in America. *United States* v. *Castillero* involved the title to the New Almaden quicksilver mine in California, then one of the richest in the world. Bitterly contested by Benjamin and the other lawyers for the rival claimants, the suit was fought through the California courts and finally decided by the United States Supreme Court in 1862, more than ten years after the start of the litigation. The report in 2 *Black* is one of the longest in the earlier history of the Supreme Court, while the record of the hearing before the circuit court in California fills four octavo volumes; the argument of one counsel alone covers three hundred pages.

Better than any other case in which Benjamin figured in America, *United States* v. *Castillero* shows his characteristics as a mature and experienced lawyer. The suit is often included among the so-called fraudulent mining cases that arose in California during the early period of her statehood. Judah P. Benjamin, Reverdy Johnson, and Archibald Peachy, the chief counsel opposing the Government, are cast as villains in the play, whereas Attorney-General Black, Edmund Randolph, and the other lawyers for the United States are portrayed as the heroes who saved the public from the rapacious rich company and its hired attorneys. This is not only the way the story is frequently written, but it is the conclusion one may well reach unless a large amount of complicated and none too accessible evidence is examined.

Undoubtedly there were many fraudulent land and mining claims in California during that hectic early period of its history. The United States Government did some notable work in sifting the good claims from the bad, and in exposing clear instances of dishonesty; for this action it has received deserved recognition. Yet the role of the Government was not always as noble as it was portrayed. Certainly it did not play an altogether heroic part in *United States* v. *Castillero*.

The New Almaden mine, the cause of the lengthy litigation, was located on a rancho about fifteen miles south of San José, California. The quicksilver mine there had been known since early times, and had been acquired in 1845 by a Mexican officer, Captain Andres Castillero. California was then part of Mexico, and Castillero carried out various formalities to confirm his claim according to the local mining law. This procedure was later declared to be insufficient to prove title, but it seems safe to say that his claim would not have been seriously questioned if California had not meantime become a part of the American Union. The progressive Americans were then none too loath to confiscate the property holdings of the benighted Mexicans in the interest of a higher civilization.

Under ordinary circumstances Castillero might have been stripped of his claim without great ado. But the mine was leased from him by wealthy English mining interests, Barron, Forbes and Company, and a million dollars' worth of quicksilver was soon being extracted annually. When rival claimants to the mine, Fossat, Berreyesa, and the United States Government, purporting to represent the public interest, contested the Castillero title, the mining company had plenty of money to employ the ablest lawyers available.

When in 1852, two years after California had become an American state, Castillero asked the United States Land Commission to confirm his title to the mine with two square leagues of land, his claim was opposed by the United States land agent in California. The commission confirmed his claim to the mine but refused to give him the land. The case was appealed to the United States District Court and there was a terrific legal battle.[34] In a letter written on behalf of the mine owners on 10 March 1859, Benjamin, Reverdy Johnson, and J. J. Crittenden were offered $10,000 each to contest all cases affecting the title of the mine and $25,000 each if they were successful.[35] Several California lawyers were also employed in the case, including Archibald Peachy for the company and Edmund Randolph as special counsel for the Government.

Peachy and Randolph were both members of old Virginia families who had come to California the year of the gold rush. Peachy, a fine-looking gentleman, tall, proud, and elegantly dressed, was considered one of the best lawyers in the state. Randolph, a grandson of George Washington's attorney-general, had inherited much of the ability of his distinguished family. A member of the first session of the California legislature—the 'Legislature of a Thousand Drinks'—where he wore a 'flop' hat and 'hickory' shirt and took a leading part in the deliberations, Randolph had later become one of the leading California lawyers, though he sometimes depended more upon invective and sarcasm than upon logic. Moreover, of noted courage, he once accepted a challenge to a duel when too weak to stand up in the field, requesting that the parties 'sit in chairs, at close distance, and crack away at each other.' [36] Now in 1858 writing to Attorney-General Black, P. Della Torre, the United States Attorney at San Francisco, recommended that Randolph be retained in the New Almaden case because of the time he had already devoted to it and his 'extraordinary ability and learning.' [37]

In the same letter Della Torre stated that it would 'require months of undivided attention on the part of any counsel to master the details and intracacies [sic] of the case.' Such attention Benjamin must have applied to it, for when it was argued in the California District Court late in 1860, he proved himself fully able to cope with Randolph or any of the opposing lawyers. If all the litigation should be finally decided in his favor, Benjamin's $25,000 fee would be perhaps the largest he had ever received.

In 1859 the Government secured an injunction restraining the further operation of the mine, and the company countered by stirring up opposition. They held public meetings and accused the Government of helping a rival claimant (Fossat) and even of attempting to secure for itself all the mineral lands in the state. In an effort to secure political support, Peachy was elected to the state senate and Latham, the company candidate, to the United States Senate.

The San Francisco press had been 'subsidized,' a Government partisan wrote Jeremiah Black, and 'a spurious public opinion manufactured. The Judge's opinion is denounced in leading editorials, and these recopied by certain country presses.'

'In a word, the New Almaden Company is fast getting to be to California what the old United States Bank was to the Union,' he concluded.[38]

The trial of *United States* v. *Castillero* before the United States District Court (acting as a circuit court) began in San Francisco on 8 October 1860. The argument for the mining company was opened by Peachy, who spoke for a week. Meantime, on the 14th, Judge McAllister, evidently tired of Peachy's endless argument, moved an adjournment, since 'the court wanted to go out to the Fair Grounds and see the bulls.' Already, according to the *San Francisco Sun*, the expenses of the case had been enormous: the company had spent 'over $150,000 in procuring testimony, paying counsel, etc., and it will probably cost them $50,000 more.'[39]

After Peachy finally concluded his pleading, he was followed by Randolph, who occupied another week.[40] Then he was succeeded by Benjamin, whose speech continued through 22, 23, 24, 25, 26 October and 5 November.[41] The large courtroom was crowded with spectators curious to hear the 'great intellectual struggle,' wrote a correspondent of the New York *Times*. Benjamin,

being a distinguished stranger, and not having dulled the edge of his reputation by lecturing . . . drew beautifully . . . Ladies, lawyers, and Judges—for none of the Civil Courts were in session during the week—thronged [the courtroom] even to the steps leading to the Bench . . . The Senator is making this terribly tedious case interesting, and reducing the complications of its history to its lowest terms.[42]

Benjamin offered what appears to be ample evidence to show that Castillero had discovered the mine. He showed that the fact was communicated not only to the public authorities of California and Mexico, but to a United States Consul and General John C. Frémont. He also offered documentary evidence from the Mexican archives to prove that the claim had been properly filed, and presented the testimony of numerous witnesses to establish the genuineness of the documents.

'A great deal of money,' he frankly admitted, had been spent in bringing the Mexican witnesses of high position up to San Francisco for the trial. He and his associates had gone so far as to charter a steamer for their work. He took the Government to task for asserting that the witnesses were perjurers and the documents forged 'without a solitary word in the entire Transcript to back these assertions.' Edmund Randolph's action in the case came in for particular criticism.

How effectively Benjamin satirized Randolph's procedure is shown, for example, by the following extract from the printed argument. Benjamin stated that every official in Mexico City whom he and his associates felt could be useful in explaining and verifying any of their papers in the case

had been brought up here before the Court—and, need I say it, *cross*-examined. These cross-examinations are a part of the judicial history of the country—a remarkable portion. Upon that cross-examination I may have something hereafter to say. It is something totally unprecedented in the whole history of jurisprudence. Six or seven hundred questions to one witness are what is termed, in familiar language, a mere flea-bite. That constitutes a mere commencement. Every possible thing which human ingenuity could devise in the shape of a cross-question in such a case, is brought up and propounded. Men are not only asked their age and birth-place; their entire domestic relations are inquired into. They are asked where they went to school, who were their school-mates and *school-masters*.

They are asked whether they are the men they profess to be, *and if they have brought proof of their own identity!*

Castillo Lanzas is called upon the stand. My brother Randolph asked him: 'Who are you? What is your name? Can you *prove* that you are the person you say you are?'

Well, I am Castillo Lanzas, is the reply. Mr. Buchanan knows me. I knew the whole diplomatic corps in London, when he and I were there together. It did not suggest itself to me to come here with certificates of identity.

Who knows you here? inquired brother Randolph.

I think that there is a gentleman here by the name of Arce who keeps a tobacco store, who knows me, and to whom I gave a passport in London.

Well, says brother Randolph, I give you permission to summon this witness in order to prove that you *are* Castillo Lanzas.

Now my friend Mr. Peachy plays rather a scurvy trick. Brother Peachy pretended that he was very apprehensive that Castillo Lanzas would be proven to be not Castillo Lanzas. At least I take this to be so, for he objected very strenuously. Brother Peachy would not allow the introduction of this tobacconist on the stand. Brother Randolph then insisted upon his own right to bring him forward, and summons him in behalf of the United States. Well, in comes Mr. Arce. Castillo Lanzas is pointed at, and the question is put 'Do you know that man?'

'Yes. That is Castillo Lanzas.'

'Where did you know him?'

'I knew him in London. He was Mexican Minister there.'

'Well, now,' exclaims brother Randolph, 'Who are you, sir? Who knows you?' That is the question next put to the witness.

[The Marshal had to call 'order' in the Court, the laughter and demonstration of applause being very loud.]

Benjamin condemned the Government for attempting to take property in violation of its plighted word as given in the treaty of cession of California. He accused Jeremiah Black of deliberate partisanship in that he called certain Mexican documents forgeries, but refused to send his 'own officers to Mexico at our expense to examine' them.

Benjamin was speaking as an attorney for the company and being richly rewarded for his efforts. Nevertheless, we cannot help but be impressed by his concluding remarks:

There is no treaty of the Government of the United States pledging the faith of a great nation in favor of one single quartz-miner in the State of California; but there is a published treaty pledging the faith of a great nation in favor of a Mexican mine-owner, whose Government ceded this territory to the United States; ceding to us nought but what it held itself. We acquired from Mexico nothing but what Mexico owned, and she did *not* own this mine when she ceded this territory to the United States. It belonged to one of her citizens. She did not claim it—did not pretend it was hers. Whence then the right of the Government of the United States? . . .

I know not what your Honors may think of the past, but I think I can share what you feel now. I think I can share the satisfaction, the glow of honest pride with which you will be actuated when you are enabled to say, 'Now, now, we are able to undo what we have done because our consciences are informed. We know now the rights of the parties; and no longer shall the equity powers of this Court be made the instruments of spoilation and oppression!'

At the conclusion of Benjamin's argument the applause was so 'loud and prolonged' that the Court called on the Marshal to preserve order.[43]

The New Almaden case was given to the judges early in November, and Benjamin sailed from San Francisco on the 10th.[44] Already a Government adherent, none too sure of the decision in the case, had written Attorney-General Black a highly colored review of the events connected with the trial. He apparently wanted Black to feel that their defeat, if such, would be due to the nefarious methods of the company and its hired attorneys, rather than to any weakness in presentation of the Government's case. The letter was sent by 'the pony,' since Randolph wanted Black to receive it as soon as possible.

The writer explained the alleged efforts of the company to manufacture distress after the closing of the mine. And then he continued with a number of strong accusations.

Thus the Company has acquired a vast hold upon the feelings of the laborers of this state. Moreover, the partners in it are immensely rich. For years back they have subsidized newspapers and paid hireling scribblers, with a lavish hand, to maintain their cause and spatter mud on their antagonists. With the coarse, insulting, and slandering articles which these wretches have been paid to write, you are sufficiently familiar. Moreover, there is a social influence . . . of balls, dinners, suppers, old wine, rare segars and juicy birds, which have been plied in this city with immense effect. For one man who is capable to comprehend the justice of a case like this, or curious to understand its details, there are a thousand whose digestion is perfect, appetite excellent & whose relish for a good dinner is nowise impaired by the reflection that it is possible it has been paid for with stolen money. All hungry and party-loving people have thus been drawn into the net of the Company, are its advocates & fierce, fast friends . . .

Then Benjamin and Reverdy Johnson were brought to San Francisco to plead the case. The correspondent continued,

No pains were spared to lend éclat to their coming, & since they came they have been most diligently puffed. During the progress of the trial, whenever it was known that either of these distinguished gentlemen meant to regale the Court with a speech, the Almaden people drummed up all the ladies in the place who could be got to come, including, of course, their own wives, sisters, aunts, & cousins, leaving nobody at home but the 'babes & sucklings.' The next day the audience was of course described by the newspapers of the Company as 'brilliant,' 'beautiful,' 'delighted,' and the speech as 'one of the most able and unanswerable efforts of the distinguished Senator,' with other stuff of the same kind. As the trial progressed a dinner was given by John Parrott, one of the owners of the mine, to Benjamin and Johnson, to which Judge McAllister & eight of his family sat down. Halleck gives a ball at the close at which the same high functionary & his family appeared in large numbers.

Moreover, during the progress of the trial, Johnson & Benjamin delivered lectures in behalf of the Church of the Advent, whereof a young McAllister is pastor, thus putting some two or three thousand dollars directly into the fingers of the Judge's son. When you consider that Benjamin is a Jew, his labors in behalf of a Christian Church display a spirit of toleration pretty nearly unexampled. These are only specimens of the art & address with which this whole affair has been managed from first to last . . .

Such was the version of this unidentified partisan (probably one of the Government counsel).[45] In his annual message to Congress the next month Buchanan made special mention of the 'distinguished services' of Attorney-General Black, in 'defense of the Government against numerous and unfounded claims to land in California purporting to have been made by the Mexican Government previous to the treaty of cession.'[46] Was the Castillero title one of these 'unfounded claims'? Certainly there was much dissent among those who had been close at hand during the litigation. The *New York Times*[47] correspondent in San Francisco wrote that Benjamin and Reverdy Johnson took back with them 'the admiration of all our people.'

Nor did they lack judicial support. The decision of the circuit court, handed down on 18 January 1861, confirmed the title of the New Almaden Company to the mine with part of the land which it claimed.

Unfortunately, the company was not satisfied and entered an appeal to the United States Supreme Court. The hearing did not take place until 1863. Although Benjamin was then Secretary of State for the Southern Confederacy, the counsel for the company, Reverdy Johnson, Charles O'Connor, and J. J. Crittenden, filed a copy of his brief with the court—a noteworthy proof of their regard for the legal ability of the 'rebel.' By a very doubtful decision, with three justices dissenting, judgment was rendered in favor of the Government.

Edmund Randolph did not take part in the arguments before the high court, since his 'prolonged and exhausting labors' in the case had already led to his untimely death. But Benjamin, as a member of the Confederate cabinet and Jefferson Davis's right-hand man, was working even harder than before.[48]

*　*　*

On Monday, 14 May 1860, members of the Senate were treated to a drastic change from their usual political diet. Adjourning after the roll call, they witnessed the arrival in Washington of one of the most bizarre—and in a sense significant—groups of visitors that had appeared there during its varied history. These visitors, who came up the river on the new steamer *Philadelphia* and were conducted to their quarters at the Willard by an honorary military escort, were, according to the *Intelligencer*, little men with dark brown eyes and dark skin 'with a tinge of copper.' They shaved part of their heads and gathered up the remaining hair in a 'lock, suggestive of a scalp-lock.'

But this did not indicate that they were Indians. They were Japanese, members of the Embassy that had come to return the visit of Commodore Perry and bring the new treaty with the United States. Portending a whole trend in history, the *Intelligencer* noted, 'Some of [the Japanese] have shrewd and intelligent physiognomies and obviously have very quick perceptions.'

Then there was this story, which, retailed in the Capital and printed in the *Intelligencer*, must have reached Benjamin's ears. One of the Japanese went to a barber shop near the Willard and had his head shaved 'quite to his liking.' He paid the barber 'in strict accordance with tonsorial prices in the Empire'—that is a copper cash equal to one eighth of a cent. Then he 'walked leisurely away.' [49]

Along with some of the Japanese, Benjamin probably joined the society folk who gathered Saturday afternoon 21 May on the White House grounds to listen to the concert by the Marine band. It was the last spring he ever spent in Washington, and to outward appearances there had never been a more delightful one. Congress usually adjourned at four o'clock, so that he had time for a carriage drive out to Georgetown along the avenue of flowering crabapple trees, to drop in at the Bayards or Yulees, or on Saturdays to join the ladies and gentlemen who strolled on the President's grounds during the band concert or, sitting in open carriages, talked about everything but the dangerous subject of politics. 'Easy compliments to the ladies fell from the lips of the men who could apply to each other in debate abuse too painful to remember.' [50]

And yet beneath this gaiety there was always the undercurrent of impending danger. On 8 December 1859, three days after the opening of the Thirty-sixth Congress, John Brown had been hanged at near-by Charles Town, Virginia, standing 'upright as a soldier' until the trap door was sprung. Not long afterwards, amid much bitterness, a conservative Republican had been elected speaker of the House of Representatives. And then in April 1860 the Democrats by a peculiar blunder had held their presidential nominating convention in Charleston, South Carolina. For although this city of Benjamin's boyhood was as charming as ever that spring, it was no place for political compromises. Indeed, it is doubtful if any significant ones could have been agreed upon anywhere by the Democratic delegates. After a majority of them refused to endorse the Southern demand that Congress guarantee slave property in the territories, the representatives from Louisiana and the other states of the Lower South withdrew from the convention; their action was warmly approved by Benjamin in a Senate debate on 8 May with Clingman of North Carolina. Benjamin appears to have spoken truly, however, when he said that he had never 'felt such an utter shrinking' of his whole being, never felt his heart sink within him as it did at the news of the impending sectional division.[51]

After the disruption of the Charleston Convention, the remaining delegates adjourned to meet at Baltimore on 18 June, while the delegates who withdrew decided to meet at Richmond a week earlier. Although Benjamin had praised the action of the seceding members, he signed, with eighteen other Southern Senators and representatives, an 'Address to the National Democracy' urging these delegates to attend the Baltimore Convention with the Douglas men; only upon the failure of agreement there should they join the remaining Southern delegates in Richmond.[52] But sincere as Benjamin was in his efforts for compromise—or at least for concession by the Northern Democrats—he did not encourage any such action by his philippic against Douglas in the Senate the following 22 May. The Republicans would soon meet in Chicago to choose their candidate for President, and it was highly probable that he would be opposed by Douglas as the candidate of the Northern Democrats. Since the Southern Democrats also would probably nominate a candidate of their own, it might well be that the Democratic party, with a split ticket, would lose the critical election. With Douglas, in Benjamin's opinion, largely to blame for this division, it is not surprising that his speech against the Illinois Senator was one of the bitterest he ever delivered.

Placed by the Dred Scott decision in an embarrassing position before his Northern supporters because of his advocacy of popular sovereignty in the territories, and baited by Lincoln in the famous Freeport debate, Douglas had advanced the doctrine that the people of a territory by unfriendly local legislation could still prevent the introduction of slavery in their midst. 'No matter what the decision of the Supreme Court might be on the abstract question,' he contended, 'still the right of the people to make a slave territory is perfect and complete under the Nebraska bill.'

One result of this statement was that Douglas was regarded by the Southern leaders as a traitor to his party. John Slidell secured his removal from the chairmanship of the Committee on Territories, and Senator Fitch of Indiana got himself involved in a near-duel with the Illinois Senator during which Benjamin served as Fitch's intermediary.

Now when Douglas was being arraigned before the Senate, Jefferson Davis and Benjamin were the leading prosecutors. During the course of Benjamin's speech he upbraided Douglas for intimating that his Southern opponents were guilty of duplicity. Douglas had said that 'no consideration of political expediency can relieve an honest man' from supporting a congressional slave code for the territories if he believed it was constitutional. Yet he stood up in the Senate hour after hour and attacked the Southern party for doing what he said their oaths and consciences required them to do. Through his interpretation of the Dred Scott decision Douglas was being 'driven step by step . . . to the Black Republican camp. Let him beware before return becomes impossible.'

After referring to Douglas as his idol, whom he had 'been obliged to pluck from his place on high,' Benjamin said that 'the precise point, the direct arraignment, the plain and explicit allegation' made against Douglas by his Democratic opponents was that 'having bargained with us upon a point upon which we were at issue, that it should be considered a judicial point; that he would abide the decision, and consider it a doctrine of the party; that having said that to us here in the Senate, he went home, and under the stress of local election, his knees gave way; his whole person trembled . . .' Two men, Douglas and Lincoln, Benjamin continued, were struggling before the people of Illinois 'on two great sides of a political controversy that was dividing the Union, each for empire at home. One stood on principle—was defeated. To-day—where stands he? The other faltered—received the prize; but to-day, where stands he? Not at the head of the Democratic party of these United States. He is a fallen star . . .'

Benjamin also advanced some arguments to prove that Lincoln was more conservative and true to the South than Douglas. The speech, which made a strong impression, was printed in pamphlet form by the Democratic National Committee and used as a campaign document by supporters of John C. Breckinridge, the presidential candidate of the Southern Democrats.[53]

Two days after making his violent attack on Douglas, Benjamin gave the Senate a notable proof of his inherent kindliness and sense of honorable obligation. On 24 May he reported from the Committee on the Judiciary a bill authorizing the President to enter into contracts to return to Africa certain Negroes taken from captured slave ships. The helpless Negroes, of whom there were about 1,200 detained at Key West, were to be decently maintained for six months after their landing in Africa, at a cost of not over $100 per person. The bill was opposed for one reason or another by Davis, Mallory, Mason, and Toombs. But Benjamin successfully maintained that the United States Government was 'bound by treaty stipulations to aid in the suppression of the slave trade. If that treaty binds us, it is our duty to carry it out in good faith.' Nobody could suggest such a proposition as casting the Negroes loose upon the shore, he said; they must be fed for a short time and clothed and sheltered until they could take care of themselves.[54]

It was only one of several incidents in which Benjamin had given expression in the Senate to a human sympathy not to be expected in a reputed champion of the privileged classes. Thus he had helped Senator Hamilton Fish of New York with his bill to improve the miserable travel conditions of the overcrowded passenger steamers used by the emigrants from Europe (it was a bill 'in which the best interests of humanity are involved,' Benjamin said);[55] and he advocated a law to prohibit the doubtful if not worthless bank notes so often issued by associations or individuals in the District of Columbia. 'The money that circulates in the hands of the people, the money that is in the hands of the hucksters in the market place, the money that passes through the hands of small and poor families into the grocer's hands, the money with which provisions are bought, with which laborers are paid—that ought to be beyond the possibility of doubt or suspicion.'[56]

VIII. Secession

'You know how absurd is the fiction put forward by our enemies in the Northern States that the great Civil War which raged between 1861 and 1865 would never have taken place but for Jefferson Davis and myself,' Benjamin told a friend the year before he died. 'Such mighty convulsions which amount indeed to revolutions, are never the work of individuals, but of divided nations.'[1]

Such was Benjamin's answer to the accusation that he was a leader in a conspiracy to disrupt the American Union. But does he tell the whole truth? Is there other evidence to consider?

There is no denying that Benjamin was a leader of the extreme Southern party in the Senate; that he was one of the ablest and most eloquent defenders of the Southern point of view on slavery and States' Rights. In a letter to Thomas F. Bayard in 1858 he even went so far as to state, 'I believe that the great error of the South has been in supineness, in neglect to meet and expose fallacies which to her appeared too shallow to serve any purpose of her enemies.'[2]

But that is not the whole story. The aggressive stand Benjamin advocated was to be made within the Union. There is no indication that he ever advocated secession prior to December 1860. Then, apparently against his best judgment, he took a number of decisive steps, culminating in his resignation from the Senate. But his action merely accelerated a movement which, without his help, would still have grown beyond control.

On 18 August 1860 it was reported that Benjamin had arrived in San Francisco on the last steamer.[3] From the time of his landing there until the end of the trial of *United States* v. *Castillero* in early November he was absorbed with this case. Indeed, he was but slightly concerned with politics from the time he left Washington in June until his return there in December.

A prominent political figure, however, is liable to be a target at any time for misrepresentation, if not deliberate falsehood. This is all the more likely if he is as secretive as Benjamin, as indifferent, at least at times, to personal criticism. And, above all, if he has taken a strong stand on controversial issues, such as give rise to a bloody civil war.

What appears to have been an example of such historical perversion was the effort to link Benjamin with a dubious letter published some years after the war in the *Memoir* of Thurlow Weed, the New York politician. This letter, purportedly written by Benjamin in August 1860 to the British Consul at New York, sought co-operation in securing the return of the Southern states to their 'allegiance to Great Britain, our mother country.' The writer requested the aid of the Consul in properly approaching Her Majesty's minister at Washington City, with a view to the accomplishment of 'his great end.'

Reposing that confidence in you, which your [the Consul's] position in life warrants me in doing, you must at present excuse me from not signing my name, for fear of an accident. This much you may know. I am a Southron, and am a member of Congress, whose untiring perseverance will never cease until the object I have thus boldly undertaken is fully accomplished. Be so kind as to answer this as early as possible. Allow me a personal interview, and, if you cannot come to New York, address your answer to 'Benjamin' in care of some one at your office.[4]

Fortunately, this rather fantastic letter was published before Benjamin's death. He categorically denied that he was the author, and there is every reason to believe his assertion. Aside from the wording of the letter, which raises strong doubts as to his authorship, it was dated from New York on 11 August 1860 and he was then several thousand miles distant on his trip to California. The name of the real author of the letter remains a mystery, but Benjamin's reply to the accusation leads one to believe that it was someone who had twisted his remarks for a special purpose.

The letter is a fiction, but to some extent founded on fact. I have always gone on the principle of speaking to fools according to their folly. There was, twenty years ago, among the upper class in England a general desire to believe that the republican form of government was an impossible one. They went in for Maximilian in Mexico, and when Otho was turned out of Greece began to look around for another Prince to raise to the throne from which he had fallen. It was imagined that all the British colonies were future kingdoms for children of the Queen, and I was constantly asked by letter and verbally by Englishmen not only of high position but more than average intellect, whether it would not be better for the South to have a monarch than a President.

I humored this idea or fancy, and said on many occasions to persons who I thought would advantageously echo my words that the best thing that could happen to the Southern[er]s would be for Queen Victoria to make them a present of her second son and place her third son over Canada. This produced an effect in certain clubs as I had intended. The Duke of Argyll was strongly of opinion that there would be monarchical governments all over America before the end of the century.[5]

By October 1860 the presidential campaign was in full swing. It was now obvious that Lincoln, the Republican nominee, had an excellent chance of being elected and there was real fear that the Southern states would then carry out their threat to secede from the Union. In a letter written in California on 8 October [6] to some German-Americans there who had requested a statement of his views 'on the present condition of public affairs,' Benjamin promised that after the end of the New Almaden trial he would endeavor to explain the position of the Breckinridge supporters, 'the true Democratic party,' and 'to repel the absurd and self-contradictory charge that we seek to dissolve the Union . . .'

On 7 November, the day after Lincoln's election, Benjamin did offer a more elaborate statement of his political views. This was in an address at the Episcopal Church of the Advent in San Francisco, on the theory and practice of the American Government. He could not look 'with aught but kindling eye and glowing heart,' he said, '. . . at the majestic march of our Union, which, like the great river upon whose banks I dwell, still pursued its resistless course into the unknown ocean which lies beyond, swelling as it advances, receiving its tributaries each distinct yet each uniting in forming one common reservoir of wealth and power, and each, I trust, to remain so united . . .' He said also that he regretted the encroachment of

Congress upon the rights of the states but hoped that the people would come to a better understanding and appreciation of the Constitution. 'Then, and only then, will the horrid sectional disputes, which now stun our ears with their discordant din, be hushed forever.' [7]

On the morning of 11 November, the *Sonora*, bound for Panama, sailed out of the Golden Gate,[8] and Benjamin gazed for the last time on the shores of California. The trip there had proved a satisfactory venture. His argument in the New Almaden case had crowned his legal career in America. And yet, his future was far from certain. Although he had sounded a confident note in his speech at the church benefit, he had expressed his real sentiments when he said that the true patriot felt 'gloomy forebodings.' [9]

* * *

While in California Benjamin had not been able to keep in close touch with affairs in his home state. Opinion of the people there on the secession issue was much more sharply divided than is generally realized. It seems safe to say that for several weeks after the November election the majority of the Louisiana voters were opposed to leaving the Union.[10] Indeed, the *New Orleans Bee* reported as late as 9 January 1861 that the public sentiment in the city was 'nearly equally divided, with a slight preponderance in favor of secession. We willingly admit that the Co-operationists in our city number a large and formidable minority, whose honest convictions every high-minded and patriotic citizen should feel bound to respect.' [11]

But once the opposition forces began to lose, they crumbled fast. The Ordinance of Secession was adopted by a majority which appears surprisingly large considering the recent temper of the state. The result, disastrous as events proved it to be, had been accomplished by a determined minority. The people were swept away by a wave of emotion. It is doubtful if they would have given much heed to the cool and logical arguments of experienced leaders like Benjamin, even if such leaders had been more daring in expressing them.[12]

The presidential election, held while Benjamin was in California, had resulted in a victory for the Breckinridge ticket in Louisiana as well as in the other states of the Lower South. But the returns showed that the strong Breckinridge parishes were in general those made up of small farmers and other poorer whites with few or no slaves. In wealthy and cosmopolitan Orleans Parish, Stephen A. Douglas actually polled 2,998 votes to 2,645 for Breckinridge, while Bell secured 5,215; in the entire state the vote was Breckinridge 22,681, Bell 20,204, and Douglas 7,625. Moreover, Lincoln's election disturbed Louisiana citizens less than it did those of South Carolina and some other Southern states. Cotton and sugar had brought satisfactory prices and the people were in a mood to enjoy themselves rather than to engage in rash political action. In New Orleans the winter gave promise of being even gayer than usual; money was plentiful and the opera was playing to large crowds.[13]

'We should not be frightened from our propriety because Abraham Lincoln is elected President,' stated a 'communicated' article in the *Picayune* on 15 November;[14] over two weeks later, after the secession agitation had begun to make fast headway, it was still skeptical. Will the movement 'ever extinguish agitation, can it restore confidence and prosperity' already so shaken by the mere anticipation of the event, the *Picayune* inquired, and its sentiments were echoed by 'the old Whigs' and 'other high-class conservatives' as well as many other citizens of the state.[15]

All the available evidence shows that Benjamin was then in accord with their position. He had not changed from the attitude he took in California. On 11 December the Washington correspondent of the *Picayune* wrote, Benjamin 'opposes secession, except in the last resort.'[16]

But already the ground was being swept from under him. The determined minority—ministers, small planters, provincial lawyer-politicians, young hot-bloods, and others with no great stake involved—were stirring up the emotions of the people. Reverend B. M. Palmer, an influential Presbyterian minister of New Orleans, used his pulpit to advocate disruption of the Union.[17] His famous Secessionist sermon of 29 November was based on texts from Psalms 94.20 and Obadiah 7:

Shall the throne of iniquity have fellowship with thee, which frameth mischief by a law?

All the men of thy confederacy have brought thee even to the border; the men that were at peace with thee have deceived thee, and prevailed against thee; they that eat thy bread have laid a wound under thee: there is none understanding in him.

This sermon was printed in pamphlet form and the *Delta* reported less than a week later that the supply for their office alone had exceeded 30,000 copies.[18] It was typical of the hysteria which breeds revolution. Soon many opponents of Secession were afraid to express themselves.

'Things have come to a pretty pass,' wrote an influential citizen of North Louisiana to Governor Moore on 5 December, 'when the decent people of the state are unable to speak for fear of compromising their future . . . Right you were when you predicted that the more conservative and less impetuous men would be forced to remain silent.' Most deplorable was the fact that his elder son with 'all his impetuous friends of similar views' favored rash action.[19]

By 10 December Moore had found it expedient or advisable to request the legislature to summon a convention to consider the propriety of secession; it was called to meet on 23 January. By that time the Secessionist feeling was running riot and there was no longer any very formidable opposition from the Co-operationists or Unionists.

We must be careful not to do injustice to Benjamin, Moore, and the other political leaders of Louisiana who were swept away by the tide. They were unquestionably influenced by the example of the other Southern states that had left the Union or were preparing to do so, and they could not but fear the destruction of the immensely valuable slave property, to say nothing of the other dangers of emancipation.[20] William Tecumseh Sherman, then superintendent of the Louisiana State Military Academy, had written:

All the Congresses on earth can't make the negro anything else than what he is. He must be subject to the white man, or he must amalgamate or be destroyed. Mexico shows the result of general equality and amalgamation, and the Indians give a fair illustration of the fate of negroes if they are released from the control of the whites.[21]

Sherman was a native of Ohio and had spent only a few years in the South. We could hardly expect a less conservative opinion from Benjamin.

For a number of reasons, therefore, Benjamin was influenced by the Secessionist agitation. But he still appears to have felt privately that the new movement was unwise. There is only too much evidence to indicate that Benjamin, as well as Moore and Slidell, 'thought it wise to fall in line and even when possible to lead the fast-growing parade . . . lest their office-holding futures and reputations as loyal Southerners be seriously impaired.'[22]

On 11 December Benjamin had been reported as opposed to secession except as a last resort; on the 23rd the *Delta* published a letter from him dated 8 December in which he asserted that it was now necessary for the Southern states to secede through separate state action. South Carolina had left the Union three days before the letter was printed, and it was highly probable that a number of other states would soon follow in her footsteps. Benjamin's letter, it should be noted, was dated at Washington on 8 December. Why was it not published earlier? Could he have ante-dated it or delayed its publication until he could observe the trend of events?

The feeling of a large number, (if not a majority,) of the people of the North is utterly hostile to our interests . . . This feeling has been instilled into the present generation from its infancy; . . . it is founded on the mistaken belief that the people of the North are responsible for the existence of slavery in the South . . . that no just reason exists for hoping for any change in Northern feeling, [or of the South] being permitted to live in peace and security within the Union.

And he asserted that the Southern states should, therefore, promptly secede.[23]

If this letter was correctly dated as of 8 December, the next statement by Benjamin on the issue was on 14 December. He was one of the thirty Senators and Representatives who signed and sent from Washington this 'Address of Certain Southern Members of Congress to Our Constituents':

The argument is exhausted. All hope of relief in the Union through the agency of committees, Congressional legislation, or constitutional amendments is extinguished . . . The Republicans are resolute in the purpose to grant nothing that will or ought to satisfy the South. We are satisfied the honor, safety, and independence of the Southern people [require the organization of] a Southern Confederacy—a result to be obtained only by separate State secession . . .[24]

Three days later the *Picayune* correspondent stated that Benjamin was 'relied upon by advocates of secession to make a powerful speech in favor of the right of secession, and the expediency of its exercise.'[25] On 31 December he finally made this address before the Senate—one of the ablest he ever delivered.[26]

After reminding the Senate of his warning of 2 May 1856 that the aggression of the Republicans would lead the South to defend herself, Benjamin said that in regard to the secession of South Carolina, the issue was whether to recognize her independence or to coerce her. And this decision was of vast consequence because of the other states that would follow in her footsteps. Since the American people had won their freedom, the right to self-government had been a cardinal principle of their liberty. Whenever a form of government became destructive of their interests or safety, the people had a right to alter or abolish it and institute a new government, and South Carolina, therefore, in convention duly assembled, had repealed an ordinance passed by her people in 1788. In proof of this legal right, so exercised, Benjamin quoted a statement by Daniel Webster in the *Rhode Island Case* and Madison's statement in his *Debates in the Federal Convention*.

But suppose one state, Benjamin continued, were to allege that the compact had been broken and others denied it. Who was to judge? The Constitution had provided a supreme judiciary to determine cases in law or equity which involve the construction of the Constitution or of laws concerning pecuniary interests. But what if the infringements on the Constitution were in political matters which, from their very nature, could not be brought before the court?

Here Benjamin followed with two illustrations of his point,

which to an impartial reader seem far-fetched and extreme. Suppose, he said, a majority of Congress would, in contravention of the Constitution, permit South Carolina to have only one Senator. There was no power to force the dominant majority to repair the wrong. The Constitution was designedly silent on the subject. Under such a condition, if South Carolina withdrew from the Union, this would not be a revolutionary remedy, but the exercise of a right inherent under the very principles of the Constitution. Again, if the North did not have a majority in the Senate, it would have it very soon. Suppose the Northern Senators, inasmuch as the Southern Senators represent states that had large numbers of slaves, should decide that the Northern states should have three Senators? If the Southern states refused to submit, that would not be revolution but the exercise of clear constitutional right.

But assume, Benjamin continued, that South Carolina was altogether wrong in her contention that the compact had been violated to her prejudice and that she had a right to withdraw in peace or to declare war, what should be done with her? Benjamin quoted Vattel and Webster to show how untenable was the attempted distinction between coercing the state and coercing the individuals. He argued that it was absurd to attempt to 'go into a State and execute the laws of the United States against individuals without a judge or jury there, without a marshal or attorney, with nobody to declare the violation of the law, or to order its execution before you attempt to enforce it . . .'

And, Benjamin said, not merely what the North had done but what she proposed to do should be considered in the issue.

The Northern states did not propose to enter the South to kill her institutions by force. They did not propose to break their promise and fell the tree. They merely proposed to girdle it so that it would die. They had examined the Constitution thoroughly, had searched it with a fair spirit, and found warrant in it for releasing themselves from the obligation of giving the South any of its benefits; but their oaths forced them to tax her; they could dispense with everything else, they protested upon their souls, [but] would be sorely worried if they did not take her money [Laughter].

In conclusion Benjamin declared:

And now, Senators, within a few weeks we part to meet as Senators in one common council chamber of the nation no more forever. We desire, we beseech you, let this parting be in peace. I conjure you to indulge in no vain delusion that duty or conscience, interest or honor, imposes upon you the necessity of invading our States or shedding the blood of our people. You have no possible justification for it. I trust it is in no craven spirit, and with no sacrifice of the honor or dignity of my own State, that I make this last appeal, but from far higher and holier motives. If, however, it shall prove vain, if you are resolved to pervert the Government framed by the fathers for the protection of our rights into an instrument for subjugating and enslaving us, then, appealing to the supreme Judge of the universe for the rectitude of our intentions, we must meet the issue that you force upon us as best becomes freemen defending all that is dear to man.

What may be the fate of this horrible contest, no man can tell, none pretend to foresee; but this much I will say: the fortunes of war may be adverse to our arms; you may carry desolation into our peaceful land, and with torch and fire you may set our cities in flames; you may even emulate the atrocities of those who, in the war of the Revolution, hounded on the blood-thirsty savage to attack upon the defenseless frontier; you may, under the protection of your advancing armies, give shelter to the furious fanatics who desire, and profess to desire, nothing more than to add all the horrors of a servile insurrection to the calamities of civil war; you may do all this—and more, too, if more there be—but you never can subjugate us; you never can convert the free sons of the soil into vassals, paying tribute to your power; and you never, never can degrade them to the level of an inferior and servile race. Never! Never!

Though Benjamin did not fully develop this phase of his case here, a good constitutional argument could then be made for the right of secession. And although this argument was never emphasized by Benjamin and his school of Southern protagonists, there remained the right of revolution—the right that had been asserted by the ancestors of many Northerners during the first war with England. In the light of future events, the action of South Carolina seems sadly inexpedient, even though the Abolitionists did propose to free the slaves without just compensation to their owners. Yet to coerce her (and the other Southern states who later joined her) would be at the cost of a terrible civil war. Though we may differ with Benjamin's arguments, we must agree that he posed some difficult questions.

Benjamin's speech was delivered during the Christmas season, and the galleries of the Senate were filled to overflowing. After he had finished, the applause was so loud that Senator Mason demanded the galleries be instantly cleared; a motion to adjourn was defeated until after the gentlemen's gallery, from which the noise came, had been vacated.[27] Benjamin's address was probably the greatest he had ever delivered and even a Northern newspaper, the *Philadelphia Bulletin*,[28] declared that he had made a 'capital speech.' His manner was 'self-possessed and resolute,' the *Bulletin* continued.

He went over the whole ground of Southern causes of complaint against the North as coolly and dispassionately as if arguing a case before the Supreme Court. [His] reiteration of the word 'never' was as free from emotion as if he had been insisting on some simple point of law, which could not be decided in any different way. But, free from emotion as it was, it produced the greatest effect. The whole gallery, on all sides, burst out as in one voice, in uncontrollable applause.

The *New York Times*[29] and *Cincinnati Commercial*,[30] however, were severely critical. The *Times* asserted Benjamin's closing statement that the South could never be subjugated had been greeted by the galleries 'with disgraceful applause, screams, and uproar'; evidently the galleries had been 'purposely packed.' As a result of the vociferous demonstration, they had been promptly cleared, but as the people passed out such remarks as the following were 'current among the mob': 'that's the talk'; 'now we will have war'; Benjamin's a brick'; 'd—n the abolitionists'; 'Abe Lincoln will never come here.'

The *Cincinnati Commercial* took Benjamin personally to task. No one who understood his 'brilliant powers,' the *Commercial* wrote, 'could fail to feel the deepest sorrow that a man of such splendid gifts should have abused them so miserably in a cause so hopeless.' He might have saved 'Louisiana from the desperate experiment of secession . . . thus entitling himself to the gratitude of the country, and adding to the lustre of his reputation as an orator the brighter and better fame of enlarged and elevated patriotism.'

But the *Delta* [31] replied that the Secession movement in Louisiana had become irresistible before Benjamin's return from California. The idea prevailing in the North that it originated with politicians was 'the greatest error ever committed by a sagacious people. There has been no excitement or movement in our political history with which the politicians have had so little and the people so much to do. Men in high places and honors are not eager or prompt to engage in revolution.'

To a large extent the *Delta* was right. It is very doubtful if the Secession movement in Louisiana was irresistible when Benjamin returned from California, but in Louisiana as elsewhere in the South it certainly outran the politicians. 'From the first to the last the Southern politicians have been stumbling blocks in the way of Southern advancement,' declared the Charleston *Mercury*,[32] organ of the Secessionist Rhetts. Aside from Robert Barnwell Rhett and William L. Yancey, the leading Secessionist agitators were not men of national prominence; they were usually young men, or older men with no important positions to lose. But for Benjamin, Jefferson Davis, and other Southerners in high civil posts the problem was not so simple. It was not that they denied the right of secession, but that they doubted the necessity of its exercise at the time. In a debate with Senator Baker of Oregon on 2 January 1861 [33] Benjamin had stated what he considered the constitutional basis for secession. Baker, who was later killed in action during the war, contended that the Constitution formed a government over the whole people as a mass; there was no provision for secession by individual states.

But Benjamin argued that certain amendments to the Constitution showed distinctly that it was formed by a delegation of power by the states—they reserved all powers not specifically given the central government. He called attention to the seventh and last articles of the Constitution, which provided that 'the ratification of the conventions of nine States shall be sufficient for the establishment' of the Constitution. Then, after a little more debate, he concluded:

If the right of secession exists at all, under any circumstances, revolutionary or not, it is a State right. Now, the question of

whether it exists under the Constitution or not, can only be determined in one way; first, by examining what powers are prohibited
to the States; and next, whether the powers not prohibited are reserved. This power is nowhere prohibited; and the tenth amendment declares that the powers not prohibited by the Constitution
to the States are reserved to the States.

Undoubtedly, Benjamin was sincere in this argument. But how
much his decision was influenced by policy and how much by natural feeling and emotion we shall never know. So far he had proved
himself to be one of those politicians who followed rather than
directed opinions and events. At the same time his ability to foresee
political change enabled him to appear to lead when he was really
drifting with the current. What may have been his real point of
view as late as January 1861 has since been revealed in a diary [34]
purportedly written by one of his political acquaintances during
that period. The alleged author had a private conversation with
Benjamin in regard to the seizure of federal posts in Louisiana without the formality of secession, and other matters concerning the
state of the Union.

Benjamin was 'too able and clearheaded a man not to feel how
monstrous and indefensible' was the seizure of the forts before
Louisiana had seceded, he wrote. But

he evidently feels the ground giving way under him, and is but a
child in the grasp of his colleague [Slidell], who, though not to be
compared with him intellectually, has all that he lacks in the way
of consistency of purpose and strength of will.

Mr. Benjamin thinks that the ablest of them [the Secession lead-
ers] really regard the experiment of a new confederation as an
effectual means of bringing the conservative masses of the Northern
people to realize the necessity of revising radically the instrument
of union. In his judgment the Constitution of 1789 has outlived its
usefulness . . . The Presidential term must be longer, the President
must cease to be re-eligible, and a class of Government functionaries,
to hold their places during good behavior, must be called into being.
I could detect, I thought, in his views on these points, a distinctly
French turn of thought, but much that he said struck me as eminently sound and sagacious. He thinks not otherwise nor any better
of President Buchanan than Mr. Douglas, though his opinion of
Mr. Douglas is anything but flattering.

It is unfair to accuse Benjamin of being a child in the grasp of
Slidell, but it is highly probable that Slidell influenced him. Benjamin had cast his lot with the Secessionists and he soon took a position which would admit of no compromise on the issue. He was a
member of the caucus of Senators from the Lower South which
met on 5 January 1861 and advised their states to secede and form
a separate confederacy to be organized in a convention at Montgomery. On the 9th, Mississippi separated from the Union, followed
on the 10th by Florida, and on the 11th by Alabama.

One of Benjamin's last important efforts in Washington to further the Secession movement was in connection with the Crittenden
resolutions. After the secession of South Carolina, Crittenden of
Kentucky offered several compromise proposals in the Senate, with
the hope of saving the Union. One of these was an amendment to
the Constitution extending the Missouri Compromise line to the
Pacific, and Benjamin was one of six Southern Senators who materially contributed to the defeat of this measure in the Senate.

Clark of New Hampshire offered a substitute to Crittenden's proposal to the effect that no amendment to the Constitution was
necessary and that the laws should be enforced. Along with Slidell,
Hemphill and Wigfall of Texas, Iverson of Georgia, and Johnson
of Arkansas, Benjamin stayed in his seat and refused to vote. 'To
the surprise of everyone,' so Senator Bragg of North Carolina wrote
in his diary on 16 January, the Clark substitute was adopted. The
vote was 25 to 23. Later Benjamin was reported to have telegraphed
to Louisiana, 'We cannot get any compromise.' [35]

This little episode was certainly not to Benjamin's credit. It is
very doubtful, however, if the Crittenden Compromise would ever
have passed both houses of Congress, for the Republicans wanted
compromise as little as did the Southern extremists.

Louisiana seceded from the Union on 26 January, and on 4 February Benjamin and Slidell withdrew from their seats in the Senate.
Slidell announced the secession of Louisiana and Benjamin made a
few farewell remarks [36] during which he forcefully denied that the
people of Louisiana were or could be precluded from seceding because they occupied territory purchased by the United States or
that the right of secession connoted anarchy. He quoted Representative George H. Pendleton, 'whose northern home looks down

on Kentucky's fertile borders,' as saying, 'Armies, money, blood cannot maintain this Union; justice, reason, peace, may!' And he said that 'no intelligent people ever rose, or ever will rise, against a sincere, rational, and benevolent authority . . . the people of the South imitate and glory in just such treason . . . as encircles with a sacred halo the undying name of Washington.'

Benjamin's often quoted peroration was:

And now to you, Mr. President, and to my brother Senators, on all sides of this Chamber, I bid a respectful farewell; with many of those from whom I have been radically separated in political sentiment, my personal relations have been kindly and have inspired me with a respect and esteem that I shall not willingly forget; with those around me from the Southern States, I part as men part from brothers on the eve of a temporary absence, with a cordial pressure of the hand and a smiling assurance of the speedy renewal of sweet intercourse around the family hearth. But to you, noble and generous friends, who, born beneath other skies, possess hearts that beat in sympathy with ours; to you, who solicited and assailed by motives the most powerful that could appeal to selfish natures, have nobly spurned them all; to you who, on our behalf, have bared your breast to the fierce beatings of the storm, and made willing sacrifice of life's most glittering prizes in your devotion to constitutional liberty; to you, who have made our cause your cause, and from many of whom I feel I part forever, what shall I, can I say? Naught, I know and feel, is needed for myself; but this I will say for the people in whose name I speak today; whether prosperous or adverse fortunes await you, one priceless treasure is yours—the assurance that an entire people honor your names, and hold them in grateful and affectionate memory.

But with still sweeter and more touching return shall your unselfish devotion be rewarded. When, in after days, the story of the present shall be written; when history shall have passed her stern sentence on the erring men who have driven their unoffending brethren from the shelter of their common home, your names will derive fresh lustre from the contrast; and when your children shall hear repeated the familiar tale, it will be with glowing cheek and kindling eye, their very souls will stand a-tiptoe as their sires are named, and they will glory in their lineage from men of spirit as generous and of patriotism as high-hearted as ever illustrated or adorned the American Senate.

To modern readers this peroration may seem a collection of trite phrases and clichés. But we must remember that Benjamin, his pistol at his side, was speaking on a burning question and to a country on the verge of sectional war. And his style, grandiloquent as it was, suited the taste of his audience, even though one Northern opponent said that 'he drew from his spectators many plaudits for his rhetoric which he could not evoke for his logic.'

Senator Bragg of North Carolina wrote that the galleries were crowded during Benjamin's remarks and occasionally they burst into applause. The speech was 'one of the most eloquent' he had ever heard. 'The Senate was hushed into positive stillness, so that every word, in his [Benjamin's] soft but distinct utterance, fell clearly upon the ears of his hearers.' Portions of the speech were 'most touching and pathetic, drawing tears from many.' Bragg confessed that he was overpowered and unable to restrain himself. Both Benjamin and Slidell shed tears at parting from the Southern Senators; Bragg silently shook their hands. He was 'too full to say a word.' [37]

High praise for the speech came also from other sources. Sir George Cornewall Lewis, a prominent Englishman of pro-Union sympathies, present at its delivery, is reported to have exclaimed that it was better than 'our Benjamin himself [Disraeli] could have done.' [38] And Captain (later General) E. D. Keyes, deeply impressed, declared that despite his 'incomparable abilities and the fact that he became a Secessionist with great reluctance' Benjamin did not excite animosity in him or any other Northern man so far as he was aware. 'When I listened to his last speech in the Senate,' Keyes continued, 'I was transported out of myself . . . There was neither violence in his action nor anger in his tone, but a pathos that lulled my senses like an opiate that fills the mind with delightful illusions. I was conscious that it was Senator Benjamin who spoke, and that his themes were mighty wrongs and desperate remedies; but his words I could not recite, nor can I yet recall them.' [39]

The next day, 5 February, Andrew Johnson replied boldly, if immoderately, to Benjamin on the Senate floor. Johnson enumerated some important omissions which he said Benjamin had made in discussing the text of the Louisiana treaty, and asserted that his speech, despite its 'euphonious utterances' and 'seeming sincerity,' was 'a complete lawyer's speech, and the authorities were summed up simply to make out the case on his side.' He also accused Benjamin of hypocrisy in that he had opposed secession during his speech at San Francisco. But Benjamin was not present on the floor to hear this criticism.[40]

* * *

With Benjamin's resignation from the Senate he ended his office-holding career under the American flag. Although there still remained his eventful life under the Stars and Bars and the Union Jack, he had—despite some obvious failings—already achieved a remarkable success. During the twenty years since he first ran for public office in New Orleans he had been an influential member of the Louisiana legislature and of two state constitutional conventions and for the past eight years a member of the United States Senate. He had become known as one of the leaders of the Southern Democrats in the upper house, only overshadowed by a few men such as Davis and Toombs. He had refused the offer to be Minister to Spain and only Natalie's reputation, it appears, had kept him from being tendered a cabinet position. He had not only won greater distinction than any other member of his race who had lived in the United States, but had become one of the outstanding Jews of the world. The only Jew who held a more important political position was Disraeli, and he was not yet prime minister.

Considering the difficulties that Benjamin had overcome, we may easily be tempted to praise him indiscriminately. He had not yet attained the proportions of a statesman. He had continued to be too absorbed with money-getting; he had at times not been above suspicion of Machiavellism. Like many of his contemporaries in the South, he had devoted much of his time and energy to defending Negro slavery. He had been one of the leaders of the final Secessionist movement, apparently against his better judgment.

But if Benjamin was not one of the rare men who would sacrifice his political future and stand against the crowd, he was no Hotspur, no extremist like Rhett, Yancey, or the Reverend Mr. Palmer. He offered the Northern extremists some wise advice, which fell by the wayside; he might have offered them much more. He warned that political events were pointing to civil war; that the South could not be coerced. On the slavery question he was too conservative; he stood for the *status quo* and had not yet offered any satisfactory solution to the terrible internecine problem. Yet Benjamin knew the Negro—knew him as Seward, Sumner, and Harriet Beecher Stowe would never know him. What a pity abolition could not have been planned and administered with the help of men like him! Perhaps it might have been carried on as equitably as in the British colonies —that is, over a moderate period of years and with compensation to the slave owners. How much suffering might thus have been averted, both for the Negro and for the white man!

Although in his political career Benjamin had not yet proved himself to be more than an able politician, in other fields he had won notable fame. He had become one of the leading American lawyers, one of the greatest of the contemporary orators and debaters. Although his career as a business promoter had been cut short, he had shown some of the vision and skill, if not always the prudence, of a Vanderbilt or Rockefeller.

When Benjamin was only thirty-five years old he had been described as 'the *Commercial* Lawyer of New Orleans' [41] and eight years later he was offered an appointment as justice of the United States Supreme Court. During the 'fifties his firm made the largest earnings of any in New Orleans. He also appeared in more cases before the Supreme Court during this decade than any other lawyer except Reverdy Johnson.[42] For some years after the death of Daniel Webster, Reverdy Johnson was considered the leading American lawyer, while a few others such as Jeremiah Black and Edward Stanton overshadowed Benjamin in the importance of their cases. But Benjamin was fast coming into his own, and it is doubtful if there was an abler or better-equipped lawyer at the American bar. There were some attorneys who were his superior in arguing a case before a jury, but as a commercial lawyer and particularly in litigation involving land claims and before an appellate court Benjamin was probably unsurpassed.

From the standpoint of style and content, Benjamin's political speeches were vulnerable to attack by his opponents. But several of his later speeches in America are included in collections of famous orations, and still make interesting reading. His addresses on 31 December 1860 and the following 4 February 1861 and sections of a few of his other speeches still deserve to be ranked among the best specimens of the contemporary American oratory.[43]

So much for Benjamin's reputation as a public speaker. He also won deserved fame as a debater; the reports of his debates in the Senate show that he usually more than held his own with his opponents. J. L. M. Curry, a contemporary congressman, wrote that there was no better debater in the Senate. 'Benjamin was collected and self-possessed in debate, had a voice as musical as the chimes of silver bells, a memory like Macaulay's.' He did not use any 'notes, and while earnest in manner and delivery, seemed as fresh at the close of a discourse as when he uttered the first sentence.' [44]

Many years later Senator Vest of Missouri asked Dennis Murphy, the official reporter of the Senate for nearly forty years and himself a lawyer of considerable ability and wide information, who in his opinion 'was the ablest and best-equipped Senator he had known during his service as reporter.' Without hesitation Murphy replied, 'Judah P. Benjamin of Louisiana.' [45]

It is interesting to speculate what Benjamin's future would have been if the Civil War had not cut short his career under the American flag. He would not have attained the presidency. But he would doubtless have won even greater distinction at the American bar. He would perhaps have held a cabinet position, and, in all probability, have done some more important work as a promoter of large business enterprises. Benjamin had caught the vision of the United States not as disparate sections but as a nation spreading across a great continent, rich with opportunities for the advancement of civilization. In one of his last Senate speeches he described his recent visit to a range of mineral deposits in the Sierra Nevadas, 'probably the richest on the face of the earth.' Within forty-four hours after he left San Francisco, he was in the plains of Utah, and, arriving in the mining country, he found that places which in May had contained only a few canvas tents were now crowded with people; he was delayed on the road for hours at a time by the teams loaded with ore and provisions.[46]

That trip symbolized for Benjamin the new America. His varied experience had separated him widely from the provincial type of Southerner. Conservative as he was in some respects, he would not 'die of an abstraction,' as Henry A. Wise had feared would be the fate of old Virginia. Possessing wide business interests, he owned a goodly slice of the Tehuantepec railroad stock, lands in Texas,[47] and, doubtless, numerous other assets, to say nothing of his law practice in New Orleans, Washington, and California. He was an outstanding representative of the new capitalism in the booming Mississippi port—a capitalism that was becoming more American than Southern.

Because of his political conservatism as well as for reasons of policy, Benjamin was a strong defender of Southern rights. But suppose the issues that brought about the Civil War had not come to a head in 1861? Suppose their settlement could have been postponed for another generation? Would not the economic development in which Benjamin was participating meantime have done much to break down sectional boundaries? Would not many members of the awakening industrial classes in the South have seen that slavery was inimical to their interests? Perhaps the picture is too optimistic, but there is much reason to believe that such events might have averted the war.

If Benjamin had had further opportunity to be a leader in this economic revolution, he would not have proved to be a rascal like Fisk or Gould. But it is likely that he would not have been entirely squeamish. Though generous with his family, he was much absorbed with the crasser forms of money-getting. There are no recorded instances of his taking legal cases without fees, as did Reverdy Johnson.

A good deal about Benjamin's character at this time is revealed in a contemporary photograph preserved in the Brady collection.[48] Benjamin is appropriately dressed in frock coat, waistcoat, high hat, and gloves, probably purchased from expensive haberdashers. But there is a certain slouchiness about his dress, perhaps partly the result of his quasi-bachelor existence. He had become quite stout, with a comfortable fullness of the stomach and waistline. In the photograph, however, he appears considerably younger than his fifty years. His hair and beard are black; his eyes bright and rather enigmatic; his face shows none of the lines usually etched in by age and worry. When he left Washington and accepted a cabinet position in the new Southern Confederacy, he was at the height of his physical and mental if not of his moral powers.

IX. *Confederate Attorney-General*

18 February 1861. Jefferson Davis inaugurated as provisional president of the Southern Confederacy.

25 February. Benjamin appointed Attorney-General.

12 April. Fort Sumter fired upon.

21 May. Confederate Congress votes to move capital to Richmond.

21 July. Northern army routed at First Manassas.

27 July *et seq.* General George B. McClellan appointed commander of Northern Army of the Potomac; beginning of tremendous preparations for decisive campaign against the South.

Was the birthday of George Washington, the father of the Union, a fitting occasion to celebrate secession from it? That depended upon your political complexion, upon the section of the country in which you happened to live.

In New Orleans on 22 February 1861 twenty thousand people assembled at the race track to see a stand of colors given to the crack Washington Artillery, the pride of the city; Benjamin made the presentation speech.

It was the last public address that he ever delivered in New Orleans, and before probably the largest crowd that ever heard him speak. 'An uprising of the entire population, in a spirit of reverence to the name of Washington, took the place of an indifference, or a close mercenary adherence to business, once peculiar to a large majority of our residents here,' the *Delta* declared.

The sunrise was welcomed by a royal salute from the guns of the Washington Artillery. Later it and the other local military units paraded in Jackson Square and Lafayette Square. Then the troops marched through the streets, bedecked with flags and garlands, to the cheers of young and old crowding the housetops, windows, and balconies, and proceeded to the review grounds at the old Creole race course. And here Benjamin presented to the Artillery 'one of the handsomest flags ever seen in this country,' made of yellow and red satin cloth woven in France and 'the handiwork of Louisiana's fair daughters.'

When he said ' 'tis for no hireling soldier that their fair hands have emblazoned its silken folds,' Benjamin indicated that he was not unaware of the feminine part of his audience. But at this time of delirious enthusiasm and overconfidence he did not indulge in the customary boasting. On the contrary, he expressed his belief that 'our independence is not to be maintained without the shedding of our blood. I know that the conviction is not shared by others. Heaven grant that I may prove mistaken.' Then, as if not to throw too much of a damper on the enthusiasm of his audience, he added:

Yet fearful as is the ordeal, and much as war is to be deplored, it is not the unmixed evil which many consider it to be. By a beneficent dispensation of the Creator, that which to mortal seems most calamitous is not unfrequently converted into a blessing at his hands. The fire sweeps over the stubble, and the charred and blackened surface of the field attests its ravage. Yet a little while and the spring rains descend, and the heated earth quickens into vigorous growth the germs that else had lain dormant in its bosom . . .

Benjamin and the New Orleans ladies would never be able to say that the Washington Artillery did not heed his charge that the colors 'be ever borne upon the battle's crest,' that 'its smoke-stained and tattered fragments attest the daring gallantry with which it was borne.' Nor does it appear that the dashing artillerymen, in whom Benjamin continued to take a beneficent interest, forgot 'in the hottest passion of the strife, the mercy due to the yielding foe.' But their gallantry in fifty battles was, as Benjamin at least partly foresaw, at the price of many promising youths left lying on distant battlefields.[1]

And so Benjamin had helped to usher New Orleans into the coming war. A little apprehensive that he might be arrested if he lingered in Washington, he hurried home after delivering his farewell speech in the Senate. Soon after his arrival a country newspaper, the *Bastrop Weekly Dispatch*, which was quoted in the *Delta*,[2] had offered Robert Toombs for President and Benjamin for vice-president of the proposed Southern Confederacy.[3] But though this movement died a-borning, just after his Washington's birthday speech Benjamin's sisters found him packing his belongings.

He told them he had been called to Montgomery to consult with Mr. Davis; he anticipated some service under the new government that would probably keep him too busy to see much of them.[4] A few days later, on 25 February, the Confederate Congress confirmed his nomination as Attorney-General by a unanimous vote.[5]

Benjamin was hardly suited for the post. In fact, with the exception of John F. Reagan of Texas, the Postmaster-General, and perhaps Stephen R. Mallory, the Secretary of the Navy, none of the members of the first Confederate cabinet was well chosen. Jefferson Davis had failed to select a harmonious and efficient group of ministers. Bob Toombs, the Secretary of State, was the same tempestuous figure whom Benjamin had known so well in the Senate. Capable but choleric and outspoken, he did not care for his civil post in wartime and was said, with some little truth, to have 'carried the state department in his hat.' Soon he resigned to become a brave but none too tractable brigadier-general. Pope Walker, an Alabama lawyer who had been chairman of his state delegation at the Charleston convention, lacked sufficient administrative experience to be Secretary of War. Temperamentally, also, he was unfit for the place. It is doubtful if any man could have satisfactorily handled the problem of financing the new government. Certainly it proved beyond the capacity of Christopher G. Memminger, the Charleston lawyer and businessman, who was given the position.

Benjamin was unsuited for the attorney-generalship in the sense that it was too unimportant a place for a man of his ability. Well equipped as he was to serve as a diplomatic commissioner to Europe or as Secretary of State, he was denied a full opportunity. The emissaries the government sent to Europe in early 1861 were his inferiors in ability and experience, and he was not appointed to the State Department until 1862, when it was too late for him to do his most effective work.

Why did Davis make such unwise appointments to his first cabinet?[6] Mrs. Davis wrote that the ministers 'were chosen not from the intimate friends of the President, but from the men preferred by the States they represented,' though she added somewhat platitudinously that 'it would have been difficult to find more honest, capable, fearless men than they were.' Specifically, in regard to Benjamin, Mrs. Davis said that his 'legal attainments caused him to be invited to be attorney-general.' [7] And Jefferson Davis himself declared, 'Mr. Benjamin of Louisiana had a very high reputation as a lawyer, and my acquaintance with him in the Senate had impressed me with the lucidity of his intellect, his systematic habits and capacity for labor. He was therefore invited to the post of Attorney-General.' [8]

In connection with Benjamin's service in the Senate, Davis must have also remembered the cool manner in which he had challenged him to a duel; the Confederate President could appreciate such sensitiveness about points of honor. Nor had he forgotten that Benjamin was from Louisiana. It would have been bad politics not to have had a representative of that influential state in the cabinet. Benjamin was given the lowest of the cabinet positions.

What was the attitude of the Southern people toward his appointment? The attorney-generalship was a civil position in which military-minded Southerners had no great interest; it is difficult to find many contemporary comments either favorable or unfavorable. The Montgomery correspondent of the Charleston *Mercury* [9] declared that 'no better appointment for legal ability and learning could be made,' but T. C. DeLeon, after extravagantly praising Benjamin's mental ability and legal knowledge, stated, 'So the people who shook their heads at him—and they were neither few nor far between—did it on other grounds than that of incapacity.' [10] Here again we run into that more elusive side of Benjamin's character, which makes him so interesting yet difficult for the historian.

There appeared, however, to have been little or no opposition to him because of his Jewish blood. A few days earlier, the Wilmington *Journal* had quoted an article from the *Mercury* written before his appointment, praising the Jews as 'amongst the most faithful and patriotic of the people of South Carolina.' It added,

In the Senate of the United States they furnished two Senators, and both of these Senators were from the South, and both of them have been foremost in vindicating the rights, interests and liberties of the South. Mr. Benjamin and Mr. Yulee are worthy to sit in any assembly of statesmen in the world.[11]

In Montgomery, Benjamin is reputed to have lived at Mrs. Cleveland's. It was at this boarding house, a simple frame residence, that Alexander H. Stephens, the Confederate vice-president, had been serenaded after he arrived in town. From Mrs. Cleveland's it was only a short walk to the Exchange Hotel, the political center of the capital, and to the Executive Office Building. Benjamin's office was in a room on the second floor of the latter building; next to it was one shared by the Adjutant-General and Chief Clerk and another used by the Secretary of the Navy; across a court in the building was that of Jefferson Davis. Such small quarters sufficed for their business in this nascent period of the Confederate Government.[12]

Almost overnight Montgomery had changed from a pretty country town to an important city, buzzing with new life. To the new Confederate capital there was flocking a crowd of patriots and place-seekers: officeholders under the old Washington Government and others on hand for the bestowal of new and, it was hoped, juicy political plums; applicants for military commissions, and assorted adventurers. 'Things here now have a very practical appearance,' wrote the *Mercury* correspondent. 'In the evenings you might almost imagine yourself in Willard's Hotel—the same talk—men in the same groups and many of them the same men.'[13]

Among other news from Washington, Benjamin heard in early March that his old associate, Justice Campbell of the Supreme Court, had resigned. He could appreciate the sentiment that Mrs. Chesnut,[14] wife of the former United States Senator from South Carolina, confided to her *Diary*: 'Lord! how he [Justice Campbell] must have hated to do it. How other men who are resigning high positions must hate to do it.'

Only a few days before a crowd had assembled to watch the raising of the new Confederate flag. There was an appropriate ceremony with an artillery salvo. But the daughter of a former United States consul complained of the deadness of the mob.

'It was utterly spiritless,' she said, 'no cheering, or so little, and no enthusiasm.'

A former captain in the old navy, however, suggested that gentlemen were 'apt to be quiet.'

This was 'a thoughtful crowd, the true mob element with us just now is hoeing corn,' he asserted.

Benjamin was doubtless in that 'thoughtful crowd,' which contained more recent officeholders under the old government than would be found at public gatherings elsewhere in the new Confederacy. At any rate, as Mrs. Chesnut noted, the bridge was broken. As a practical man of the world he must needs make the best of the situation. It was the Southern Confederacy, do or die; failure might well mean a halter for the leaders of the revolution.

On 16 March 1861 the Montgomery Government sent a rather ineffectual delegation to seek European aid for the Confederacy: William L. Yancey, 'the orator of secession,' Judge Rost of Louisiana, and A. Dudley Mann of Virginia.[15] About this time Benjamin was disturbed by the circulation in the Northern press of the story that he had left Yale after being detected in thievery, but decided that it was best to ignore the unpleasant affair.[16] Writing to James A. Bayard [17] about the incident on 19 March, he also took the opportunity to express some hopeful views on the new government:

Our experiment is succeeding admirably. You have no conception of the feeling in these states. I do not believe honestly that you could get them to return to the Union with Northern States on condition of putting an article in the constitution guarantying [sic] to them the right of governing the North at their own pleasure.

The feeling everywhere is one of intense relief at getting rid of an insupportably odious conviction. You will be with us in November in spite of everything.

Since neither Bayard nor his native state, Delaware, ever affiliated with the Confederacy, Benjamin was too hopeful. But, war or no war, Benjamin retained a number of his friends in the North.[18] When an effort was made to expel him from the Union Club in New York, it failed, and some dissatisfied members formed a separate organization, the Union League Club.[19]

In the same letter to Bayard, Benjamin referred to the new Confederate constitution. Experienced legislators representing the individual Confederate states had met in Montgomery and drawn up a constitution for the new government. The Constitution of the United States was used as a model; it was the only instance in American history when that document was revised to meet more modern needs. There were, however, only a few significant changes: more specific stipulations were included to safeguard slavery and states' rights, provisions were added whereby the President could veto specific items of appropriation bills, and department heads were given seats in Congress. And in the light of contemporary American history, it is worthy of note that the process of ratification of amendments to the constitution was somewhat simplified and that the President was to serve only one term of six years.[20]

As a former United States Senator and an eminent constitutional lawyer, Benjamin found these changes of great interest. He expressed his keen satisfaction with the Confederate constitution in the concluding sentences of his letter to Bayard.

Is it not close to perfection? It has been adopted by 87 to 5 in Alabama, *unanimously* in Georgia, will be, I think, unanimous in Louisiana and indeed in nearly every one of our States. It might have been possible to reform the old instrument still more, but how soberly and prudently have the amendments been made! God grant your little state a chance to live under it, & that we may once again sit side by side in a Senate of patriots and Statesmen free from your night-mare of *Red* and mine of *Black* republicanism.[21]

Thus Benjamin sought to fill Bayard with his optimistic propaganda. Doubtless he was pleased with a number of the developments under the new government. Already he must have begun to feel for it some of the love a man has for his own creature—a creature to whom he helped give life and for whom he must fight and bleed.

Actually, however, the future of the Confederacy was highly uncertain. Benjamin's letter was written less than a month before Fort Sumter was fired on and Lincoln issued his call for troops to subdue the seceded states. Before the new government could secure its independence it had to fight a determined enemy with greatly superior resources in men, ships, money, and all the sinews of war. And no one knew this better than Benjamin. He was in favor of stern military preparations even before the cabinet authorized the bombardment of Fort Sumter, as is revealed by an incident later recalled for Pierce Butler by Judge D. M. Shelby, a law partner of L. P. Walker, the Confederate Secretary of War.

Shelby said that when he was in the old Exchange Hotel on one occasion many years after the war, Walker pointed out to him the very room, near the parlor, where the first Confederate cabinet meeting had been held, indicating even the relative positions of the ministers and the President. Said Mr. Walker,

At that time, I, like everybody else, believed there would be no war. In fact, I had gone about the state advising people to secede, and promising to wipe up with my pocket handkerchief all the blood that would be shed. When this cabinet meeting was held, there was only one man there who had any sense, and that man was Benjamin. Mr. Benjamin proposed that the Government purchase as much cotton as it could hold, at least 100,000 bales, and ship it at once to England. With the proceeds of a part of it he advised the immediate purchase of at least 150,000 stand of small arms, and guns and munitions in corresponding amounts—I forget the exact figures. The residue of the cotton was to be held as a basis for credit. For, said Benjamin, we are entering on a contest that must be long and costly. All the rest of us fairly ridiculed the idea of a serious war. Well, you know what happened.[22]

The repetition of this story after the lapse of many years may have led to some inaccuracies. There is strong reason for believing that Jefferson Davis also feared a serious war.[23] At any rate, Benjamin's proposal was not adopted; if it had been, the Civil War might have ended differently. The funds from the sale of cotton might have enabled the Confederacy to organize a superior army to secure a decisive military victory and European recognition before the North could gather her great resources, or they might have provided the sinews with which to withstand a protracted conflict.

Lacking sufficient arms with which to equip them, the Montgomery government rejected many thousands of volunteers. Within a few months after the formation of the Confederacy, wrote Secretary Walker, 360,000 men, the flower of the South, volunteered for service in the army, and by May he was 'worn out with personal applications of ardent officers.' Indeed, he was so harassed by the young braves that he would actually walk the back way from his office to the Exchange Hotel in order to avoid them! But even then he was waylaid by men offering their lives for the Confederate cause.[24] In April a Confederate purchasing agent did sail for Europe and by the following winter large shipments of arms and munitions were reaching the South, but precious time had been lost.

After he failed to get his plan adopted, Benjamin seems to have acquiesced in the program of the administration. With nearly all the members of the cabinet he appears to have voted to authorize General Beauregard to fire on Fort Sumter if he felt it advisable.[25] The Fort was bombarded on the 12th, and three days later Lincoln issued the call for 75,000 troops. In Montgomery the cabinet read his proclamation 'amid bursts of laughter.'[26] Poor cause for mirth it now seems, even though Lincoln did call for relatively few soldiers.

Then, after news of the proclamation spread about the city, a mass meeting was held in front of the Exchange Hotel, where speeches were made by Benjamin and Reagan, and, it was reported, 'the sentiment enthusiastically expressed that as Lincoln had declared war, the Southern forces should march to Bunker Hill monument and demand peace.'[27] This was the kind of talk a politician might have given a crowd of ardent Confederates on that spring day. About the same time, however, Benjamin declined an invitation to deliver the annual address to the literary societies at the University of Georgia, on account of 'the present condition of public affairs when we know not what a day may bring forth.'[28]

* * *

Those were busy days in Montgomery, even for the less important cabinet officers. Benjamin was expected to be present at the various cabinet meetings as well as to attend to his departmental duties, and was often busy for long hours. On 10 April, for instance, the Montgomery correspondent of the Richmond *Dispatch*[29] wrote that a cabinet meeting had been held on the previous Tuesday evening 'where serious conclusions were arrived at, and warlike orders issued'; 'the Secretaries were at their Departments until past midnight.' A month later Jefferson Davis seemed to one critical observer to be taking up all his time with the cabinet,

presumably planning future operations. Sometimes the Cabinet would depart surreptitiously, one at a time, and Mr. Davis while making things as plain as did the preacher the virtues of the baptismal, finds his demonstrations made to one weak, weary man, who has no vim to contend.[30]

With all the important if tedious cabinet meetings, Benjamin's other duties seemed rather insignificant. Yet they had to be attended to. As Attorney-General he had been made head of the Confederate Department of Justice. This was the first American department bearing that name, for in the United States the Attorney-General then directed an office rather than a department; it was not until 1870 that the present Department of Justice was established.[31] Under the Confederate set-up as provided by the acts of 21 and 27 February and 7 March 1861, their somewhat similar department was to include the offices of the Attorney-General and the Assistant Attorney-General, and the bureau of public printing under the superintendent.[32] Furthermore, Benjamin also recommended immediate legislation on the subject of patent rights. By the end of April applications for patents were coming in at the average rate of seventy per month, and on 21 May 1861 the Patent Office in the Department was established under a commissioner of patents. This office—like the Confederate post-office—was required to be self-sustaining, and was such despite the vicissitudes of the war.[33]

Although the duties of the Attorney-General were varied and required considerable professional experience, they offered no great difficulty for Benjamin, even though including some that under the old Government belonged to the Secretary of Interior. One of the most important was the supervision of the Confederate courts. He had to organize these courts and the board of sequestration commissioners. And he was also supposed to argue Government cases before the Supreme Court, a task which perhaps no other lawyer in the South could have handled with greater ability. But the Confederates never carried out the constitutional provision to establish this court. When their last impotent Congress adjourned in March 1865, it left a bill on the table for the appointment of a Chief Justice and four associates at annual salaries of $8,000 and $7,000 respectively.[34]

Among other duties, Benjamin had to give legal advice to the President and heads of departments, and on 1 April he wrote his first opinion as Attorney-General. Secretary Memminger wished to know if lemons, oranges, and walnuts were duty-free under the terms of a recent act of Congress that exempted certain commodities, including all agricultural products in their 'natural state.' With the Confederacy on the brink of a bloody war, Benjamin wrote a rather lengthy opinion on the momentous subject, finally concluding that 'the lemons and oranges are not subject to duty under the law, but that the walnuts are.' [35] During the following months he prepared a few other opinions, largely dealing with the application of the military law. One written on 8 July was copied by Jules St. Martin, who had been made a clerk in the Department.[36] Natalie's conduct had not broken up his friendship with Benjamin, and Jules remained close by his brother-in-law during the critical war years.

Benjamin lost no time in organizing his department and by 5 April the *Mercury* correspondent could write that it was in good working order. Wade Keyes of Alabama had been made Assistant Attorney-General and George E. W. Nelson of Georgia, Superintendent of Public Printing; a list of judges, marshals, and district attorneys for the Confederate States had been completed except for a judge in Louisiana and another in Texas.[37]

As a cabinet officer, Benjamin was of course expected to attend certain social functions. On the morning of 6 March he was probably present at Mrs. Davis's first 'levee' which was 'largely attended by the fashionable belles of Montgomery, and a great number of the distingué' who were flocking to the capital.[38] Mrs. Chesnut, however, who spoke of a few dinners in the town, added 'what a rough menagerie we have here.' [39]

Back in his office, Benjamin had to help receive some of the visitors who streamed into the departments. Among them none was more interesting than William H. Russell, the famous correspondent of the London *Times*. Having covered the Crimean War for his newspaper, he now was on hand for the troubles brewing in America.

Russell was a keen observer and did not fail to write his impressions frankly. Fair-minded as he tried to be to the South, he could not react favorably to some aspects of life in Montgomery, among them a slave auction. Walking from his hotel, his attention was attracted to a small crowd of people gathered near by, and he joined them despite the hot day. Besides the auctioneer and the Negro for sale, they included 'five or six other men in long black coats and high hats, some whittling sticks, and chewing tobacco and discharging streams of discolored saliva,' and a few soldiers in 'makeshift' uniforms. 'Only nine hundred and seventy-five dollars,' the auctioneer was saying; the Negro was sold and, Russell continued, 'walked off with his bundle, God knows where.' 'Niggers is cheap,' was the only comment of the bystanders.

Although Russell had not been particularly disturbed by the slave markets he saw while in the East he now found it 'painful to see decent-looking men in European garb engaged in the work before me. Perchance these impressions may wear off . . .' [40]

Among other activities, Russell interviewed both Davis and Benjamin, 'a very intelligent and able man,' and was particularly impressed with Benjamin's 'brisk, lively, agreeable manner, combined with much vivacity of speech and quickness of utterance'; he was 'the most open, frank, and cordial' of the Confederates Russell met. Soon the two men were engaged in conversation on matters relating to the new Government.

Benjamin began by stating to his visitor the policy of the Confederacy in regard to privateers and letters of marque and reprisal, and Russell commented that it was likely the North would not respect the Confederate flag and would treat their privateers as pirates.

'We have an easy remedy for that,' Benjamin replied. 'For any man under our flag whom the authorities of the United States dare to execute, we shall hang two of their people.'

'Suppose, Mr. Attorney-General, England, or any of the great powers which decreed the abolition of privateering, refuse to recognize your flags?'

'We intend to claim, and do claim, the exercise of all the rights and privileges of an independent sovereign State, and any attempt to refuse us the full measure of those rights would be an act of hostility to our country.'

'But if England, for example, declared your privateers were pirates?'

'As the United States never admitted the principle laid down at the Congress of Paris, neither have the Confederate States. If England thinks fit to declare privateers under our flag pirates, it would be nothing more or less than declaration of war against us, and we must meet it as best we can.'

In fact, reported Russell, Benjamin did not appear afraid of anything. His confidence was, in Russell's opinion, based a good deal on his 'firm faith in cotton, and in England's utter subjection to her cotton interests and manufactures.'

'All this coyness about acknowledging a slave power will come right at last. We hear our commissioners have gone on to Paris, which looks as if they had met with no encouragement at London; but we are quite easy in our minds on this point at present,' Benjamin asserted.

Although Benjamin had the reputation in Montgomery of being somewhat aloof, Russell found him a congenial spirit. After their interview he dined with him in the evening; Jules St. Martin was likewise present. Jules had difficulty with his English and the conversation was 'Franco-English, very pleasant, for Mr. Benjamin is agreeable and lively.'

Referring to the blockade of the Southern ports, Benjamin declared that he was certain the English law authorities must advise the Government it was illegal so long as President Lincoln claimed them to be ports of the United States.

'At present,' Benjamin continued, 'their paper blockade does no harm; the season for shipping cotton is over; but in October next, when the Mississippi is floating cotton by the thousands of bales, and all our wharfs are full, it is inevitable that the Yankees must come to trouble with this attempt to coerce us.'

After Benjamin had, as he hoped, impregnated Russell with his optimism, he walked with him back to the hotel; Russell's room being full of 'tobacco-smoke, filibusters, and conversation,' and, sleep being impossible, they joined in the talk.[41]

Benjamin's remarks to Russell about the future of the Confederacy are somewhat puzzling in view of his earlier statements that he feared a severe war. This conversation was one of those instances when Benjamin's mind, so often coldly realistic, became too greatly fired with enthusiasm. Years later while living in London, he admitted his mistake. He and Russell walked together from a 'pleasant' dinner party in Mayfair, and Russell reminded him of their conversation in Montgomery.

'Ah, yes,' Benjamin said, 'I admit I was mistaken! I did not believe that your government would allow such misery to your operatives, such loss to your manufacturers, or that the people themselves would have borne it. And, let me tell you, though I have done now with politics, thank God! I consider your government made a frightful mistake which you may have occasion to rue hereafter.' [42]

Another visitor to Montgomery during that period was James Morris Morgan, who came to offer his 'services and the sword I intended to buy, to the Government.' Morgan said he found numbers of department employees rushing about the building in a great state of excitement, with nothing to do.

None of them could tell me where I could find the Secretary of the Navy. At last I ran across an intelligent official who informed me that 'there warn't no such person.' It appeared to be the custom of the attaches, when in doubt, to refer the stranger to Mr. Judah P. Benjamin, the 'Poo Bah' of the Confederate Government . . . He informed me that there was not as yet any Confederate Navy, and further humiliated me by calling me 'Sonny.' However, he was very kind and took me into the private office of President Davis. [43]

While meeting visitors and attending to his various departmental duties, Benjamin was not neglecting the art of flattery. He told J. B. Jones, a clerk in the War Department, that while in Washington he and Senator Bayard had been interested in his *Story of Disunion*. Jones, obviously pleased, was then much more complimentary of Benjamin than he became a few months later. He noted in his *Diary*,

Mr. B. is certainly a man of intellect, education, and extensive reading, combined with natural abilities of a tolerably high order. Upon his lips there seems to bask an eternal smile; but if it be studied, it is not a smile—yet it bears no unpleasing aspect. [44]

This was written on 21 May. As the months passed Jones wrote many items in his *Diary* about Benjamin. A middle-aged Marylander with considerable experience as a writer and editor, Jones had come to Montgomery 'to write and preserve a *Diary* of the Revolution.'

He was a self-righteous little man, captious, complaining, and some-what credulous, and he had a number of fixed antipathies—Jews, West Pointers, and 'non-combatants who were not members of his own family.' [45] Nevertheless, he gives a realistic picture of men and events at the Confederate capitals.

Meantime, North Carolina was considering secession from the Union. Late in May her state convention adopted an ordinance of secession, which is said to have been prepared by Benjamin in Montgomery and brought to Raleigh. The ordinance, which was quite brief, announced the dissolution of the union between North Carolina and 'the other States united with her under the Compact of Government, entitled, "The Constitution of the United States," ' and declared that she was 'in the full possession and exercise of all those rights of Sovereignty which belong and appertain to a free and independent State.' [46]

Already by the middle of May the weather had become quite hot in Montgomery and Jones was complaining. 'The mosquitoes bled me all night . . . And as they never cease to bite till killed by the frost, the pest here is perennial.' [47] Virginia had joined the Con-federacy and the Confederate capital was now moved to Richmond. Hardly a summer resort, this city was still a more healthy location than Montgomery. Removal of the capital there also provided a more commodious place, and served as a politic gesture to the influential state of Virginia.

From the standpoint of his own comfort and pleasure, Benjamin was probably pleased, for Richmond, the historic Virginia capital, afforded him more attractions than Montgomery. Now that he was a cabinet officer and unable to go to Europe for part of the summer, he could particularly appreciate the relatively cooler climate of Virginia. Yet Benjamin definitely opposed the transfer.

'It was in my judgment, expressed at the time, a mistake to have moved the seat of government from Montgomery to Richmond,' he later declared.[48]

We should like to know whether his disapproval was based on military reasons. For the new capital was in a highly vulnerable position. Situated in the northernmost state of the Confederacy, Richmond was only some 115 miles from Washington, the capital of the Northern Government and the most important seat of its military power. Nor was it even necessary for the enemy to rely upon the direct overland route to Richmond, since with her vastly superior sea power the North could use the York and James Rivers to facilitate the advance of her land forces to close striking distance. The long defense of Richmond is one of the heroic episodes of history. But the Confederate capital should never have been located there in the first place. Chattanooga, Atlanta, Charlotte, even Montgomery would have been a wiser choice.[49]

In any event, the Confederate Congress decided to make the change. On 1 June the Richmond *Examiner* reported that Mr. Benjamin, the Attorney-General of the Confederacy, had arrived in the city the day before and was at the Spottswood, the fashionable hotel where Davis and his party had taken a suite a few days before. Benjamin's appearance was almost unnoticed. General Beauregard, 'the hero of Fort Sumter and conqueror of the toad-spotted traitor to his section, Major Anderson,' arrived the same day and perhaps on the same train, and immediately took the limelight. The 'manifestations of enthusiasm' for him, the *Examiner* declared, were as 'great in their welcome of him to the hospitality and confidence of our beautiful and renowned city, as the calumny and threats of his Abolition enemies have been black with falsehood and atrocious in offers for his cowardly assassination.' General Beauregard was then a friend of Davis, and the President had great confidence in his military ability. There was also no sign as yet of any impairment in Beauregard's friendship with Benjamin.

At the Spottswood were many of the notables and socially elect who flocked to the seat of the new Government. The day of Benjamin's arrival, 'Rooney' Lee and General W. H. Cocke were registered, and on 4 June came three cabinet members, Walker, Mallory, and Memminger. The next night Jefferson Davis was serenaded by a band and a crowd of several thousand people. They called for him to make a speech, and there were also shouts for Governor Wise, Lamar, Wigfall, and others.[50]

As the months passed, Benjamin became a popular figure in Richmond—at least in social circles. As in Montgomery, there had not yet been time for society to 'form,' and it consisted of the established Richmond families plus a swarm of vigorous if disconcerting people now moving into the new capital. In this mixed society Benjamin was readily accepted not merely because of his official position but his own personal attractions.

As Thomas De Leon later recalled,

One ubiquitous and most acceptable social factor of the official circle [was that] polished and smooth brevet bachelor, Hon. Judah P. Benjamin, attorney-general with the plus sign. There was no circle, official or otherwise, that missed his soft, purring presence, or had not regretted so doing. He was always expected, almost always found time to respond, and was invariably compensating. He moved into and through the most elegant or the simplest assemblage on natural rubber tires and well-oiled bearings, a smile of recognition for the mere acquaintance, a reminiscent word for the intimate, and a general diffusion of placid *bonhomie*. A Hebrew of Hebrews, for the map of the Holy City was traced all over his small, refined face, the attorney-general was of the highest type of his race. Small and rotund, he was yet of easy grace in manner, and his soft voice was not only pleasant of sound, but always carried something worth hearing. That he was a great and successful lawyer all knew, and that he was an omnivorous devourer of books and of wonderful assimilative capacity.

Hebrew in blood, English in tenacity of grasp and purpose, Mr. Benjamin was French in taste, jusque au bout des ongles [sic].

Socially, De Leon continued, Benjamin was 'delightful and many-sided, and as popular with the young as with the older set about him.' Such attractions could help him while away the odd hours, and they could make useful friends. They could ingratiate him with Jefferson Davis and his family—particularly since Benjamin, 'astute and best informed,' was also 'greatly regarded by Mr. Davis as an adviser.' [51]

* * *

During the hot weeks of June and early July, Benjamin had to transact the routine work of the Attorney-General's office and attend the cabinet meetings. On the whole, his official duties were not very heavy—at least as compared with those of L. P. Walker, the Secretary of War. Strenuous preparations were needed to prepare the Confederate forces for the threatened invasion of the South; Walker had an irksome and responsible office, for which, it was fast becoming evident, he was ill adapted. On 20 July [52] J. B. Jones noted in his *Diary*,

The Secretary works too much—or rather does not economize his labor. He procrastinates final action; and hence his work, never being disposed of, is always increasing in volume . . . Mr. Walker is a man of capacity, and has a most extraordinary recollection of details. But I fear his nerves are too finely strung for the official treadmill. I heard him say yesterday, with a sigh, that no *gentleman* can be fit for office.

Well, Mr. Walker *is* a gentleman by education and instincts, and is fastidiously tenacious of what is due a gentleman. Will his official life be a long one? I know one thing—there are several aspiring dignitaries waiting impatiently for his shoes. But those who expect to reach the Presidency by a successful administration of any of the departments, or by the bestowal of patronage, are laboring under an egregious error. None but generals will get the imperial purple for the next twenty years—if indeed the prematurely made '*permanent*' government should be permanent.

But Jones did not yet fully realize the influence Benjamin was gaining with Davis. The very next night (21 July), however, there was further proof of it, which the diarist did not fail to note. Bull Run, the first great battle of the war, was fought that day; in the evening an excited group, including the cabinet members, were assembled at the War Department to hear the successive dispatches. Benjamin went to the Spottswood, where the Davises were still living, and returned with news of the victory. He had obtained from Mrs. Davis the contents of the dispatch she had just received from President Davis, and, saying that he could repeat it from memory, he did so for the newspaper men present. According to Jones, Benjamin's face

glowed something like Daniel Webster's after taking a pint of brandy. [The] men in place felt that now they had their offices for life, as the *permanent* government would soon be ratified by the people, and that the Rubicon had been passed in earnest . . . All men seemed to think that the tide of war would roll from that day northward into the enemy's country, until we should win a glorious peace.

A week later, on 28 July, Benjamin came again to the War Department with a message to Walker to the effect that two specified civilian prisoners were not to be released without the President's consent. Jones now declared that he was pleased to note that Benjamin was so zealous. Later, on 10 August he added,

Mr. Benjamin is a frequent visitor at the department, and is very sociable; some intimations have been thrown out that he aspires to become, some day, Secretary of War. Mr. Benjamin, unquestionably, will have great influence with the President, for he has studied his character most carefully. He will be familiar not only with his 'likes,' but especially with his 'dislikes.'

Then on the next day Jones noted:

There is a whisper that something like a rupture had occurred between the President and Gen. Beauregard; and I am amazed to learn that Mr. Benjamin is inimical to Gen. B. I know nothing of the foundation for the report; but it is said that Beauregard was eager to pass with his army into Maryland, immediately after the battle, and was prevented.

And now the events move rapidly to their sequel: the appointment of Benjamin as Acting-Secretary of War. On 19 August Secretary Walker left for Orange Court House to see a dying officer, and that morning Jones, meeting Benjamin near Walker's door, asked him if he did not think some one should act as Secretary during his absence. Benjamin

replied quickly, and with interest, in the affirmative. There was much pressing business every hour, and it was uncertain when the Secretary would return. I asked him [Benjamin] if he would not speak to the President on the subject. He assented; but, hesitating a moment, said he thought it would be better for me to see him. I reminded him of my uniform reluctance to approach the Chief Executive, and he smiled. He then urged me to go to the presidential mansion, and in his, Mr. B's name, request the President to appoint a Secretary *ad interim*. I did so, for the President was in the city that day, and fast recovering from his recent attack of ague.

After the temporary stay at the Spottswood, Davis had now moved with his family to the Brockenbrough residence, a gray stucco mansion on Clay Street with many memories of John Randolph, his sweetheart, Maria Ward, and other persons and events connected with old Richmond. Here Jones went, according to his

version, and delivered the message 'not omitting to use the name of
Mr. Benjamin.' Davis thereupon signed an order making Walker's
assistant, Colonel Bledsoe, the Acting Secretary. This proceeding in
which Jones had played an important part was called an 'outrage'
by several of the department employees; some even intimated that
Benjamin's 'motive was to have some of his partisans appointed to
lucrative places in the army during the absence of the Secretary.'

That night Walker returned. Jones doubted if Walker would
ordinarily have given a second thought to what had happened during his absence; but some friends called his attention to the matter
and the following afternoon Jones saw a note on the Secretary's
desk addressed to the President. Already hints had been circulated
that Walker was planning to resign.

On 14 September he did resign and was appointed a brigadier-
general in the Confederate Army. Benjamin then stepped into his
shoes.

X. *Acting Secretary of War*

17 September 1861. Walker leaves Benjamin a 'bed of *roses*'?; he is appointed Acting Secretary of War.[1]

1 October. Meeting of Davis, Beauregard, Jos. E. Johnston, and G. W. Smith at Centreville, Va. Decision to remain on the defensive.

21 October. Minor Confederate victory at Ball's Bluff, Virginia.

6 November. Jefferson Davis elected President for six years of 'permanent' Confederate Government.

7 November. Capture of Port Royal, South Carolina.

8 November. Mason and Slidell, Confederate commissioners to Great Britain and France, seized on British merchantman by Northern naval officer.

8 November. Minor insurrection against Confederacy breaks out in East Tennessee.

BENJAMIN was appointed Acting Secretary of War on 17 September 1861. Until 21 November he also remained at the head of the Department of Justice, although he relegated the chief duties to Assistant Attorney-General Wade Keyes.[2] As Benjamin fully realized, his duties would not only involve great responsibility but would be exceedingly arduous. L. P. Walker had never organized the War Department on an efficient basis, nor had the Confederate Government met the appalling need for arms and supplies—not to mention adequate manpower. And the Southern forces, thus handicapped, would have to meet the largest and best-equipped armies so far assembled on the American continent.

Would it be Benjamin's ill fortune to hold his most important official positions when the cards were stacked against him? When success was unlikely no matter how hard—how capably he worked?

His appointment was received with favor. The *Charleston Courier*[3] wrote that, except for Jefferson Davis, Benjamin was perhaps the best man in the Confederacy for the post, and had 'the thorough confidence of the President.' And the *Richmond Examiner*[4] declared that the office was 'filled by a man of most varied ability who had never failed to master any business he undertook, and whose wonderful capacity for work will qualify him for grappling with the Herculean labours of his position.' But the *Examiner* struck a discordant note when it wrote that the general conduct of the war would of course still be determined by Davis.

It would not be many months before this powerful newspaper would turn against Benjamin. But now it not only praised his appointment as Acting Secretary of War, but mentioned him as one of the men qualified to be vice-president under the new Government to be inaugurated in February 1862.[5]

History has proved that the ideal war minister in a republic is a civilian with military experience. In an autocracy such as imperial Germany, the most suitable appointee was a soldier like von Roon, working in co-ordination with a von Moltke and general staff. But in a democracy it is necessary to give more heed to politicians and public opinion. Although notable success as war ministers has been attained by civilians without military training, such as Newton D. Baker, they are better qualified if they have had such experience.

Benjamin possessed a number of useful, if not entirely admirable, qualifications for his position. He had keen intelligence, which nearly always enabled him to master new problems; he had versatility, imagination, tremendous industry; he realized that in war the end must often justify the means. He understood the wiles of politicians, the art of flattery; above all, he knew how to ingratiate himself with Jefferson Davis. And yet there were two factors that soon began to cause Benjamin serious difficulties, and in the end were chiefly responsible for his failure as Secretary of War. They were his unmilitary temperament and training and his domination by the President. Of course Benjamin could make no pretense to knowledge of military art. In a note of congratulation to Beauregard after he had captured Fort Sumter, Benjamin had said he was only a poor civilian 'who knows nothing of war.'[6] Probably he now wished that letter unwritten!

'Mr. Benjamin was a brilliant lawyer, but he knew as much about war as an Arab knows of the Sermon on the Mount,' a clever Confederate soldier commented, not without some point. 'The pages of Vattel and of Grotius were more familiar to him than Upton [sic] tactics or Jomini's precepts.' [7] And with his inexperience in military affairs went inexperience with military men. If a Southern gentleman was punctilious about matters of personal dignity, he was none the less so after receiving the stamp of West Point and the Army. Even more important was the knowledge he had acquired of military forms and procedure. Later secretaries of war like Randolph and Breckinridge, who had served as Confederate officers and learned the workings of the army mind, had a definite advantage over Benjamin.

Always felt in the Department was the strong hand of Jefferson Davis. Often neglecting to propitiate the civil officers and population, he devoted most of his time to military affairs. He spent long hours poring over military reports and directing the general movements of the armies. Although it is impossible to determine just how much Davis was responsible for the mistakes for which Benjamin bore the burden, there is some definite evidence. The President undoubtedly suggested or approved a number of the sharp letters that caused Benjamin trouble with certain generals. Indeed, there was little of importance in the central military administration which did not come under Davis's supervision. In one extreme case late in October 1861, he wrote Beauregard that his letters of 20 and 21 October 'had just been referred to him'; then added 'and I hasten to reply without consulting the Secretary of War.' [8] Benjamin gained an increasing influence with Davis, but he probably acquiesced in many decisions against his best judgment.

* * *

DEFECTS IN OUR COMMISSARIAT
SHORT RATIONS

No department in our army is more important than the commissariat, and none in which more mismanagement, waste and recklessness are exhibited . . .

began a bold article in the *Examiner* for 2 October 1862, which Benjamin must have read.

We are 'credibly informed,' the *Examiner* continued, that there has not been a day within the past two months when full rations were served to the army. There has been 'great and almost constant want of candles and soap'; sometimes no bacon and for the past ten days allegedly no sugar or rice.

'There is fault somewhere. If it does not arise from an absence of material in the country, or want of funds in the Government, then it must be chargeable to incompetency and recklessness in the Commissary Department,' a department which, the *Examiner* did not need to add, was under the general control of Benjamin.

Quite properly the newspaper had featured this ominous article—indicative of events behind the lines that would contribute largely to the downfall of the Confederacy—rather than the minor military or naval bulletins such as news of the troop movements in Missouri or the recapture of the Confederate steamer, *Clara Bell*, off Mobile. For, as Napoleon had said, an army marched 'on its stomach.' And the Confederate food rations, never too varied at best, had to be moved over an inadequate transport system, under the direction of an incompetent commissary-general, Jefferson Davis's 'pet' and West Point college-mate, the crusty Colonel Northrop.

Well, the *Examiner* did point to one specific remedy. While the army in Northern Virginia had been deprived of soap for the past two months (at a cost in cleanliness and odiferousness that one could easily imagine), the railroad depot at Manassas was encumbered with hogsheads of spoiled bacon, easily converted into soap. But, as Benjamin soon learned, even to take such a small step would be to start a series of charges and counter-charges among the commissary agents and army officers. For no one would ever admit that he was to blame. And behind it all was the difficult Colonel Northrop, whom Jefferson Davis would not remove from office even if Benjamin dared to make the request.[9]

Such was the life of an administrative chief in war time! It was one problem after another, wearisome, complicated, if not insoluble. Nor was this to mention specifically the numerous military duties more often associated with the office of Secretary of War.

At any rate, immediately after his appointment Benjamin had set out to familiarize himself with all these duties and responsibilities. Cheerfully and courageously, too, despite the enormity of the task.

First let us review with him the situation of the rival armies at this date, some two months after the Northern rout at First Manassas.

While the Confederate Government was at Montgomery, preparations for war had been entirely inadequate. But after the removal of the capital to Richmond, Jefferson Davis and his advisers greatly increased their efforts. Among various measures Davis employed Robert E. Lee as his military adviser—a position somewhat similar to that of a chief of staff. An experienced officer with a realistic attitude toward Confederate problems, Lee had no foolish hopes of foreign recognition at that time, and was convinced that the war would be long and costly. During his brief tenure of the post he did much to improve the organization of the Confederate armies.[10]

On 21 July, a week before Lee left Richmond for another post, the Confederates routed the Northern army at Manassas. Richmond got its first taste of the grimmer side of war when many badly wounded soldiers began to be shipped into the city, to say nothing of the dead in coffins and wooden boxes. On the 29th a number of wounded, on crutches or with arms in splints, appeared on the streets and 'created a sensation.' But what could the people expect? Benjamin, more realistic, probably agreed with the comment of J. B. Jones: 'A year hence and we shall be accustomed to such spectacles.'[11]

But it took worse sights than this to dampen the military spirit of the Confederates. News of the victory at Manassas was greeted with delirious enthusiasm. The Southerners now developed an even more exaggerated opinion of their military superiority. They believed that the result of the battle had greatly impressed the European powers, and came to rely more upon foreign recognition than upon their own natural resources. Instead of following up the victory, they relaxed and slackened their efforts.

But in the North the surprising result of the battle was met with grim determination. The day after the defeat, the House of Representatives voted for the enlistment of 500,000 volunteers, and Major-General George B. McClellan was assigned to the command of the troops in and about Washington, at once beginning to devote his great talents to their training and organization. Between 4 August and 15 October at least 100,000 men were added to McClellan's forces, and there seemed to be 'no limit to the resources and patriot-

ism of the North.' The Confederate forces under General Joseph
E. Johnston near Manassas, numbering only about 40,000 men,
would have to face a vast army, healthy, well trained, and with
splendid morale.

It was not surprising that Johnston's troops were discouraged by
the news of these preparations that trickled down to them. And all
the more so since they had scarcely enough clothing and shelter,
and were already feeling the results of the inefficiency of Commissary-General Northrop in the straitened food supply. The ranking
officers of the army felt that the coming winter would have a bad
effect upon the health, spirits, and discipline of the men.

Never noted for his optimism, Joe Johnston realized the increasing advantage being obtained by the enemy. He wrote Benjamin
suggesting that Jefferson Davis, the Secretary of War, or someone
representing him meet Johnston for a conference. Characteristically,
Davis chose to go himself and the meeting was held at Centreville,
Virginia, on 1 October; Generals Beauregard and G. W. Smith
were also present. Although a strong effort was made to get Davis's
consent to reinforce Johnston and assume the offensive in Northern
Virginia, Davis declined on the ground that there were not enough
troops and munitions available.[12] Yet, despite the woeful deficiency
of the latter, he may have lost a golden opportunity. For he placed
the army on the defensive at a time when every day meant an increase in the military strength of the North. Even if the proposed
Confederate offensive had been unsuccessful, it would have served
a useful purpose in stripping the South of her false confidence.

Jefferson Davis was an experienced military administrator and
usually showed considerable judgment in directing the Confederate
armies. Despite his stubborn loyalty to such favorites as Braxton
Bragg and Lucius B. Northrop, he usually made good appointments:
Lee, Jackson, Joseph E. Johnston, Albert Sidney Johnston, and the
other able generals. And yet Davis was overcautious, and 'this was
a vital fault, for the Confederacy was a bold experiment.'

As for Benjamin, he was apparently in sympathy with the President's defensive policy. For on 24 September the Richmond correspondent of the *Mercury* [13] had reported that there were wide
disagreements in the cabinet concerning the future conduct of the
war, with Benjamin 'understood to be a strong advocate of a *purely*

defensive policy.' His attitude was, in all probability, based partly on his desire to agree with the President and partly on his knowledge of the serious lack of arms and supplies. It is unlikely that he had a full understanding of the strategic principle involved. An amateur in military matters, he apparently did not perceive that this was a case where an offense might well be the best defense.

But if Benjamin failed to grasp the underlying strategy most likely to bring Confederate success, no one could assert that he did not enter upon his administrative work with vision and energy. On 27 October he wrote Joe Johnston [14] that 'news from Europe to-day assures us of a very early recognition of our independence and of the breaking of the blockade,' but his optimistic remarks are again not to be taken too seriously. He attacked his problems in the War Department in a manner that proved that he fully realized the gravity of the situation.

In a letter to L. P. Walker, Benjamin said that the former Secretary had certainly left him a 'bed of roses.' [15] Walker could understand such facetiousness. Even if there had been no pressing danger of Northern invasion, the administrative work of the department was enough to overtax the strength and ability of any ordinary man. The war theater which Benjamin took over stretched from Virginia to Texas and westward, and to Missouri and the territory of the Indian tribes. He was in charge of the coast defense of the individual states, many of which were fearful of invasion and none too anxious to subordinate their interests to the good of the Confederacy; he supervised the large Confederate armies in Virginia and Kentucky as well as the scattered forces and garrisons throughout all the Southern states. This unwise dispersion of troops, it should be noted, was one of the fatal errors of the Confederate Government. It added greatly to Benjamin's labors and made it difficult for him to meet a threatened attack.

Moreover, his problems were accentuated by the inadequate railroad, telegraph, and postal systems, and the wretched dirt roads. Sometimes it would be weeks before Benjamin would know what was happening in Texas or the Indian territory, and there would often be anxious hours before he would even receive communications from near-by states. Difficulties also arose from the fact that the Confederate troops were volunteers, usually enlisted for periods of not over a year. Unless these volunteers could be enrolled for a longer time, the armies might melt away before they could be used against the enemy—the lessons of the American Revolution and the War of 1812 had not yet been fully learned.

It has been intimated that Secretary Walker left the management of the War Department in a rather bad state; Benjamin brought to its administration the methods of the trained executive and man of affairs. Although every letter had to be written in longhand, Benjamin greatly increased the speed of correspondence. He made a point of trying to answer letters within a few days of their receipt. Those like the following could be dashed off hurriedly or written by a subordinate for his signature. To Brig. Gen'l. Walker, Manassas, Va., 2 Oct. 1861:

Col. Richard Taylor of the 9th Louisiana Regiment being sick at my house and unfit for duty, I have extended his leave of absence for fifteen days.

Or this letter the next day to E. Gardner, Portsmouth, Va.:

Sir. In reply to your letter of 30th ult, asking passport for yourself and wife to return to England, I have to inform you that no permission can be given to any persons not engaged in the military service of the Confederate States to pass without our military lines. No objection, however, will be interposed against your returning in any other manner.

Of course Benjamin could not reply to many queries until he had given them extended study. And he would often have to move with great secrecy and circumspection, as in dealing in late October with information from several Confederate spies: the celebrated Mrs. Rose Greenhow and 'Callan,' clerk of the Senate Committee in Washington, and H. A. Stewart, in care of 'Mr. Hermange, Sun Office,' Baltimore. But when necessary he acted quickly and decisively. Thus on 22 September we find him writing Quartermaster-General Myers about the cause of delayed transportation of flour for the army:

. . . Who was the delinquent? I must insist that the investigation be pursued until the question is satisfactorily answered.

Please to report as early as possible.[16]

How many letters and telegrams Benjamin wrote during the six months' period he was in the war office we shall never know, but originals or letter-book copies of several thousand are still preserved.[17] The work required of him was enormous. In early October he wrote to one of the Southern governors, 'The labors of this Department deprive its chief of the repose even of Sundays, as your excellency will perceive by the date of this letter.' [18]

No wonder that by 5 October the *Courier* was writing:

. . . Renewed vigor and industry characterize the War Department. The new Secretary, Mr. Benjamin, (let us hope he will be the permanent appointee) is just the man for the position. No one comes from an interview with him who does not speak in terms of wonder and admiration at his quickness of perception and promptness of decision. He dispatches more business in one hour than most men could accomplish in a day. Though he entered the Department comparatively unacquainted with its details, in a few days he has made himself thoroughly conversant with the whole scope and range of his duties as a War Minister. Mr. Benjamin is one of the most extraordinary men in America, and is almost indispensable to the Confederacy. No public man has a larger share of the confidence of the President . . .

In his difficult office there were few personal qualities that stood Benjamin in better service than his sanguine temperament and ability to endure criticism. No one could hold his position and escape bitter censure. Often it would be based upon false or insufficient evidence, and he could not reply for fear of giving information to the enemy. Yet few men in his position have endured criticism more easily than he did; he was even accused of lack of deep feeling. This much is certain: he would give his best ability to the solution of a problem, and if things then went wrong, he simply would not worry. There is something admirable about his letter to a Confederate brigadier:

. . . It gives me pleasure to assure you that there is not a syllable in Gen. Lee's report that reflects in the remotest manner any discredit on you, and I hope you will not feel offended at my expressing surprise that you should attach any importance or feel any sensitiveness in relation to sensation articles or reports in the newspapers. I have the pleasure of seeing my own action and opinion almost daily misconceived 'on the most reliable information' with perfect equanimity and you may well trust to your own well earned reputation as a perfect shield against all anonymous attacks.[19]

Obviously, the most pressing problem was to prepare for the expected Northern invasion. Before Benjamin could take the necessary steps to supply the lack of men and supplies, he needed to obtain systematic reports of the military resources of the Confederacy. The results of this inventory are given in the two reports which he made to the President during the following December and February.[20] The first report was, as he stated, necessarily very imperfect, since his experience was still too brief to give him a thorough mastery of such 'a vast and complicated organization' as the War Department. Nevertheless, we secure from the two a clear impression of the resources of the department at the time of his appointment.

In the February 1862 report Benjamin first alluded to the inadequate preparations for war made by the Government at Montgomery, which, he argued, should be attributed to the false sense of security manifested by Congress and most of the people rather than to any failure of the Executive. After the removal to Richmond, efforts were specially directed to preparing an army in Virginia to meet the threatened Northern invasion. Yet the Confederate army at Manassas was only 28,000 effective men. In order to meet the 'vast preparations' for their 'subjugation,' the Confederate Congress on 8 August authorized the President to call for 400,000 volunteers and on 21 August voted an additional appropriation of $57,000,000.

During this five months' period, according to Benjamin,

the increase in the armies on both sides; the expansion of the area over which hostilities are conducted . . . the defense of the sea-coast . . . the desperate efforts of the enemy in putting forth the utmost of his gigantic strength and lavishing all his available resources in the vain hope of our speedy conquest, have combined to throw upon the Department a weight of responsibility and a burden of labor almost beyond human endurance. Even with adequate supplies and instructed officers the task would have been formidable in the extreme.

But these were not available. The South lacked sufficient manufacturing establishments and often even the raw material for manufacturing. She had no adequate navy, and since foreign nations acquiesced in the Northern 'paper' blockade, such arms and munitions as could be purchased abroad were imported by vessels specially bought for the purpose by the Government.

There were barely enough trained officers for an army of ten regiments, Benjamin continued, yet forty times that number were in the field. The regiments furnished by the different states had to be organized; their staffs appointed and their needs supplied, 'the whole through agency of citizens selected from civil pursuits and entirely ignorant of the office they were selected to fill.' Altogether, he concluded, 'the difficulties presented in the performance of duties so varied and so onerous, with means so inadequate, would have been absolutely insurmountable but for the generous and earnest support and co-operation of the people.'

One point that Benjamin touched on needs further explanation. Why did the Confederate agents abroad find it difficult to purchase sufficient arms and munitions? The answer is that by the time they arrived the threat of war in Europe and the activities of Northern agents had largely pre-empted the market. If the Confederates had started a month or two earlier, it might have been a different story. One agent, Captain Huse, did report in August 1861 [21] that a shipment of military supplies was being dispatched, but in February 1862, five months after Benjamin became Secretary of War, only 15,000 stand of arms had yet been received.[22] The result was that Benjamin, like L. P. Walker, was unable properly to arm thousands of ardent volunteers when they offered to enlist—including some of the best men in the South.

After the serviceable rifles and muskets were put in the hands of the troops, the Government had on hand in August a bare 3,500 muskets, chiefly antiquated flintlocks that needed to be passed through the workshop.[23] Most of the available cannon powder was in forts on the sea coast, and there were only about 200,000 pounds of musket and rifle powder, the report continued. Lack of powder was one of the most serious difficulties with which Benjamin had to contend while Secretary of War. Although he mentioned orders that had been issued to purchase 650,000 pounds abroad, the deficiency was very seriously felt as late as the following March.

Deplorable also was the condition of the Quartermaster's Department. A month before Benjamin's accession to office, L. P. Walker had stated that importation would be 'immediately necessary' of not less than 1,000,000 pairs of shoes, 800,000 yards of gray woolen cloth, 500,000 stout flannel shirts, and 500,000 pairs of Irish woolen socks.[24] Of his budget of $57,000,000 for the year ending 18 February 1862, Walker wrote Memminger on 4 September [25] that $12,000,000 was allotted for the Commissary-General's Department, $1,000,000 for the Surgeon-General's Department, $3,500,000 for the Ordnance Department, $1,000,000 for the Engineering Department, and $39,000,000 for the Quartermaster-General's Department—twice that for the other four departments combined. The Quartermaster's never succeeded in supplying all the equipment needed by the army, and to the end of the war the Confederate soldier could only too often be distinguished by his tattered nondescript uniform, his worn-out shoes, or even his bare feet.

With such an enormous task to perform, much depended on the character and ability of Benjamin's subordinates. Although the bureau heads with whom he worked were not his selections and included several men who were not equal to the heavy responsibilities of their positions, most of them were possessed of good if not exceptional ability. Less known than many minor brigadiers, these key men had almost as heterogeneous a background as the cabinet members. Josiah Gorgas, the only genius among them, was a Pennsylvanian, and two of the most inefficient, the portly Colonel Bledsoe,[26] chief of the Bureau of War, and Colonel Northrop, had been fellow-cadets of Jefferson Davis at West Point.

The Chief of the Bureau of Ordnance, Colonel Gorgas, is deserving of special mention. This bewhiskered Yankee (with an Alabama wife) was one of the ablest officers in the Confederate army, a man upon whom Benjamin could depend for steady and intelligent, even brilliant co-operation. A West Pointer with wide experience in ordnance work, he was in April 1861 appointed the Confederate Chief of Ordnance and soon proved his capabilities for this position. General Joseph E. Johnston declared that Gorgas 'created the ordnance department out of nothing,' which was not

II. SOME BENJAMIN HOMES

A. His probable home at 8 B and C Company St., Christiansted, St. Croix.

B. 327 Bourbon St., New Orleans (in center) where he lived about 1835-45.

C. Bellechasse, his plantation mansion near New Orleans.

D. The Decatur House on Lafayette Circle, his residence in 1860. (*Courtesy Historic American Building Survey*)

E. 9 Main St., Richmond. His home as a Confederate cabinet minister. (*Cook Photo*) undue praise for his remarkable work. However much the Confederate soldiers may have lacked food and clothing, they were, after the early difficulties had been solved, usually supplied with enough arms and munitions; and amusingly enough, this was due largely to the efficient Yankee who presided over the Ordnance Bureau.[27]

There were also a few other bureau chiefs in the Department. To a provincial Southerner these administrators must have seemed an odd lot: two Yankees, a Jew, a Washington lawyer, several oldish officers from the former United States Army, and so on.[28] But, despite what carping critics had to say in certain instances about their background, these men proved a devoted and on the whole competent group—perhaps as satisfactory as Benjamin was likely to secure, considering the tendency among the ablest Confederates to volunteer for field service.

* * *

In his report to Congress Benjamin mentioned that the War Department had secured quarters in the Mechanics Institute. This was on Ninth Street in the heart of the Richmond business district and close to the offices of Jefferson Davis and other high officials. We also know that by early October Benjamin had moved from the Spottswood Hotel to a private residence.[29] Located at 9 West Main Street, it was an unimposing two-story brick house, leased from Griffin Davenport. Here Benjamin lived with Jules St. Martin and a 'mess' of Louisiana congressmen—Duncan Kenner, Charles M. Conrad, and others—until the end of the war.[30]

The Davenport house, like many *ante-bellum* Richmond homes, has long since been destroyed, and the site is occupied by a mercantile establishment. Some of the near-by residences, remaining from Benjamin's time, have a neglected, run-down appearance; only the stately stone mansion of Ellen Glasgow, the novelist, a few doors distant, retains its former dignity. In 1861, however, Benjamin found the Davenport house not merely conveniently located but suitable in other ways. It was in the fashionable west end of Richmond, and, though only about a mile up the street from his office, was somewhat remote from the wartime confusion, the suffering and the sordidness that now lay heavy over the city.

From a state capital of some 37,000 population, with a considerable business development, a charming and cultivated if conservative society, Richmond had grown within a few months to a noxiously thriving metropolis. To the new Confederate capital had now swarmed all the elements, bright and drab, heroic and cowardly, noble and vicious, which come to the fore in war time. There were thousands of able-bodied soldiers passing through the city on their way to the battlefields; there were the sick and wounded in improvised hospitals. There were government officials and their families, Negro slaves, spies, speculators, and a swarm of gamblers, prostitutes, and other underworld elements.[31]

The gamblers and prostitutes in particular were now finding a rich harvest. A few of the more elegant gaming establishments at least were not unwelcome to Benjamin, for gambling was one of his principle means of relaxation from his heavy labors. As for prostitution, it flourished in various sections of the city; names and places were often printed in the newspapers—notably the *Examiner*, which continued to publish news with a frankness remarkable for a war period.

Again, it is surprising that temperance advocates make so little capital of excessive drinking in war time. Some months after Benjamin had become Secretary of War the *Examiner* wailed:

One cannot go amiss for whiskey in Richmond. The curse and filth of it reek along the streets. It is eating into the vitals of society. It is killing our soldiers, making brutes of our officers, 'stealing the brains' of our generals, taxing our army with endless court-martials, and *sinking our great struggle into a pandemonium of revelry, recklessness, and mad license.* Scarcely a night passes in Richmond but the sound of drunken riot may be heard on the streets, as the revellers pass from brothel to brothel, or reel along the streets seeking for shelter and home. One has only to go into the streets of the city to see hundreds of good-looking young men, wearing the uniform of their country, imbruted by liquor, converted into bar-room vagabonds, or ruined perhaps forever.[32]

Exaggerated as this account was, it contained an unpleasant element of truth. But to prevent drinking in the army was about as difficult as to dry up the James River. No extremist on the subject, Benjamin sipped his sherry or julep with as much pleasure as any

New Orleanian. In a letter the next year [33] to Blanton Duncan Esq., Columbia, South Carolina, he wrote,

I acknowledge with many thanks your very acceptable present of four bottles of brandy which was duly received and sampled yesterday to my entire satisfaction—It was the more welcome as none of *any* quality can be got here, and yours is really uncommonly fine—

And yet it was obvious to Benjamin that liquor was beginning to play havoc among the troops; he would do what he could to curb the evil. When Colonel Northrop, the Commissary-General, proposed that a whiskey ration be issued to the troops to supplement the inadequate coffee ration, Benjamin replied firmly in the negative. 'The deleterious effects of a ration of spirits, issued regularly to our volunteers, and many of whom are very young and totally unaccustomed to the use of liquor would in our opinion be very great.' The deficiency in the coffee ration might be partly supplied by tobacco, which 'would go far to satisfying a large majority of the troops, and your experience will suggest to you other articles . . . But I have an invincible objection to issuing whiskey as proposed.' [34]

Furthermore, there is some evidence that Benjamin was trying to promote temperance among the Confederate officers. In a letter regarding a Colonel Campbell who was recommended for promotion to brigadier-general, Benjamin declared, 'Will you communicate with this Department at your earliest opportunity whatever you may know of his *habits* as regards *temperance*.' [35] Benjamin's efforts to encourage sobriety seem to have had an appreciable effect. At least no critical blunders are known to have been committed during this period by befuddled officers. But the liquor problem, like a number of others he wrestled with during that critical fall and winter, could never be completely solved. Within a month after he made the inquiry about Colonel Campbell, several prominent East Tennesseans were excitedly telegraphing that the Army of the Cumberland was routed, their section in a panic, and 'a new leader is needed—one who is brave, skillful, prudent, and *sober, sober, sober.*' [36]

Another problem to which Benjamin devoted much attention

during his first months as Secretary of War was sickness among the troops. That this problem came close home is shown by a letter which he wrote in early October regarding his old friend, 'Dick' Taylor. Taylor, a colonel in the Ninth Louisiana, had arrived in Virginia with his regiment too late to share in the glory of Bull Run, but in plenty of time for the disillusioning aftermath. When an epidemic of sickness swept the Confederate troops in Northern Virginia, his own Louisianians had been 'fearfully smitten' and he had spent long hours in the hospital nursing the sick and trying to comfort the last moments of the dying. Finally, he himself had come down with a malignant fever and he spent some time with Benjamin while recuperating.

With his friend in the house, Benjamin could get first-hand evidence—if any was needed—of the alarming amount of sickness in Johnston's army. The Confederate troops in Northern Virginia, like most of the Southern volunteers, had been recruited chiefly from the rural districts. Now in camp thousands were being debilitated by mumps, whooping cough, and measles—diseases that in urban populations are often only a passing manifestation of childhood. Measles in particular assumed a serious form, and was as virulent as smallpox or cholera. On 30 September the total number of sick in the Manassas hospital was estimated at 15,000, or about a third of the army. During the following week Benjamin spent a large part of his time trying to organize reform measures for the sick. This was his 'first and holiest duty,' he wrote, and other matters would have to be postponed until the men were properly cared for. Time and various remedial efforts did somewhat decrease the sickness in Johnston's army, but similar problems continued to arise.[37]

Meantime, what of the threatened Northern offensive? It might be postponed until spring, but Benjamin could not hope for his luck to hold out any longer. Possibly before the end of October and certainly not later than March he would have to meet the attack. Would he have enough troops and munitions to do so? However strenuously his ordnance chief, Gorgas, might endeavor to increase the amount of arms and ammunition manufactured within the Confederacy, the production would remain insufficient for months to come. It was of vital importance that the Confederate purchasing agents in Europe dispatch a large supply of munitions at an early date.

Already in August Secretary Walker had sent Captain Huse, the chief purchasing agent abroad, an urgent plea to hasten his shipments.[38] In addition, Benjamin took such measures as were feasible. He sought to purchase as much as possible of a shipment of arms which arrived in September off the Georgia coast;[39] he resisted the importunities of state authorities who demanded arms which he needed for Confederate troops;[40] and he made arrangements for several hundred thousand pounds of powder to be obtained in Europe for the Government by Fraser and Company of Charleston —besides renewing instructions for Huse to obtain powder through the Fraser house in Liverpool.[41] After all, there was not much else Benjamin could do to hasten the shipments. There was no transatlantic cable; the pressing letters he sent through the blockade might not arrive for a month or more, and there was increasing danger of their interception. While waiting on the European purchases he could only make the best of the munitions that were available or could be manufactured in the South.

To struggle with the multifarious problems of the war office was no light matter even for a man of Benjamin's temperament. But he could take comfort in the fact that he was rising high in the favor of his chief, President Davis. On 14 October, J. B. Jones noted an incident in point. He wrote that Benjamin had refused an application of a Marylander to return temporarily to his family, although he was vouched for by his relative, Secretary of State Hunter. 'I infer from this that Mr. Benjamin is omnipotent in the cabinet,' Jones said.[42]

Actually, it was to be several months before Benjamin could be sure of his position with the President. But he was steadily increasing his hold on Davis; no other cabinet minister was meeting with comparable success. 'It was a curious spectacle,' Mrs. Davis later recalled, 'the steady approximation to a thorough friendliness of the President and his War Minister. It was a very gradual rapprochement but all the more solid for that reason.'[43]

Davis suffered from neuralgic pains and had lost the sight of one eye; he was harassed and worn by the burden of his office. Almost inevitably he came to depend upon Benjamin, calm and cheerful, capable and industrious. Mrs. Davis noted the 'industry, judgment, and ardor'[44] with which Benjamin entered upon his duties in the war office, and although she did not say so, we may infer that she was a good-will agent for Benjamin with her husband. Although it would be incorrect to say that Mrs. Davis dominated the President, she had a strong influence upon him and was in truth a power behind the throne. Certainly Benjamin could not have found a better ally in his campaign for the presidential favor.

Benjamin had now become not only the most important member of the cabinet but one of the most influential men in the new Confederacy. As he attended to the duties of his responsible position he could not but reflect on the queer tricks fate had played upon him within the past six months. It all seemed like a dream, he wrote Thomas Jordan, one of Beauregard's officers, on 27 October. And so it did to Jordan, who in his reply added 'the most dreamlike thing in the world's history is the presence here in Fairfax County . . . twelve months from the time you were in San Francisco, of two hostile armies, of formidable size, such as now confront each other.'[45]

But if the events of the past six months had seemed like a dream to Benjamin, he had been nothing if not practical and clear-minded. Among numerous visitors to the department on which this fact was impressed was John Lewis Peyton, later a European agent for the State of North Carolina. Lewis noticed Benjamin's natural manner and his obvious ability. During their conversation he made a great many 'witty and pleasant' remarks and 'seemed in a short time to appreciate the characters of those with whom he associated . . . Many regarded him as the ablest member of the cabinet,' Lewis declared.[46]

But however great his capacity or influence, Benjamin was still on probation. He was still Acting Secretary of War and he would have to grapple with more difficult problems before he would be given a permanent appointment. He would have to meet the highly explosive issue of states' rights in the Confederacy, an issue which was already beginning to handicap the administration at every turn; to deal with two minor military campaigns and their incidental problems; worst of all, from the standpoint of his future, to continue or bring to a head his quarrels now brewing with several ranking Confederate generals. In many respects the outlook was discouraging.

An able historian has stated that 'the seeds of death' were sowed in the Confederacy at its birth and those seeds were states' rights.[47] With so many complex problems involved, the downfall of the Confederacy cannot be attributed to any one cause. But the point is obvious: when fighting a strong and formidable enemy, a nation must concentrate its resources. Whatever the importance of preserving the rights of the individual citizen or federal state in normal times, during a critical war they must be curtailed or sacrificed for the benefit of the whole country. The American Revolution and the War of 1812 offered abundant proof of the evils that could follow from the failure to co-operate effectively with the central government.

And yet many prominent Southerners could not or would not heed the lesson of history. A number of state governors in particular were thorns in the flesh of the Confederate administration. During the very first week of his tenure Benjamin had trouble with Governor Joseph E. Brown of Georgia over some badly needed railway stock which Brown refused to turn over to the Confederacy,[48] and similar difficulties continued to crop up throughout his entire term of office.[49]

When Marlborough wished to use the troops of his Dutch allies in the Blenheim campaign, he slipped them out of Holland before the political authorities were aware of his purpose. But Benjamin could not deal with the problem so simply. The individual Southerners—particularly in the older Southern states—had a deep-set respect for states' rights. And some, like Governor Brown, an able if provincial-minded politician with an intuitive ability to sway the masses, were formidable opponents. If Benjamin valued his political life he must handle the states' rights problem with care and circumspection.

When Joe Brown wrote the Secretary on 25 September that he could not send another gun out of Georgia and requested the return of certain Georgia troops to meet an expected invasion of the state, Benjamin placated him by sending 1,000 rifles.[50] But in November he stoutly refused a similar request. Brown telegraphed for Georgia troops from the army in Virginia on the ground that Savannah was menaced by the enemy; the men were trained and armed by the state and 'her safety now requires their service . . . Please answer immediately.' But Benjamin replied the next day that there were 'reasons of public policy which would make it suicidal' to comply with Brown's request to withdraw troops from the front at the moment.

The Government would co-operate with all its power for the defense of Georgia, Benjamin continued, but

[it] must do so in the manner it deemed most certain to produce the desired effect of repulsing the enemy at all points, and cannot scatter its armies into fragments at the request of each governor who may be alarmed for the safety of his people. Be assured that no effort will be spared to aid you, and be good enough to communicate your confidence in this assurance to your people, thus allaying all needless panic.[51]

Governor Clarke of North Carolina was only a mild precursor for Governor Zebulon Vance of this state, but he caused the Confederate Government trouble enough. Clarke began to annoy Benjamin with his somewhat importunate if well-meaning letters soon after he entered the department. Cape Hatteras had been captured only a month before and North Carolinians naturally feared an invasion of their coastal counties. On 24, 25, and 27 September, Clarke wrote letters on this subject to Benjamin, who replied to the three on 29 September with denial of the charges of neglect.[52] Benjamin admitted that he had not been able to furnish North Carolina all the cannon powder she desired, but in this respect she shared 'the fate of South Carolina, Alabama, and Louisiana, all of which make the same complaint.' The Confederate Government was 'straining every nerve' to obtain the powder and 'was distributing its supply as fairly as it can between the points threatened with immediate attack.'

Nevertheless, only a month later Clarke [53] again appealed to Benjamin for aid, because of rumors of 'large fleets and expeditions' being fitted out, supposedly to attack the North Carolina coast. Clarke's own force was restricted almost to militia, unarmed, undrilled, and unorganized, but they saw just over our lines in Virginia near Suffolk, two or three North Carolina regiments, well armed and well drilled, who are not allowed to come to the defense of their homes and two of them posted remote from any point of attack. This is not a criticism on their military policy, but rather a suggestion to have their services when we are so seriously threatened.

To this letter Benjamin replied with some of the customary assurances he used for such cases, and added that a regiment, a battalion, and a battery of artillery had been ordered to Goldsboro before receipt of the governor's letter, while three more regiments were held in readiness in Richmond. 'The safety of all parts of the Confederate States engages equally the solicitude of the Government, and the people of North Carolina' are assured that no possible assistance would be denied them, he continued.[54]

Although there were similar letters from every other section of the Confederacy, Benjamin remained firm in his determination not to weaken the main Confederate armies any more than was absolutely necessary. With the Confederate armies in Northern Virginia and Kentucky already smaller than those of the enemy, he fully appreciated the importance of concentrating his available troops. And yet he might have been more tactful in his correspondence with the anxious state officials. Some of his letters and telegrams seem unnecessarily terse and pointed. For example, when Governor Rector of Arkansas requested arms to enable him to meet a threatened invasion of his state, Benjamin did not bother to express regrets at his inability to comply but merely telegraphed, 'I cannot give a single arm to any but troops mustered into the Confederate service for the war.' [55] Evidently Benjamin's patience was wearing a bit thin.

* * *

Among other letters in the miscellaneous correspondence that poured into Benjamin's office was one from a private soldier, Charles Leavitt, who had developed plans for a submarine gunboat. This boat, Leavitt asserted, would submerge, 'leap' to the surface when within a short distance of the enemy's ship, fire a shell that would blow in its side, then submerge again and steam noiselessly toward another ship. And in this manner, he contended, the Confederacy could break the blockade by the Union fleet.[56]

Since there was little or no chance of the South's securing enough war ships of the conventional type, Benjamin must have realized that she would need to consider any new method of warfare. He had seen more miraculous inventions during his lifetime than that Leavitt suggested. Perhaps a boat could be made to move under the water, then rise to the surface to attack the enemy! Leavitt was discharged from military service, 'his labor being required for other important Government work.' [57] His plan proved unsuccessful, but the Confederates later developed another type of submarine boat that enjoyed a slight success.

With the ironclad introduced in 1862, they deserve the credit for experimenting with two of the most important types of modern fighting craft. Some of the Richmond administrators—Benjamin, Mallory, Gorgas, and a few others—were more progressive than is generally realized.

* * *

In view of his skill and industry in conducting the business of the department, it is clear that Benjamin had been successful as Acting Secretary of War. But he was not escaping severe criticism. Although some of it was rather trivial, as when J. B. Jones and the *Examiner* took exception to his administration of the passport law,[58] there were other difficulties of a far more serious nature. Within a month after Benjamin became Acting Secretary he was embroiled in quarrels with Joseph E. Johnston and P. G. T. Beauregard, two of the most prominent Confederate generals; and he had hardly improved his personal relations with some other prominent Confederates. Just how much Benjamin was responsible for these unhappy quarrels, big and little, it is difficult to determine. Although he had proved in his previous career that he would not submit to insults, he had never had the reputation of being contentious or vindictive. Why, therefore, should his tenure of the war office be marked by a succession of personal controversies?

To begin with, some difficulties of this nature were to be expected during a critical war. For the generals and key officials involved, it inevitably meant heavy if not almost crushing work and a variety of disappointments and disillusionments. The result was only too often unbridled tongues and serious personal friction. With this problem still serious in 1943, how much more aggravated was it in 1862 when the Confederacy was full of men adhering or professing to adhere to the old Southern code of a gentleman? Sensitive though many of these men were in matters of personal dignity, they should perhaps not be criticized too severely for maintaining at a sacrifice their concept of the prevalent social code. Yet a debunking historian might be tempted to strain the point and say that the Confederacy died of having too many gentlemen in her hierarchy. Certainly they were very troublesome for Benjamin.

In his encounters with aggrieved gentlemen Benjamin was often taking up the gage for Jefferson Davis in his personal altercations or was acting upon the orders of the President. At times also Benjamin blundered through ignorance of military procedure. The style of some of his letters was better adapted to a business firm in New Orleans or New York. Like many people with facile minds, he was prone to overestimate the knowledge he acquired. Believing that he knew more than he really did about military matters, he got himself into unnecessary predicaments.

As a leading supporter of the administration, Benjamin found the quarrel with Joe Johnston ready-made when he assumed office. Between Jefferson Davis and the peppery little Virginian there had been a serious altercation, which was to bring repercussions until the end of the war.[59] Joe Johnston, devoted and high-minded as he was in many respects, was at times hypersensitive in matters of personal dignity. Out-spoken and combative, if not actually quarrelsome, he was aggrieved because Davis had not given him first rank among the Confederate generals.

There was a technical question of procedure involved and the two men appear to have developed a sincere difference of opinion. Only a few days before Benjamin became Acting Secretary, Johnston sent Jefferson Davis a long letter of protest against his ranking. He wrote a lengthy disquisition on the legal points involved, added some histrionics about tarnishing his 'fair fame' as a soldier and his father's Revolutionary sword, and concluded with a reference to the 'studied indignity' offered him—an action for 'the benefit of

persons neither of whom has yet struck a blow for the Confederacy.' [60]

This was strong language: the letter was better unwritten—and
particularly so since it was addressed to Jefferson Davis. The Confederate President was in most respects a man of noble character—
brave, self-sacrificing, incorruptible. A sick man, he was attempting
an exceedingly difficult task, a task which few if any of his critics
could have handled more capably. Yet Davis was as sensitive as
Johnston; he was peevish and dogmatic with an 'overweening respect for authority.'

In view of Davis's disposition it is not surprising that he replied
to Johnston's tactless letter with one even more unfortunate:

I have just received and read your letter of the 12th instant. Its
language is, as you say, unusual; its arguments and statements utterly one-sided, and its insinuations as unfounded as they are
unbecoming. [61]

Such bouquets were being exchanged between the President of the
Confederacy and the commander of its most important army about
the time that Benjamin entered the war office. He must have heard
a good deal more about the background of the quarrel from Dick
Taylor, who tried unsuccessfully to act as mediator between his
relative, Jefferson Davis, and Joe Johnston. The estrangement grew
wider and Benjamin himself was soon involved.

With Johnston pursuing his grievances, almost any letter to him
from Benjamin might be enough to arouse his ire, and it was
aroused by one Benjamin wrote him on 28 September in regard to
certain information he needed about the Manassas army. Benjamin
stated that he did not have a single report of the quantity of ammunition, means of transportation, sick in camp and hospital in
Johnston's army to enable him to form a judgment of its necessities.
'Completely foiled' by the total lack of systematic returns from
Johnston, he begged to call attention to the fact, since it would be
obvious that the department could not be administered without 'a
thorough reform' in this regard. [62] This was certainly a reasonable
request, but it displeased Johnston, who probably looked on Benjamin as little more than a smart lawyer-politician. How could he

presume to tell a high-ranking West Pointer what to do about military matters?

There were other difficulties of minor but cumulative importance. The blame lay mostly in Johnston's sensitiveness but also to some extent in Benjamin's tactlessness and inexperience with military administration. When Benjamin became aware of his mistakes and of the necessity of treating Johnston with circumspection, he tried to be more tactful, as is shown by the following letter, dated 20 October 1861. It is one of several propitiatory ones that Benjamin wrote the general at this period:

MY DEAR SIR: I have just seen General Wigfall and find from my conversation with him that you cannot have understood my note in relation to Capt. Montgomery. I had no funds in the appropriations from which I could pay for recruiting, and not knowing what to do with him, left him subject to your orders, but with no idea of interfering in any way with any arrangement you might make for the command of the battery. I merely suggested (not knowing that there was any charge against him) that it might be well to let him learn how to manage his battery under the command of the officer you had chosen, but even this was a mere suggestion, to be adopted or not at your discretion. Wigfall says that the men won't obey Montgomery, and that he is not fit to command, but that you wish to avoid a court-martial, as they are ineffective and troublesome machines with volunteers. This may all be very true, but what are we to do? I know of no other means of getting rid of an incompetent or unworthy officer. The President has no power to dismiss him. I leave the whole matter to you to do the best you can, and have written these few lines only to remove the impression that I desired at all to interfere with the command of the battery, as ordered by you . . .[63]

But Joe Johnston was not to be assuaged. Within a few months the quarrel between Benjamin and the able but temperamental general was to reach serious proportions.

If Benjamin's background—his 'French turn of thought'—was not appreciated by Joe Johnston, a prominent Confederate from an older Southern state, it should have strengthened Benjamin's friendship with the Creole, Beauregard. And the two men probably would not have become involved in controversy if there had not first been a growing estrangement between Davis and Beauregard. But quarrel with him Benjamin did, and more bitterly than with any of his other antagonists during his early period in the war office.

After First Manassas the victorious Beauregard had been lauded as the South's greatest military hero. The rival of Jefferson Davis in influence, he was unwilling to subordinate himself properly to the civil administration. It is not surprising that ill feeling began to develop between him and Davis or that Benjamin began to break lances in behalf of the President. On 11 August, J. B. Jones spoke of 'a whisper that something like a rupture' had occurred between Davis and Beauregard: he was 'amazed to learn that Mr. Benjamin is inimical to Gen. B.' [64]

And then on 30 October Jones noted that a 'dreadful quarrel is brewing' between Beauregard and the Secretary. The President and vice-president of the Confederacy under the permanent constitution were to be elected on 6 November for six-year terms, and it was apparent that there would be no real opposition to Davis and Stephens; Beauregard was the only person 'even hinted at' as an opponent of Davis for the presidency. Benjamin fought Beauregard, therefore, 'on vantage-ground,' and likewise commended himself to the President. And all the more so because of some highly inadvisable correspondence Beauregard had carried on with Davis and others about the general's role in the Manassas campaign and subsequent events.[65]

There had been a petty difficulty between Benjamin and Beauregard over a rocket battery, which would probably have been settled without serious trouble if it had not been for the ill-will already engendered. Beauregard felt that it would be advisable to add a rocket battery to his command at Manassas, and began to organize it without securing Benjamin's authorization; the Secretary was not informed of the plan until his co-operation was sought by an officer whom Beauregard sent to Richmond to enlist volunteers for the battery. Benjamin told the Beauregard representative to wait until the President could pass on the matter; then a few days later the officer was informed that his orders were invalid, and he was to return to the army. Clearly, it appears, Benjamin was carrying out the orders of Jefferson Davis, and Davis was largely responsible for the violent quarrel that ensued between Benjamin and Beauregard.[66]

As in many such controversies, there was a silly misunderstanding. Davis and perhaps Benjamin thought that Beauregard was deliberately usurping authority, but the fact that his emissary came openly to Richmond and later sought Benjamin's assistance seems to indicate the contrary. Moreover, the plan for the battery had been approved by Adjutant-General Cooper. We can imagine the general's surprise and anger at the turn of events, for not only did his officer return from Richmond empty-handed but, almost simultaneously, Beauregard himself received a stiff letter of censure from Benjamin.

He expressed 'no small surprise' that Beauregard should have 'committed an act without warrant in law,' and then he informed him that he could be excused 'and go unpunished' only because of the character of his motive and his defect of judgment. Small wonder that, as a Beauregard biographer states, the letter 'staggered' the general, particularly since it 'seemed improbable that Mr. Benjamin had ventured it on his own responsibility.' Doubtless, Beauregard recalled that Benjamin had written him in the spring that he was 'only a poor civilian who knows nothing of war.' Ignoring the Secretary, Beauregard wrote Davis as follows:

I feel assured I need not attract your attention to the unusual and offensive style adopted by the Secretary for the War Department on this occasion; but I would respectfully request that he may be instructed that it is not the custom to indulge in that manner of correspondence with your Lieutenants in the field and that he be directed to be more circumspect in the future.

Davis's reply was patronizing. After assuring Beauregard that Benjamin had intended no offense and asking the general to overlook the technical language of a letter 'written like a lawyer,' he said, 'Now my dear sir, let me entreat you to dismiss this small matter from your mind. In the hostile masses before you, you have a subject more worthy of your contemplation . . . My prayers always attend you, and, with confidence, I turn to you in the hour of peril.' [67]

But before Davis's letter reached Beauregard another had arrived from Benjamin in regard to a different matter. The forces of Johnston and Beauregard in Northern Virginia had not yet been combined by any order of the War Department and to avoid difficulties, Johnston, the senior officer, had been acting as commander of all the troops while Beauregard retained command of his own soldiers. But the War Department acted on the theory that Johnston was in direct command of the whole army. So much confusion resulted that Beauregard wrote the Secretary that if he was no longer in command of an army corps, he requested to be relieved forthwith of his false position. Although his letter was not unreasonable, Benjamin replied,

I beg to say, in all kindness, that it is not your position which is false, but your idea of the organization of the Army as established by the act of Congress . . . You are second in command of the whole Army of the Potomac . . . if you will take the pains to read the sixth section of the 'Act to provide for the public defense' approved the 6th of March, 1861 . . .[68]

Upon receipt of this letter Beauregard's 'Creole blood boiled with rage,' and he wrote another hot letter to the President. But this time Davis was worse than patronizing.

I do not feel competent to instruct Mr. Benjamin in the matter of style. There are few whom the public would probably believe fit for the task . . . It cannot be peculiar to Mr. Benjamin to look at every exercise of official power in its legal aspect, and you surely did not intend to inform me that your army and yourself are outside of the limits of the law. It is my duty to see that the laws are faithfully executed and I cannot recognize the pretension of anyone that their restraint is too narrow for him.[69]

Beauregard had appealed over Benjamin's head to the President. Davis had supported Benjamin. Soon Beauregard, who was defeated in more long-range debate with his skillful opponent, left Virginia to assume another command in the West.[70] The ill-feeling aroused by the quarrel, however, not only lowered the efficiency of the army at a critical time but made for Benjamin another powerful enemy. Even though he had strengthened his position with Davis, there were danger signals ahead—the more so since he had some unpleasant if unavoidable difficulties about the same time with General A. R. Lawton [71] and General Henry A. Wise, the recent governor of Virginia.[72]

* * *

By November Benjamin had been Acting Secretary of War for six weeks. As yet there had been no important battles or campaigns during his incumbency but in his official report to Congress in December he would make as much as possible of Ball's Bluff and several other minor victories. On the debit side there was the capture of Port Royal, South Carolina, and of Tybee Island, near Savannah, but such reverses were to be expected with the Confederate Government lacking sufficient forces to protect the entire coast.

Except in his personal relations with certain generals—and this problem had not reached an acute stage—Benjamin's administration had been an almost unqualified success. In early November he would give further evidence of his capacity by his energetic suppression of disaffection in East Tennessee. He was indeed proving himself to be the ablest member of the cabinet; not Hunter, Mallory, Memminger, or Reagan was displaying commensurate talents. On 6 November Jefferson Davis was unanimously elected President of the Confederacy and on the 21st he gave Benjamin a full appointment as Secretary of War. Doubtless the President was all the more willing to bestow the honor upon him since he had been a leading supporter of the administration and had incurred the ill-will of some influential men in pursuing Davis's policies.

The position of Attorney-General, to which Benjamin had been able to devote little or no time since his appointment in September as Acting Secretary, was now given to his former senatorial colleague, Thomas Bragg of North Carolina.

XI. *Mounting Difficulties*

21 November 1861. Benjamin given full appointment as Secretary of War.

30 January 1862. Benjamin recalls part of 'Stonewall' Jackson's command from Romney, West Virginia, and nearly precipitates his resignation.

6 February. Capture of Fort Henry, Tennessee.

8 February. Capture of Roanoke Island, North Carolina.

16 February. Capture of Fort Donelson, Tennessee.

WHEN Benjamin became Secretary of War on 21 November it was only a year since he had left California on the *Sonora*, and nine months since he had resigned his seat in the Senate. Did the events after he left Washington still seem to him like a 'dream'? Could it be true that he was the war minister of a new Southern Government waging a desperate fight for her existence? But he must have had little time for such reflections. In addition to his usual administrative problems, he was still busily engaged in the effort to stamp out a minor insurrection in East Tennessee, and he knew that this was only a hint of worse troubles to come.

Although the industrial resources of East Tennessee were then undeveloped, this mountainous region was of considerable importance to the Confederacy. It was traversed by several railroads of economic and strategic value, and as a grain and cattle country it provided an appreciable counterweight to the cotton areas of the Lower South. But what, negatively speaking, made East Tennessee of even more importance was the fact that its population was loyal to the Union. Under the leadership of Andrew Johnson and 'Parson' Brownlow, the opposition to the Confederacy in the remote Tennessee glens took almost the character of a crusade. With material aid from the Union Government it might spread to the moun-

taineers of Kentucky and other adjacent states and become a serious
threat to the Confederacy.

Warnings about the disloyalty in East Tennessee had reached
the Confederate authorities even before Benjamin became Acting
Secretary, but disturbed by alarms from many directions they had
delayed action, hoping that the situation would not become serious.[1]
On 9 November, however, Benjamin was informed that an insurrection had broken out in the region: several railroad bridges had
been burned and bands of armed men were assembled.[2] The situation was now clearly out of hand and, to meet the pressing danger,
he moved with admirable celerity. Indeed, the very day or day
after he received notice of the bridge burnings, he telegraphed
General W. H. Carroll at Memphis and General Braxton Bragg at
Pensacola to send reinforcements to the scene.[3]

There was a slight delay in forwarding some of the troops because of the lack of arms, and two regiments at least were sent to
East Tennessee armed with shot guns, 'country' rifles, and old
muskets.[4] But within five days after the bridge burnings Benjamin
had ample reinforcements moving into the region so that there was
a quick collapse of the insurrection. A considerable number of the
Unionists were captured, including Judge Patterson, the son-in-law
of Andrew Johnson, Colonel Pickens, and several members of the
Legislature; Colonel W. B. Wood, the Confederate commander at
Knoxville, wrote Benjamin to ask what he should do with the
leaders. They had encouraged the insurrection, Wood declared, but
had managed not to be found in arms. To turn them over to the
civil courts would be a 'mere farce,' for they 'really deserve the
gallows,' and, 'if consistent with the laws, ought speedily to secure
their deserts.'[5]

Benjamin's reply was one of the severest letters he ever penned
while a Confederate cabinet officer. The insurrectionists not proved
to be bridge burners were to be held as prisoners of war, he said,
while those firing them who could be identified were 'to be tried
summarily by drum-head court-martial, and, if found guilty, executed on the spot by hanging. It would be well to leave their
bodies hanging in the vicinity of the burned bridges.'[6] Several of
the bridge burners were actually hanged and one was saved only by
a telegram sent by his despairing young daughter to Jefferson

Davis.[7] Benjamin's conduct may seem unnecessarily harsh, but it is doubtful if milder methods would have prevented a recurrence of the uprising.

After the suppression of this insurrection, Benjamin had to deal with the captured Unionist leader, William G. Brownlow. A Methodist minister and editor of the Knoxville *Whig,* 'Parson' Brownlow had during the generation before the Civil War attained a widespread reputation because of his upright if self-righteous character, dogmatic beliefs, and fierce crusading spirit. From his own statement, he was a paragon of human virtues. He was honest and fearless; he did not smoke, drink, or swear, and had courted only one girl, 'and her I married.'

Bitterly opposed to secession, Brownlow continued his heroic fight against the movement until he at last said that 'one man alone could not fight the whole Southern Confederacy.'[8] As the most influential factor in keeping East Tennessee loyal to the Union, he was naturally suspected of having some connection with the bridge burnings, the more so since he was absent from home at the time.[9] Anxious to get the 'Fighting Parson' out of the Confederacy, Benjamin suggested to General G. B. Crittenden, the Confederate commander at Knoxville, that Brownlow be permitted to go through the Confederate lines. Crittenden promised Brownlow to make the arrangements but postponed action; in the meantime, Brownlow was arrested on a warrant issued by J. C. Ramsey, the Confederate district attorney at Knoxville, accused of treason, and lodged in jail.

Benjamin deeply regretted Brownlow's arrest and was determined to uphold the good name of his Government. On 22 December 1861 he wrote Ramsey that it was better for 'the most dangerous enemy' to escape than for the honor and good faith of the Confederate Government to be 'impugned or even suspected.' If Brownlow was exposed to harm from his arrest, Benjamin said that he would urge the President to pardon him for any offense of which he might be found guilty. Brownlow was permitted to leave the Confederacy unmolested. As he crossed the lines he exclaimed, 'Glory to God in the highest, and on earth peace, good will toward all men, except a few hell-born and hell-bound rebels in Knoxville.'[10]

With the East Tennessee campaign and the 'Fighting Parson'

now disposed of, Benjamin could again devote his main efforts to preparing for the Northern offensive. During the next few weeks there were the usual calls and alarms from every section of the Confederacy, and he responded in accordance with what he (and of course Jefferson Davis) deemed the urgency of the case and the availability of resources. On 19 November, in response to an appeal from General Albert Sidney Johnston, commander of the main Western army, Benjamin authorized him to call out all the armed men he could secure from Mississippi, northern Alabama, Kentucky, and Tennessee; he was not, however, to issue any arms except to troops who enlisted for the duration of the war.[11] And on 7 December when General John B. Magruder telegraphed excitedly that he had 'reliable information' that Yorktown would be attacked within a week by 40,000 troops, moving by land and water, Benjamin replied that he did not believe the report but was sending the unarmed regiment that Magruder requested to receive the arms at his disposal.[12]

Another problem that caused Benjamin considerable anxiety at this time was the short term of enlistments in the army. Such enlistments had nearly caused Washington's army to melt away in the face of the British, and had been largely responsible for the miserable defeats in the War of 1812.[13] Yet a large part of the Confederate soldiers were now enlisted for a year, and their terms would probably expire at a time when they would be vitally needed. This was the most important problem facing the incoming Confederate Congress, Benjamin wrote Jefferson Davis in November; and, although there had been heavy expense in arming and maintaining the one-year volunteers, it was 'insignificant' when compared to the loss of efficiency. The extent to which the army would be weakened by replacing seasoned soldiers with raw recruits could not be estimated.

It was then highly doubtful if enough Confederate volunteers could be prevailed upon to enlist for the duration of the war, but Benjamin advocated that the twelve-month volunteers be granted a liberal bounty and moderate furlough upon condition that they re-enlist for the war, an argument he largely reiterated in his official report to the President in early December. At the same time he stated that he had steadily resisted all demands to receive troops for a shorter period than three years or the war unless they furnished their own arms.[14] It should be noted that he made no mention of conscription, a drastic plan that the administration was not yet ready to propose.

As the Christmas holiday season approached, Benjamin could look forward to a brief respite. Unlike many of the Confederate officials, he did not have a wife or children with him in Richmond; Natalie and Ninette had remained in Paris and it was highly doubtful if he could hope to see them until the end of the war. Nor did he have the pleasure of visiting his friends and relatives in the Lower South. Jules St. Martin had remained with him, however, and numerous other Louisianians were now in the city, besides his friends at the 'mess.'

The stream of visitors to Benjamin's office also offered him some relief—if not always pleasant—from the burden of paper work. Among them was John Herbert Claiborne, a Virginian, who reported for assignment with the Confederate forces. Claiborne had been elected a member of the state senate and, being forced to resign either this office or his military commission, had chosen to remain in the army.

'I told you a month ago to take your seat in the Senate of Virginia,' Benjamin told him.

Claiborne explained the course which he had pursued, whereupon Benjamin looked at him in a rather quizzical manner. Was the man 'a little daft' to wish to leave Richmond and to go back to the army?—but he made no further remarks and wrote the necessary order.[15] Apparently Benjamin did not feel that the brief glory and excitement of the battlefield compensated for all the weary months of cold, hunger, fatigue, and general disillusionment. But he was also inclined to be cynical of men and motives, a tendency probably increased since he had become Secretary of War and seen more than his share of bickering and petty jealousy, of selfishness and pseudo-patriotism.

At Christmas he does appear to have secured a short holiday,[16] but by the twenty-seventh he was back again at his correspondence.[17] Among the letters and telegrams requiring attention was one from Joe Johnston, written Christmas Day, which transmitted some alarming information from a 'friend' in Washington. If any confidence whatever could be placed in anything said by those in high authority, the 'friend' asserted, an advance of the Federal Army of the Potomac would take place before 5 January; General Porter had said that it would in all probability be made that week.[18] With this false alarm and the usual routine business, Benjamin ended the old year 1861.

It was the most eventful year of 'the present century,' wrote the Richmond *Whig*, and certainly it was the most eventful of Benjamin's career to that date. Many of his associates would sit up late to drink toasts to the New Year—to drink too many toasts if they were like one Tennessee general recently reported to Benjamin as having been 'drunk not less than five years.' Yet the *Whig* sounded a note of caution in this respect: 'The times are such as to demand the serious and sober contemplation of every individual.'[19]

* * *

If the weather was a good omen, the new year promised to be more auspicious than the old. The first of January 1862 was a bright, sunny day, as bright and beautiful as spring, even though the wind did stir up the dust none too pleasantly. And for such a fine day fine events! Among them was the President's reception, attended by government officials, Confederate officers, pretty women, prominent citizens—all the colorful array that gathered in Richmond for such occasions. The reception began at eleven o'clock and continued for four hours. Jefferson Davis, tall and dignified, stood at the door of the 'parlour,' and a continuous throng of people took advantage of the opportunity to give him a friendly grasp of the hand. The occasion was enlivened by the Armory band and everything was reported to have passed off 'delightfully.'[20]

At such times it was satisfying to be Secretary of War, to enjoy the respect, the smiles and adulation that went to one becoming known as the President's most important minister, his right-hand man. But with power went responsibility: during January, Benjamin would, besides his usual troubles, have to face a bitter quarrel with the redoubtable 'Stonewall' Jackson, and in February more quarrels, more wearisome administrative problems, the opening of the Northern offensive, and a series of military disasters. And worst of all, from the standpoint of Benjamin's future, there would be a rising tide of criticism of his conduct of the Department from press and people.

Fortunately, his difficulties as war minister had not yet caused any serious repercussions among the Southern people. In December 1861, Herschel V. Johnson wrote his friend Alexander H. Stephens that the members of the cabinet 'ought to quit,' but Benjamin was 'able and I think the man for his place.' [21] Coming from the former vice-presidential candidate on the Douglas ticket and an opponent of the Davis administration, this was praise indeed, and it probably expressed the opinion of the average Southern citizen in so far as he had any opinion. Absorbed with the more exciting activities of the battlefield, he knew less about cabinet ministers than he did about some of the minor brigadiers. He was impressed with Benjamin's intelligence and industry, what little he knew about it; he was content for him to remain in the war office.

But soon Benjamin's troubles began in earnest. Inspired largely by certain generals and politicians, the opposition to him spread among the common people, where it grew and festered.

There were too many individualists living in the South for Benjamin to have peace after his early conflicts with the generals. He now became involved in a controversy with the rising Stonewall Jackson, which nearly caused Jackson's resignation from the Confederate service. Without the presence of his 'right arm,' Lee would hardly have won some of his notable victories in the following campaigns, and the war would perhaps have ended a year or two earlier. Benjamin's action nearly deprived the world of the Valley Campaign and the flanking movements at Second Manassas and Chancellorsville, military operations rivalling in brilliance those of Hannibal and Napoleon. What is less glamorous, he might have unwittingly saved the lives of thousands of brave men who were killed in the later campaigns of the war.

After the Confederate victory at First Manassas, Jackson had been bitterly disappointed at the refusal of President Davis to permit the Southern army to invade the North, and appears to have been somewhat unfavorably disposed toward the administration.[22] On 21 October, however, Benjamin put him in charge of the Valley district with headquarters at Winchester. And here, although he had only a few thousand men under his command, he began with characteristic daring to consider where he could take the offensive.[23]

Facing Jackson on the north side of the Potomac was the Union commander Banks, a raw political general with 18,000 men, while to the westward in the West Virginia hills was another Northern general, Rosecrans, with some 27,000 widely scattered troops. One of his detachments, 5,000 men under General Kelly, was at Romney, thirty-five miles northwest of Winchester, and Jackson asked permission to attack the isolated detachment. For this purpose Benjamin reinforced his command to 11,000 men.[24]

On 1 January Jackson's little army set out for Romney, and by the 14th had occupied the village, despite the terrible suffering of the men during the midwinter march across the mountains. He also desired to move against Grafton, seventy-five miles to the west, but the troops were now muttering loudly over their privations, and it was doubtful if some would have followed him further. It was not enough that when some of the men rose grumbling from a bed of snow they likewise saw Stonewall Jackson rise out of the snow near them.[25]

Jackson abandoned the plans for a further advance and returned to Winchester, leaving Loring's Division in winter quarters in 'the exposed and cheerless' village of Romney. Altogether, the expedition had required slightly over three weeks and, despite the difficulties, had recovered three counties for the Confederacy, secured the fertile valley of the south branch of the Potomac, and placed the enemy, who was preparing to assume the offensive, upon the defensive.[26]

But soon afterwards Benjamin thrust himself harshly into the scene. On 30 January he ordered Loring's Division back from Romney. This step was not taken precipitously, for Benjamin had received a memorial, signed by eleven of Loring's officers and approved by their commander, asserting that Romney was of no strategic importance and expressing fear that the continued hardships would keep many of their troops from re-enlisting. Only picked men could stick it out with Stonewall Jackson! [27]

Furthermore, there is evidence that pressure may have been put on Benjamin by at least one influential person in Richmond.[28] Jackson himself wrote Benjamin that it was 'very desirable' to hold the position, but, not assured, Benjamin wrote or telegraphed on 26 January for the opinion of Joe Johnston, saying that 'they' were particularly concerned because of the fact that Johnston had reported movements of large bodies of the enemy to Harpers Ferry. It was to be presumed that Benjamin had consulted Jefferson Davis, and this is definitely proved by his following statement that the President wanted Johnston to examine the situation and report whether any action was needed.[29]

After Johnston replied on 29 January that he was sending his acting inspector-general to report on the case, Benjamin did not wait for further word from him. Taking the bull by the horns, on 30 January he telegraphed Jackson as follows:

Our news indicates that a movement is being made to cut off General Loring's command. Order him back to Winchester immediately.

The next day Jackson replied that Benjamin's order had been received and promptly complied with.

And then he added:

With such interference in my command I cannot expect to be of much service in the field; and accordingly respectfully request to be ordered to report for duty to the superintendent of the Virginia Military Institute at Lexington, as has been done in the case of other professors. Should this application not be granted, I respectfully request that the President will accept my resignation from the Army.

This astounding letter was, in accordance with military procedure, sent through Jackson's superior officer, Joe Johnston, at Centreville. And Johnston endorsed it, 'Respectfully forwarded, with great regret. I don't know how the loss of this officer can be supplied. General officers are much wanted in this department.' [30]

In another letter, to Major Thomas G. Rhett, an assistant adjutant-general serving under Johnston, Jackson said he had been informed that Loring's command was in danger of being cut off but that this danger did not exist either then or, in Jackson's opinion, when Benjamin wrote the order. Jackson, therefore, respectfully recommended that the order be countermanded and Loring be required to return with his command to the vicinity of Romney. This letter was bluntly endorsed by Johnston on 6 February as follows: 'Respectfully referred to the Secretary of War, whose orders I cannot countermand.' [31]

In view of the difficulties that had arisen, a case might perhaps be made for Benjamin's action in ordering Loring's command back from Romney. But surely there was no need for taking the drastic step without first notifying Jackson's superior officer, General Johnston. There is some evidence that partly absolves Benjamin, but seventy-eight years after the unhappy affair it is still obscured.

In a letter to Johnston on 3 February Benjamin explained that he had telegraphed Jackson to recall Loring 'at the President's instance . . . as we had news of a contemplated movement by McClellan to cut off Loring's command . . . I fear with you (as shown by your correspondence forwarded to the Department) that General Jackson has scattered his forces quite too far for safety.' [32] It is curious that this letter, in the printed war records, has not been given more attention by the older war historians. Obviously, the President had ordered Benjamin to send the obnoxious telegram. He might have taken similar action if left to his own initiative, but there is no proof of this.

Although Jackson was with difficulty prevailed upon to retain his command, his correspondence reveals how bitterly he and his friends felt toward Benjamin. Among the men who had written him in regard to his pending resignation were Joe Johnston, Governor Letcher, J. M. Bennett, the Virginia Comptroller-General, and an aged minister, Francis McFarland.[33] Johnston stated that under ordinary circumstances his dignity would demand his pursuing the course Jackson proposed, but the character of the present war, with the North showing 'greater energy' than the South, required sacrifices from all those who had been educated as soldiers.

The somewhat unpredictable Johnston now felt it was his duty to be conciliatory, yet his feelings were clear enough. 'I received my information of the order of which you have such cause to complain from your letter,' he continued. 'Is not that as great an official wrong to me as the order itself to you? Let us dispassionately reason with the government on this subject of command—and if we fail to influence its practice, then ask to be relieved from positions the authority of which is exercised by the war department, while the responsibilities are left to us.'

Governor Letcher, who had been Jackson's friend in Lexington, wrote that there was a rumor about the Capitol that the order had been countermanded and an apology would be issued. Jackson's resignation would be a 'calamity to the country and the cause' and if he could hold on consistently with his sense of duty, 'it would be well, and would give great satisfaction throughout the country.' In an even stronger letter Comptroller Bennett said that Benjamin's order was 'a most remarkable specimen of indiscretion, lack of judgment, and disregard of the courtesies'; he was happy to learn that it had met with 'almost universal condemnation.' After making an unpleasant reference to 'Mr. Benjamin (the Jew),' Bennett declared the Secretary would not commit the action again and urged Jackson to remain in the service if he could do so without dishonor, for 'Your name alone is worth ten thousand men.'

McFarland, the old minister, also expressed 'the universal desire that Jackson not be compelled in honor to quit the army.' If a God-fearing man like him felt it necessary to resign, McFarland would regard his action as evidence of the frown of the Lord upon the Southern cause.

He added that God would give Jackson victory above those who put their trust in the strength of the flesh. Did he put Benjamin in this latter class? At any rate, he was accumulating numerous and powerful enemies. A few more such crises and even the loyal Jefferson Davis would not be able to retain him in the War Department.

* * *

To add to Benjamin's difficulties, Joe Johnston wrote him that he was causing 'great confusion and an approach to demoralization' by giving orders to the army in matters of military detail, which should come only from the commanding general; leaves of absence, discharges, acceptances of resignation, and similar orders had all been given upon application to Benjamin in Richmond and without consulting the officers concerned. That very day Johnston had been surprised to receive an order from the War Department detailing a private for a working party. 'I hazard nothing in saying that in time of war a Secretary of War never before made such a detail,' Johnston asserted. He realized fully the demands upon Benjamin's time and attention, but by leaving to him the internal control of his army Benjamin would be relieved of much that must divert his mind from the general supervision that was the 'part' of his 'exalted station.'

Was Johnston being sarcastic? He said that he was writing in 'no spirit of captiousness' but with 'perfect frankness,' in order to remove any causes of misunderstanding and to obtain concert of action.[34] Not securing satisfaction from Benjamin, he appealed on 5 February directly to Jefferson Davis. Indeed, he even requested that he be relieved of responsibility for the Valley District. 'A collision of the authority of the honorable Secretary of War with mine might occur at any critical moment. In such an event disaster would be inevitable.' In his reply Davis admitted 'the propriety in all cases' of transmitting orders through the general to those under his command, but said that it was not surprising that the Secretary 'should, in a case requiring prompt action, have departed from the usual method.' On more than one occasion, Davis asserted, Johnston had failed to carry out Benjamin's instructions when forwarded to him 'in the proper manner.' [35]

Benjamin could point to several instances when Johnston had delayed—perhaps deliberately neglected—to carry out his instructions, while his interference with the general's command was no doubt often at Davis's suggestion or with his approval.[36] Yet that did not prevent his running quarrel with Johnston from reaching a more acute stage. In March it would reach a crisis and be an important reason why Davis could not secure the reappointment of Benjamin to the war office.

* * *

But the single event responsible for Benjamin's loss of office was the capture of Roanoke Island. A quiet, sandy spot, pleasantly ensconced in the North Carolina inland sea above Cape Hatteras, Roanoke Island was the site of the ill-fated 'Lost Colony' of Sir Walter Raleigh. It shows little evidence today that it was also the site of a Confederate military débâcle. A concrete road crosses the place where the little Confederate force was overwhelmed, and summer cottages dot the sandy shore at near-by Nags Head, where their commander, the brave and tempestuous General Wise, had his headquarters.

The North Carolina coast has a peculiar formation. Along nearly two-thirds of the sea front there is a narrow bank of sand—the real line of the ocean, while back of this sand bank is a crescent-shaped inland sea, connecting with Norfolk, the ocean, interior rivers, and inlets. In this sea are two large sounds: Albemarle in the North, and Pamlico in the South. Lying between these two sounds in a placid blue waterway, open to vessels of light draught, is Roanoke Island. It is about forty-five miles north of Cape Hatteras, where there is a navigable opening into the ocean, and about seventy miles south of Norfolk, then reached only by a combined land and water route.

Located at this strategic point on the Carolina inland sea, Roanoke Island was in position to defend much of the coastal area of North Carolina, an important railroad to Richmond, and the back door to Norfolk. Nine miles long and at some points as much as three miles wide, the island contained ample room for land defenses and a good location for batteries to sweep the ship channel between the island and the opposite inland shore. In fact, it would not be too difficult to obstruct this channel and prevent passage by enemy vessels sailing up from Cape Hatteras, the only practicable route in early 1862 for a naval expedition against the island.

Benjamin had hardly been appointed Secretary of War when Governor Clark of North Carolina began urging him or General Benjamin Huger, commander of the Norfolk district that included Roanoke Island, to see to the defense of the North Carolina coastal area.[37] An aristocratic Charlestonian, Huger had attended West Point for a year with Jefferson Davis and later won some distinction in the old army while serving in the Mexican War and as an ordnance officer. But Huger lacked adequate knowledge of the topography of his command and was too inactive to secure it. He does not appear to have even visited Roanoke Island, and his efforts to fortify the island were wholly insufficient. Although batteries were erected there, they were placed on the upper shore as if the enemy were expected to attack from the north—perhaps after the capture of Norfolk. On the southern part of the island where there was critical danger of attack by an invading force from Cape Hatteras, no fortifications whatever were placed.

A Northern fleet could enter the inland sea near Fort Hatteras, which had been captured from the Confederates the previous August, sail up to a point off the lower end of Roanoke Island, and land an expeditionary force without facing any real danger from the shore batteries or being stopped by obstructions in the channel. Further up the island, however, near the present bridge to the mainland, the Confederates had built a redoubt some seventy yards in length, flanked by marshy ground, and erected a battery to sweep the single road from the southern end of the island. This was indeed an 'ugly' place, but if it were turned or otherwise captured the shore batteries would be at the mercy of the enemy.[88]

With Roanoke Island in such a hapless condition Governor Clark, now with more than enough cause for alarm, tried to arouse the administration to the necessities of the situation. After writing Benjamin, Clark in December appealed directly to President Davis. Although the channel in front of the batteries at the island was three and a half miles wide, Clark said, there was no obstruction to aid the guns and impede a hostile fleet.

It was understood that this was to be done immediately after the fall of Hatteras, but it is as yet so imperfectly done as to amount to no protection. A little promptness may even now effect much; for the possession of Albemarle Sound would entail one of the heaviest calamities of the war.[89]

Clark certainly did his best to awaken the authorities and his appeals were seconded by letters from several Confederate generals.

But the Confederates continued their orgy of mismanagement of the situation. Although Roanoke Island was under the control of General Huger, during the period from May to December 1861 it had four immediate commanders who were little if at all more active. Finally, on 21 December 1861, the island was put under the command of General Henry A. Wise, who could be depended upon to bring plenty of energy (and talented swearing!) into his operations. The order, however, distinctly placed him under the command of General Huger.[40]

After making a survey of Roanoke Island, Wise notified Huger that it was defenseless. He wrote that he needed 4,500 infantry, additional artillery, ammunition, pile drivers, and supplies of every kind; and he called Huger's attention to the improper locations of the shore batteries.[41] But Huger would not give Wise adequate assistance. In fact, he even wrote the general, 'I think you want supplies, hard work and coolness among the troops you have, instead of more men,' a criticism that must have been galling to that sensitive and high-spirited Virginian.[42] Furthermore, on 13 January Huger wrote Benjamin, 'I do not consider large forces necessary for the defense of the island. If the batteries can keep off the gun boats and transports, the infantry will have little opportunity to act.'[43]

Naturally, Benjamin relied upon the judgment of Huger, a trained soldier, rather than that of Wise, a 'political' general whom he had recently recalled from western Virginia. When Wise began to make direct appeals to the War Department, Benjamin did not at first give them any serious attention. In reply to Wise's request for more ammunition, Benjamin wrote him on 12 January that he believed he could furnish a moderate supply of fixed ammunition for field pieces, but the supply of cannon powder was 'very limited. At the first indication, however, of an attack on Roanoke Island a supply will be sent you. With the number of batteries now requiring a supply we have a very small reserve, that we can only part with to the point that may be actually attacked. I am in daily hope of the receipt of a handsome importation from abroad, and the instant it arrives you shall be supplied.' Benjamin's supply of powder was indeed 'very limited' and he was saving it for what he considered more pressing use. But Wise replied that if he had to wait for an enemy attack before receiving powder from Richmond, it would be too late.[44]

To complete the chronicle of ineptitude, there are still other facts to be recorded. There were stupid delays in driving piles to block the channel west of the island, so that when the attack was made in February 1,700 yards of the passage remained open despite the strenuous efforts of General Wise.[45] Moreover, the relations were strained between Wise and Commander Lynch, the Confederate naval officer in the vicinity. With mistaken zeal Commander

Lynch took all but one of the tugs in the vicinity and converted them into feeble gun boats, leaving Wise with little means of water transportation and thus seriously handicapped in his effort to strengthen the defenses. The 'mosquito fleet,' as he derisively termed it, made a valiant effort at the time of the Northern attack but did little damage.[46]

Such was the deplorable state of affairs on the island shortly before the expected Northern attack. But Henry A. Wise, the recent Virginia governor, was still an influential political figure as well as an old-fashioned Southern gentleman and individualist. Refusing to submit to the situation, he hurried back to Huger at Norfolk and, according to Wise's gifted son, John S. Wise, 'doubtless harassed that easy-going and high-living officer with his importunities.'[47] Then, unable to obtain sufficient assistance from Huger, General Wise went without orders to Richmond and appealed personally to Benjamin.

Wise was thus violating military law, and his conduct would under ordinary circumstances have led to his summary arrest; but in the Civil War such regulations were often violated with impunity. Arriving in the Confederate capital where he had so recently lived as governor of Virginia, and had many influential friends, he called upon Benjamin in a last desperate appeal for assistance. He was allowed only 'a short and cursory interview,' but 'in the most importunate manner' urged 'the absolute necessity of strengthening the defenses' upon the island with additional men, guns, and ammunition.

In answer to Wise's appeal for reinforcements, Benjamin said he had none to spare. But Wise pointed out that Huger had about 15,000 men in front of Norfolk, who had been lying idle in camp for eight months; a considerable number could be spared for the defense of Roanoke Island, especially in view of its importance to the defense of Norfolk. Despite General Wise's strenuous efforts, so John S. Wise contended, he failed to make much impression upon the Secretary. Benjamin 'was an attorney and not a soldier,' Wise declared.

He looked for instruction to his client, who in this case was General Huger. He doubtless thought that the West Pointer knew much more of such matters than the civilian, and regarded it as little less than insubordination for a brigadier-general to seek the department direct. Then, too, Mr. Benjamin was an easy-spoken, cool, suave Jew, quiet and diplomatic in speech, never excited. It disturbed his nerves to have General Wise in his department,—ardent, urgent, pressing, declaring that past neglect had been criminal and present delay was suicidal, and even guilty occasionally of some indignant swearing at the galling indifference shown to the urgent peril of the situation.[48]

General Wise remained in Richmond from 19 January to 22 January. Knowing his character, we can well imagine that he spoke his mind freely, not only to Benjamin but to his own friends in Richmond. But, meantime, the Secretary received a communication from Commander Lynch at Roanoke Island, describing the pressing danger of attack there and advising that Benjamin urge the immediate return of General Wise. Probably Benjamin needed no further suggestion; he must have been thoroughly tired of Wise's presence in the city. In any case, on the 22nd he issued a peremptory order for the immediate return of the general to his post.

Wise, not assuaged by a propitiatory letter the next day from Benjamin, set out in wrath and perturbation for Roanoke Island. Apparently, he did not know that Benjamin had telegraphed Huger on the previous day: 'The President would approve of your taking or sending from Norfolk into North Carolina all the forces you can spare without endangering the safety of your command.'[49]

Delayed by the weather and difficulty with transportation, Wise did not arrive at the island until 31 January. The next day he was seized with a severe attack of pleurisy—his second illness in the past four months—and confined to his bed at his headquarters at Nag's Head on the mainland.[50] Thus, to his great distress, he was unable to take a very active part in preparations for the Northern attack, which was now imminent, or indeed in the later battle.

At that period of the Confederacy, when there may have been a spy even in the Davis household,[51] it is likely that the poorly fortified condition of Roanoke Island was reported to the Northern Government. At any rate, in early 1861 a joint naval and military expedition was sent to the North Carolina inland sea, consisting of three brigades of over 13,000 men under the command of General

Burnside, and some 20 war vessels. Leaving Fortress Monroe on 11 January 1862, within a week the expedition passed the shoals of Hatteras Inlet and stood within easy striking distance of Roanoke Island.[52]

On 7 February the fleet sailed to a point off the lower island. After it had attacked the three Confederate batteries and met strong resistance from the only one that could be brought to bear effectively upon it, Burnside landed troops at a point near the middle of the island. This was said to have been after valuable information had been supplied by a Negro slave. To quote the Northern account:

Behind the gunboats came the transports, with the Union troops on board. By the side of General Burnside stood a colored boy, Tom. He was only twenty years old. He had been a slave of John M. Daniel, of Roanoke [Island]. He longed for liberty. He knew that there was a Union fleet and Union soldiers at Hatteras Inlet, and one morning when his master called him, Tom did not answer. He had crept away in the darkness, and managed to get across the water and into the Union lines. He knew all about Roanoke Island, the forts, the piles and sunken vessels in the sound, and the number of Confederate troops on the island. He knew where there was a landing-place—Ashby's Harbor—a little inlet on the west side of the island, half-way up to Fort Bartow; the troops could land there and save wading through the marshes.[53]

On 8 February, a raw foggy morning, they moved northward in three divisions to attack the main Confederate position, one advancing up the road in front of the redoubt, the other two trying to flank the position by crossing the marshes.

To meet this heavy attack the Confederates could muster only about 2,000 men. Moreover, most of these were ill-trained North Carolina recruits, although they included two companies of the Richmond Blues, the prize battalion of the Confederate capital, one under the command of General Wise's son, Captain O. Jennings Wise. Buttressed by the more experienced troops, the Confederates spiritedly resisted the force in their front for several hours. But, meantime, the flanking Union division succeeded, after strenuous efforts, in working its way through the supposedly impassable swamp. The combined Northern forces then made an assault upon the redoubt, forcing the small Confederate command there to give way.

The Confederate loss in killed and wounded was small, but 2,500 were made prisoners, including some troops who arrived too late for the battle. Among the wounded was Captain Wise, who died the next morning. Although only twenty-eight years old at the time of his death, Wise had already been editor of the *Richmond Enquirer* as well as captain of the Blues, and was considered one of the most promising young men in Virginia. Furthermore, the small Confederate fleet exhausted its ammunition, retreated, and was captured or destroyed. Elizabeth City, New Bern, and Little Washington were then taken, followed later by Fort Macon, guarding the harbor of Beaufort, and the Northern expedition was in a position to make dangerous forays farther into the state and perhaps upward into southeastern Virginia.[54]

The feeling against Benjamin, already criticized as one of the officials chiefly responsible for this disaster, was increased by the much publicized funeral of Jennings Wise. Held at Saint James's Episcopal Church in Richmond, and attended by many prominent people, it was one of the most impressive funerals that had ever taken place there. Benjamin may not have been present, feeling that he would be *persona non grata* at the funeral of the most prominent casualty of the battle. Attracted by the 'plaintive' music, however, he had probably watched the public procession escorting the bodies of Wise and another Roanoke Island victim as it slowly moved from the railroad station to the state capitol.[55]

What were his thoughts as this sad sequel to the defeat dramatized it in the eyes of the city? For many of the events leading to the miserable débâcle he could not be proved responsible. But others looked only too damning. In Richmond, in North Carolina, and elsewhere in the Confederacy, he had aroused a formidable opposition that would not be satisfied until he was removed from the War Department.

'I intend to "accuse" General Huger of nothing! nothing! nothing!' exclaimed General Wise. 'That was the disease which brought disaster at Roanoke Island.' Wise not only claimed that he had been deprived of some badly needed cannon through the countermanding of an order by General Huger, but also made accusations of criminal neglect against Huger and the Confederate Administration.[56]

Against Benjamin he was extremely bitter. Nearly seventy years later, one of Wise's grandsons wrote that Benjamin's name was 'anathema in [his] family. My uncle was killed at Roanoke Island and my grandfather always charged Benjamin with the murder.' [57]

Moreover, there was plenty of other criticism. 'The Secretary of War and General Huger were both warned, time and again, that the island was in danger; but they turned a deaf ear and General Huger had never even visited the island,' wrote the *Raleigh Standard*. 'Mr. Benjamin is the subordinate of the President. Why did not the latter see to it that his officer did his duty?' [58] In a letter on 21 February to Major Bryan Grimes from the Convention Hall at Raleigh, F. B. Satterthwaite spoke of 'the loud and deep complaint at the gross and unpardonable neglect by the Richmond authorities. Roanoke Island *could* and *ought* to have been defended.' [59] The *Raleigh Register* demanded an investigation of the causes of the defeat, while the *Charleston Mercury* quoted the *Newbern Progress* as saying that 'a few thousand men and a few heavy guns could have checked the enemy . . .'

'The people are beginning to complain a good deal about the way in which things are managed in Richmond, and certainly they have some cause,' the *Progress* continued.[60]

Benjamin laid the proposal for an investigation before the Confederate Congress, which appointed a committee for the purpose with B. S. Gaither of North Carolina as chairman. Its report, which did not appear until late March after Benjamin had become Secretary of State, showed a tendency to obscure a few aspects of the case. But it did ask this pointed question: 'If they [Benjamin and Huger] had not the means to reinforce General Wise, why was he not ordered to abandon his position and save his command?' And it concluded, 'Whatever of blame and responsibility is justly attributable to anyone for the defeat of our troops at Roanoke Island should attach to General Huger and the late Secretary of War Benjamin.' [61]

It was a body blow aimed not merely at Huger and Benjamin

but, inferentially, at Jefferson Davis. And the verdict, which had already been anticipated in the press, seems to have met with general approval.

* * *

Reviewing the evidence after three quarters of a century, we must agree that Benjamin was deserving of censure. He had relied too much upon the inept Huger and had failed to heed Wise's calls until too late; he had overestimated the ability of Huger, the West Pointer, and underestimated the ability of Wise, the political general. Attorney-General Bragg made the following comments in his diary:

[Benjamin] will say he left all to Huger and he will say he had no troops to spare. The truth is Mr. Benjamin could not be brought to believe that Burnside was going to North Carolina. And as there was much difficulty in defending so many points, and from whence to spare troops for a point that he did believe to be in danger he did not take any active steps to defend the Island until it was too late. It is true General Huger was invested with full direction, and the importance of the place required more energy and industry on his part, and he ought to have made provision for defending it at all hazards. Both were to blame and that will be the verdict of the public.[62]

Yet there is much to be said in extenuation of Benjamin's conduct. He was harassed by calls from every section of the Confederacy, and could meet only a fractional part of them. And with Jefferson Davis directing the Department even in matters of minor importance, he had doubtless followed the policy which the President dictated. On 23 January Bragg, an administration supporter, had written, 'We have had no cabinet meeting—The President and Secretary of War keep military matters to themselves—they have been in conference today.' [63] But it was Davis who directed military matters, and Benjamin who carried out the orders.

Moreover, Benjamin was only slightly responsible for the incompetent work of the officers who fortified the island prior to the appointment of General Wise; he was little to blame for the batteries being placed at the wrong end of the island or for the failure to obstruct the ship channel. And only to a limited degree did he deserve the emotional outburst following the death of the chivalrous Jennings Wise. During the battle Captain Wise wore a redlined cape or blanket, which when thrown open must have attracted the attention of the enemy; and, recklessly brave, he disdained to seek shelter from the hot fire. Indeed, his own brother admitted that his bravery was carried to such an extreme that it was 'almost suicidal.' [64]

Another count in the indictment was the failure of Benjamin to meet the urgent requisitions of General Wise for powder and other supplies. Twenty-five years later, at the unveiling of the R. E. Lee monument in Richmond, the able and respected Colonel Charles Marshall, a former member of Lee's staff, read an extract from a letter of Benjamin's in which he explained his alleged neglect of duty. He said that he had directed General Huger to send powder from Norfolk to Roanoke Island, but Huger replied that to do so would leave Norfolk without ammunition. Benjamin continued,

I consulted the President, whether it was best for the country that I should submit to unmerited censure or reveal to a congressional committee our poverty and my utter inability to supply the requisitions of General Wise, and thus run the risk that fact should become known to some of the spies of the enemy, of whose activity we were well assured. It was thought best for the public interest that I should submit to censure.[65]

The Northern soldiers, after the Confederate prisoners were rounded up at Roanoke Island, added to their woes by informing them of the capture of Fort Henry in Tennessee; and this was soon followed by the capture of the near-by Fort Donelson. There was much gloom in the South and increasing attacks on Benjamin and other members of the administration.

Once Benjamin had got into difficulties he seemed to be beset by them on all sides. Among his duties as Secretary of War was the direction of a number of secret agents, then operating between Richmond and the North. On 12 February the *Examiner* reported that they had information from 'a source of undoubted reliability' that two spies who had been trusted with the confidence of Secretary of War Benjamin had turned traitors. Letters and private dispatches had been committed to them for delivery to certain persons within the Federal lines and 'more particularly in Washington City.' One of the spies was said to have conveyed information to the enemy 'of great importance and to have been the means of incarceration in loathsome prisons of some of the most worthy citizens of Virginia, who unluckily lived within reach of the Federal lines.' And, more important, facts had been revealed concerning all the Confederate inland and coastal defenses.

Captured by the Confederates, the two spies, Scully and Lewis, confessed and implicated a so-called 'Englishman'—really a Northern secret agent—Timothy Webster. Webster was tried and, despite his boast of influence with the War Department, was condemned and executed. Perhaps it was symptomatic that the rope, doubtless drawn from defective supplies of the blockaded Confederacy, broke when he was hanged, and he had to be strung up a second time. 'This is hard, isn't it? I suffer a double death,' Webster said.[66]

To help fill Benjamin's cup of woes to overflowing, the disorderly elements in Richmond, bred by the war, were now too strong for the civil authorities. The situation had been bad enough in October when he was making his first efforts to curb the liquor evil, but it had later got almost completely out of hand. During the winter of 1861-2 the Confederate capital was one of the most disorderly cities in America. On 5 February the *Dispatch*, aroused by a deadly brawl at the Metropolitan Hall, called on 'the strong arm of power . . . to hold in check the spirit of lawless brutality . . . rampant in Richmond.'

The row at the Hall had occurred in the gallery, the *Dispatch* said,

where a number of brazen women were surrounded by a crowd of drunken, unprincipled men. Oaths and curses, shrieks and yells, intermingled with the rapid discharge of deadly weapons, the sudden panic and flight of the throng in other portions of the house, made up a picture of Northern [sic] rowdyism which could not be looked upon without a shudder.

In so far as Confederate soldiers were responsible for the disorder in the capital, at least during the middle of February, they were certainly deserving of sympathy. Hundreds of the soldiers, now streaming through the city on return from a furlough granted by the War Department, found they could not obtain or afford hotel accommodations. For the Department paid privates but $11 a month.

With 'exorbitant' hotel rates of $2.50 and $3 how could even an economical soldier manage to pay his travel fare for four or five days, much less stop at a hotel, the *Examiner* asked on 12 February. The result was that many, then in the city without over-night accommodations, were at the mercy of bar keepers ready enough to swill them with whiskey and turn them out of doors. 'Hundreds of these soldiers are found in the streets at night exposed to the weather, without shelter, or wandering about either in drunken vagrancy or on errands of riot and vice.' Could not the Government do something to prevent this evil and repair its shameful neglect of the soldiers' comfort by establishing a lodging house for the soldiers on furlough or leave passing through Richmond, the *Examiner* concluded?

What with the opening of the Northern offensive, Benjamin must have felt that he had more than he could do already without taking up such problems. A few days after the newspaper complaints about the conditions in the city, however, he did make a further effort to curb the liquor evil. Bragg noted in his diary on 15 February a proposal made at a cabinet meeting that Benjamin be authorized to 'seize the corn of distillers which they were procuring in great quantities, to the injury of the Government, endangering the supply of food and forage, and corrupting and destroying the army by intoxicating drink.'

When a vote was taken on the measure, the cabinet was found to be equally divided, Benjamin, Mallory, and Bragg being in favor of seizing the distillers' corn, whereas Hunter, Memminger, and Reagan opposed the measure as 'a dangerous and unauthorized exercise of power.'

Benjamin then said that since the cabinet was equally divided he could not advise the President to sanction the proposal. The cabinet thereupon agreed that Davis should issue a proclamation and call upon the states to pass laws to stop the distilling of grain; but, as Benjamin well realized, to request the governors to carry out such drastic action and to get it accomplished were two entirely different things.

Later, on 19 February, at a joint session of Congress, Representative Smith of Virginia offered a resolution that if any officer in the army be found intoxicated, he should be deprived of his commission; and if any officer receive knowledge of the intoxication of another officer and fail to report him he also should be deprived of the same. Smith proposed that the resolution should lie on the table and be printed, but he was opposed by Conrow of Arkansas. Conrow did not believe there was so much drunkenness in the army; at any rate, he was opposed to the printing of the bill, for he did not want such a fact made public. The bill was defeated.[67]

Some relief from the disorderly conditions, however, was given early in March, when Jefferson Davis temporarily proclaimed martial law in Richmond and, with the consent of Congress, suspended the writ of habeas corpus in this city and certain other places in danger of attack by the enemy. In all likelihood, this drastic action was taken with Benjamin's approval if not at his actual suggestion.

XII. *Censured but Promoted*

25 February 1862. Federal forces occupy Nashville, Tennessee.
9 March. Battle between ironclad warships, the *Merrimac*, and the *Monitor*.
17 March. Benjamin appointed Secretary of State.

FOR nearly three years beginning on 22 February 1862, Benjamin took time to keep a sketchy diary.[1] On this date—Washington's birthday—there is a bare mention of the inauguration of Jefferson Davis as President for six years of the permanent government. Perhaps Benjamin did not care to write more about the inauguration, for the weather and the critical times had combined to make it anything but a pleasant occasion. Shortly before noon the members of the Confederate Congress and the Virginia legislature with a few other notables gathered in the hall of the House of Delegates to await the President. 'The lady of President Davis,' a Miss Howard, Joseph Davis, and Judge Halyburton sat on the front seat directly facing that designated for the chief executive, while near by were Benjamin, Memminger, Mallory, and Reagan. 'The galleries were full of ladies, to the entire exclusion of gentlemen, who could only occupy the lower and upper floors of the rotunda.' It was a 'grave and great assemblage . . . silent tears were seen coursing down the cheeks of gray-haired men, while the determined will stood out in every feature.'

Upon the arrival of Jefferson Davis at noon a procession was formed and moved from inside the Hall to a stand on the Capitol grounds. As if to presage ill for the beleaguered government, the heavens now opened and a heavy rain began to fall. Some lucky persons were able to secure a place under the awning but most of the assembled crowd—including hundreds of the devoted ladies—had

to brave the cold and rain, even as they were to brave worse difficulties during the next few years.

After having prayed in his room 'for divine support I need so
sorely,' Jefferson Davis delivered his inaugural address and took the
oath of office. 'As he stood pale and emaciated, dedicating himself
to the services of the Confederacy,' he seemed to Mrs. Davis 'a willing victim going to his funeral pyre.' The idea affected her so
strongly that she returned to her carriage and went home.[2]

Benjamin's thoughts on this occasion are not recorded. If the
worst came to pass, however, he felt that he had done his best to
avoid it. On 25 February Davis referred in his regular message to
Congress to the disasters at Roanoke Island and Fort Donelson, and
Benjamin was pleased to quote in his diary an extract from the
President's remarks:

An impartial judgment will, upon full investigation, award to the
various departments of the Government credit for having done all
which human power and foresight enabled them to accomplish.

But whatever comfort Benjamin might derive from Davis's support, it was becoming more and more doubtful if the President
could retain him in the War Department. The setbacks at Roanoke
Island, Fort Henry, and Fort Donelson were followed by further
military reverses. Retreating before the superior Northern forces,
Albert Sidney Johnston had to abandon Nashville on the 23rd and
retreated southward in the direction of Corinth, Mississippi. General
Pillow at Memphis excitedly contended that the government should
abandon the sea-coast defenses, except New Orleans, and concentrate all their forces in Tennessee. 'If we do not relieve heart of the
country, Mississippi River will be opened and then cause of South
is desperate,' he telegraphed.[3]

Before the end of February Bragg was referring in his diary to
the 'great clamor' against Benjamin by some congressmen. Certain
of the President's friends expressed fears that his nomination for
Secretary of War under the permanent government would be rejected, and, although Bragg thought otherwise, he stated 'it is evident the opposition is great and growing.[4] On 4 March a resolution
was offered in the Confederate Congress asserting that Benjamin
lacked sufficient confidence of the army and the people, and his

retirement was 'a high military necessity.' [5] Moreover, in the Senate the bold and caustic Foote of Tennessee, an old enemy of Jefferson Davis, engaged in bitter tirades against the Secretary, whom he labored assiduously to remove from office by enlisting the support of the Confederate people.[6]

But, if we may accept Foote's account, it was not he but General Joe Johnston who delivered the *coup de grâce*. With some twenty congressmen, including James Orr, the Speaker of the House, and others of equal rank, Foote and Johnston were invited about this time to a dinner party in Richmond. During the course of the dinner Benjamin's 'gross acts of official misconduct' became the subject of conversation, and one of the company present asked General Johnston whether he thought it even possible that the Confederate cause could succeed with Mr. Benjamin as War Minister.

'To this inquiry, General Johnston, after a little pause, emphatically responded in the negative,' Foote asserted. 'This high authority was immediately cited in both houses of Congress against Mr. Benjamin, and was in the end fatal to his hopes of remaining in the Department of War.' [7] Davis waited for nearly a month before sending his nomination for cabinet ministers under the permanent constitution, in the hope of persuading the Senate to confirm Benjamin as Secretary of War. Then he gave up the effort, and on 17 March appointed him Secretary of State in 'the very teeth of criticism.' After the Senate approved the appointment the next day, a motion to reconsider by Orr of South Carolina was lost 13 to 8, the following Senators voting in the affirmative: Burnett, Clay, Clark, Dortch, Haynes, Orr, Preston and Semmes.[8]

* * *

Benjamin had served as Secretary of War for six months. As administrator he had in some respects shown himself to have the qualities of a great war minister. The department was now organized on an efficient basis and running smoothly, despite the enormous pressure upon it; George Wythe Randolph, James A. Seddon, John C. Breckinridge, the war ministers succeeding him, were all to benefit from his work.[9] In his industry, his organizing ability, his facility in dispatching immense quantities of business, Benjamin had indeed proved that he had much of the genius of a Carnot.

To a notable degree the victories of the Confederate armies during the following summer and fall were due to Benjamin's efforts. A summary of his successful operations up to February 1862 is contained in his report to Congress during that month, and it can be supplemented with data derived from other correspondence while in the department.[10] When the Confederate purchasing agents arrived in Europe they found the market 'swept,' so that they had finally been reduced to the necessity of contracting with European manufacturers for their deliveries as fast as they could be made. The combined deliveries of the various manufacturies would total 91,000 stand of arms within the next two months, but only about 15,000 stand had yet been received within the Confederacy. The purchases necessary for supplying gun-powder, rifle cannon, and military equipment of all kinds had also been made abroad and since 'most of them could be obtained ready-made they had been received in considerable quantities and as rapidly as they could be imported.'

'Large quantities of medicine, blankets, and equipments of all kinds' had reached 'the Government, and within the past six weeks' the Department had 'received fifty-five tons of gun-powder of its own importation and sixty-five tons imported by private citizens.' Early attempts had also been made to purchase military supplies in Canada, Cuba, and Mexico, but they provided only limited resources. The department had contracts for the importation of 2,000 tons of saltpeter and was already supplied with an abundance of sulphur.[11]

But since the foreign markets were restricted, the report continued, it was to the development of the domestic resources, including the establishment of arsenals, foundries, powder mills, and workshops, that the attention of the War Department was 'more specially directed.' Contracts had been made in the Confederacy for 1,105 tons of saltpeter. Powder mills in the South were capable of making at least ten tons of powder per day if supplied with the raw material; but the powder manufacture had recently been at the rate of only three tons per day and no increase would be made until some of the cargoes ordered from abroad were received. There were outstanding contracts for about 40,000 tons of iron, about 27,000 tons of shot and shell, in addition to 350,000 projectiles for artillery. In addition to the seacoast and siege guns and mortars already obtained, 890 were now under contract while three field pieces per day had been delivered from the Confederate foundries since the first day of August.

Moreover, contracts were in process of execution for 66,500 muskets and rifles as well as large numbers of pistols and sabres. The Government armories at Richmond and Fayetteville were supplying 1,500 muskets and rifles per month, 'and the supply could be doubled but for the deficiency of skilled labor and the great demand for workmen in private workshops.'

Summarizing, Benjamin asserted that 'with the single exception of small-arms, of which the supply is quite too slow for our pressing need in this great war, the Confederate States have, in the brief period which has elapsed since June last, evinced the capacity of providing all that is necessary to the maintenance of their independence.'

The reports for the Quartermaster's Bureau and for the Commissary-General also showed that energetic efforts had been made. With regard to the former, Benjamin stated that it would hereafter be in their power to meet the demands upon them, for they could rely not only on the supplies of blankets, cloth, and shoes already imported from Europe, but also on the productions of manufacturing establishments at home. His prediction in this respect, however, was not verified. The Confederate soldiers were never properly clothed or shod, and, occasionally, were even reduced to stripping dead Yankees before their bodies were cold. At any rate, Benjamin listed the total expenditures of the Quartermaster's Bureau from 3 April to 31 December 1861 as nearly $62,000,000, with many hundreds of accounts still unexamined.

He also accorded high praise to the Commissary-General for his success with his difficult task, though admitting that there had been a deficiency in certain articles of the rations as the result of the cessation of foreign commerce. Even in that early period of the war there were many Confederates who found more serious fault with the Commissariat—and particularly with the difficult Colonel Northrop.

Again, as to the strength of the Confederate army, Benjamin

stated that there were about 435 regiments, of which about 400 were infantry and the remainder cavalry and artillery. The records are incomplete but it appears that, despite the inaction in the field during the previous winter, there had been an increase of some hundred and twenty-five regiments since Benjamin succeeded to office.

Lastly, after reviewing the military campaigns—on which he could not dwell so happily—Benjamin 'respectfully invoked' the attention of Congress to the absolute necessity of an increase in the clerical force of the department. He and the chiefs of bureaus were compelled 'to extend their labors beyond reasonable limits; the clerks have been directed to attend at their desks two additional hours in the evening, and yet the details of business have accumulated with such rapidity that the accounts of disbursing officers to the amount of many hundreds remain unsettled, and correspondence is in arrears in all the bureaus,' Benjamin added.

Benjamin had not been overly modest in explaining his own work in bolstering the resources of the Confederacy. The report was a brief in his own defense as well as propaganda for the Confederate cause. Yet the document, with other evidence available in the official records, gives ample proof of Benjamin's success in obtaining the matériel of war so sorely needed by the new government. His achievements are all the more noteworthy in view of the slight industrialization of the South at the beginning of the war and the strengthening of the Northern blockade. Although much credit was due his subordinates in the department, especially the able Gorgas, it was nevertheless clear that Benjamin was a man who would get results whatever the difficulties.

In this connection few of his personal characteristics stood him in better stead than his continued willingness to endure criticism for the good of the Confederate cause. Many years later Mrs. Davis wrote in reference to Benjamin's appointment as Secretary of State, 'The President promoted him with a personal and aggrieved sense of the injustice done to the man who had become his friend and right hand.' [12] This comment is highly significant. Of course it states clearly the connection between Davis and Benjamin: no man in the Confederacy now stood in a more intimate and important relation to the Confederate President. But Mrs. Davis implied more than that. Jefferson Davis had 'a personal and aggrieved sense' of the unjust criticism heaped upon Benjamin. Probably that meant criticism not merely of Benjamin's own actions, for which Davis felt the Secretary was unjustly censured, but of those actions for which the President was primarily responsible and Benjamin took the blame.

With his cosmopolitan background and wide experience, Benjamin was able to view the Confederate problems with a broad perspective. He was a Southern nationalist and could see beyond his beloved Louisiana; he could think in terms of the South as a whole. Despite his occasional outbursts of unjustifiable optimism, it is clear that he usually viewed the war with hard realism. Benjamin had doubted the wisdom of secession, he had prophesied that there would be a long and bloody war, he had proposed that large shipments of cotton be sent to Europe as security for the purchase of arms, he had opposed the movement of the capital to Richmond, and he had devoted all his brains and energy to preparing for the new Northern offensive in 1862. Surely all these actions indicated a man who saw clearly the difficulties in winning the war and was willing to make the necessary sacrifices to do so. Surely here was a revolutionist of the breed of Danton and Lenin, not Dumouriez or Kerensky.

Because of his realistic attitude toward Confederate problems as well as his ability to put it to practical application, Benjamin had in most respects been successful as Secretary of War—that is, successful up to the time of the strong demand for his removal. But this success did not mean that he should remain in office longer. Owing partly to his tactlessness and lack of knowledge of military niceties, and partly to circumstances beyond his control, he had offended many powerful persons and they had used their influence to his detriment. Among the common people also there was now an increasing murmur against him.

It was not only that some prominent Confederates had concluded —rightly or wrongly—that Benjamin was difficult to work with, but that many people of all classes lacked confidence in his fitness in other respects to deal with military matters. The feeling was later epitomized by a Confederate veteran, the son of General John C. Breckinridge, who said he talked with many friends who were in the Virginia area throughout the war and the common opinion they expressed was that Benjamin's great talents did not extend to the military field.[18]

Of course, much of Benjamin's unpopularity arose from lack of adequate knowledge of his problems and the popular desire for a scapegoat. Speaking with unwonted frankness when he was in prison after the war, Jefferson Davis said that the Confederate Congress was in some respects slow to advise against reverses but it was never lacking in promptness to find a scapegoat. Davis also intimated that the anti-administration party in the South, not deeming it wise at that time to attack him personally, would assail any man in whom he was supposed to have a special interest.[14]

Again Benjamin was the victim of the bad luck that dogged him during so much of his Confederate career. He happened to be Secretary of War at the time of the great Northern offensive of 1862 when the out-numbered and ill-prepared Confederates were almost certain to meet some reverses—reverses that 'no human activity or foresight could have averted.' Had it not been for these reverses, he probably could have remained in office, and the War Department would not have lost the benefit of his brilliant executive qualities, his understanding of the sensitive and somewhat difficult Davis. In most respects Benjamin had learned his job; and he was abler than any of his successors in office. He had done an excellent job in preparing the South for the critical campaigns, and it seemed hard that he did not get more credit for his work. Yet he could no longer hope for full success in a position where he was opposed by such powerful enemies—particularly among the generals. It was now much better for him to be in the State Department.

*   *   *

On 19 March 1862 announcement was made of the cabinet appointments which had been confirmed by the Senate: Memminger, Mallory, and Reagan retained their old posts, and there were three new appointments. Benjamin was transferred to the State Department, where 'his great mind will soon find ample employment'; George Wythe Randolph of Virginia who would bring to his office 'high military attainments' was made Secretary of War; and the

Attorney-General's place was given to Judge F. H. Watts, an Alabama jurist who was an old-line Whig and recent candidate for governor.[15]

The news of Benjamin's appointment seems to have met with little open disapproval, for as yet there was not a great deal of outspoken criticism of the administration. But the silence of many influential newspapers was ominous. His promotion in the face of such bitter criticism of his conduct in the War Office caused the first serious lack of confidence in the Davis Government. We will recall that the congressional investigating committee did not submit its report on the Roanoke Island débâcle until late March. It was unfortunate for the Administration to have as Secretary of State a man who was censured by the committee. Even though much evidence could be offered in his favor, it was not all known to the people of the Confederacy.

Obviously, Benjamin's unpopularity would add considerably to his difficulties as Secretary of State. Aside from his following in New Orleans and Louisiana, he could not bring to the Davis government the popular support of which it already stood in need. In this respect he was in strong contrast to his old rival, William H. Seward, who brought to his position as Secretary of State in the Union government more political strength than Lincoln could have obtained from perhaps any other man in the North. Yet conditions were quite different in the South. A man was needed for Secretary of State there who could get the best possible results while working under Jefferson Davis. And in these circumstances who was better suited for the place than Benjamin?

In late March when the Virginia spring was opening up and McClellan was preparing to move his great host up the Peninsula toward Richmond, Benjamin succeeded inauspiciously to the position of Secretary of State. After the unhappy interlude as War Secretary, he was now in a position for which he was qualified by both training and temperament, if not in some other respects. A good linguist and with numerous European contacts, he could approach foreign affairs with more familiarity than the great majority of Confederates. He was a brilliant lawyer and not without experience in international law. He had served with James M. Mason, the Confederate minister to England, in the United States Senate; he

had been the political lieutenant and senatorial colleague of John C.
Slidell, the Confederate representative in Paris; he had been pitted
in the Senate against his Northern rival, William H. Seward. He
was in excellent health and able to continue his enormous labors;
he was resourceful and not entirely loathe to use Machiavellian tactics if they were necessary in order to gain his objective. Even his
unpopularity in the South would not necessarily handicap him in
his dealings with foreign diplomats. And he was learning from experience, and becoming more tactful in all his public relations.

Despite the unpopularity he provoked while Secretary of War,
despite the heavy burdens of the office, Benjamin would have been
willing to remain in the post if Jefferson Davis could have secured
his reappointment. But now there was no need of repining. When
it looked as if his political career was over, he had seen it rise to
new life; his appointment had been confirmed—if by a rather narrow margin—to a still higher position.

And yet, being human, he doubtless indulged in some bitter reflections. He could hardly have enjoyed, for example, the *Dispatch's*
extravagant eulogy of his successor in the War Department, General
Randolph. Would Randolph have been praised so highly if he had
not been a gentleman who needed 'no introduction to our Virginia
community,' if he had not been a Virginia Randolph, a grandson
of Thomas Jefferson? [16] Did that background necessarily make
Randolph abler than Benjamin? Did it necessarily make his blood
better than that of the de Mendes or even the Benjamins?

At any rate, Benjamin was never the man to waste much time in
bemoaning the past. As Secretary of State he would find congenial
duties and perhaps would not have to labor under such a terrific
strain as he had undergone during the past six months. While the
head of the War Department he had seen the worst side of the war,
the worst side of human beings. Perhaps he would now have more
opportunity to see a brighter side. Although he was now the most
important Confederate cabinet officer, perhaps he would have a
little more opportunity to enjoy the society, the cards, theaters, and
other diversions, with which many of his brother officials were
finding relief from the burdens of the war.

On 17 March, the day Benjamin was appointed Secretary of State,
Harry Macarthy, the celebrated Arkansas comedian, author, and

'vocalist,' began a re-engagement of six nights at the Metropolitan Hall. A few nights later *Richard the Third* was being played by request at the Richmond Varieties. And then on the 25th there was 'the last opportunity' to hear Macarthy. To quote from the blurb in the *Whig*, he would appear at the African Church and it would be 'a treat to hear and *see* him sing "The Bonnie Blue Flag," his own composition.' [17]

We are a band of brothers, and native to the soil,
Fighting for the property we gained by honest toil;
And when our rights were threatened, the cry rose near and far:
Hurrah for the Bonnie Blue Flag that bears a single star.

Chorus

Hurrah! Hurrah! for Southern right, hurrah!
Hurrah for the Bonnie Blue Flag that bears a single star.

As long as the Union was faithful to her trust,
Like friends and brethren kind were we, and just;
But now, when Northern treachery attempts our rights to mar,
We hoist on high the Bonnie Blue Flag that bears a single star.[18]

XIII. Secretary of State

6-7 April 1862. Confederates defeated in desperate battle at Shiloh, Tenn.

25 April. Surrender of New Orleans.

25 June-1 July. Confederate victory in Seven Days' Battle near Richmond.

17 September. Indecisive battle at Antietam, Md., but Confederate invasion curbed.

1 October. Lincoln issues Emancipation Proclamation.

8 October *et seq.* Indecisive battle at Perryville, Ky., followed by Confederate retreat into Tenn.

11 November (circa). English and Russian governments reject French offer for joint intervention in American war.

13 December. Confederate victory at Fredericksburg, Va.

2-4 May 1863. Confederate victory at Chancellorsville, Va.

1-4 July. Federal victory at Gettysburg, Penn.

4 July. Surrender of Vicksburg, Miss.

WHILE Benjamin was Secretary of State, he had offices in the same building with Jefferson Davis. With unhappy forethought the United States Government had built a spacious and handsome Customs House in Richmond shortly before the war. Conveniently located on Main Street in the heart of the business section, it was confiscated by the Confederate Government and used as an executive office building. The vaults and offices on the first floor were 'appropriated' by the Honorable Christopher G. Memminger, Secretary of the Treasury, and the 'elegant and convenient' offices on the upper floor by Jefferson Davis and the State Department.[1]

Benjamin's private office was thus not only on the same floor with Davis but hardly a hundred feet distant. And scarcely a day passed that he did not visit the President in his office, at first usually to obtain the army news, 'of which Mr. Davis was sure to be informed, if anybody was,'[2] but as the war progressed, more and more to consult and advise with him on important matters of state.

His office was described by a sharp-eyed Yankee who attended a conference there in 1864 after Benjamin had obtained a number of books and office supplies slipped through the blockade. After his audience had been arranged, the visitor entered a door over which was the legend 'State Department.' Facing him in the center of the room was a black walnut table, covered with a green cloth, and filled with 'a multitude of "state papers." ' From this table his eyes moved to the walls hung with a few maps and battle plans, and to a corner containing a tier of book shelves. Here in this workaday office were none of Benjamin's beloved classics, but chiefly books of official use or interest: Headley's *History,* Lossing's *Pictorial History,* Greeley's *American Conflict,* and one or more volumes of Frank Moore's *Rebellion Records;* a dozen separate copies and several bound volumes of the *Atlantic Monthly;* Parton's *B. F. Butler in New Orleans,* and probably the *Parliamentary Debates,* diplomatic reports, and similar books that Benjamin bought in England or elsewhere.[3]

His office, along with his staff and various problems, simple and complex, Benjamin had inherited from his predecessor, R. M. T. Hunter. The former Virginia Senator was a man of ability and experience, and he left considerable evidence of his work in the department. He had drafted some foreign dispatches that presented for the European powers the Southern case for secession and offered commercial inducements to recognition of the Confederacy; he had appointed Mason and Slidell to their ministerial posts and sent Henry Hotze, a gifted young Mobile journalist, to Europe as a propaganda agent; and he had built up a small administrative staff.

Unlike the War Department, which had thousands of employees in Richmond and elsewhere, the State Department had only a few assistants. There were then few women clerks, and after Benjamin became Secretary of State nearly all the work of the department was performed by him and some half-dozen men. These he was to know intimately during the next few years and one was to leave some brief but valuable reminiscences of him. Like his chief administrators in the War Department, they were a varied lot, not every one conforming in the strictest sense to the words of the *Bonnie Blue Flag:* 'We are a band of brothers and native to the soil.'

When the foreign-born Benjamin became Secretary of State, he retained as Assistant Secretary the British-born William M. Browne, a former Washington newspaperman appointed by R. M. T. Hunter. Browne, a cultivated gentleman of some ability, would probably have been of considerable help to Benjamin if he had not resigned, 22 April 1862, in order to accept a position as aide-de-camp on 'His Excellency's [Jefferson Davis's] personal staff.' In doing so, Browne wrote Benjamin that his chief regret was that it would mean 'the consequent cessation of the close and agreeable association with yourself with which in your confidence you have honored me.' [4] Benjamin appears to have worked smoothly with his subordinates in all his cabinet posts.

Browne's place as Assistant Secretary of State was not filled and his duties devolved upon the chief clerk of the department, Lucius Quinton Washington, a distant relative of the illustrious George. Washington had been acquainted with Benjamin for some years before 1861 and while they served together in Richmond the relation ripened into intimacy. In a letter to Jefferson Davis written in 1879, William Preston Johnston described Washington as 'an upright, chivalrous, intelligent, laborious gentleman. He had clung to our primitive [sic] ideas with unswerving loyalty and devotion.' Although, according to Colonel Johnston, Washington had 'some peculiarities,' [5] he appears to have worked for Benjamin faithfully and harmoniously.

Records of the State Department show that on 1 July 1862 Benjamin's salary was $6,000 a year, and that by 1864 it had been increased to $9,000 a year. As for the remaining personnel of the Department—hardly enough to supply a minor bureau in the present State Department at Washington—they were listed on 30 September 1863 as follows:

	Office	Salary
L. Q. Washington	Chief Clerk	$1,750.00
Wm. J. Bromwell	Clerk	1,500.00
Wm. J. Bromwell	Disbursing Clerk	200.00
James B. Baker	Clerk	1,500.00
Geo. W. Paul	Messenger	750.00
Philip Green	Laborer	45.00
		per month

Philip Green, a Negro slave hired from his master, doubtless had his own curious slant on Confederate statecraft.[6]

After familiarizing himself to some extent with the work of the department, Benjamin wrote on 5 April the first of his many dispatches to the Confederate emissaries in Europe. Preparation of these dispatches—chiefly in connection with the effort to secure European recognition for his government—and the study of those sent to him from abroad were to be two of his principal duties for the next few years. By examining them we are able not only to learn the extent to which he followed the policy of R. M. T. Hunter but to watch the development of his own more daring plans.

In a dispatch sent later in April to James M. Mason, the Confederate minister at London, Benjamin intimated that the department was having great difficulty in communicating with him, for no letter whatsoever had been received from Mason with the exception of a short, informal letter to Hunter written immediately after Mason's arrival in London. Benjamin did not doubt that he must have forwarded dispatches more than once by such means as he found available, but they had not been received.

'In the absence,' therefore, 'of reliable information' about the situation in England, the President did not deem it advisable to make any change in the instructions communicated by Hunter in his dispatches of 3 September 1861 and 8 February 1862, Benjamin said.[7]

This last statement is highly significant. As the result of faulty communication with Mason, Benjamin was afraid to change the old policy of Secretary Hunter; and when he did he was groping in the dark. The difficulty in corresponding with the Confederate foreign representatives was one of the most serious problems that confronted Benjamin. Unwilling to risk sending instructions that would be outdated or that were based on inadequate information, he preferred to wait for an opportune time to write the representatives or to give directions only on matters about which there could be no mistake. The State Department did obtain news—often distorted—from Northern newspapers; and, in addition, *The Times*, *Daily Telegraph*, and other London journals as well as various magazines were regularly received at the department and 'most carefully scanned, especially the debates in Parliament.'[8] But the information Benjamin secured from the foreign periodicals was usually at least ten days or two weeks old and often woefully inadequate.

In fact, all his communications with Europe until May 1863—shortly before the decisive Federal victories at Gettysburg and Vicksburg—were so irregular and infrequent as to nullify to a large extent his efforts to control the Southern foreign policy. This becomes strongly evident when we examine a chart of the mailing and receipt dates of Benjamin's dispatches to and from Slidell, Mason, and Hotze during this potentially hopeful period of his diplomacy.[9]

None of Benjamin's dispatches to Slidell arrived until 5 July 1862, and later he heard from the Secretary on 25 October 1862, 31 December 1862, 6 February 1863, 27 February 1863, and 19 March 1863. The most important dispatch he sent Slidell—Number 5 of 14 April 1862—did not arrive until early July, and Benjamin did not receive a reply until late October. That was a delay of six months, long enough for many important changes in the foreign situation.[10]

Moreover, there were similar difficulties in communicating with Mason. For several dispatches that Benjamin wrote him in April 1862 arrived in late June; then one or more on 14 January 1863 and probably about the last part of April 1863. During these long intervals of three months, seven months, and three months, Mason probably received no dispatches from Benjamin at all. Although Mason's dispatches to Benjamin during the period arrived with greater frequency, here also there were serious delays.[11] Nor was the situation more encouraging in the case of Hotze and the other foreign agents.

So serious was the problem that Benjamin sometimes referred to it frankly in his correspondence. Thus he wrote in a letter of 24 January 1863 [12] to Fraser and Company of Charleston:

It appears that Major Sanders who was authorised by me to take charge of dispatches for Europe, and to whom I requested you to confide a bundle of dispatches, has been guilty of the folly (if not worse) of taking them on board of a sailing vessel and allowing them to be captured to the detriment of the public interest. Major Sanders was specially instructed to go on one of your steamers.

I write to beg that in future you will not permit any dispatches to be taken by any other conveyance than by a steamer even when a special messenger may be sent by the Department.

Anticipating possible loss of the dispatches (sometimes Benjamin could sourly peruse captured ones in the Northern newspapers) he often wrote in cipher. An extract from Slidell's cipher to him of 9 October 1863, with the decoded words, is given in the printed records. Thus 'of any significance' appears as 'hw yjf wzkyqgmttlfa' and 'Imperial master' as 'mxawkpec qikfct.' The cipher was based on poly-alphabetic substitution, using the numerical value of the normal alphabet plus the numerical equivalent for letters in a key phrase ('Where liberty dwells there is my country').[13] Of the same type as that then used by the United States State Department, it is much simpler than some present-day ciphers.

Benjamin also tried to prevent the loss of state papers by sending them through Mrs. Davis to Slidell's daughter, Rosine. Mrs. Davis used an assumed name and the answers were returned by Rosine in the form of friendly letters, in which the 'high contending parties' also were referred to under pseudonyms. Incidentally, Mrs. Davis's relations with Benjamin were on such a friendly basis that he made no objection to her reading the letters, which she found 'most interesting.'

His tact 'was exhibited . . . in a pleasant way about the letters,' she recalled many years later. 'He never put on a manner of reserve towards me, nor did he caution me "to observe the utmost secrecy towards every one about their contents" as another man who knew less of secret affairs did. Of what he knew I must be cognizant, he spoke freely when alone with me, but no more reticent man ever lived where it was possible to be silent.'[14]

Nor is it to be inferred that—with the vital European communication frequently disturbed—Benjamin did not make other efforts to improve it. By 9 May 1863 he was able to call the attention of Slidell to an improved means of communication, using the daring blockade runners to Nassau or Bermuda, by which, he asserted, dispatches were received with regularity in about thirty days. Although the time required was often nearer two months than one (the derelicts pounding on the shores near Wilmington offered mute evidence of the boats which did not arrive), there were few more serious complaints about delayed or captured dispatches until near the end of the war.[15]

To summarize, it was Benjamin's misfortune that the improvements in communications with Europe had come too late for him to use them to any great advantage. By early July 1863, Gettysburg and Vicksburg had been lost and with them the best opportunities for foreign recognition. It was now unlikely to be won except by the use of some desperate bait, such as emancipation of the slaves— and that was not offered until too late.

During the spring of 1862, while McClellan was moving on Richmond, Benjamin's long working hours were filled with cabinet duties, interviews, and a variety of other matters in addition to his diplomatic work. At such critical periods Jefferson Davis held frequent and protracted cabinet meetings, despite what W. M. Brooks, late president of the Alabama Secession Convention, wrote to the contrary. For as Davis caustically wrote him:

You inform me that 'the highest and most reputable authors' say that I 'have not had a cabinet council for more than four months.' I read your letter to a member of my cabinet today [was it to his confidant, Benjamin?]; he was surprised at the extravagance of the falsehood, and did not believe that so much as a week had at any time occurred without a cabinet consultation.

Continuing, Davis categorically denied that he treated Benjamin as a mere clerk. 'If you know Mr. Benjamin you must realize the impossibility of his submitting to degradation at the hands of anyone,' he wrote.[16]

As the military crisis continued, the strain on the frail Jefferson Davis was severe. On 18 April 1862, J. B. Jones described him as thin and haggard. It was whispered on the street that Davis would immediately be baptized and confirmed, Jones said, and he added with his not infrequent acerbity, 'I hope so because it may place a great gulf between him and the descendant of those who crucified the Savior.' Confirmed in the Episcopal Church, Davis afterwards worshipped regularly at fashionable St. Paul's. But this did not place a 'gulf' between him and Benjamin, as Jones so fondly hoped. If anything, Benjamin's influence over the President was increasing, as was indicated by an incident that took place the following month.

On 12 May Jones complained to General Winder, the courageous and hard-boiled old Provost-Marshall in Richmond, that certain tobacco stores had not been destroyed in accordance with an act of Congress. But Winder answered that he was acting under the authority of the Secretary of State. Indignant, Jones wrote severely, 'What has the Secretary of State to do with *martial law?* Is there really no Secretary of War?' [17] Later, on 8 October, Jones heard 'a foolish North Carolinian' abusing the Administration; he not only criticized Davis but enumerated the Northern men who were in high positions in the Confederate Government. 'He was furious, and swore all the distresses of the people were owing to a Nero-like despotism, originating in the brain of Benjamin, the Jew, whose wife lived in Paris.' [18]

Although the North Carolinian expressed the opinion of only a small minority, it is true Benjamin's power in the Administration was growing still stronger.

The next month the able George Wythe Randolph, feeling that he was being unduly dominated by Davis, resigned as Secretary of War. Yet Benjamin continued—if at a sacrifice—to keep on good terms not only with Davis but even with his more unpopular administrative chiefs. Typical was a letter he wrote on 1 December to Blanton Duncan. After confessing that he owed Duncan an answer to several letters, he added:

. . . frankly I have been embarrassed in answering you by a reason which I wish to state candidly. Your letters carry complaints against a colleague in the Cabinet which it is not proper in me to receive without protest. The relations between the members of the Cabinet involve mutual support and confidence, and it would be a violation of an implied pledge of honor for one member of the Cabinet to endorse even by silent acquiescence complaints against his colleague. The only proper remedy for you is by appeal to the President and such appeal for justice is never made in vain. [19]

With the military situation so precarious, it was vitally important for Benjamin to make every possible move to secure foreign recognition. In this effort was embodied the very heart of his foreign policy.

In the first place, Benjamin's hopes for European aid always rested on the bayonets of the gallant Confederate soldiers. The French and British Governments were not willing to help a country which showed little ability to maintain itself; the Confederacy might fail and leave them to face the wrath of the United States, to say nothing of the opposition in their own countries. In general, Benjamin found the foreign nations most cordial after Confederate victories and coolest after defeats, and this interdependence of the Confederate military and diplomatic activities must be kept in mind. To a very considerable extent his success depended upon that of a military machine which he did not direct and for which he was not greatly responsible.

In the second place, there was the interrelation of the French and British phases of his diplomacy. For purposes of clarity, these phases are treated separately, but it must be remembered that they were often dependent on many of the same forces; the attitude of London was often reflected in Paris. In fact, though Benjamin was not yet fully aware of this situation, the French Government was afraid to recognize the Confederacy except by joint action with England, while no independent action in this matter was to be expected of any other European country.

As we have noted, Benjamin's diplomatic relations with Louis Napoleon during the Civil War were probably not the first contacts he had made with the French emperor. It was only by a superficial judgment that he could be dismissed as 'Napoleon le petit.' One of the wiliest rulers of his age, he realized that after seizing the imperial crown he must satisfy the traditional French love of glory; and he had fought successfully in the Crimea and Italy.

But after his victories at Solferino and Magenta not only did Napoleon's glory begin to fade, but the French liberal elements strove to make the government conform more to the spirit of the age. Realizing the need for further action, he saw in the American war an opportunity to regain some of his lost prestige. He might be influenced to make a move in favor of the South—provided he was offered sufficient inducements and the risks were not too great. It was a chance to play the devious game of international diplomacy on a grand scale—and both Napoleon and Benjamin soon grasped at it.

After Slidell's arrival in Paris in January 1862, Benjamin did not hear from his old colleague for six months, but long before that time Benjamin had made a definite move for French recognition. On 12 April, less than a month after he became Secretary of State, he sent Slidell an important proposal for transmission to the French emperor. Based on Benjamin's knowledge of the character of Napoleon and such information about the French attitude towards the Confederacy as he could secure in Richmond, the dispatch was a frank appeal to material considerations. One of the ablest state papers written by Benjamin during the war, it may be read with profit by any student of American history.

Benjamin definitely broke away, at least for the time, from the King Cotton theory. Indeed, it might be contended that he was offering to place the Confederacy in commercial dependence on France.

Benjamin stated that it was 'of course, quite impossible at this distance and with communications so imperfect to ascertain precisely the extent' to which the French Government was committed by the understanding reported to exist between it and the English Government in relation to Confederate affairs.

As a general rule [he continued], it is undoubtedly desirable that our relations with all countries should be placed on the same common footing . . . But in the exceptional position which we now occupy, struggling for existence against an enemy whose vastly superior resources for obtaining the material of war place us at great disadvantage, it becomes of primary importance to neglect no means of opening our ports, and thereby obtaining the articles most needed for the supply of the army. If therefore by a convention conceding to the French Emperor the right of introducing French products into this country free of duty for a certain defined period it were possible to induce his abandonment of the policy hitherto pursued . . . the President would approve of your action in making a treaty on such a basis.

Then Benjamin made the definite proposition to Napoleon. Slidell was, if it seemed advisable after inquiry, to offer him

a certain number of bales of cotton to be received by the merchant vessels of France at certain designated points. In this manner one hundred thousand bales of cotton of 500 pounds each, costing this Government but $4,500,000 would represent a grant to France of not less than $12,500,000 or francs 63,000,000, if cotton be worth as we suppose, not less than twenty-five cents per pound in Europe. Such a sum would maintain afloat a considerable fleet for a length of time quite sufficient to open the Atlantic and Gulf ports to the commerce of France.

Nor was this all. 'I do not state this as the limit to which you would be authorized to go in making a negotiation on the subject, but to place clearly before you the advantage which would result in stipulating for payment in cotton,'[20] Benjamin continued.

After sending this dispatch to Slidell, Benjamin had to reconcile himself to the long wait until he could learn Napoleon's answer. In early May, however, he had the opportunity to see his old friend, Count Henri Mercier, the French minister to Washington, during a visit to Richmond, and assure him that the Confederacy would not consider peace without independence.

'I know your good feeling for us, and we require no proof of it,' Benjamin said. 'But you know we are hot-blooded people and we would not like to talk with anybody who entertained the idea of the possibility of our dishonoring ourselves by reuniting with a people for whom we feel unmitigated contempt as well as abhorrence.'[21]

Convinced by his interviews with Benjamin and other prominent Confederates that the South was determined to gain her independence, no matter what the cost, Mercier sent the information to his Government and it was used as a basis for future moves toward mediation in favor of the Confederacy.[22]

And then the tide of the battle turned in favor of the South. In late June and early July 1862, Lee defeated McClellan in the Seven Days' Battle, while two months later, after another notable victory at Second Manassas, the Confederates launched a grand offensive. Never did the Confederate hope for European recognition have a firmer basis than in September of that year, when Bragg was threatening Louisville and Lee was crossing the Potomac into Maryland. And although the Southern armies suffered setbacks at Perryville and Antietam, they were still ready for hard fighting.

What did Benjamin do to develop the opportunities offered him by Lee's victories? First, let us return to his diplomatic relations with Louis Napoleon. After writing Slidell in April 1862 to make the offer of the cotton subsidy and free trade, Benjamin did not communicate with him again until 19 July. Not receiving any word from Slidell until that month, and 'having no opportunity affording reasonable prospect' of his own dispatches receiving their destination, he could only wait anxiously for news of the mission.[23] A letter from Slidell received on 5 July [24] had relieved him somewhat, but there was still no word regarding Benjamin's proposition to the Emperor.

Early in July, however, Slidell had received the dispatch containing the offer, and on the 16th had conferred with Louis Napoleon. During a frank conversation of over an hour, Slidell not only offered Napoleon the cotton subsidy and free trade but also the assurance of Southern support for his schemes in Mexico. In 1861 Benito Juarez, the Republican leader, had overthrown the conservative government in Mexico and proceeded to apply radical measures against the Catholic Church and to repudiate the public debt contracted by his predecessor. Now given the opportunity he was looking for, Napoleon persuaded Great Britain and Spain to intervene with him in Mexico to secure a forceful settlement of the debts owed them by her government. Then, after the forces of the other powers were withdrawn, his troops remained in the country. When Slidell talked with Napoleon at Vichy it was already evident that his ambitions were more grandiose than he would openly admit; probably he was even planning to establish a French empire in Mexico.

With all these facts in mind, Slidell now proceeded to offer Louis Napoleon the definite *quid pro quo*. He mentioned the offer that Benjamin had outlined, and said that the cotton subsidy was offered exclusively to France; his colleague in London 'was not aware' of his authority to make it. Moreover, as to Mexico, he referred to the help the United States was giving Juarez and her unfriendly attitude toward France in other respects, and even went so far as to declare that since the Lincoln government was the ally and protector of Napoleon's enemy Juarez, the Confederacy 'could have no objection to make common cause with him [Napoleon] against the common enemy.' The crafty Napoleon would not commit himself definitely, but Slidell got 'the decided impression that if England long persevered in obstinate inaction, he would take the responsibility of intervening by himself.' [25]

After Slidell had talked with him again in October and renewed Benjamin's proposition and the offer of Southern aid to his Mexican venture,[26] the Emperor tried in late October and early November to get the British and Russian Governments to join with him in proposing to the belligerents a six months' armistice and suspension of the blockade. It was a critical step. What would be the answer of England and Russia? If it were favorable Benjamin's diplomacy would probably be crowned with success and the war ended.

XIV. *Southern Diplomacy*

THE autumn weeks of 1862 were the most hopeful of Benjamin's diplomatic career. Although there was still no late news from Slidell and Mason, his diary for this period contains numerous encouraging items from his newspaper files. The hot Virginia summer was now ended, and his quickened spirit was reflected in the gay foliage on the streets of the West End, the bracing air and cheerful firesides. In late September and early October, it is true the newspapers contained numerous items about the issuance of Lincoln's Emancipation Proclamation, but so far these did not indicate that it had done much harm to the Confederate cause; in fact the evidence was quite to the contrary. On 2 October Benjamin, receiving European 'advices' to 18 September, read in the Paris *Patrie* that the war was 'about over' and in the *Constitutional* that 'Europe cannot wait any longer before recognizing the Southern Confederacy.' [1] And there were also other highly encouraging items, with details about the armistice proposed by Napoleon III, not merely in the Northern and French 'advices' but also in the British during the next two months.[2]

On 1 December [3] Benjamin learned that Earl Russell had rejected the French overture, but he continued to feel that he had much ground for hope—particularly after the Union defeat at Fredricksburg later in the month.[4] Apparently, he did not yet realize that his best chance of securing French recognition had passed. Although Slidell, at Benjamin's prompting, could still dangle bribes before Louis Napoleon, he was afraid to take any decisive step without British support. Just why this support was not forthcoming and why Benjamin was unable to change the recalcitrant British ministry is revealed when we examine Benjamin's relations with Mason since the previous spring.

* * *

When arriving in London in January 1862, Mason found much sympathy for the Confederate cause, particularly among the upper classes. But the aristocracy was no longer England—not even when it was supported by much of the middle class. Opposition to the Confederacy had spread among certain liberal and lower-class elements and the Government, already inclined to caution, preferred to await the result of the impending battles. After an interview with Earl Russell, the British foreign minister, Mason wrote Benjamin that he found Russell's 'personal sympathies not with us, and his policy inaction.' [5] Altogether, it was obvious to those on the scene that neither France nor England was likely to recognize the Confederacy during the next few months—that is, unless her armies won important victories or she offered other strong inducements to action.

If Disraeli had by then attained his great ambition to climb 'the greasy pole,' the world might have seen some brilliant diplomatic moves, with Benjamin working in conjunction with the other Sephardic statesman. There might have been some earlier feats comparable to Disraeli's acquisition of the controlling shares in the Suez Canal, or his clever maneuvering at the Congress of Berlin. But Disraeli had not yet become prime minister.

During the past few decades there had continued to be curious parallels in the lives of Benjamin and Disraeli. Both men had married Gentile wives, both were dynamic political conservatives, and both were the leading representatives of their race in their respective countries. But, unhappily for Benjamin, the similarities here ended. In old-world England Disraeli had found that it took longer to rise to political heights than Benjamin did in new America; and Benjamin had to deal with Earl Russell—cold-blooded, slow-moving, and not entirely sympathetic to the South.

Committed to a conservative course in his dealing with the English Government, Benjamin now relied on such points as the invalidity and ineffectiveness of the blockade and the stability of the Southern Government. In his No. 2 to Mason of 8 April 1862 (written on the second day of the battle at Shiloh), Benjamin argued cleverly against Earl Russell's policy concerning the blockade. He enclosed a list of over a hundred ships that had traded between the South and foreign ports during the preceding November,

December, and January, despite the blockade that it had 'pleased neutral nations heretofore to respect as binding on their commerce.'

Seven European nations, including the five great powers, he continued, had 'fixed by common agreement and "solemn declaration" the principle that "blockades, in order to be binding must be effective—that is to say, maintained by a force sufficient really to prevent access to the coast of the enemy." ' The Southern Confederacy, after being recognized as a belligerent by France and Great Britain, was informally requested by both of these powers to agree to this declaration, and accepted therewith.

'Great then, was the surprise' of President Davis (was it after Benjamin had prompted him?) at finding in the recently published reports of the English Parliament the following statement of Earl Russell in his letter of 14 February 1862 to Lord Lyons:

Her Majesty's government, however, are of opinion that, assuming that the blockade was duly notified and also that a number of ships is stationed and remains at the entrance of a port sufficient really to prevent access to it, *or to create an evident danger of entering it or leaving it,* and that these ships do not voluntarily permit ingress or egress, the fact that various ships may have successfully escaped through it (as in the particular instances here referred to) will not of itself prevent the blockade from being an effectual one by international law.

Benjamin showed conclusively that Earl Russell's words that he [Benjamin] had underscored—'or to create an evident danger of entering it or leaving it'—were an addition to the definition of a blockade in the Treaty of 1856 and were extracted from the Convention of 1801, which had been superseded. Moreover, Benjamin noted that Earl Russell premised his declaration by 'assuming that a number of ships is stationed and remains at the entrance of a port sufficient really to prevent access to it.' But the 'plain answer to this' was that 'the admitted fact of "various ships escaping through the blockade" ' was inconsistent with Russell's argument. The absurdity of pretending that the 2,500 miles of Southern seacoast was guarded by a force which was sufficient to prevent access was 'too glaring to require comment.' President Davis trusted Mason would 'lose no suitable opportunity of pressing these views on the British Government.' [6]

Altogether, the dispatch comprised nearly 3,000 words and must have filled at least 15 or 20 pages of Benjamin's script. How long did it take Benjamin to write such dispatches? Could he compose them quickly, his thoughts moving with easy precision? Or were they studied efforts, perhaps even the labored result of midnight vigils? No one could answer these questions better than Benjamin's chief clerk, Quinton Washington.

Probably Benjamin took more time with the earlier dispatches than he did with those written after he became familiar with the duties of Secretary of State. But we have Washington's word that Benjamin's

grasp of a subject seemed instantaneous. His mind appeared to move without friction. His thought was clear. His style, whether in composition or conversation, was natural, orderly and perspicuous. I do not affirm that his compositions were wholly unstudied, but, whatever art there was, he had the art to hide. I have known him often to compose a long dispatch or State paper with great rapidity, with hardly a word changed or interlined in the whole manuscript.[7]

Although handicapped by the cool attitude of the English Government, Mason worked faithfully though not brilliantly to carry out Benjamin's instructions; and he was helped materially by young Henry Hotze, the clever Confederate propagandist at London. Under the direction of Mason, Hotze, and their British sympathizers, increasing pressure was put on the Palmerston government, but it continued to await the turn of events in the South. After the Confederate victories in the Seven Days' Battle, Mason tried to force the issue and asked for a personal interview with Earl Russell. But on 2 August Russell sent him a refusal. 'Her Majesty's government are still determined to wait,' he said. Disgusted with his treatment, Mason wrote Benjamin that he was considering whether to make one more request for recognition. If it was rejected, he did not feel it would be compatible with the dignity of the Confederate Government for him to remain longer in England and he would retire to the continent to await further instructions from Richmond.[8]

Mason's letter, which arrived on 25 August, was received by Benjamin with grave anxiety. If Mason left London, it would upset

Benjamin's plans for Confederate diplomacy in Europe. Cautiously, therefore, he wrote the sensitive Virginian that he and Davis agreed that Mason should not take 'any attitude susceptible of being construed into that of a supplicant'; but, nevertheless, such a drastic measure as Mason proposed should be taken only 'after the most grave and mature deliberation.'

In order to encourage Mason and, doubtless, to provide propaganda for his use in England, Benjamin called attention to the 'enormous' losses suffered by the enemy during the recent campaigns. They totalled 349,500, he solemnly averred.[9] If these figures were correct, the whole race of Yankees was fast being exterminated; Mason had every reason to take heart. Perhaps Benjamin actually believed that the Northern casualties were so high, but it appears that he was loading Mason with propaganda.

In any case, the Union army had recently suffered some serious defeats, both in the Seven Days' Battle and at Second Manassas. If only the Confederates had been able to clinch them through successful invasion of the North! Then England and France would most likely have recognized the Confederacy and turned the scale in her favor. And with independence secured, in what hopes might not Benjamin indulge! Under the provisions of the Confederate Constitution, Jefferson Davis could serve only one term of six years and Benjamin was not barred from succeeding him because of his alien birth. That was indeed day-dreaming. Yet he might continue as Secretary of State, becoming an even stronger power behind the throne. Or he might resume practice as a leading Southern lawyer, with his plans for commercial development finding a national and even an international scope.

To a great extent Benjamin's future depended upon the foreign news. At the beginning of November it was still highly encouraging, for he quoted in his diary the celebrated remarks of Gladstone, the Chancellor of the Exchequer, on 7 October at Newcastle: 'Jefferson Davis and other leaders of the South have made an army; they are making, it appears, a navy; and they have made what is more than either—they have made a nation.' In the latter part of October the British cabinet was considering a meeting at which it would make a decision favorable to the South.

On 11 November the cabinet did meet and there was a two-day

debate on Napoleon's proposal for joint mediation, received 10 November. Earl Russell, now temporarily favorable to the South, urged that the Government accept the French offer. But the cabinet rejected Russell's proposal chiefly because of the refusal of Russia to co-operate, the failure of the Southern offensive, and, above all, the grave risk of provoking a war with the United States.[10]

Already on 16 October the *Examiner*, sensing the diplomatic defeat, had published a strong editorial blast against the Administration.

The chief source of failure in the policy of the Confederate Government, is the fact that it is composed of men incapable of originating ideas or measures . . . all its projects were long discussed by persons unconnected with it, and made entirely public, months before the Confederate Government concluded to adopt them as principles of its own conduct.

Specifically, the *Examiner* blamed the Government for its failure to use the cotton crop to provide funds for arms and supplies: the cotton 'was only gold in the bowels of the earth and undiscovered to man,' unless the Government would make use of it. The Davis administration would have found it difficult to answer adequately this criticism, for there had indeed been a lack of original 'ideas or measures' in certain high quarters. But the newspaper apparently was not aware that Benjamin had proposed at Montgomery a plan for the purchase of cotton, or that he had tried to bribe Louis Napoleon with a cotton subsidy.

Nevertheless, Benjamin had failed thus far to secure European recognition for his Government. He had played one of his best cards against Louis Napoleon and it had brought inadequate results. Would Benjamin now try another daring move, or would he sit back waiting for decisive Confederate victories or other events less likely to bring European recognition?

There was one trump card he had not played, which, if he could have played it in time, might well have secured the independence of the Confederacy—the emancipation of slaves. The evidence that opposition to slavery formed one of the strongest rallying cries for the Northern war party was too obvious for comment; without this issue it would have been far more difficult for the Lincoln Government to maintain the necessary morale. Equally obvious was the fact that slavery was a strong obstacle to foreign recognition of the South. As events proved, the North won the Civil War only after four years of bloody fighting with many serious defeats and internal difficulties. If the slaves had been emancipated and European recognition secured, it is far less likely that the Union Government could have carried the war to a successful conclusion.

But with the maintenance of slavery a key point in the Southern policy, Benjamin was seriously, perhaps fatally, handicapped in his foreign negotiations. As early as 21 May 1861, Yancey and Mann had written Secretary Toombs from London that 'we are satisfied . . . the public mind here is entirely opposed [to the Confederacy] on the question of slavery, and that the sincerity and universality of this feeling embarrasses the Government in dealing with the question of our recognition.' [11] Moreover, their opinion was strongly seconded by Edwin De Leon, a propagandist whom Benjamin sent abroad to 'enlighten' the European press. Writing from Paris on 30 September 1862, De Leon incorrectly informed Benjamin that the slavery question had been dropped in England, but he said it was 'the great bugbear in France, and those who professed to be our advocates were pleading pitifully an extenuation of our sins in this respect and shuddering at the epithet *esclavagiste* with which the paid partisans of the North are pelting them.' [12]

An avid reader of the foreign press, and, as we know, with many European contacts, Benjamin realized that there was only too much evidence of this moral opposition to the Confederacy in both England and France. He must have also perceived that it would be overcome only by emancipation.

Of course the South, which had seceded from the Union largely because of the Northern opposition to slavery, was not prepared even to consider the necessity of emancipation—despite the fact that slavery was no longer in keeping with the spirit of the age. But what of an experienced and cosmopolitan-minded statesman like Benjamin? In late 1862 and, indeed, until the last desperate months of the war, he very probably believed that any proposals for emancipation on his part would have meant political suicide.

And yet there is considerable evidence to show that Benjamin was not actively hostile to the idea. Not until near the end of the war did he deem it practical to propose emancipation in return for

European recognition. Yet his attitude toward the Negro issue at this early period was both curious and significant. We wonder if he would have taken more positive action even before Gettysburg had he been able to secure the support of public opinion and his chief, Jefferson Davis.

As is often true in an analysis of the reticent Benjamin, we are stopped by a wall of mystery. Still, there are a number of facts to indicate that he may have been guilty of unorthodox ideas on the Negro question. In Richmond there were few people, if any, who were closer to him than his messmate, Duncan Kenner. Old friends and associates, now living together in the same house, they must often have talked confidentially about the prospects for Confederate success. Although a large slave owner and a prominent member of the Confederate Congress, Kenner was less conservative than many of his contemporaries in Richmond. He had a broad perspective upon Southern problems that must have been affected by his Northern university education and his extensive travel both in the United States and in Europe.

After the fall of New Orleans in April 1862, Kenner was convinced the Southern Confederacy could not succeed if it adhered to slavery and, consequently, failed to secure the support of England and France. Upon his return to Richmond to attend the Confederate Congress, Kenner informed Jefferson Davis of his conclusion and added that he was determined to move in Congress that a commission be sent to Europe to propose to the English and French governments that if they would acknowledge the Southern Confederacy it would abolish slavery. There is strong reason to believe that Kenner must also have talked over his proposition with Benjamin, probably before consulting Davis. However, Davis did not approve of Kenner's proposal. He told Kenner that the affairs of the Confederacy were not so desperate as to warrant the plan, and persuaded him not to make the motion in Congress at that time.[13]

During the remainder of 1862 and early 1863, questions relating to the Negro continued to come before Benjamin in various forms. On 11 November 1862, for example, Hotze wrote Benjamin that the Lancashire cotton operatives as a class were inimicable to the South; they looked upon slavery 'as did the people of New England' and regarded it as the source of the miseries they had to endure as a result of the cotton scarcity.[14]

As the months passed English sentiment against slavery was increased by the conviction that the Northern Government seriously planned to emancipate the slaves. By April 1863, the London *Quarterly Review* wrote that 'Mr. Lincoln has, within the last two months found a set-off in the increasing moral support which he has received.' Emancipation meetings held in England in the spring of 1863 were 'numerously attended,' and in a letter to Benjamin in April Hotze said that there was 'a latent danger in the agitation in this subject and of this public men are aware, which may account in part for the timidity of their American policy.' [15]

Meantime, the emancipation issue had also been brought before Benjamin by an unexpected medium—James Spence, an influential Liverpool merchant. The author of *The American Union,* a defense of the Confederacy that had gone through four large editions in less than a year, and the organizer of two London associations to help the South, Spence was rewarded by an appointment as a Confederate financial agent in England.[16] But to the embarrassment of many prominent Confederates, Spence not only held forbidden views on the explosive subject of slavery but did not hesitate to air them!

Writing to Benjamin in October 1862, the month of the issuance of Lincoln's Emancipation Proclamation, Hotze regretfully stated that Spence had

of late rendered the idea of ultimate emancipation unduly conspicuous. The public mind had ceased to expect any promises of this kind from us, and to understand that the merest self-respect would prevent us from making them. Mr. Spence, however, appears of late to have become impressed with the belief that his moral influence with the Southern people, derived from his eminent services to them, might be sufficient to effect that in which all other human influences must fail.

Hotze admitted that Spence was sincere in his philanthropic convictions and devotion to the Confederacy but 'at this juncture of affairs' he almost dreaded 'the direction his friendship and devotion seem about to take.' [17]

It is significant to note that Benjamin did not reply to this criticism of Spence for more than a year, and, when he did, the objection that he made to the Englishman's opinions appears to be based largely on the grounds of expediency.[18] Moreover, as late as early May 1863, not one word of direct reproof from Benjamin is known to have reached Spence. By then the situation was somewhat scandalous, in the opinion of some die-hard Southerners, and the Richmond *Enquirer* published a strong editorial criticizing the State Department for employing Spence, an Englishman of known antislavery views. The *Enquirer* declared that Spence had enlarged on the evils and immorality of slavery and made it one of the motives for speedy recognition of the Confederacy that 'this abomination would be put in the way of ultimate extinction.'

'As a reward we suppose, for his book,' the influential newspaper continued, Spence had been made the Confederate commercial agent at Liverpool

so that here we are paying a man for abusing us as a nation of criminals steeped in moral evil! The operation of our State Department seems to be against us, not for us . . . Is it, indeed, the case that we do not quite recognize ourselves? that we hesitate to stand upon our own feet, and assert the rights of our own conscience? Are we not very sure, either that we are really independent until Europe has said so, or that the institutions and principles or our society are sound and rightful until Europe has passed upon them? [19]

The Spence incident, of which we have not heard the last, offered the best evidence that Benjamin may have been developing unorthodox views on the Negro question at this time, but there were also other straws in the wind. Because of rumors that had been circulated by Northern agents in Europe, that the Confederacy proposed to reopen the African slave trade as soon as peace was restored, Benjamin issued a circular to several of the Confederate diplomatic representatives in Europe calling attention to the fact that the Government was specifically denied this power under the terms of the Constitution.[20] Again, in his diary during early 1863, the use of Negro soldiers by the Northern Government is mentioned several times. On 13 June 1863, for example, he noted that the Union General Banks had praised the bravery of the Negro troops at Port Hudson.

Altogether, there is considerable evidence that Benjamin may have been considering another bold move comparable to his effort to win French recognition by the cotton subsidy. But after his diplomatic failure in October 1862, he did not actually attempt any more *coups* for the next eight months before Gettysburg—that is, during the remainder of the hopeful period of his diplomacy. His inaction was not only the result of political expediency but also of the favorable military situation. With a few exceptions his diplomatic activities during this time were of a routine nature.

From the testimony of his friend, Prince de Polignac, and other available evidence, it is clear that Benjamin was now entirely too hopeful of Confederate success—and his diplomatic efforts were suffering accordingly. De Polignac, in Richmond awaiting promotion to brigadier-general and, perhaps, a diplomatic appointment, spent a good deal of time with Benjamin and commented in his diary [21] at some length on the Secretary's political views:

Dec. 1st 1862. Called in the evening at the President with whom I referred to my journey. He says Mr. Benj. still wishes to wait for the French Consul before taking a decision.

6 (dec.) The French Consul has just come back from the North, says that the Democratic party intend resisting the Lincoln Administration in all anti-constitutional measures. A strong peace party is springing up. They propose calling Convention together, in the various states. Pennsylvania is said to have taken the head in the counter-revolution. The French Minister is looking for European intervention at an early day, not before the month of March however when the term of the present Congress shall expire as the new members intend compelling the Presdt. to call a session.—So Mr. B. must be more buoyant with hopes than ever and will probably not deem it necessary to send anyone abroad.

8 (dec) Nothing worthy of record. Mr. B. did not send for me, showing that his hopes about foreign intervention are brighter than ever.

9 (dec) Long conversation with Mr. P. [the French Consul], who did not take exactly the same point of view I did of European

politics in reference to this country, but was won over to my side. He will talk with B. on the subject. I hope he may enlighten his prejudiced mind . . .

And then came the first reports of the great battle at Fredericksburg:

13 (dec) Conflicting reports from Fredericksburg of a fight . . . This much we know, viz; that the Federals are in possession of the town.—Dined with Mr. B. always buoyant with hopes—he looks forward to the next step of the Emperor of France, who, he believes, will follow up the intentions evinced in his late note to Russian and English Cabinets. His mind is made up to it, he infers from different circumstances among others from the hints of the Northern press on the subject.

In a letter to Dudley Mann of 17 January 1863,[22] Benjamin was still writing that 'we trust that our early general recognition can not now long be delayed.' But two weeks later de Polignac noted that he had called at the Secretary's home and found Benjamin had 'given up his hopes about interference at this moment.'[23] By May he believed that the European powers would intervene in behalf of the South only after their help was no longer needed, but soon afterwards he talked in a more optimistic manner.[24]

During June there was another noteworthy visitor to Richmond, Martin Gordon of New Orleans, who was sent through the lines by General Banks in order to ascertain the 'feeling' of the Confederate people. After talking with the Secretary of State and other prominent people, and sifting the public opinion, Martin said that there was one man in the capital who 'believes or talks of intervention— Mr. Benjamin.'[25]

Like some of Benjamin's other optimistic remarks this may indeed have been a case of professing rather than believing; it was highly important that he keep a cheerful front. But his statement, if sincere, can be explained by his own sanguine temperament, the Confederate victories at Fredericksburg and Chancellorsville, and the still friendly attitude of Louis Napoleon. During that month the Davis government was preparing for an invasion of the North, and there was indeed reason for hope that Lee's splendid veterans would win a decisive victory that would lead to foreign recognition. But there was also the chance of his suffering a crushing defeat, which would have the opposite effect. The situation already looked bad in the West, where Vicksburg was in critical danger of capture.

Surely a man in Benjamin's position needed to bridle his enthusiasm—not to be the one prominent Confederate in the city 'who believes or talks of intervention.' Such a state of mind was a positive weakness in a foreign minister of a country fighting to win her independence from another with so much greater manpower and resources.

Benjamin's false optimism undoubtedly curtailed his effectiveness as Secretary of State. Yet it is only fair to note that there was no apparent let-up in his activities. One important matter that he dealt with in January 1863 was the Erlanger loan to the Confederacy. Erlanger and Company of Paris, a wealthy and influential banking firm, offered to underwrite an issue of 5,000,000 francs in Confederate bonds. Bearing interest at 8 per cent and payable in cotton at six pence per pound—then far less than the market price—the bonds would be an attractive bait for speculators. And the Erlanger syndicate generously agreed to handle them provided they got all the profits in excess of 70 per cent of the sale price—plus a 5 per cent commission for disposing of them, plus an 8 per cent discount for anticipating any or all of the installments, plus a 1 per cent commission for handling the sinking fund and interest!

Thus the Confederacy would receive only about 3,300,000 of the 5,000,000 francs and even this amount would be whittled down under the redemption and commission provision. Yet the money would still be of great value to the Southern Government, particularly since Slidell wrote Benjamin that he had 'the best reason to believe that even in anticipation of its [the contract's] acceptance the very strongest influences will be enlisted in our favor.' Erlanger was reputed to have great influence with Louis Napoleon and he was believed to look with favor upon the scheme.

Nevertheless, to Benjamin a bad trade was a bad trade. He could not see Erlanger making such enormous profits, whatever his political influence or connection with Slidell. The Confederate Government agreed to make the contract with Erlanger, but it was to be for 3,000,000 instead of 5,000,000 francs; Erlanger was to have the profits above 77 per cent instead of 70 per cent, and the interest was to be 7 instead of 8 per cent. The contract would have been declined altogether, so Benjamin wrote Mason, 'but for the political considerations indicated by Mr. Slidell, in whose judgment in such matters we are disposed to place very great confidence.'

The Erlanger contract did prove a boon to the Confederacy: there was a considerable sale of cotton bonds in Europe, which provided funds for the hard-pressed Confederate purchasing agents abroad; Erlanger backed a plan to build ironclad ships for the Confederacy, and work was begun upon them with the covert approval of Louis Napoleon. Because of the loan and other considerations Napoleon was still willing to recognize the Confederacy—provided he would have English co-operation. He was particularly receptive after the Southern victory in April 1863 at Chancellorsville.[26]

Among his minor activities during the spring of 1863 Benjamin wrote a letter to Senator Clement Clay complying with his request for suggestions regarding a national seal for the Confederacy, a device for the national coin, and on other matters relating to coinage, weights, and measures. The ideas which Benjamin advanced in this connection never had any great practical importance for his Government but do much to help one understand the conservative social philosophy to which he still adhered in some respects. In view of the strong influence of Benjamin in the Davis administration, they give a significant impression of the type of government that would have existed in the South if the Confederacy had succeeded—an impression that must be weighed against his more progressive ideas.

For the seal Benjamin proposed 'a cavalier,' copied from the equestrian statue of Washington in Capitol Square at Richmond. The cavalier would be applicable to the Confederates, a nation of horsemen.

[It would do] just honor to our people. The cavalier or knight is typical of chivalry, bravery, generosity, humanity, and other knightly virtues. Cavalier is synonymous with gentlemen in nearly all the modern languages . . . The word . . . is eminently suggestive of the origin of Southern society, as used in contradistinction to Puritan. The Southerners remain what their ancestors were, gentlemen.

Benjamin even proposed that the Confederacy issue a $5 gold coin to be called a cavalier, and that there be $10 and $20 pieces known as double cavaliers and quadruple cavaliers.[27]

During the hot days of late June 1863 another foreign dignitary interviewed Benjamin—Lieutenant-Colonel Fremantle of the British army. While discussing the European situation, Benjamin asserted that England had always had it in her power to terminate the war by recognizing the Confederacy and making a commercial treaty with her. He denied that the Yankees really would dare to go to war with Great Britain for taking such action, however much they might swear they would do so.[28]

Only a few weeks after this interview the Confederates were defeated at Gettysburg and Vicksburg, making it quite unlikely that foreign recognition could be secured except by desperate measures. And these Benjamin would not fail to attempt during the next two years, though too late to save the sinking Confederate Government.

XV. *Life in Richmond*

LIKE Earl Harold of England Benjamin 'had little stillness the while he ruled.' Only about two weeks after he entered the State Department, McClellan's blue-clad host moved from Fortress Monroe in a grand assault on Richmond but was halted by the Confederate forces thrown across the lower Peninsula. And then on a Sunday in late April, when the Yankees were besieging Yorktown, word came of the fall of New Orleans. Since Benjamin still had large business interests in that city, he perhaps reacted to the news much as did his brother-in-law, Jules St. Martin. Walking with some friends after church, Jules was given the bad tidings.

'This must hit you hard,' someone said.

'I am ruined, voilà tout,' Jules replied, ('with a characteristic gesture of throwing care to the winds.') [1]

A few days later Yorktown was evacuated, and Joe Johnston's army retreated up the Peninsula to make a stand on the high ground in front of Richmond. Would Johnston be able to defend the capital? Fearing the worst, several of the cabinet officers sent their wives and children out of the city, while the archives were shipped to Lynchburg and Columbia.[2]

Jules volunteered and served for a time as a private in the trenches in front of Richmond. A debonair Creole, cheerful, witty, and with an 'exquisite courtesy,' he had made friends everywhere and become a favorite in Richmond wartime society. When he had first appeared on the streets his 'nicety of dress' after the 'Parisian style' had been the subject of comment, but now in the field he roughed it with the other soldiers.

Some years afterwards, in Paris, Jules enjoyed telling two visiting Virginia ladies a story of his 'camp life in the freezing trenches.' Once while he was camping on cold ground a friendly Confederate colonel told him to follow him without informing anyone, for he had found a place where they could 'sleep warm.'

Eagerly Jules followed his guide, only to be introduced to an enclosure full of dirty, grunting animals. It was a pig sty, and here they slept until morning in the 'oozing mud.'

'It is true that their [the pigs] noses disturbed me now and then,' Jules said, 'But que voulez vous! I was freezing!' [3]

By 31 May Benjamin heard the rumblings of the guns at Seven Pines, only a few miles from Richmond. General Joe Johnston was severely wounded in the battle, and was succeeded as commander of the main Confederate army in Virginia by Robert E. Lee. With Lee, Davis and Benjamin were to work in entire accord until the end of the war.

Now with McClellan's army at the very outskirts of Richmond, Lee had a task to test even his great military genius. Shortly before, when Lee was serving again as Davis's military adviser, the President had called him to meet with the cabinet and asked his opinion on the best line of defense in case the capital had to be abandoned. After discussing certain aspects of the question, with Benjamin and his colleagues doubtless hanging on his words, he answered that the next best line was at the Staunton River. 'But Richmond must not be given up—it shall not be given up,' he said with tears streaming down his cheeks. Some of the cabinet members were to see Lee on several other occasions when the fate of the Confederacy hung in the balance, but on none of them perhaps did he show deeper emotion.[4] Soon afterwards in the Seven Days' Battle (25 June-1 July 1862) he drove the Union army from their position in front of Richmond to a base on the James River, some twenty miles below the city.

* * *

One summer night in 1862 Riley, a colored servant at Benjamin's sisters' home in New Orleans, entered with the dread news that there was 'a Yankee right at the door.' Mrs. Levy and Miss Harriet Benjamin temporarily fled, leaving the former's daughter, Mrs. Popham, to go to the door—and face the young Federal lieutenant whom she found there.

The house was needed by the military authorities, the lieutenant said, and would be taken over in the morning and used as a hospital. Mrs. Popham was permitted to carry away such possessions as were absolutely necessary; a squad of soldiers was sent to protect her during the night.

Arrived at the house, the soldiers proved to be Germans who had known her husband. 'By humoring them and plying them with what was left of some rare old Bourbon and Cognac, once highly prized by Mr. Benjamin and his guests,' Mrs. Popham related, 'we prevailed on them to move nearly all of the furniture to the house of a neighbor, kindly put at our service, which was practically empty. Owing a small amount to the German groceryman, whose yard adjoins ours, I pulled some palings off the fence and drove the cow into his yard. By this payment in kind, our only debt was cleared.'

All through the night the ladies worked, packing and moving. In the morning, as Mrs. Levy was sitting on the front porch upon almost their last bundles of belongings, another squad of soldiers, with an insolent young fellow in command, came to relieve the complaisant guard of the past night.

'Madam,' said the officer, 'are you the sister of the arch Rebel, Benjamin?'

Mrs. Levy admitted that she was.

'Then you are not to remove anything from this house. It is a military necessity.'

Thus did the war reach the Benjamin family circle, not merely Judah and Jules, as we have noted, but his loved ones in New Orleans. How anxiously Benjamin had waited for news of them after the fall of the city we can easily imagine when we read the accounts of the depredations of 'Beast' Butler and his soldiers.

Actually, none of Benjamin's family in the city suffered any bodily harm because of their relation to the 'arch Rebel.' But it would have been too much to expect Butler not to disport himself with Benjamin's possessions.

The officer who had forbade the ladies to remove the remaining possessions they needed was soon replaced by a more reasonable one. They rented two rooms in the French Quarter, where they lived several weeks. Then they received word from Benjamin advising them to make their way into the Southern lines. Soon afterwards they escaped to La Grange, Georgia, where he kept them in comparative comfort until the end of the war.[5]

As for their residence in New Orleans (Benjamin's property), it was seized, and also certain other possessions which Butler could readily lay hands on, including the black tin box full of Tehuantepec bonds and other papers.[6]

* * *

During the latter years of the Civil War, Jefferson Davis had only two intimate advisers: the inept, though well-meaning Braxton Bragg, and Benjamin. Since Bragg was in the West with the army during a great part of this period, Benjamin was then Davis's only close adviser in the capital. In the realm of military affairs his influence was not so strong or salutary as in civil affairs. Although continuing to be his own chief of staff, Jefferson Davis did on a number of important occasions seek Benjamin's opinion on pressing military problems. Yet the advice Davis received was somewhat amateurish, for as much as Benjamin had learned while Secretary of War, he still had not advanced beyond the layman's conception of strategy.

Before the critical Gettysburg campaign during the summer of 1863, Benjamin was probably one of the cabinet members who supported Davis in his fateful decision to send Lee's army into Pennsylvania. The cabinet met early one Saturday and remained in anxious session until after nightfall, the President and all the ministers fully realizing the grave character of the problem under discussion. Postmaster-General Reagan, a shrewd though ill-educated Texan, offered a plan to relieve pressure in the West.

First he would have had false information disseminated to the effect that the army in Virginia would be sent north of the Potomac and the defenses of Richmond strengthened and supplies collected for a six months' siege. Then at the proper time, twenty-five or thirty thousand of Lee's troops would be sent west and concentrated with other troops to relieve Vicksburg, threatened by Grant.[7] If Reagan's plan had been followed it might have changed the course of the war. But it was not adopted and Lee's army moved northward to its defeat at Gettysburg.

Again, the next year Benjamin was to favor the removal of General Joseph E. Johnston from command of the army in front of Atlanta, another decision with evil results for the Confederacy.[8]

In the other numerous and pressing governmental activities, Benjamin's influence was more helpful. His friend, Dr. Moses Hoge, testified that it was Davis's custom to refer to Benjamin all matters that did not clearly belong to any department,[9] and L. Q. Washington added, 'Benjamin loved work and absorbed it not only in his own department, but from other branches of the service.' Occupying the adjoining room to Benjamin's at the State Department, and sharing 'his confidence and friendship to an unusual extent,' Washington was able to estimate Benjamin's capacity as a public official and 'weigh and appreciate his many personal gifts and admirable qualities.'

'A man of society, his tact in personal intercourse was unfailing; his politeness, invariable,' Washington asserted. There would have been strong dissent to this statement from Joe Johnston, Beauregard, and a number of other prominent Confederates, who looked on Benjamin as far from tactful. Nevertheless, he was now smoother in his personal relations than he had been while Secretary of War.

'His opinions were generally decided but courteously expressed, even when he differed most widely from others,' Washington continued. 'In his most unguarded moments I cannot recall that he ever uttered an oath or a violent expression. He was ever calm, self-poised, and master of all his resources.'

Not an early riser, Benjamin would arrive at the State Department about 9 A.M., and remain until 3 P.M. unless some special work required him to stay longer.[10] But this was not usually the case. He dispatched his business rapidly and would permit no work to lie over or accumulate. It was such habits that helped to make him so useful to the hard-pressed and overwrought Jefferson Davis.

From the State Department Benjamin would often go to the adjacent offices of the President, where he worked with Davis for long hours. During the earlier period of his incumbency in the State Department the pressure of work was probably not so severe as in the months preceding the capture of Richmond. But Mrs. Davis has vividly described the burden under which he labored.

Mr. Benjamin was always ready for work, sometimes with half an hour's recess he remained with the executive from ten in the morning until nine at night and together they traversed all the difficulties which encompassed our beleaguered land . . . Both the President and the Secretary of State worked like galley slaves early and late.

The pace was too severe for Davis, and his wife stated that he 'came home fasting, a mere mass of throbbing nerves, and perfectly exhausted.' But Benjamin 'was always fresh and buoyant.'

Curious to know how the Secretary could hold up under such a physical strain, Mrs. Davis once asked him for an explanation.

'I always carry to these long cabinet meetings a small cake which I eat when I begin to feel fatigued, and it freshens me up at once,' Benjamin answered. It was an interesting explanation but did not take into account either his remarkable physical endurance or the calm temperament which helped so much to prevent nervous exhaustion.

There was one striking peculiarity about Benjamin's temperament, Mrs. Davis added.

No matter what disaster befel [sic] our arms after he had done all in his power to prevent or rectify it, he was never depressed. No reverses tortured him exceedingly, as it did Mr. Davis, who though he was too reticent and self-controlled to betray his anguish suffered like one in torment. Mr. Benjamin was serenely cheerful, played games, jested and talked as wittily as usual.[11]

It was that placid temperament which led the critical John S. Wise to refer to him as caring no more for the Confederacy 'than a last years' bird's nest.' [12]

So puzzled were the President and Mrs. Davis by Benjamin's demeanor that she asked him what comfort came to him. Was he hopeful of a fortunate ending of the war?

Benjamin answered that he believed there was a fate in the destiny of nations, and it was wrong and useless to disturb oneself and thus weaken one's energy to bear what was foreordained.[13]

* * *

Absorbed with his heavy governmental responsibilities, Benjamin did not mingle often in Richmond society. While Secretary of War and now Secretary of State he had little time or inclination for social life; he enjoyed the company of a few friends from Louisiana and elsewhere but did not care for crowds or general society. It was not that he had lost his taste for good living but merely that he preferred to live quietly. At the 'comfortable' house which he and Jules had 'set up' on West Main Street they entertained their friends 'in as elegant a manner as blockaded *bon vivants* could do,' Mrs. Davis wrote.[14]

There were some social functions that Benjamin doubtless attended whether from policy or inclination—for example, the dinner which Lewis Harvie, President of the Richmond and Danville Railroad, gave at 'Dykeland' in Amelia County for Jefferson Davis and the cabinet.[15] And he also dropped in at a number of other well-known homes.

The charming Constance Cary (Mrs. Burton Harrison) recalled seeing Benjamin at a reception at the Semmes's. 'The drawing rooms were crowded with smart people, the President and Mrs. Davis, Mr. Benjamin, the silver-tongued Secretary of State, Mr. and Mrs. Mallory and their sparkling little Ruby with all the high world of the government.'[16]

Another place where he might be found was Mrs. Robert C. Stanard's, the nearest approach in Richmond to a salon. Mrs. Stanard gave delightful teas and dinners, collecting many of the brightest luminaries in the Confederate civil and military administration. At her home one could meet Pierre Soulé, Judge Campbell, Wade Hampton, John B. Gordon, Alexander H. Stephens, and Benjamin, as well as 'the most polished and promising youth of the war,' and 'the best of her own sex that the tact and experience' of Mrs. Stanard could select. Here Benjamin brought 'his charming stories, his dramatic recitation of scraps of verse, and clever comments on men, women, and books.'[17]

There is a characteristic story told of Benjamin, apparently during this period. At a dance he attended, there was 'a very modest quiet girl, by no means pretty, and quite uninteresting,' who during the course of the party, suddenly discovered that her dress was too decolleté, and retired into a corner, unwilling to dance under such circumstances. While she was there, Benjamin happened to pass by and, noticing her predicament, stopped and sat down by her, though he had rarely spoken to her before.

After a little desultory ballroom talk, he said, 'How very well you are dressed. I could not suggest any improvement in your costume.'

The young girl brightened up. And, so the story goes, Benjamin took some 'grist to her mill' in the form of dancing partners.[18]

Again, one of his favorite recreations in Richmond was gambling. When he fled from the city in 1865, he left a cribbage board at his West Main Street house,[19] which may have been used occasionally for this purpose. In all likelihood, however, he indulged oftener in the commoner forms of gambling, and frequented one or more of the gambling establishments that now flourished in the capital.

Although the Richmond newspapers had continued to inveigh against gambling, Benjamin and others of like mind still enjoyed their private games. Thus on 3 January 1863 the *Examiner* launched forth with a crusading editorial against 'the gamblers of Richmond' who had 'multiplied as the lice of Egypt.' Only a few months before 'a virtuous deacon' had been captured in a gambling saloon of the city, the *Examiner* wrote, and on the same occasion 'it is said that a cabinet minister, who was in one of those inner chambers reserved for distinguished guests and sacred to the mysteries of "blue checks," effected his escape by jumping from the window.'

If Benjamin had to make his exit in such a manner, it must have been a strain upon even his good nature, not to speak of his dignity. The *Examiner* was not above retailing gossip about prominent Confederates and may have had its story on hearsay. Benjamin appears, however, to have been the member of the cabinet most addicted to gambling. Reverend Moses Hoge, a most reliable source of information, said that Benjamin secured his chief recreation at Richmond in this manner. And another reliable friend, Henry Capers, the Confederate Treasury official, wrote more specifically on the subject. In a prefatory comment he said he had never met a man whose intellect was superior to Benjamin's, and extravagantly praised his achievements in both America and England. Then Capers continued with a vivid account of Benjamin's visits to Worsham's faro bank, much frequented by the sporting element in the capital, and the extreme criticism of him as a result by the *Examiner*.[20]

There have been other accusations against Benjamin during the Richmond years which must be given more serious attention. The historian, James Ford Rhodes, wrote that he was suspected of corruption during the war, and another story to this effect has been repeated in recent years. Upon careful examination of the evidence, however, none of the charges can be definitely substantiated.[21]

Moreover, Jefferson Davis, against whom there was never any proof of dishonesty, would not have kept Benjamin in his position if he had believed that he was corrupt. And if Benjamin made money through illicit practices during the war, what did he do with it? There is nothing necessarily suspicious in the fact that he lived well during the war, for he made a relatively good salary and probably retained some of his private fortune.

Further doubt is removed when we examine certain of his private business correspondence that survived the war and subsequent misadventures. In a letter to Fraser, Trenholm, and Company of Liverpool on 27 July 1864 [22] Benjamin acknowledged receipt of their current account showing a balance against him of about £653, subject to a credit of about £96, the amount of insurance recovered on a cask of sherry bought for him. He also referred to thirty-three bales of cotton he was having shipped to Europe on his private account (part of fifty ordered from Mobile), and supposed that the thirty-three bales 'will suffice to cover the balance against me and to provide for the remittances to Mrs. Benjamin for the current year.' Confirmation of the general extent of these cotton transactions is also found in a letter which he received on 12 September 1864 from W. D. Brewer and Company, his Mobile agents. There is no proof of purchases larger than Benjamin could normally have made from legitimate funds.[23]

Many of the suspicions against him arose from the fact that he was in a public position that made him susceptible to criticism, and from his manner of living. Thus to attempt to bring the cask of sherry into lean, suffering Richmond of 1864 was to invite suspicion of corruption even more than gambling. There was an exaggerated story in the army about 'that damned Jew,' living on 'fine wines, fruits—the fat of the land,' and keeping open house in Richmond. But doubtless Benjamin felt that he was making tremendous sacrifices for the Confederacy and fully earned his little pleasures. At times he seemed so indifferent to criticism that some of his associates may have been inclined to suspect the worst. They would have been surprised by a letter he wrote Blanton Duncan:

Let me thank you for your kind offer to supply me with a part of the brandy you have bought in Charleston. I do not well know how to refuse your offer without wounding your feelings, yet I should much prefer that you would permit me to reimburse the cost of what I receive. I made no scruple of receiving the presents that you sent me previously, because they were of small pecuniary value and were regarded by me as testimonials of friendship which were cordially accepted; but a demijohn of brandy at present prices represents quite a sum of money and in my public position it makes me feel somewhat uncomfortable to accept presents of any value.

I trust you will fully appreciate my motives and will not think that requesting your permission to reimburse the cost of the brandy I am actuated by any but the kindest feelings towards yourself.[24]

It should be added that Benjamin's bitterest opponents could not offer positive proof of corruption in his administration of his cabinet posts—the State Department any more than the War Department and the Department of Justice. In this respect they were in refreshing contrast to some offices in the Union Government. Benjamin's business associates and employees throughout life were superior men in character as well as ability. How he could deal with a subordinate in whom he lacked confidence is shown by the following letter to Quartermaster-General Myers, written when Benjamin was Secretary of War. For some reason the letter does not appear in the printed war records.

You are requested to assign Captain —— Asst. Quartermaster at New Orleans to some other post where he will have no other contracts to make, supplies to purchase or money to spend.

Assign some other officer of your Bureau in whom you have full reliance for duty at New Orleans.[25]

But let us return to the life in Richmond during the wartime. The winter of 1862-3 had been slow to depart and as late as 20 March 1863 Benjamin awoke to find the snow six inches deep on the ground and still falling fast. All that morning Hood's division filed through Main Street near his office. Mostly Texans, these men were becoming known as Lee's prize shock troops, and he had used them in several desperate fights where only nerve and cold steel could carry the day. Soon many of them would be killed in the critical battles of the new campaign, but now they were in high spirits and merrily snowballing each other. One would not have suspected that they had slept out in the snow the night before, without tents.[26]

If all the bulwarks of the Confederacy had been as firm as Hood's men, there would have been far less danger that the Government would be overthrown. But behind the lines were only too many people who saw the war in a different light. The currency inflation, the extortionate prices for food, and all the dull suffering that comes to those who wait at home while the soldiers fight led to a serious civil disturbance in Richmond, a disturbance with ominous possibilities for the future of the Confederacy.

Entering his office at nine o'clock on the morning of 2 April 1863, Benjamin could have seen from his rear window a motley crowd, chiefly women of the poorer class, moving out of the Capitol grounds. Early that day a few hundred of them had gathered there, grumbling that they were hungry and must have food. Now, with their number swelled to over a thousand, they were marching out of the western gates of the Square, down Ninth Street, and across Main in the direction of Cary.

As they walked they continued to gain recruits at every step until they were a truly formidable array; but so far they preserved reasonable silence and order.

Asked by the ubiquitous J. B. Jones where the crowd was going, a young woman, 'seemingly emaciated but yet with a smile,' answered that they were going to find something to eat.

And this they did. Entering the stores of the 'speculators' on Cary Street, they proceeded to empty them of meal, flour, shoes, and anything else they wanted. Then, growing bolder, they turned back into Main Street near the State Department, and, breaking open shops, began to pillage them of silk, jewelry, and other luxuries. For some time there was no halting the rioters. Then the militia appeared and threatened to fire.

But just at the critical moment Jefferson Davis arrived. Deeply moved, he mounted a dray and succeeded in persuading the rioters to disperse. He was willing to share his last loaf with the suffering people, he said. But he urged them to bear their privations with fortitude and thus remain united against the Northern invaders who were the authors of all their sufferings. Thus by a narrow margin the riot was ended without bloodshed and, perhaps, serious repercussions among other suffering people of the Confederacy.

Was Benjamin reminded of the 'March of the Women,' which ushered in so many terrible events of the French Revolution? For not only the conduct of the mob but, if we may believe the newspaper accounts, the very appearance of their ringleaders was not unlike that of the fish wives and market-women who had brought the French royal family back from Versailles to Paris.

Thus Minerva Meredith, a leader of the rioters, was described in connection with a pardon application, granted by Governor Letcher, as a poor illiterate woman and a grandmother. But the *Whig* and *Examiner* depicted her as a 'virago, full six feet tall, raw-boned and muscular.' And Mrs. Mary Jackson, another of the ringleaders, was 'an athletic woman of forty, with straight features and a vixenish eye.' She wore a silk dress, plaid shawl, man's bonnet with a long cape, and shortly before the riot was seen with a six-shooter pistol and a bowie knife. It was she who said that the women were determined to have bread or blood and to shoot down every man who attempted to interfere with them.

The *Whig*, co-operating with the local authorities in the effort to minimize the affair, asserted that the 'petticoated foray' was political in origin. There had been fewer applications for charity that winter than in any one for many years. The writer of the article had encountered but two beggars during the winter, one an 'obvious imposter' while the other 'set upon him with the stunning petition for a "quarter to buy a catechism." '

Characteristically, Benjamin made no mention of the event in his diary. We do not know if he used his influence to help secure the generous treatment that was accorded the rioters, but an incident that occurred a few days after the outbreak may throw some light on the attitude toward him of some malcontents in the city.

A surgeon was arrested for saying there was 'a power behind the throne greater than the throne.' Summoned into court before Mayor Mayo, and asked to what power he referred, he answered, 'the people,' and was released. But had he really meant Benjamin? [27]

Whether or not the recent civil disturbance affected his condition, by 17 April Jefferson Davis was described as 'very feeble and
nervous,' and 'really threatened with the loss of sight altogether.' [28]
But he labored on, and Benjamin was his usual bulwark of strength.
Fortunately, the Administration could still count on the loyal support of the great majority of the white population, and in the rare
cases when a slave showed bumptious tendencies he was quickly
put in his place.

For instance, there was Henry, a slave hired by James Quin, a res-
taurant keeper on Main Street. 'Found out in the street, after hours,
smoking a cigar and carrying a cane, and having no pass,' Henry
was hailed before the Mayor's Court, given ten lashes for his 'night's
promenade,' and sent back to his master.[29]

As a sign of the times it may be noted that in August 1863—a
month after Gettysburg—J. B. Jones was complaining of the high
prices in Richmond. Sugar was selling for $2 a pound and it had
been more than a year since the Jones family had had coffee or
tea. He had not even seen a rat or mouse for months, and lean cats
were 'wandering past every day in quest of new homes.' Some little
good, however, can usually be found in any form of misery, and
temperance advocates could soon rejoice that corn whiskey was selling at $20 to $25 a gallon, rye whiskey at $38 to $40, and apple
brandy at $25 to $30.[30] With liquor selling at such prices it might
indeed seem that there would be less drinking in the army, but
apparently the soldiers still secured their whiskey one way or another. Benjamin's efforts when Secretary of War to curb this evil
had not stood the strain of wartime.

*   *   *

Among Benjamin's friends in Richmond during the latter part of
the war was Francis Lawley, the Richmond correspondent of the
London *Times*.[31] A son of Lord Wenlock and with influential English connections, he became devoted to Benjamin, who doubtless
helped to color his vivid dispatches with a sympathetic attitude towards the Confederacy. In the spring of 1864 Grant took personal
command of the Union Army in Virginia and, with a heavily superior force, began his bludgeoning assaults on Lee's weakened but

grimly determined troops. By June Lawley was writing that 'once more have the shouts of the combatants . . . been heard in the streets of Richmond,' once more the near-by hills and valleys were 'stained with blood and ploughed by cannon balls, and the night air made hideous by the wail of the wounded and the groans of the dying.'[32]

With the future so critical for Davis and his chief ministers, did Benjamin turn more to religion? Did he now find in Judaism the faith that sustained so many of his forefathers in their hours of trial? The undeniable fact is that he was seldom among the crowds who flocked to the churches during the war. A Richmond Jew remembered his being 'called up' to the reading of the law at Beth Ahabah synagogue, but he never attended there more than a few times. Yet Benjamin did not forswear Judaism and he 'remained always a firm believer in immortality and in a personal Divinity.'[33] It appears to have been a genuine, if none too active faith.

Incidentally, he was friendly but not partial to the Jewish soldiers, of whom over 10,000 served the Confederacy, some with conspicuous bravery.[34]

Soon Grant crossed the James River and the fighting was renewed in front of Petersburg. But Benjamin, whatever his reasons for hope, was not disheartened, and, if he had been, would have derived new strength from the attitude of the Richmond people. Brave and devoted, they also, as Lawley put it, trusted in 'St. Lee as much as Mecca in Mahomet, or Spain in St. James of Campostello.' Walking on Franklin Street on a summer evening Benjamin could see on 'every porch a group of gaily-attired ladies,' could hear 'many a light laugh, many a song issuing from open casements.'[35]

For another phase of Benjamin's life during this desperate period let us turn again to the account by his friend, Mrs. Davis. Toward the end of the war, she wrote, Benjamin's

intimate friends received verbal invitations somewhat in this fashion, 'Do come to dinner or tea; we succeeded in running the blockade this week'—which meant 'real coffee' after dinner, preserved fruits, loaf sugar, good tea, and sometimes some anchovy toast, which was always acceptable to Mr. Benjamin's palate. He used to say that with bread made of Crenshaw's flour, (a noted miller of Virginia) spread with paste made of English walnuts, from an immense tree in our grounds, and a glass of McHenry Sherry, of which we had a scanty store, 'a man's patriotism became rampant.'

Once when he was invited to partake of beefsteak pie of which he was very fond, he wrote 'I have never eaten it in perfection except on the Cunard Steamers (my cook had been chef on one) and I shall enjoy the scream of the sea birds, the lashing of the sea, the blue above and the blue below, while I eat it; so you may expect me.'

Mr. Benjamin was a gourmet after the most refined and abstemious model. He ate little, but if that little happened to be coarse and badly cooked, he really suffered. He loved 'lollipops' as he called candy, like a child; and he has often been heard to declare that the absence of hors d'œuvres depressed his vitality and mentality, though when he had them he partook of them most sparingly.

. . . One day when there happened to be a prospect of our having some very good brains *en papillotte*, and afterwards some mayonnaise, we invited Mr. Benjamin to dinner. He stopped midway in a criticism upon 'Les Miserables,' of Victor Hugo, (which had just reached the Confederacy), and whispered to me—'I do not enjoy my dinner, for Jules would like these dishes so much, and he is young and values such things. I begged him to let me send some of the dinner to his house—but he declined saying, 'The papillottes would fall flat, and the salad would fade: but if I might take him some cake and lollipops, I should feel very happy.' He would not allow a servant to carry them, but took them in a parcel with a napkin, and walked home, beaming with the hope of conferring pleasure upon his beloved Jules.

On one occasion Jules, feeling that his small figure required more 'stateliness of address' than if he had been taller, protested when Benjamin showed his tender feeling toward him by some caressing words. 'You will make Mrs. Davis think that I am a child,' he said. Benjamin looked apologetically at him, and answered, 'No man ever loved his child any better, but love like ours must be founded on respect, at least mine for you.'

Throughout their visit, Benjamin, by his 'gentle deference' toward Jules, 'showed such a craving for affection, such unwillingness to offend that it almost brought tears to my eyes,' Mrs. Davis declared.[86]

To the last Benjamin continued to be one of the hardest workers in the cabinet, often toiling until past midnight. But however desperate the situation, he seldom lost his equanimity. The thin Confederate lines might be stretched almost to the breaking point, Benjamin might have been up until a late hour conferring with Jefferson Davis about one of the plans that he (Benjamin) so strongly supported to stir up civil disaffection in the North, to employ Negro soldiers, or even to emancipate the slaves in return for English recognition. Yet the next morning as he went by Dr. Hoge's on the way to his office he was 'dressed faultlessly and always with a bright, cheerful aspect.'

'There goes Mr. Benjamin, smiling as usual,' Mrs. Hoge would often comment.[37]

On 5 November Benjamin wrote a note to his landlord, Griffin Davenport, leasing his house at 9 West Main for another year. The terms of the lease, as stated in a memorandum from Davenport, were that Benjamin should pay $250 per month; there should be no ladies or children in the house, and the bed linen should be returned to the owner.[38] Ten days later Sherman began his march to the sea. And Benjamin, struggling desperately to help save the sinking Southern Government, spent only a few more months in Richmond, months when his private life was almost completely submerged in his grave public responsibilities.

XVI. *The Lost Cause*

19-20 Sept. 1863. Confederate victory at Chickamauga, Ga.

23-25 Nov. Federal victory at Chattanooga, Tenn.

May-June 1864. Lee checks Grant at the Wilderness, Spottsylvania Courthouse, and Cold Harbor, Va.

15-16 Dec. Federal victory at Nashville, Tenn.

20 Dec. Sherman captures Savannah, Ga.

9 April 1865. Lee surrenders at Appomattox Courthouse, Va.

S YMPTOMATIC of the declining fortunes of the Confederacy was a letter written by Judge Campbell, head of the Confederate Impressment Bureau, to Secretary Seddon, three weeks after Gettysburg. There was 'a great necessity,' Campbell said, 'for some practical dealing with the crime of desertion, if so general a habit [was] to be considered a crime.' From fifty to a hundred thousand soldiers were evading duty in one way or another, of whom 'probably forty or fifty thousand' were absent without leave.[1] Although the troops who stuck to their posts—and they were in a great majority—fought with dogged courage, the military situation was growing slowly but steadily worse, and it was only briefly improved by Bragg's abortive victory at Chickamauga in September. Clearly, strong measures were needed and the fact was brought home to Benjamin by severe attacks upon him in two of the leading Confederate newspapers.

On 11 August 1863 the *Charleston Mercury*, in a leading editorial spread on the front page, called attention to the crisis facing the Confederacy, and among 'the most matchless blunders' responsible for the situation listed the gross abuse of the appointing power by Jefferson Davis in 'thrusting away ability and character, and keeping dependents of favor like MALLORY, and BENJAMIN, and NORTHROP, and MYERS about him.' Then, a little over a month later, the *Richmond Enquirer* was back on the offensive, renewing its open war on Benjamin because of the retention of James Spence, the anti-slavery advocate, as a Confederate financial agent, and even renewing the old charges of Benjamin's maladministration of the War Department.[2]

Altogether, the situation must have been disturbing to Benjamin, even though he did refer philosophically to 'croakers' who were to be expected in times of disaster. In one of his rare references to the Deity, he wrote in August 1863 that 'after Providence' the army was 'our reliance' for success.

And yet many wars had been won by countries in worse condition than that of the Confederacy in late 1863. There was much that a cool and determined statesman could do—provided he had sufficient power—to achieve final victory.[3]

The Negro question, which offered a key to the situation, again bobbed up before Benjamin during August in the form of a letter from B. H. Micou, a brother of his old law partner. Micou, who owned cotton-mill interests in Alabama, was a man who believed that desperate times require desperate remedies. He now proposed that Negro soldiers be used to recruit the Southern armies.

But Benjamin did not feel that it was wise for him to express himself categorically in favor of the proposal—however much it may have appealed to him. The question of arming the slaves had awakened attention in several quarters lately, he wrote Micou. 'With many and obvious advantages,' such as Micou suggested, there were 'very grave practical difficulties in the execution of any general scheme of employing negro slaves in the army.' To begin with, the President had no authority to initiate such a scheme; and it would have to be devised and matured by Congress. Whether Congress would do so Benjamin did not know but he hastily suggested a few of the difficulties:

1st Slaves are property. If taken for public service, they must be paid for. At present rates each regiment of 1000 slaves would cost $200,000 at the very least, besides their outfit, and the Government would become a vast slave holder, and must either sell the slaves after the war, which would be a most odious proceeding after they had aided in gaining our liberties, or must free them to the great detriment of the country.

2d. If instead of buying, the Government hire them, it would stand as insurer for their return to their owners; it would be forced to pay hire for them besides the outfit and rations; and it would have to pay hire according to the value of their services on a fair estimate. Now negro men command readily $30 a month all through Virginia. How could we possibly afford such a price, and what would be the effect on the poorer classes of whites in the army, if informed that negroes were paid $30 a month, while the white man receives only $11.

3d. The collection and banding together of negro men in bodies, in the immediate neighborhood of the enemy's forces, is an experiment of which the results are far from certain. The facility which would be thus afforded for their desertion in mass might prove too severe a test for their fidelity when exposed to the arts of designing emissaries of the enemy who would be sure to find means of communicating with them.

Finally it was far from certain that the male slave population was not doing just as valuable and important service already as they could do in the army.

A nation cannot exist without labor in the field, in the workshop, in the rail-road, the canal, the high-ways, and the manufactory. In coal and iron mines, in foundries and in fortifications we could employ the total male slave population that could possibly be spared from the production of supplies for subsistence. This is the appropriate field for negro labor to which they are habituated, and which appears at first sight to be altogether less liable to objection, than to imitate our enemies by using them in military organizations.

I have not thoroughly studied the subject [Benjamin concluded], but throw out these suggestions as food for thought, although they have probably been considered by you already. On one point however I think all must agree and that is, the absolute necessity of withdrawing all male slaves from any district of country exposed to the approach of an enemy. This is a military precaution which commanders in the field may lawfully take, and to which I shall invoke the attention of the proper department.

Far from deeming your letter intrusive or improper, I see in it nothing but an evidence of patriotism and desire to serve your country, but of course I required no proof that you could entertain any other sentiments.[4]

It should be noted that Benjamin did not offer any objections to Micou's plan except on practical grounds—he was not repelled by the radical nature of the proposal. Obviously, Negroes could not be expected to fight well in the Southern armies unless it was to their advantage. Suppose the Negro soldiers were offered their freedom in event of a final Southern victory. Were they loyal enough to their masters to fight on the Southern side when they stood to win their freedom anyhow if the North won? Later Benjamin was to propose that the Negroes be offered the doubtful bait, but he now apparently felt that the plan would not only be summarily rejected by the Confederate people but would arouse a fierce antagonism that might sweep him out of the State Department.

The Negro question came to Benjamin's attention again in late 1863 through his relations with Spence, the English agent. The opposition to Spence's antislavery views finally in September 1863 caused the Government to strip him of many of his powers and finally in December was to cause his dismissal from his post. Meantime, in October Spence wrote a letter to Benjamin giving his views on emancipation. In the reply on 11 January, delayed a month by 'severe extra labor' caused by the convening of Congress, Benjamin not only thanked Spence for his efforts on behalf of the Confederacy in England but stated that 'the intemperate attacks' against him by some of the Richmond newspapers were regarded with 'pain and mortification by all just men.' Benjamin felt the criticisms 'all the more sensibly' because he was aware that they were really directed against himself, launched at Spence's expense by 'unscrupulous partisans. The liberty of the press at present degenerates into unbridled license but it is better to endure this evil than to impair the independence of a great bulwark of public liberty.'

As for Spence's opinions about emancipation, Benjamin admitted that he felt 'some embarrassment in replying' to them, but said he would be entirely frank. He freely admitted that as a private gentleman entirely unconnected with the Confederate Government Spence could not with self-respect 'conceal or color' his true sentiments on this or any other question in which principles were involved, and he confessed that Spence's opinions made his advocacy of the Southern cause more effective with people who agreed with him.

Furthermore, Benjamin said that 'as a man of the world' he would
meet Spence 'on the most cordial terms without the slightest reference' to his views on the subject, and he did not add a single word
to indicate that they were abhorrent to him. Nevertheless, he said,
it would be impossible to keep him in the service of the Department after the publication of his opinions.[5]

Not long afterwards Benjamin—was he again tied down by reasons of policy?—apparently helped to defeat a proposal originating
with several generals in Bragg's army, to enlist Negroes in the Confederate military service.[6]

* * *

As events proved, Benjamin's operations for nearly eighteen
months after Gettysburg were of no great significance. Yet before
criticizing him it is only fair to take into consideration the difficulties under which he labored. For neither the people nor the administration was ready for radical measures.

In a letter of 8 August 1863 to R. O. Hubard, who had written
to communicate his views on the proper foreign policy of the Government, Benjamin said that the operations of the Department of
State 'are and must from their very nature always be kept secret
. . . censure must be endured by every public man worthy to serve
his country, however unjust that censure may be . . .' Apparently
Benjamin wrote this statement without any idea of its publication,
but when he felt it advisable he could wield a vigorous pen in his
own defense, to say nothing of enlisting the help of various administration supporters. He is known to have contributed to the *Richmond Sentinel*, a newspaper now being recognized as the Government organ,[7] and he probably wrote or supplied material for the
able article in this newspaper on 27 September 1863 answering the
latest criticism from the *Enquirer* about the retention of Spence.

When Jefferson Davis, because of this criticism as well as complaints about the honesty and efficiency of some of his foreign
agents, decided to reorganize the Confederate financial set-up in
Europe, he ordered Benjamin to draw up the necessary plans. All
the European purchasing agents were placed under the control of
Colin J. McRae, who accomplished his task satisfactorily until the
end of the war.[8]

By two other moves also Benjamin helped to satisfy public opinion and live up to his own convictions about the proper course of action: he recalled James M. Mason from his English mission, and dismissed the remaining British consuls in the Confederacy. Writing to Mason on 4 August 1863, Benjamin said that the perusal of the recent debates in Parliament had satisfied the President that the British Government had no intention of receiving him as the Confederate minister and that his continued residence in London would be 'neither conducive to the interest nor consistent with the dignity' of the Confederacy.[9] Although Mason was retained in Europe as a special commissioner to foreign nations, his work was now of little significance.

Twenty years later Benjamin told the Paris correspondent of the *New York Tribune* that he and Davis calculated well their chances (in England), and that they were beaten by small and secret influences that reminded him of the mouse gnawing through the net in which the lion was caught. The point seems over-strained but Benjamin was at the same time quoted as reducing this anti-Southern activity to a few personal equations: the influence brought to bear on Lord Russell by G. M. Crawford of the *London Daily News* through Sir John Harding, then Queen's Advocate; T. B. Potter, 'a worse opponent than Mr. Cobden because he had then health and wealth, and would stop at nothing'; Thomas Walker, then editor of the *Daily News;* and Edward Pigott, the foreign editor. Benjamin's London agent and later Benjamin did their best to get around the last two gentlemen. They did win over a millionaire who had an interest in the *News*, and Benjamin wrote an article that the financier copied and sent as his own to Walker for publication; but Walker, a man of high and independent spirit, refused to publish it on the ground that it was not in keeping with the policy adopted by his paper.

Benjamin declared that if England had refused to recognize the blockade, France would have gone with her and the North must have yielded.

Moreover, he was 'greatly amused' at the credit Thurlow Weed, who served as one of Lincoln's European agents, gave himself for having influenced Napoleon's minister, the Duke de Morny, 'by appeals to national feeling and other such sentiments.'

Morny only understood Bourse considerations. He was cold-headed and cold-blooded, and fond of luxury as a King Charles dog. Slidell's daughters would have been invaluable at the Tuileries had England refused to recognize the blockade and the Emperor followed suit. Louis Napoleon was completely with the South. He used to go to the meetings of the Confederate Committee, which were held at the Tete Noire tavern at St. Cloud twice a week, when the Court was in the neighborhood. To attract him some comical persons used to be invited whose business it was to deal in a sort of conversation which is euphemistically termed here *gauloise*.[10]

In addition to terminating the Confederate mission to England, Benjamin within the next few months evicted the remaining British consular agents in the South. Moreover, when so doing he took in early October 1863 another action that, in the words of one informed commentator, 'no other man in the Confederacy would have dared' to take, an action for which there have been few precedents or examples in history. While Jefferson Davis was on the way to Tennessee to try to settle a quarrel between Bragg and some of his generals, Benjamin called a meeting of the cabinet on his own responsibility. After he had brought the matter before them, they decided by 'unhesitating and unanimous action' to expel all the remaining British consular representatives still in the Confederacy. Robert Lansing, Secretary of State under Woodrow Wilson, was to convene several cabinet meetings in the absence of the President and without his sanction. Yet Lansing's action met with a rebuff, whereas Benjamin quickly secured an approval by telegraph from Jefferson Davis. And that despite Davis's usual touchiness regarding any efforts to restrict his authority.[11]

* * *

John Slidell was retained at Paris after the withdrawal of Mason from London, but Benjamin now saw little chance of French recognition of the Confederacy. On 4 August 1863 [12] he vainly wrote Slidell to ask if it would be practicable to sell directly to the French Government some eight million dollars' worth of cotton, available in the South at eight to ten cents a pound. He continued to communicate with Slidell at intervals until near the end of the war, but the correspondence is of little value except for its revelation of Benjamin's lack of faith in Louis Napoleon, the oscillations of his hopes and fears regarding Confederate success, and details of the departmental routine.

During late 1863 and early 1864 Benjamin also devoted considerable efforts to a number of diplomatic side issues, including one that was now closely connected with his French diplomacy—his relations with Mexico. The story of the Confederate relations with Mexico goes back to May 1861, when Secretary Toombs sent John T. Pickett, a former United States consul at Vera Cruz, as an agent to that country. Pickett was better fitted, however, to be a soldier or a filibuster than a diplomat; he revealed his attitude toward his mission when he wrote that, 'a million or so of money judiciously applied' would purchase Mexican recognition of the Confederacy. 'The Mexicans are not over-scrupulous, and it is not our mission to mend their morals at this precise period.' [13]

In Mexico Pickett became better known for a personal affray, which caused him to be incarcerated in a local jail, and for other misadventures than for any positive help he rendered the Confederacy. He was faced with serious difficulties in any case because of Mexican suspicions arising from earlier imperialistic designs of Southern leaders, the clever diplomacy of the Northern Government, and the interception of much of his correspondence with Richmond. Attaching little importance for some time to Mexican relations, however, Benjamin was not disturbed by Pickett's failure and did little about Mexico beyond maintaining him and a few minor agents there.[14]

But early in January 1864, after the Archduke Maximilian of Austria had been made the puppet emperor of a French-supported government in Mexico, Benjamin saw an opportunity for effective diplomacy there. The Confederate Government now appointed William Preston of Kentucky, former American minister to Spain, as envoy extraordinary and minister plenipotentiary to Mexico, with authority to sign a treaty upon matters of interest to the Confederate and the Mexican Governments. In an accompanying dispatch to Preston, Benjamin not only gave him general instructions but outlined some of the difficulties he would have to face.

Bitterly Benjamin wrote that Seward would 'know no scruples

. . . would hesitate at no promises and even offer an alliance with the United States in order to secure the rejection of the Confederate overtures.' In order to overcome this diplomacy and to secure the Confederate aims, Preston was to endeavor to convince the Mexican Government not only that the United States planned to annex Mexico but that they now cloaked their purpose under the theory of 'one war at a time.' Benjamin likewise referred to the denunciation in the Northern press of the recent change in the Mexican Government, and the resolution offered in the United States Senate to declare war on France because of her violation of the Monroe Doctrine.

Of course, Benjamin's plans meant that the Confederacy was willing to repudiate the Monroe Doctrine in this instance, but he was playing for what to his sorely pressed Government seemed a more important stake. Yet the Preston mission failed. Maximilian, at first receptive to the Confederate overtures, soon turned a deaf ear, apparently because of pressure from Louis Napoleon.[15]

Another of Benjamin's diplomatic efforts during this period was the attempt to curb the enlistment of Irish volunteers for the Union army. By the middle of 1863 perhaps 75,000 Irishmen had enlisted, all in what he considered flagrant disregard of British neutrality (and this was not to mention the German and other foreign recruits). On 3 July 1863, therefore, he appointed Lieutenant J. L. Capston, C.S.A., special agent to proceed to Ireland and 'by strictly legitimate' methods to combat the work of the Northern agents. Capston was to explain to the Irish that if they joined the Union army they would have to meet in battle other Irishmen and perhaps kinsmen in a quarrel which did not concern them. And he was to contrast the former treatment of foreigners in the North and in the South, particularly during the Know-Nothing movement, which, based 'on hatred to foreigners and especially to Catholics,' was 'triumphant' in the North but 'crushed' in the South.[16]

Two months later Benjamin also sent a Catholic priest, Father John Bannon, to Ireland with similar instructions to those given Capston. But neither of the two agents had much success, 'the poor naive but combative Irish peasants [being almost willing to sell their souls] for a thousand years extra service in purgatory' for the $500 enlistment bounty from the United States Government.[17]

It was of little avail to send Dudley Mann to Rome in the hope that Pope Pius IX would curb the flow of Catholic recruits. The Pope was impressed with Mann's statements about the decoying of 'innocent Irishmen from their homes to be murdered in cold blood,' although he said that it might be judicious for the Confederacy to consent to gradual emancipation.[18] But Benjamin was hardly surprised when the interview proved abortive, for he was now attaching slight importance to such ventures. It would not be long before he would concentrate his chief efforts outside the Confederacy on Secret Service operations in Canada and the North, operations in which he had already become the key man under Davis.

* * *

Shortly after Lee's surrender Edward Frazor of St. Louis, a Confederate secret agent, confessed that in the summer of 1864 he had been introduced to Benjamin. 'He asked me if I knew all these claims for destroying U. S. property were right and correct,' said Frazor. 'I told him they were, as far as I knew. He then offered $30,000 in greenbacks to settle. I told him I could not take that. Then he said he would take time to study again.'

There was some dickering and the matter was settled for $35,000 in gold and $15,000 to be paid in four months, provided certain claims for burning Federal medical stores in Louisville the previous year 'were all right.'

Shortly afterwards Frazor went with Benjamin to see Jefferson Davis and Davis discussed with the agent a plan to destroy the 'long bridge' near Nashville. 'Benjamin said the pay would be $400,000 for burning the bridge. After we got all ready to leave Mr. Benjamin gave us a draft for $34,800 in gold on Columbia, S. C.'

Thus Frazor, 'probably weary of imprisonment' and hoping for a reprieve from his Northern captors, presented one silhouette of this phase of Benjamin's work in the latter part of the war. Even though 'no more reticent man ever lived where it was possible to be silent,' we can piece together a good deal of information about Benjamin's Secret Service operations—a few of the private, closely guarded conferences in Richmond with their dramatic conspirational elements, as well as the more obvious activities. And we can sketch a general picture of the results even though there is never a plethora of evidence, particularly for the minor activities.

In the case just cited, Edward Frazor was one of a group of men arrested near the end of the war for destroying Northern shipping and other property. Largely through the confession of Frazor and another man, who admitted that they were originally paid by Benjamin, we learn that the conspirators burned in September 1863 some ten or fifteen boats on the Mississippi River and then or later a number of buildings in the Northern states; and that they were probably responsible for the loss of a large proportion of the seventy or more steamboats, owned at St. Louis, which had been destroyed by fire during the war.[19] Small-time work it seems for a man in Benjamin's position, but the war was reaching such a desperate stage that he had to grasp what opportunities were available.

Again, in Benjamin's miscellaneous correspondence for January 1864 there is a letter from L. E. Orris suggesting that it would be worthwhile for him to get in touch with ex-President Pierce. There is no proof that the Confederate agents in Canada or the North actually attempted to contact Pierce. Yet the Orris letter opens up an interesting speculation on just how many Northern political leaders had surreptitious contacts with the Confederate Government, particularly since two of the agents, Clement Clay and Jacob Thompson, were later in touch with a considerable number of Northern men.[20]

Another phase of Benjamin's work was to secure intelligence reports on various sections of the Confederacy. Thus in a letter of 31 July 1864 from Duncan Kenner, and another, six weeks later, from C. M. Conrad, who enclosed a letter from E. Warren Moïse, Benjamin got a dismal picture of the military situation in western Louisiana. 'Want of shoes, want of hats, want of ammunition [sic], want of everything—except want of will and want of capacity will be alleged' as responsible for the inactivity there, Benjamin was informed.[21]

Imagine his private comments when he read, also in the Moïse letter, that the commanding general in the area, Kirby Smith, had been in Texas 'nursing his wife who has been introducing a new "Smith" into the world as if Smiths new or old were very remarkable things.' For more than two months a force of over thirty thou-

sand men had been kept in entire inactivity, while the armies of
Stephen Lee and Joseph E. Johnston were sorely pressed on the
other side of the river, one letter continued. Kirby Smith was an
able General but in this case Benjamin was informed that he could
not be induced to make any move, although General Lee had informed him that Canby was marching on Mobile with twenty thousand men and sent dispatch after dispatch urging his co-operation.
The endorsement on the back of these letters shows that copies
were referred by Benjamin to Jefferson Davis.[22]

* * *

The most important Secret Service operations in which Benjamin
was engaged during the entire war were those directed by his agents
working out of Canada in conjunction with disaffected elements in
the Northern states. As early as 9 November 1863 Colonel B. H.
Hill, a Northern officer at Detroit, had reported the rumors reaching his ears of plans by Confederate refugees in Canada for the
temporary occupation of the 'northern lakes,' the release of Southern prisoners at Johnson's Island and Chicago, and the seizure of
the steamer *Michigan*. At first Colonel Hill had not paid much attention to the rumors, but now he said that agents had arrived at
Windsor, Ontario, with certificates of deposit for over $100,000 and
a letter of recommendation from Benjamin.[23] The Lincoln government had as yet learned little about the operations that the Confederates were planning from their Canadian bases, but a dangerous
conspiracy was being hatched. With effective co-operation from
the Northern anti-war Democrats, it might prove more effective
than anything Benjamin could now expect from his diplomatic
negotiations.

For the direction of the Canadian work, a discreet and energetic
leader was needed, and on 25 March 1864 Benjamin's old Whig
friend, A. H. H. Stuart, the former Secretary of the Interior, received a letter from Benjamin requesting him to come to Richmond
and confer with him and the President on a subject 'too delicate for
correspondence.' Arriving at the State Department, Stuart was received cordially by Benjamin and informed that the President and

himself had agreed upon his appointment as a Commissioner of the Confederate States.

The plan was for him to proceed via Nassau to Canada, where, according to Stuart,

I should have a sort of diplomatic family or court, the mission of which, by means of a secret service, would be to foster and give direct aid to a peace sentiment which it was understood was then active along the Border States, and particularly to give aid to a peace organization known as the 'Knights of the Golden Circle,' which flourished in the Northwestern States. I was to have a large amount of money at my disposal, Congress having placed a deposit of 3,000,000 pounds in London on which I could draw; and I was to be held to no accountability for the money except my certificate upon my honor that it had been spent in aid of the mission on which I had been sent. I was to have a Secretary and other officials under me on the Commission.

Mr. Benjamin spoke with freedom and fullness of the scheme, and I soon found that he was laboring under a remarkable delusion as to the peace sentiment in the North, as well as the probable efficiency of such a Commission as he proposed.

And Stuart immediately declined the appointment on the ground of pressing family obligations.[24]

Benjamin does appear to have been unduly encouraged about the strength of the Northern peace movement. The anti-war elements, 'mighty in speech and pen,' were less influential than they seemed. Even in the darkest periods of the war Lincoln had the steadfast support of the great body of plain people in the North. Yet when Benjamin talked with Stuart there was much war weariness and discontent there, and it increased considerably after the bloody Union reverses in May and June. By midsummer the Sons of Liberty, another secret organization opposed to the Lincoln government, had several hundred thousand members, chiefly in Indiana, Illinois, Ohio, Kentucky, Missouri, Michigan, and New York. With the main Confederate armies still fighting strongly in both the East and West and the Union casualties reaching heart-rending proportions, there was considerable hope that the Democrats would carry several Northern states, if not the presidential election. And the Northern Democrats might offer peace even though the great majority of them did balk at other overt aid to the Confederacy.[25]

Over-optimistic as he was, Benjamin did have even in the spring of 1863 substantial reasons for fomenting the disaffection in the North. After Stuart's refusal to go to Canada and direct the work, the appointment was given to two commissioners, Clement Clay and Jacob Thompson, Secretary of the Interior under Buchanan.

In view of the later activities of some of the Confederate agents operating from Canada—including the wild effort to burn New York City—the instructions Clay and Thompson received from Davis and Benjamin before they left Richmond are significant. In their letter of appointment from the President they were merely directed to proceed at once to Canada and to carry out such instructions as they had received from him 'verbally, in such manner as shall seem most likely to conduce to the furtherance of the interests of the Confederate States of America which have been entrusted to you.' [26] Benjamin also wrote Slidell that they had sent Clay and Thompson 'to Canada on secret service in the hope of aiding the disruption between the Eastern and Western States in the approaching election at the North. It is supposed that much good can be done by the purchase of some of the principal presses, especially in the Northwest.' [27]

Obviously, it is important to know what were the secret instructions given the two commissioners, but on this point we have only the testimony of L. Q. Washington. He said that he was present at the confidential meeting of Davis and Benjamin with Clay and Thompson, at which they were given their directions, and that they were not ordered to do anything 'which was not in accord with the accepted methods of civilized warfare.' [28]

In Canada Clay and Thompson directed the work of a number of ex-Confederate soldiers and other agents, some of whom had been dispatched from Richmond. One of these agents, Lieutenant John W. Headley, who assisted in the effort to burn New York and other desperate ventures, later wrote a valuable account of his experiences, but almost his only mention of Benjamin was that after a conference in Richmond with Davis and Seddon he and another soldier, Colonel Robert Martin, set out for Canada with a letter written by the Secretary of State to Jacob Thompson introducing them and cautiously stating their mission.[29]

Arriving in Canada, Thompson and Clay proceeded to secure information regarding the Sons of Liberty, then the most active of the secret organizations in the North opposing the Lincoln government. For the great majority of the members its objects were, they found, restricted to such efforts as combating the draft, curtailing enlistments, resisting arbitrary arrests, and fighting the re-election of President Lincoln. But there was also a secret group within the organization whose plans, known only to a few leaders, called for the seizing of arsenals, releasing and arming of Confederate prisoners, and forming a Northwest Confederacy which would force the termination of hostilities.

Thompson, who became the real leader of the mission, got in touch with Clement L. Vallandigham, the violent anti-war Democrat now at the head of the Sons of Liberty, and hinted that he would supply money to be used in establishing the Northwest Confederacy. But Vallandigham would not accept this proffered aid. Furthermore, Thompson learned from others that 20 July 1864, fixed as the date for an uprising, had been changed to 16 August. This postponement, Thompson wrote Benjamin, had been insisted upon on the ground that it was necessary to have a series of public meetings to prepare the public mind. But could it be true that the influence of the Sons of Liberty had been overrated, that it could be counted on for little more than secret mummery and noisy agitation?

In any event, the first meeting was held at Peoria, Illinois, and, Thompson wrote, after he had supplied the necessary money, it proved to be 'a decided success; the vast multitudes who attended seemed to be swayed but by one leading idea—peace.' But in the meantime the correspondence had been published in regard to a meeting which had been held between Horace Greeley and the Confederate commissioners in Canada, and this with an accompanying manifesto by Lincoln led to a considerable feeling in the North that the South would agree to a reconstruction. Some of the politicians in the Sons of Liberty now felt that McClellan, the Democratic candidate in the November election, could be elected, and argued that this should be tried before any resort to force. After this plan was advanced the movement in the Northwest soon languished.[30]

But Thompson also attempted a few more dangerous projects. Following Benjamin's suggestions, so far as then practicable, he began soon after his arrival in Canada to urge the people of the North to convert their paper money into gold and withdraw it from the market. Thompson was satisfied that his efforts had some success: partly, it seems, for this reason gold rose to 290; but it later fell heavily. He also gave John Porterfield, a former Nashville banker, $100,000, with which he proceeded to New York City to carry out a financial operation which he had devised, consisting of 'the purchase of gold and exporting the same, selling it for sterling bills of exchange, and then again converting his exchange into gold.'

By this policy, Thompson asserted, Porterfield caused the shipment of more than $2,000,000 in gold at an expense of less than $10,000. Unhappily, however, one of his former business partners was arrested and he felt it prudent to return to Canada. Other funds were also advanced through Thompson to Benjamin P. Churchill of Cincinnati to organize a corps for incendiarism in that city, but this project proved abortive.[31]

Thompson likewise wrote Benjamin that before the arrival of Colonel Martin and Lieutenant Headley, bringing an unsigned note from Benjamin, all the different places where Confederate prisoners were confined—Camp Douglas, Rock Island, Camp Morton, Camp Chase, Elmira—had been thoroughly examined and they were forced to conclude that any efforts at forcible deliveries would be disastrous. One of Thompson's daring agents, however, Captain T. Henry Hines, was permitted to attempt the release of the prisoners at Camp Douglas, but was defeated by 'treachery' and the vigilance of the Northern authorities. Thompson's agents also failed in a reckless effort to capture the revenue cutter *Michigan*, the only armed American ship on the Great Lakes, but succeeded in a raid during October on St. Albans, Vermont, though some of the men were later captured and imprisoned in Canada.[32]

While the Confederate raiders were in St. Albans, they ran up and down the main street firing their pistols and crying out that they would burn the town as Sheridan had done in the Shenandoah Valley and Sherman in Atlanta.[33] In an editorial in the Richmond *Sentinel*, which Benjamin may have written or inspired, there had been allusions to the barbarous methods of warfare being employed by the North and an intimation that, at least to a certain extent, it was now necessary to fight fire with fire.[34] 'We may expect . . . the black flag. Let us take care to be in the right, and at the same time to shrink from no duty.

Other indirect evidence also indicates that Benjamin, embittered and desperate at the result of the long and now ferocious war, might be ready to employ some of the tactics being used by Sheridan and Sherman.[35] The next important operation, however, which Thompson's agents attempted—the burning of New York City—was initiated without any known orders from Benjamin. In his report, Thompson stated that 'having nothing else on hand, Colonel Martin expressed the wish to organize a corps to burn New York City . . . [and] was allowed to do so.' [36]

Martin and his fellow-conspirators proceeded to New York where they got in touch with some of the leading Southern sympathizers. Then on the night of 25 November—after Sherman had begun his ruthless march to the sea, cutting a destructive swath across one of the richest areas in the South—the Confederates set fires in quick succession at Barnum's Museum and about a dozen hotels. But owing to the faulty combustion of the 'Greek fire' that was used and the exertions of the local firemen, the blazes were easily extinguished. The great plot to burn New York had been badly bungled.[37]

Meantime, Benjamin was having great difficulty in effecting any quick communication with Thompson because of the activities of Northern counter-agents. One means of keeping in touch was the use of Personals published under assumed names in the pro-Southern *New York News*.[38] Now thwarted in all his major activities, Thompson wrote Benjamin in January 1865 that he inferred from his Personal in the *News* that the Secretary wanted him to remain in Canada for the present and that he would obey the orders. 'Indeed I have so many papers in my possession,' he continued, 'which in the hands of the enemy would utterly ruin and destroy very many of the prominent men in the North, that a due sense of my obligations to them will force on me the extremest caution in my movements.' [39] Not long afterwards Thompson and Clay (whose work had been curtailed by ill health) started back for the

South. On 3 December 1864 they had spent some $300,000 in their various operations, and held drafts for an equal amount that they had not collected.[40] In view of the serious plight of the Confederacy at the time, Davis and Benjamin were justified in sending them on the mission. But as events proved it had little more than a nuisance value.

* * *

As the terrible effects of the long war were felt more and more deeply in the South, Benjamin, as the chief adviser to Davis, became the target for increasingly bitter assaults from the newspapers and politicians in the Confederacy.[41] One of the loudest of his opponents continued to be the Confederate Senator, Henry S. Foote. Although not a bad-hearted man in many ways, Foote hated Davis venomously and during the last part of the war took delight in attacking and ridiculing Benjamin, whom he labeled the 'unprincipled minister of an unprincipled tyrant.' [42] In January 1864 a majority of the Senate Judiciary Committee had reported a bill vacating the offices of all the members of the cabinet at the expiration of every two years or of every Congress, but it did not pass.[43]

On 12 October a radical editorial appeared in the *Sentinel*. Probably influenced by Benjamin, it wrote that the South

would sooner sacrifice slavery a thousand times than to be conquered by the Yankees and have it sacrificed by them. If it becomes necessary we can enlist the negro element on our side. We can make all the offers that the Yankees can, and some that they cannot.

Other editorials in somewhat similar vein followed on 14 and 24 November—after Lincoln had been re-elected and Sherman was marching to the sea. In the latter editorial the *Sentinel* flatly advocated the arming of the slaves in case General Lee and the other military authorities felt it was necessary for Southern success. The Negroes who fought in the ranks were to be given their freedom at the end of the war. For it was not a case, the *Sentinel* said, where the Confederate people could cling to pre-conceived notions and prejudices about slavery. If they did not arm the Negroes to fill their depleted ranks, they were likely to lose their independence, and no sacrifice was too great to keep them from getting under the Yankee yoke.

Simultaneously with the appearance of these editorials the Confederate Congress had assembled on 7 November, and Jefferson Davis, reputedly at Benjamin's suggestion, recommended the employment of 40,000 slaves in the army but not to be used as soldiers except in the last extremity; after the war they were to be emancipated.[44] It was an opening wedge for the use of large numbers of Negro troops in the Confederate ranks—that is (and here was always the rub), if they could be relied on to fight for the Southern cause.

As might have been expected, leadership was sharply divided on the desperate proposal. General Howell Cobb, Senators Hunter and Wigfall, Congressmen Foote and Chambers, and Governor Joe Brown forcibly stated their objections, as did the Charleston *Mercury*.[45] But General Lee, Governor Smith of Virginia, Senator Brown, and Benjamin argued ably for the measure on the ground of military necessity. In a letter on 21 December to his old collegemate Frederick Porcher of Charleston, who had written him primarily to urge the arming of the slaves, Benjamin indicated that President Davis was only waiting for public opinion to ripen on the subject. Moreover, in deprecating another of Porcher's suggestions—that the Administration assume extra-constitutional power—he made the following proposal:

If the Constitution is not to be our guide I would prefer to see it suppressed by a revolution which should declare a dictatorship during the War, after the manner of ancient Rome, leaving to the future the care of re-establishing firm and regular government.[46]

It goes without saying that Benjamin would have preferred Davis for dictator, not Lee or any other prominent Confederate.

Early in February 1865, the Confederate peace commissioners, Judge Campbell, Alexander H. Stephens, and R. M. T. Hunter, returned from their unsuccessful meeting with Lincoln and Seward at Fortress Monroe.[47] A mass meeting was then held in the African Church at Richmond on 9 February to rally the people for a further desperate effort; Benjamin made the most important speech on the fateful occasion.

The African Church, then the largest auditorium in Richmond, was frequently borrowed from its Negro members for such assemblies. There had been muttered complaints about the condition in which it had been left by the white people after some of their meetings. And now on 9 February an overflowing crowd of the still-determined Richmond officialdom and citizenry gathered for the rally at the church on lower Broad.

Certainly Benjamin felt the critical importance of his speech that February afternoon. As anticipated, he made a courageous appeal that deeply stirred his audience. Vehemently he advocated taking all the cotton and tobacco in the Confederacy and holding it as a basis for the credit of the Government. Indeed, Benjamin said, he wanted more than this:

I want all the bacon, every thing which can feed soldiers, and I want it as a free gift to the country. Talk of rights! What rights do the arrogant invaders leave you? I want another thing. War is a game that cannot be played without men. Where are the men? I am going to open my whole heart to you. Look to the trenches below Richmond. Is it not a shame that men who have sacrificed all in our defence should not be reinforced by all the means in our power? Is it any time now for antiquated patriotism to argue refusal to send them aid, be it white or black? I will now call your attention to some figures, which I wish you to seriously ponder. In 1860 the South had 1,664,000 arms-bearing men. How many men have the Yankees sent against us? In 1861, 654,000; in 1862, 740,000; in 1863, 700,000; in 1864 they called out 1,500,000. Here you have figures that they brought out 3,000,000 men against 1,664,000 Confederates, who lived at the beginning of the war to draw sword in their country's service. Our resources of white population have greatly diminished, but you had 680,000 black men of the same ages, and could Divine prophecy have told us of the fierceness of the enemy's death grapple at our throats, could we have known what we now know, that Lincoln has confessed, that without 200,000 negroes which he stole from us, he would be compelled to give up the contest, should we have entertained any doubts upon the subject? I feel that the time is rapidly coming on when the people will wonder that they ever doubted.

Then Benjamin came out flatly for the arming of the slaves:

Let us say to every negro who wishes to go into the ranks on condition of being made free, 'Go and fight—you are free.' If we impress them, they will go against us. We know that every one who could fight for his freedom has no chance. The only side that has had advantage of this element is the Yankee people, that can beat us to the end of the year in making bargains. Let us imitate them in this. I would imitate them in nothing else.[48]

Benjamin's last public speech in America was also his most radical. But by now nothing he could do would please some of his bitter opponents. Already during the preceding month the Virginia delegation to Congress had demanded the resignation of the cabinet, and James A. Seddon had resigned as Secretary of War.[49] But the cabinet member against whom the bitterest criticism was directed was Benjamin; beside all the other causes for attack upon him, he now had to bear much of the odium for the proposal to arm the slaves. On 13 February 1865, the Senate divided evenly on a resolution stating that Benjamin was 'not a wise and prudent Secretary of State, and lacked the confidence of the country.'[50] Soon afterwards, on 21 February, he wrote a letter to Davis vainly offering to resign his position if this action would rid the President of embarrassment. The text is given to show that Benjamin, despite his obvious faults, possessed noble qualities—qualities he often did not bother to reveal:

Department of State
Richmond 21 February 1865

Confidential

MY DEAR SIR

I have been recently disturbed in mind on a subject which I can no longer refrain from placing frankly before you.

It is unnecessary to remind you that I accepted office with reluctance and have retained it solely from a sense of duty. Separated from my family for nearly five years past, my eager desire to see them has been repressed by the belief that my services were not without value to you: and I knew how impossible it was for any human being to sustain the burthen now weighing on you, without zealous and cordial aid.

For some months past however I have doubted whether my withdrawal from office would not rather promote the success of your administration than deprive you of useful assistance. It has been apparent that I have been the object of concerted and incessant assault by those who are inimical to me personally, as well as by all in Congress and the press that are hostile to you. These attacks have been regarded by me with entire indifference, except as suggesting the doubt above expressed. If our affairs were in a more prosperous condition, I should tender my resignation unconditionally, confident that if found desirable it would be in my power to return to your assistance in the Legislative Department of the Government. But in the present juncture I shrink from giving Color for an instant to the suspicion of a desire to shield myself from danger or responsibility by abandonment of duty.

And he concluded with this frank proposal:

I must therefore beg you to let me know your own conclusion with entire unreserve. Will your administration be strengthened or any opposition to it disarmed by substituting another in my place in the Cabinet? If so, I will at once seek the sphere of duty above referred to, in which I know I can be serviceable in sustaining you in this great struggle. If not, I shall cheerfully continue the sacrifice of private inclination and family affection to the call of duty, at all hazards, and under all responsibilities—
I am with entire regard and respect

Your friend & obt st [51]

Benjamin was singled out unjustly by some opponents of the Administration as the chief cause of all the woes of the Confederacy. J. B. Jones wrote on 17 March that one reason alleged for the refusal of Congress to suspend the writ of habeas corpus was the continuance of Benjamin in the cabinet. But in this great crisis Davis still firmly supported his favorite. Jones, who had observed the smile disappear from Benjamin's face, noted that he was again cheerful.[52]

Meantime, Benjamin had played his last diplomatic card. In December 1864 he and Davis sent Duncan Kenner to Europe to offer emancipation of the slaves in return for recognition of the Confederacy. In a dispatch to Slidell on 27 December, which was filled with a pathetic eloquence, Benjamin hinted at the nature of Kenner's mission and requested his co-operation in any communication that he should make to Slidell orally.

After a perilous trip through the Union lines to New York City, Kenner sailed for Europe, and here, since he had no previous diplomatic experience, he preferred to move through Slidell and Mason. Slidell made an unsuccessful overture to the French Government and Kenner then went to England where Mason on 14 March had an unsuccessful interview with Lord Palmerston. The old minister listened to Mason 'with interest and attention,' but would not take any positive action.

The offer of emancipation had come too late for serious consideration.[53]

XVII. *Escape from the South*

THE weather in the early spring of 1865 was as ominous as it had been that February day three years before at the inauguration of Jefferson Davis as President of the permanent government. Again, there were sullen skies, bursting forth at intervals with gusts of rain; again, pools of water underfoot adding to the depressing dampness and heaviness.[1] It was weather calculated to increase the general feeling of impending disaster—that, even if Sherman was not already in North Carolina, Lee's army not already dangerously weakened by battle, privation, and desertion.

And yet Benjamin was as usual making the best of things. His everyday life he kept as comfortable and cheerful as possible, and at 9 West Main 'blazing fires and an absolutely immaculate interior banished surface gloom and despondency.'[2]

At the same time he was making preparations for more desperate emergencies. For several weeks before the end of March when Grant's army finally broke through Lee's thinly held lines, the Government had been quietly packing some of its most valuable archives. As if to provide funds in case of removal of the capital, treasury warrants were issued to various Confederate officials. One warrant, dated 1 April 1865, which is still in existence, was issued to Benjamin on the 'Secret Service' account. It was for $1,500 in gold, and receipt for payment was signed by C. W. Volkman, a clerk in the State Department.[3]

Was Benjamin also preparing in case it would be necessary for him to escape from the South? Issuance of the treasury warrant indicated that he may have been doing so, as did the fact that by 28 March his chief clerk, William J. Bromwell, had already been sent southward with a number of boxes and trunks of valuable papers. On 5 April Bromwell wrote Benjamin[4] from Lexington, North Carolina, that they had all been stored in Charlotte, North

Carolina: six boxes of papers belonging to the State Department, which had been marked 'W.J.B.' 'to attract as little attention as possible'; two trunks marked 'J.P.B.,' one 'G.D.,' one 'D. F. Kenner,' and one 'St. Martin.'

On 1 April General Lee, feeling that his heavily outnumbered troops could not hold out much longer, informed Jefferson Davis that he was preparing 'for the necessity of evacuating our position on the James River at once.'[5] This, of course, meant that Richmond would have to be abandoned. During the remainder of that day and the following night, Benjamin, the other cabinet ministers, and Captain Clark, Davis's chief clerk, worked feverishly, assorting papers, destroying unessential ones, and packing the others to be removed.[6]

The next day, Sunday, 2 April, Benjamin was in his office by eight o'clock and attended to numerous final details.[7] A few hours later, while all the other cabinet members were at church, a telegram arrived from General Lee announcing that he could not hold his position longer than night fall; the Government must leave Richmond before the army began retreating that evening.

Soon after eleven o'clock the train bearing Davis, Benjamin, and other officials set out for Danville. The engine could go only about ten miles an hour over the war-worn Confederate railroad and the Davis party passed a gloomy night, only partly relieved by the sunshine the next morning. Although Secretary Mallory thought that Benjamin's 'deep olive complexion had become a shade darker within the last twenty-four hours,' he said,

[Benjamin's] Epicurean philosophy was ever at command, and his hope and good humor inexhaustible. In the pleasantest of human voices he playfully called attention to the 'serious family' around him as he discussed a sandwich; and with a 'never-give-up-the-ship' sort of air, referred to other great national causes which had been redeemed from far gloomier reverses than ours.[8]

Finally, at three p.m. the next afternoon, the train arrived at Danville. For a week this city, then a quiet little village near the North Carolina border, was the capital of the dying Confederacy. The most troubled and exciting period Danville had ever known, three-quarters of a century later there were still a few aged people there with a vivid recollection of those hectic days.

An old gentleman—Joseph B. Anderson—could still describe the visit of Judah P. Benjamin to a local newspaper office. On Wednesday, 5 April, Benjamin, climbing the rickety outside stairway leading to the office of the Danville *Register*, where Anderson was employed, delivered to him a proclamation by Jefferson Davis. Penned by Benjamin on poor quality foolscap paper, the proclamation had been prepared after a round-table discussion by the cabinet of the military situation, and exhorted the people to further resistance. This document, obviously the product of desperation rather than reasoned hope, Benjamin gave to Anderson for publication in the *Register;* in so doing he did not show any anxiety, so far as Anderson noted.[9]

Benjamin secured quarters in Danville at the home of J. M. Johnston, a local banker, and shared a room with another refugee, Dr. Moses Hoge. A considerate and delightful house guest, Benjamin adapted himself to the customs of the Johnston family. Although he could easily have dallied over his bath and been too late for morning prayers, a custom with which he obviously had little experience, he made a point of attending them. He also went to church with members of the household the following Sunday, instead of staying at home or accompanying President Davis and other members of the cabinet to the services.

Equally thoughtful of his roommate, Benjamin arranged his hours of rising and retiring so as to put Dr. Hoge to the least possible inconvenience. And although he and Dr. Hoge might, in the latter's words, 'have held very different opinions on some subjects,' he never made a remark that jarred upon his companion. In their devotion to the Confederacy they were in perfect accord, and they also had many long and pleasant conversations on literary subjects— especially their favorites among the great poets. When Dr. Hoge told Benjamin that Horace was his favorite of all the Latin poets, 'because of all the ancients he was the most modern,' Benjamin laughed and said that was a terse way of expressing his own reason for the same preference.

'We had some friendly arguments about the place Tennyson would occupy in history,' Dr. Hoge related. 'He was a passionate admirer of Tennyson and I think ranked him above all the English poets, Shakespeare excepted. When I would suggest that Tennyson had never written anything equal to Comus or Il Penseroso, or L'Allegro, or to Dryden in his vigorous and masterly use of the English language, or to some of the stanzas of Childe Harold, he would always be ready with a reference to some passage of his favorite author to confute my statements. He seemed to be as familiar with literature as with law and among our public men I cannot recall a more accomplished belles lettres scholar.' [10]

With these and other seemingly trivial events, official and unofficial, the time passed while the anxious people of Danville waited for news of Lee's army. But Benjamin was not unaware of the desperate military situation. While conversing with Major Hutter, commander of the Danville arsenal, Benjamin asked him if he had been paid recently and, finding that he had not, gave him $600, the amount due him, in gold belonging to the government. The Confederate soldiers had better have the gold than the Yankees, Benjamin declared.[11]

The tidings of Lee's surrender on 9 April did not reach Danville until late the next afternoon. After learning the dread news, Benjamin returned to the Johnston home, where he found Dr. Hoge talking to the ladies. There was some general conversation during which Benjamin appeared to be as cheerful as usual; then he made a sign to Dr. Hoge, led him up to their room and closed the door.

'I did not have the heart to tell those good ladies what I have just learned,' he said. 'General Lee has surrendered and I fear the Confederate cause is lost.'

Dr. Hoge was deeply affected. As soon as he recovered his composure he asked Benjamin what he intended to do, and Benjamin replied that he would go with Davis and his cabinet to Greensboro. But beyond that he did not have anything in mind.

How would it be possible for him to escape capture, Dr. Hoge inquired, travelling as it was proposed with a company of Confederate officials of the highest rank—when the Federal troops would soon be traversing the whole country?

'I will never forget the expression of his countenance or the pitiless smile which accompanied his words when he said, "I will never be taken alive." ' [12]

There was a dangerous night trip to Greensboro, about fifty miles southward into North Carolina. Just after the train arrived there, Stoneman's Cavalry burned the bridge outside the city over which it had crossed! [13]

At Greensboro the Davis party did not receive the cordial reception they had enjoyed in Danville. For some time there had been a growing Union sentiment in the North Carolina town and to this was now added the fear of Yankee vengeance upon those who gave help to the leaders of the Confederate Government. Secretary Mallory wrote that 'this pitiful phase of human nature was a marked exception to the conduct of the [other] people upon this eventful journey.' The cabinet members, with the exception of Trenholm, who received the calculating hospitality of a prominent Greensboro citizen, were quartered in a leaky, dilapidated box car, which they dubbed the 'Cabinet Car.' But they made the best of the unpleasant situation. They drew bread and bacon from their Navy Store and foraged for eggs, flour, and coffee; Colonel Lubbock of Davis's staff helped divert the little group with some of his Texas stories; Mallory, with yarns of the Seminole Indian War, and Benjamin with his inexhaustible wit and humor.

While the presidential party was in Greensboro, there was a fateful cabinet meeting, attended also by Generals Johnston and Beauregard. The two generals are reported to have estimated that the Confederacy had only 25,000 men still in the field, the United States 350,000, and Johnston also said the Government had no credit, no arms or ammunition except that in the hands of the troops. To continue the war, he declared, would be the greatest of human crimes; and he was backed in his opinion by Breckinridge, Mallory, and Reagan.

Only Benjamin, among the cabinet members present, supported Jefferson Davis in his fanatical determination to continue fighting. He 'made a speech for war,' Joe Johnston wrote, 'much like that of Sempronius in Addison's play':

> My voice is still for war
> Gods! can a Roman senate long debate
> Which of the two to choose, slavery or death!
> No, let us arise at once, gird on our swords,
> And, at the head of our remaining troops,
> Attack the foe, break through the thick array
> Of his thronged legions, and charge home upon him.

In Greensboro Benjamin and his associates were 'relieved of one great worry.' The Confederate treasury—some $500,000—was sent ahead under guard to Charlotte, North Carolina, with the exception of about $39,000 in gold, which was removed for distribution to Johnston's army, and about $35,000 in gold reserved for the President and the members of the cabinet.[14]

The surrender of Johnston's army was now imminent. Fearing capture by the Union soldiers, the Davis party started southward on 15 April with an escort of faithful cavalrymen. It was impossible to proceed farther by train, since Stoneman's raiders had cut the tracks, and travel was further impeded by the recent heavy rains. Slowly the little procession pushed its way toward Charlotte. Jefferson Davis, his staff, and several cabinet officers rode horseback, but portly Benjamin—who declared that he would not mount a horse until forced to do so—General Cooper, George Davis, the Attorney-General, and Jules St. Martin brought up the rear of the column in an ambulance. Once, riding back in search of this rear contingent, Burton Harrison found the whole party stalled in a mud-hole in the darkness.

'I could see from afar the occasional bright glow of Benjamin's cigar,' he wrote. While his companions were 'perfectly silent, Benjamin's silvery voice was presently heard as he rhythmically intoned for their comfort verse after verse of Tennyson's "Ode on the Death of the Duke of Wellington."' As long as Benjamin remained with them his cheerfulness and adaptability to 'emergencies made him a most agreeable comrade.'[15]

A few days later the Davis party finally arrived at Charlotte. Here they found the town crowded with soldiers, including many paroled from Lee's army, and refugee officials from Richmond. 'There was a lull in everything connected with the Confederacy at this time and everyone wondered what would happen next.'[16] Benjamin, along with Jules St. Martin and Burton Harrison, found quarters at the home of Abram Weill. To one of the Weill family he presented his beautiful gold-headed cane, which he said had been on one side of him and his pistol on the other when he made his final speech in the United States Senate. Later he wrote the Weills several letters from England.[17]

At Charlotte Benjamin attended a cabinet meeting at the home

of a local citizen, where he was later remembered as sitting uncon-
cernedly in a frail mahogany chair. Just why 'it did not crash beneath him was a mystery.' [18]

Also in Charlotte Benjamin learned of the assassination of President Lincoln. Whatever he may have thought of this tragedy in
other respects, he could hardly have felt that it offered hope of
successfully continuing the war. Asked by President Davis to write,
along with each of the other cabinet members, his opinion whether
the Government should accept the terms of surrender that, they
were informed, had been drawn up by Joe Johnston and Sherman,
Benjamin expressed himself in favor of accepting them. In one of the
last papers he ever wrote for the dying Confederacy, he sadly called
attention to the fact that Lee's army was irretrievably lost, Johnston's dissolving, and that the struggle could not be maintained
except by guerrilla warfare, which 'would entail far more suffering
on our own people than it would cause damage to the enemy.' [19]

But Jefferson Davis had a desperate plan for re-establishing the
Confederacy west of the Mississippi,[20] and the party resumed their
flight southward. During the course of the journey, Davis, Breckinridge, Benjamin, and the other cabinet and staff members mingled
and talked freely with their military escort, and this had an excellent effect upon the men. George Davis had left the party in Charlotte, and Trenholm, who was ill, left before they penetrated far
into South Carolina; the soldiers talked about the chances for escape
of the Confederate leaders still with the party.

Jefferson Davis had a good chance, they thought, because of the
extraordinary efforts that would be made to assist him, and they
were also encouraged about the chances for General Breckinridge
and Reagan, who had been a frontiersman and, so they understood,
a Texas Ranger. But they believed that Benjamin would 'surely be
caught, and all deplored it, for he had made himself exceedingly
popular.' [21]

At Abbeville, South Carolina, on 2 May the last council of war
was held. The indomitable Jefferson Davis made a plea for continuance of the struggle but the silence of the men present finally convinced him of the futility of his hopes. Pale and disconsolate, he left
the council room, leaning on General Breckinridge. Benjamin also
was now much depressed.[22] With Benjamin, Breckinridge, and

Reagan, the three remaining cabinet members (Mallory also had now left the party), Davis made ready to continue their flight.

While at Abbeville, Benjamin left with friends a trunk containing all his belongings except what he wore on his back and carried in a second trunk.[23] He was stripping for action. He had said that he would never be taken alive, and now he was preparing for a desperate effort to escape from the fast-pressing Yankees.

Already he had found it necessary to mount a horse, and for a time endured the discomfort of riding.[24] When the presidential party reached the Vienna Valley on the west bank of the Savannah River about twenty miles from Washington, Georgia, Benjamin finally left them on 3 May.

Unaccustomed to travel by horseback, Benjamin made an arrangement with Davis to proceed by another route and join him in the Trans-Mississippi district. Probably it was his tactful way of letting Davis know that he felt all was lost and wished to shift for himself.[25] Reagan reported him as now saying that he was going 'to the farthest place from the United States if it takes me to the middle of China.' [26]

Benjamin now set out to escape from the South. The Northern soldiers were known to be only a few hours' ride from the Davis party and bending every effort to capture the President and cabinet members. As Secretary of State and, in Yankee eyes, a leader of the nefarious rebellion, Benjamin would be a particularly rich haul.

Casting about for means of eluding his pursuers, he soon decided to disguise himself as a Frenchman, travelling through the South. He secured a horse and buggy and adopted the name of 'Monsieur Bonfals.' To make his disguise complete, he put on goggles, pulled his hat well over his face, and hid his bulging figure under a large cloak. He even pretended that he could not speak English, and a companion at this stage of his journey, Colonel Leovy of New Orleans, acted as interpreter.[27] Not forgetting his sisters at this time of peril, he left with a friend $900 in gold to be sent to them at La Grange, Georgia.[28]

A week after he left Jefferson Davis, Benjamin was overtaken by Colonel John Taylor Wood, who gave him the news of the President's capture by the Yankees.[29] For Benjamin the situation was now all the more dangerous. When he left the Davis party Reagan had asked him if he was not afraid he would be caught and recognized since his initials, J.P.B., were plainly marked on his trunk. But Benjamin replied that there was a Frenchman travelling in the Southern states who had the same initials, and that he could speak broken English like a Frenchman.[30]

Soon Benjamin crossed the Georgia border and entered the then sparsely settled state of Florida. He now changed his disguise to that of a farmer looking for land for himself and some South Carolina friends to settle upon. He induced a farmer's wife to make him some homespun clothes like her husband's, secured the roughest possible equipment for his horse, and set forth again. Taking every possible precaution, he travelled as much as practicable on by-roads, avoiding towns and the more inhabited districts.

Thus Benjamin reached 'central Florida.' How could he now hope to effect his escape? The Atlantic coast of Florida was alive with Yankee boats, patrolling the waters day and night for escaping Confederates. Fearing that he had no chance to get away by that route, he decided to try the Gulf Coast. But, unable to travel more than thirty miles a day, it would take him considerable time to reach his destination even with the best of luck. And particularly so since for reasons of safety he often travelled by night and slept by day.[31]

* * *

Of Benjamin's flight there are many stories, some of which cannot be substantiated. According to one, apparently authentic, he was travelling in Florida on a mule when he came one morning to a place where there were tracks leading in different directions. Instead of inquiring about his route, he retired a little distance into the bushes, unsaddled and tethered the mule, and lay down to sleep.

He had been asleep some time when he distinctly heard the words 'Hi for Jeff' spoken over his head. Tired and drowsy, however, he at first paid no attention to the sound. A second and then a third time he heard 'Hi for Jeff,' shrill and clear over his head. Obviously, the words did not come from a human being, and, getting up and searching about, guided by the sound of the voice, Benjamin saw a parrot, which had evidently escaped from a farmhouse, enjoying himself in a circle of small birds. Benjamin concluded that the parrot belonged to someone who was favorable to the Southern cause. But how to find the owner's house? He decided to pelt the bird with stones in the hope that it would fly back to the house. And sure enough, it did. Benjamin found the owner, a Southern sympathizer who substantially aided him in his escape.[32]

With the help of Major John Lesley of Tampa, Benjamin succeeded in reaching the Manatee River. Lesley knew the country and guided Benjamin, whom he introduced as Mr. Howard, to the beautiful mansion of Major Robert Gamble near the Manatee. Here he remained several weeks before completing arrangements to continue his flight. Captain Archibald McNeil, who then occupied the Gamble house, was also being sought by the Yankees and an almost constant watch was kept from the second story porch of the house.

One afternoon about three o'clock the Yankees did make a surprise raid on the mansion. So suddenly did they appear that Benjamin and McNeil barely had time to escape through the kitchen into the dense thicket back of the residence. And to make matters worse, McNeil's dog trailed them. They believed that his yelps could be heard at the house, and to quiet him McNeil had to take him in his arms as they hurried on into the undergrowth. Suspecting that something was amiss, the Yankees searched the thicket and at one time were within an arm's length of their prey, so that a sneeze, a cough, or a whine from the dog would have meant capture for the two men. But they were not caught. They hid in the underbrush until after dark, when the Yankees gave up the search.

This nerve-racking experience made Benjamin all the more determined to hasten his escape. He found allies in Mrs. McNeil and another lady staying at the mansion, who made him a suit of blue denim, uppers for shoes from his old green broadcloth overcoat, and had the colored cobbler sew them to leather soles. Benjamin donned his new outfit and, his sense of humor still active, he performed a few antics for the special entertainment of the children in the household.[33]

The next day he began another stage of his journey. Securing a boat from Captain John Curry, he crossed the Manatee to the home of Captain Fred Tresca, a native Frenchman who had lived in Florida for some years and knew the inside water routes down the west coast as far as Knight's Key. For about two weeks Benjamin remained with the Trescas while arrangements were being completed for him to proceed southward; years later one of the family recalled his genial disposition and love for the children. Mrs. Tresca helped him by sewing pleats in the back of his vest and waistband to carry his gold. Doubtless for the first time during his flight his fat body proved an advantage, since there was ample room in his clothes to sew the gold.

Benjamin now began the perilous journey down the Florida coast. With much difficulty Captain Curry secured a yawl, which had been sunk in a creek for two years in order to conceal it from the enemy, and in this boat Benjamin, Captain Tresca, and one H. A. McLeod set forth from Sarasota Bay on the long trip down the coast.

The lower west coast of Florida is heavily indented by numerous bays, harbors, creeks, and rivers emptying into the gulf. A skillful pilot was needed who could take advantage of all the waterways, big and little, as they proceeded southward. Fortunately, McLeod, a sturdy ex-Confederate soldier and fearless sailor, met the requirements. Tempted by the large reward offered them, he and Tresca were willing, as Benjamin put it, 'to expose their lives to the very great hazard of going to sea in an open boat.' And by 23 June they were off on a two weeks' trip down the coast, stopping occasionally to go ashore for water and provisions. Unable when setting forth to secure provisions fit for keeping at sea, they relied chiefly on fish and turtle eggs for food, and when necessary drank the milk of cocoanuts instead of water.

Soon after they set sail down the coast they had a narrow escape from the Yankees. Sighting a Federal gunboat just as it was lowering a small boat to chase them, they turned in at Gasparilla Pass and concealed themselves and their boat in the undergrowth. The pursuing boat searched everywhere for them and indeed came so near their hiding place that they could hear the Yankees talking. Benjamin and his companions hardly dared to breathe. They were so afraid the Yankees would continue to chase them that they spent two nights on Gasparilla Island.

But this was not the last sight of their enemy. Farther on their way they were sighted by another gunboat. This time they were unable to elude the boat, so Captain Tresca quickly ordered Benjamin to don the cook's apron, skull cap, etc. and to get busy around the galley. Obeying, he played his role cleverly, smearing grease and soot on himself and looking very much the cook.

It was well that he did, for some of the Yankees actually boarded the little boat and questioned Tresca. He told them that he was fishing to supply some men who were stationed at near-by points on the coast, and seeing fishing tackle, net, and freshly caught fish, they were satisfied with his story. One of the Yankees remarked, however, that he never before remembered seeing a Jew perform common labor.

About 7 July Benjamin and his companions finally reached Knight's Key, at the southern end of the Florida coast.[34] And here, in a larger boat, the *Blonde*, with a leg-o'-mutton sail, they set forth boldly into the Atlantic Ocean, steering towards the Bimini Islands, a British possession about a hundred and twenty-five miles eastward. This phase of the journey also was not without its perils, and at one time the men were in imminent danger of being drowned. To quote from the account that Benjamin wrote his sister, Mrs. Levy:

I did not write you in my last of the narrow escape I had from water-spouts when in my little boat at sea. I had never seen a water-spout, and often expressed a desire to be witness of so striking a phenomenon. I got, however, more than I bargained for. On the night before I reached Bemini, after a day of intense heat, the entire horizon was black with squalls. We took in our sail, unstepped the mast, and as we were on soundings, we let go the anchor in order to ride out the squalls in safety. They were forming all around us, and as there was no wind, it was impossible to tell which of them would strike us. At about nine o'clock, however, a very heavy, lurid cloud in the west dipped down toward the sea, and in a single minute two large water-spouts were formed, and the wind began blowing furiously directly toward us, bringing the water-spouts in a straight line for our boat. They were at the distance of a couple of miles, and did not seem to travel very fast. The furious whirl of the water could be distinctly heard, as in a long waving column that swayed about in the breeze and extended from the ocean up into the cloud, the spouts advanced in their course. If they had struck us, we would have been swamped in a second, but before they reached us the main squall was upon us with such a tremendous blast of wind and rain combined that it was impossible to face the drops of water which were driven into our eyes with such violence as to compel us instantly to turn our backs to it, while it seemed that the force of the wind was so great that it would press our little boat bodily down into the sea.

On turning our backs to this tremendous squall, judge of our dismay on seeing another water-spout formed in another squall in the east, also traveling directly towards us, although the wind was blowing with such fury from the west. There must have been contrary currents at different heights in the air, and we had scarcely caught sight of this new danger, when the two spouts first seen passed our boat at a distance of about one hundred yards (separated from each other by about a quarter of a mile), tearing up the whole surface of the sea as they passed, and whirling it furiously into the clouds, with a roar such as is heard at the foot of Niagara Falls. The western blast soon reached the spout that had been coming toward us from the east and checked its career. It wavered and broke, and the two other spouts continued their awful race across the ocean until we lost sight of them in the blackness of the horizon. A quarter of an hour after, all was calm and still, and our boat was lazily heaving and setting on the long swell of the Bahama Sea. It was a scene and picture that has become photographed into my brain, and that I can never forget.

McLeod also said that the 'squalls and the water-spouts and tropical storms came near finishing' them. The water came down in sheets. McLeod took a tin pan and bailed desperately while Benjamin used his hat.

Turning to his companion, Benjamin said with a smile, 'McLeod, this is not like being Secretary of State.' His cheerfulness and good humor helped to ease the strain on McLeod and Tresca. McLeod spoke of him as an 'awfully nervy man' though adding that 'anybody would have been frightened.'

Benjamin reached the Biminis on Monday, 10 July. Here he felt there was no longer any danger of his being captured, and thought it safe to take passage in a small sloop, loaded with sponge, for Nassau. But the morning after they left the Biminis the sloop foundered, thirty-five miles from land, and it sank so quickly that Benjamin hardly had time to jump into a small skiff, which the sloop had in tow, before it went to the bottom.

In the skiff, leaky, with but a single oar [Benjamin wrote Mrs. Levy from Nassau], with no provisions save a pot of rice that had just been cooked for breakfast, and a small keg of water, I found myself at eight o'clock in the morning, with three negroes for my companions in disaster, only five inches of the boat out of water, on the broad ocean, with the certainty that we could not survive five minutes if the sea became the least rough. We started, however, quite courageously for the land, and without any signs of trepidation from any one on board, and the weather continuing very calm we proceeded landward till about eleven o'clock, when a vessel was discerned in the distance, which was supposed to be a small schooner and which we felt sure of reaching if the weather continued calm.

We made for the vessel, the three negroes using the single oar by turns in sculling our little boat, and by five o'clock in the afternoon were safely on board H. R. M. Light House Yacht *Georgina*, a fine large brig, on board of which we were warmly received, and treated very kindly by Captain Stuart. The vessel was on a tour of inspection of the Bahama lighthouses, but Captain Stuart turned out of his way to put me back at Bemini, where I arrived for the second time on Saturday, the 15th. I immediately chartered another sloop to bring me here, and we started the same afternoon. The voyage is only about one hundred miles, but we were so baffled by calms, squalls, and head winds, that we were six days making it, and I arrived last evening only to learn that if I do not depart this morning for Havana, I may be detained a month before I get another chance to leave this island. I am thoroughly exhausted, and need rest, though in perfect health, but I must not yield to fatigue under the circumstances, and so I am passing this morning in writing letters to go by the *Corsica* steamer for New York on Monday, as I know how intense must be the anxiety of all I love on both sides of the Atlantic, until news is received of my safety . . .

I can as yet give you no idea of my plans or purposes. Until I reach England I can't tell what my condition is. I may be penniless, but I have strong reason to hope that some six or seven hundred bales of cotton which I own, reached Europe in safety. If so, I shall be beyond want for some years, and can supply all the needs of my dear sisters, and await events before determining my future course. If, however, I find that I have nothing left, I shall use my pen for a support for the present, in the English press, if I can so manage, as I have every reason to believe that I would find ready employment in that way.

I am contented and cheerful under all reverses, and only long to hear of the health and happiness of those I love . . .

It should be added that after Benjamin had returned to the Biminis he found Tresca and McLeod and it was they who finally brought him safely to Nassau. Here he not only paid Tresca $1,500 in gold for his passage of over 600 miles and reimbursed him for other expenses but sent presents for his wife and Mrs. McNeil.[35]

From Nassau Benjamin proceeded to Havana where on 1 August he wrote another letter, describing his travels and future plans to his 'darling sister' Penina (Mrs. Kruttschnitt). He planned to leave for England by the sixth and to see his wife and daughter in Paris by 1 September. Surely it would seem that the dangerous phase of his Odyssey would at last be ended and he could proceed quietly to London.

But while his boat was near St. Thomas a fire broke out in the hold and it was only 'by dint of great exertion and admirable conduct and discipline exhibited by all on board' that the flames were kept from bursting through the deck. By the narrowest of margins they succeeded in getting back to St. Thomas 'at about three o'clock in the morning with seven feet of water in the hold poured in by the steam pumps, and the deck burned to within an eighth of an inch of the entire thickness.' Two days later, however, he set out again and on 30 August he arrived without further misadventures at Southampton, England.[36]

XVIII. *British Barrister*

From Southampton Benjamin went to London where he remained a week in order to attend to some matters connected with the 'obsequies' of the late Confederacy. Then he hurried to Paris to see his family. After a separation of five years, what happiness to embrace his wife and daughter, in perfect health! His beloved Ninette, now cured of her 'lifelong disorder,' looked as 'blooming as a rose.' [1]

While he was in Paris strong inducements were held out for him to establish himself in France. Some bankers to whom he was introduced by Slidell hinted that 'it would be easy to obtain an honorable and lucrative position in the financial circles.' And his old New Orleans friend, Madame de Pontalba, was 'imperious in her urgency' that he should remain in Paris, promising all sorts of aids and influence in his behalf.[2]

Doubtless Benjamin could have adapted himself to Paris even as he had to New Orleans, Washington, and Richmond. But he was now strongly pulled to England and his old love—the law. He decided that nothing was more independent or offered a more promising future than to be a London barrister. By 29 September he was back in London and writing his sisters that he was almost fixed in his determination to practice law there. He would have to be naturalized and meet the various other rules and regulations for the admission of a foreigner, but, meantime, the English were treating him with 'great kindness and distinction.'

[I] have been called on by Lord Campbell and Sir James Ferguson . . . both accidentally in London, for the 'whole world,' as they say, is now in the country, this being the 'long vacation' in London. Both assured me that I would meet the utmost aid and sympathy, and would be called on by a large number of the leading public men here, as soon as they returned to town. Mr. D'Israeli also wrote to a friend of mine expressing the desire of being useful to me when he should arrive in town, and I have been promised a dinner at which I am to be introduced to Gladstone and Tennyson as soon as the season opens here.[3]

Above all, perhaps, he would be pleased to meet his literary idol!

Yet how would Benjamin support himself and his expensive family? Even with good luck it would be years before he could become established at the English bar.

In a letter of 20 October, however, to James A. Bayard, Benjamin declined a generous offer of financial assistance from him and his son. He said that when he first arrived in England he had been very poor with barely enough funds to support his family for a few months. But he soon received a hundred bales of cotton which had escaped 'Yankee vigilance' and sold it for the top price of nearly $20,000. With this and almost $10,000 he had made from a fortunate investment he was 'not quite a beggar.' He hoped to be called to the English bar that winter and was 'as cheerful and as happy as is possible for me to be while my unfortunate friends are in such cruel confinement, and my unhappy country in so deplorable a condition.' [4]

The Benchers of Lincoln's Inn where Benjamin applied would not yet, as his friends hoped, relax in his favor their general rules for the admission of barristers.[5] But he seems to have passed the next few months pleasantly enough, considering the reversal in his fortunes. On 20 December he wrote another letter to his relatives in America, full of affection for them and of details regarding his life in England and his view of American affairs:

The news from the other side fills me with alarm and concern, and I cannot penetrate into the dark future that seems to await my unhappy country. The unholy passions of the wretched Northern fanatics seem to require no fresh fuel in order to burn with fiercer intensity; and until the mass of the people hurl them from power, God knows what excesses they will commit.

I have made some valuable acquaintances here and shall have many more as soon as Parliament assembles. I have dined with Mr. Gladstone and was greatly pleased with him. Yesterday I returned from a visit to Kent, at the seat of a baronet named Sir Joseph Hawley, where I spent three days in the midst of the proverbial splendor and comfort of an English gentleman's country seat, and with a crowd of titled and fashionable guests. I found their tone, manners, and customs just what I would have expected,—quiet, easy, courteous and agreeable. The style of course exceeds anything to be seen on our side of the water. I was very hospitably received and warmly pressed to prolong my visit, but I have no time to yield to pleasures, till I have secured some lucrative business . . .

Then turning to the Louisiana scene, Benjamin indicated that he had not changed his old political philosophy. In his home state (as throughout the South) a large proportion of the Negroes looked on emancipation from slavery as also emancipation from work, and were a critical economic and social problem.

I hope poor Joe has become despondent about the negroes too soon, and that he may yet succeed in making a crop, though I confess that I have always looked with the utmost dread and distrust on the experiment of emancipation so suddenly forced on the South by the event of the war. God knows how all is to end! . . .[6]

In this and an earlier letter from England Benjamin had assured 'Sis' and 'Hatty' of his ability to help them if they were 'the least in want.' He could always spare a few hundred dollars and had no fears of his ability 'to make a handsome competence' at the English bar.[7] Yet it was not long before he found himself in serious need of money and even reduced to penny-pinching in order to meet his various responsibilities.

About eight months after his arrival in London, an English banking firm, Overend, Gurney, and Company, failed, carrying with it a large part of his funds.[8] He could not have made ends meet if he had not secured employment with a London newspaper, the *Daily Telegraph*. It paid him to write a weekly leader on international affairs at five pounds an article. There followed a number of leaders relating to America, which have the earmarks of coming from his pen though we now have no means of positive identification, since they were unsigned. We do know, however, that his 'brilliant' articles—as the *Telegraph* later described them—so pleased the paper that he was offered a position as sub-editor.[9]

Again Benjamin was not to be lured from his old love. He was determined to become an English barrister, no matter what personal sacrifices were entailed. Now becoming even more hard-pressed, he practiced all kinds of little economies but would not have the fact known even to his family. He lived very simply in bachelor quarters and sometimes dined only on bread and cheese at cheap restaurants, where for a person of his reputation it would have been embarrassing to be seen. After he became a full-fledged barrister, he also took to walking, since it would now be considered beneath his dignity to ride a penny bus.[10]

Nearly every Sunday Benjamin dined with some Louisianians then in London, to one of whom, in an unguarded moment, he confessed the penny-pinching.[11] It would seem that this would have gone hard with a man who had been one of the most prominent American political figures and had been able to indulge himself in all the little amenities of life. But Benjamin kept his good humor and was optimistic of ultimate success.

Modestly, he refused credit for his courage in beginning this new career. In a letter to a friend some years after he had become a leader of the English bar, Benjamin said:

You say I look on things through the *couleur de rose* of success. Not so, but through the *couleur de rose* of a temperament, blessed birth gift, that under all circumstances and every trial, took to the bright side and absolutely rebels against distrust of the future. I was complimented on my 'pluck' . . . it was simply elasticity of natural temperament: a total absence of . . . despondency and brooding over adverse circumstances.[12]

* * *

At the head of the long dining hall sat the Benchers. There were several of them who would be pointed out to the inquiring guest: the gaunt figure of Lord Brougham, in the public eye ever since the days of Queen Caroline's divorce trial; Lord St. Leonards, a former Lord Chancellor, his 'singularly refined features' hardly revealing that he was the son of Richard Sugden, a Westminster hairdresser; Sir Roundell Palmer, a former Attorney-General, with a mind as keen as that of a great medieval schoolman; and the austere Sir Hugh Cairns, 'confessedly the first lawyer of his time.'

These and other old leaders of the bar sat to themselves. Next were the barristers, some forty or fifty of them, and, beyond, about a hundred and fifty students in their simple 'stuff' gowns. Among these students, up from Oxford or Cambridge that Hilary term, sat a middle-aged man. Old enough to be their father, he yet talked to them easily and with entire abandon. The rule was that 'all are presumed to be gentlemen,' so even when he dined with a stranger he chatted with him over the soup or joint, the port or bitter beer, as if he were an old acquaintance.[13]

'After four years of the fiercest fights, unremitting labour and the exercise of great power, just escaped with his life,' as the London *Times* described Benjamin, he 'now sat down quietly to qualify himself to earn his bread.'[14]

Over the gateway in Chancery Lane, Ben Jonson had worked as a bricklayer with a trowel in one hand and Horace in the other. And here on a scaffold erected in Lincoln's Inn Fields, William Russell had died, a martyr to English liberty. Here in one Inn or another had studied Bacon, Boswell, Macaulay, Thackeray, Pitt, Canning, not to mention a long line of distinguished English lawyers and judges. Nor should one omit the Americans: William Byrd II; several signers of the Declaration of Independence;—and now, after a hundred years, Judah P. Benjamin.[15]

Enrolling at Lincoln's Inn on 13 January 1866, Benjamin was scheduled to serve his apprenticeship before becoming a barrister. He was supposed to meet the residence requirement of six dinners in hall every three-month term for a period of three years; to pay the prescribed fees; and to enter a barrister's chambers in order to learn the methods of practice.[16]

He was fortunate in being taken as a pupil into the chambers of Charles Pollock, son of Sir Frederick Pollock, lord chief baron of the exchequer. Charles Pollock had himself secured a large and lucrative practice, particularly in Benjamin's specialty, mercantile cases.[17] Like so many Englishmen, Pollock took a personal interest in Benjamin. When dining with his friend or spending an afternoon with him at Putney, Benjamin told him many stories of the Civil War. Always he cheerfully put forward 'the amusing side of things,' and spoke with 'anything like bitterness' of only two injuries that had been inflicted upon him by the Yankees. They had

burned his law library and—oh cruel blow!—had drunk his cellar
of old madeira.[18]

Benjamin was also befriended by Charles Pollock's father, the old
Baron Pollock. One of Pollock's daughters gave a graphic account
of a week end Benjamin spent at the baron's country seat at Hatton
in February 1866.

I had not met Benjamin, and had pictured to myself an American
of the Jefferson Davis type. To my surprise, when he entered the
room I saw a short, stout, genial man, of decidedly Jewish descent
with bright, dark eyes, and all the politeness and *bonhomie* of a
Frenchman, looking as if he had never had a care in his life.

Next morning Miss Pollock and Benjamin were both down early,
and he gave her 'most interesting and thrilling details of his perilous
escape' from the South.

I was much struck by his generous candor. I asked him what the
Northerners would have done to him if they had caught him and
he said that probably they would have put him to death. When I
exclaimed in horror at such an atrocity, he said, apologetically, that
as party feeling ran high just then his side might have done the
same thing had the circumstances been reversed.[19]

As for Baron Pollock, Benjamin found him a remarkable character in his own right. Although eighty-three years old, he would
rise at five o'clock, breakfast at half-past eight, take the train for
London, and arrive at half-past nine. During nine months of the
year he would sit in court every day from ten to four, before returning to the country.[20]

Although Benjamin had arrived in England when fifty-five years
old, he could find consolation in the fact that he was in a country
where age was far less an obstacle to success than in America. Had
not Wellington been commander-in-chief at seventy-seven and
Palmerston leader of the House of Commons at eighty-two? Night
after night he would take a vigorous part in debate until one, two,
or three o'clock in the morning.[21] And as for Gladstone, now fifty-
seven, and Disraeli, now sixty-two, neither had yet been entrusted
with the premiership.

James M. Mason, who was still in London, thought that there

must be something in the 'dreary' English climate that took away from long life those infirmities which could sometimes make it a calamity, while the robust longevity among the upper classes could perhaps be attributed to their exercise on horseback. In the country they were in the field all day, hunting or shooting; in town, on horseback an hour or two each day in the Park and moving 'at a round pace.' [22]

* * *

When persuading his son, who already had two pupils in his office, to take in Benjamin, Baron Pollock had argued that he needed only to familiarize himself somewhat with the procedure of the English courts and become acquainted with the lawyers.[23] Not long afterwards, a case came to the office that gave the younger Pollock ample proof of Benjamin's capacity. Pollock, as counsel for the London metropolitan police, was asked to give his opinion on a point involving the right of the police to search persons in their custody before convicted of any crime.

'Here is a case made for you, on the right of search,' he said, alluding to the Trent affair during the Civil War.

Benjamin at once set to work to consider the authorities, and when Pollock returned from court they were all disposed of. According to Pollock,

The only fault to be found was that the learning was too great for the occasion, going back to first principles in justification of each answer. Many years after, I was told that the opinion was held in high respect, and often referred to by the police and at the Home Office.[24]

Through the influence of Lords Justices Turner and Giffard, Page Wood (later Lord Hatherley), and Sir Fitzroy Kelley, Benjamin was enabled to dispense with the usual three-year legal apprenticeship and was called to the bar in Trinity term (6 June) 1866.[25] By the practice of the Inns of Court from an early period, they elected as members only gentlemen who were subjects of the realm, so on 22 May 1866 Benjamin presented a petition to the Masters of the Bench of Lincoln's Inn stating that his parents were both natural-born British subjects of British ancestry and that he, consequently, was a natural-born subject of Her Majesty. Taken when an infant

III. BENJAMIN AS A BRITISH BARRISTER

to the United States, where, during his minority, his father was
naturalized, he 'thus became entitled to all the rights of a citizen
of the United States without abjuring [his] native allegiance.' [26]

At fifty-five Benjamin had become an English barrister. It was
thirty-four years since he had been admitted to the Louisiana bar,
seventeen since he had been admitted to practice before the United
States Supreme Court, and only a year since he had been the fugitive ex-Secretary of State of the Southern Confederacy.

One of the first firms Benjamin represented in England was an
old established marine-insurance company. When just before its
annual meeting the company decided to have its unusually lengthy
rules revised, its two regular counsel refused to do the work in so
short a time despite the sizable fee. The assignment was then given
to Benjamin and the instructions were sent him late one evening.
Most lawyers would have had to study the rules of similar organizations in order to collate them and exhaust all the sources of improvement. But not Benjamin!

He got up for an early breakfast, sat down to his task, and worked
steadily, not stopping for lunch. By eight o'clock that evening—
his dinner hour—he had completed the new set of rules. And he
wrote them out 'in his own neat hand, *currente calamo*, with scarce
an alteration or correction from beginning to end, as if he had been
composing a poem.'

'I doubt if any draughtsman within the walls of the two Temples
could have done this so efficiently within the same time,' Charles
Pollock declared.[27]

As influential people began to sing his praises, Benjamin had good
reason to be encouraged at his prospects, even though relatively
few cases were yet coming to his office. In late October 1866 he
wrote James M. Mason,

I have, as you know, been called to the bar and have chosen the
Northern Circuit which embraces Liverpool. I have attended assizes
once in Liverpool and have no reason as yet to complain, though
I have done very little, as my call was just before the long vacation.
But Michaelmas Term commences on the 29th inst., and I may have
a chance to appear in some cases. My time is spent in close study
and we have not had a game of whist since your departure. I am
as much interested in my profession as when I first commenced as

a boy, and am rapidly recovering all that I had partially forgotten in the turmoil of public affairs.[28]

Although the American law was based on the English law, Benjamin nevertheless had much to learn. The English methods and technicalities of practice differed greatly from those to which he had been accustomed in America. As a barrister he only conducted cases in court, while all his briefs had to be prepared by solicitors. One advantage he enjoyed was that the Louisiana code was similar to the code derived from the Roman law, still used in several European countries and their colonies.

Benjamin was unrivalled by his contemporary barristers in arguing, before the judicial committee of the Privy Council, appeals from the former French colonies that had been ceded to England—including the profitable Canadian field. And his knowledge of the laws of shipping helped him greatly with commercial and maritime law, a type of practice especially important in London and Liverpool. On the other hand, he was at a disadvantage in that English practice was generally based on the common law, with which he had not had very extensive experience.

When Benjamin first began to appear in the English courts his method of argument was annoying to the British. English judges were sincerely regarded as gentlemen of superior character, chosen for their ability to declare and administer the law. But Benjamin, unaccustomed to the deference and respect paid the Bench, was in the habit of beginning his pleadings with a lecture on the law relating to the case in hand. He would expound the most elementary principles of this law and, if the court doubted or differed from any of his propositions, he would inform them that they were wrong. Naturally, the judges were displeased by this procedure, the more so since Benjamin used none of the phrases of courtesy or deference usually employed in addressing the Bench, and spoke with what they considered an unpleasant American twang.

Soon after Benjamin began his practice, he so offended a judge that Lord James of Hereford, who was opposing him in the case, waited for him as they left the courtroom. As they walked together from Westminster Hall to the Temple, Sir James frankly told Benjamin that he would be more effective in his arguments if he would show greater deference to the judges and not reveal that he considered their knowledge of the law inferior to his own. Fortunately, Benjamin accepted this generous advice and admitted that he had not yet fallen into the English habits of procedure. Quickly overcoming these failings, he showed as much respect and courtesy to the judges as was advisable.[29]

A lesser handicap was his personal appearance. Fat and stumpy as he was, and decidedly bizarre-looking, he did not have, in English eyes, the aspect of a distinguished barrister. There was not enough dignity in his walk or bearing.[30]

* * *

Word of the new career upon which Benjamin had embarked was slow in reaching the United States. *The American Law Review* for October 1866, however, announced his first appearance at the recent assizes in Liverpool 'where he held two briefs, and is said to have won golden opinions by his tact and ability.' The *Review* continued,

No one ever questioned Mr. Benjamin's ability. If his moral qualities had been equal to his intellectual, there was no position in his native country beyond his reach. He seems properly to have joined the Northern Circuit, and the secessionist sympathizers at Liverpool ought to give him good business.[31]

After some little trouble and delay, Benjamin secured chambers at 4 Lambs Building, Middle Temple, where he kept an office until he retired from active practice. His home addresses, however, are not listed in the city directories until 1873, when he had a bachelor flat in a fashionable neighborhood.

However many economies Benjamin might make in his private life, he would not cheapen his legal services; he would receive good fees or none at all. On one occasion a well-known firm, whose favor might have been valuable to him, sent him some work to do for them and attached a fee of five guineas. For several days the papers lay untouched on Benjamin's desk, and the clerk of the firm, calling for them and seeing them unopened, thought there had been some mistake.

'Not at all,' Benjamin said. 'The fee proffered covered taking in the papers, but not examining them.'

Twenty-five guineas were added and Benjamin took the work. Long afterwards the solicitor who sent Benjamin the papers told him that his client had insisted upon Benjamin's opinion exclusively, upon which he answered, 'If you had told me that at the time, I should not have looked at the papers for twice the fee.' [32]

Through the influence of an early Liverpool client Benjamin was secured as one of the counsel for the defense in *United States* v. *Wagner,* the first important suit brought by the United States in England in connection with litigation resulting from the Civil War. The United States sued Wagner as the legal representative of Fraser, Trenholm and Company, of Liverpool, to recover some property belonging to the Confederacy, on the ground that it had now legally passed into American hands; Vice-Chancellor Wood allowed a demurrer to the plaintiff's bill on the technical point that the plaintiff did not put on record the name of a public officer representing its interest, upon whom a cross bill could be served. The case was appealed to the Court of Appeal in Chancery, Lincoln's Inn, and on 17 June 1867 a judgment was given in favor of the United States. The Lord Chancellor, with the Appeal judges concurring, held that no injustice was done to the defendant by allowing the United States to sue in its own name, for the defendant could secure the name of a person employed by its government against whom he could bring action.[33]

During his first lean years in England Benjamin began work on a law book that he proposed to offer for sale to the profession. Over thirty years before, during his early period of practice at New Orleans, he had written his *Digest of the Louisiana Law;* now he devoted his spare time to the preparation of a treatise on Sales. In April 1867 he wrote his sisters that he expected to have it ready for publication by November or December. It was all the more important for him to hasten his work since he was barely making expenses.[34] In 1867 his fees totalled only £495,12.3*d*.[35]

The manuscript took more time than Benjamin had first anticipated and early in 1868 he wrote one of his sisters, 'My book is nearly finished, but the nearer I get to the end, the more fastidious I become about correcting, amending and improving it.' [36] Finally, the volume came out in August 1868. It was an immediate success. Although given the lengthy descriptive title, *A Treatise on the Law of Sale of Personal Property, with Reference to the American Decisions, to the French Code and Civil Law*, it was commonly known as 'Benjamin on Sales.

He followed *Blackburn on Sales* as a model for guidance in the treatment of such topics as that work embraced, but also developed the principles applicable to various other branches of the law of sales. An effort was made 'to afford some compensations for the imperfections of the attempt,' the preface explained, 'by reference to American decisions, and to the authorities in the civil law, not elsewhere so readily accessible.'

A modest statement! *Benjamin on Sales* was more than a mere attempt to accomplish this purpose. The weighty volume with its broad and authoritative treatment was almost immediately recognized as a legal classic and filled a need long felt by the British bar. It was a notable success not only in Great Britain but in the British possessions and the United States, and its publication marked a turning point in Benjamin's career.[37] One morning soon after the appearance of the book, when Baron Martin took his seat on the Bench he asked to have the volume handed to him.

'Never heard of it, my Lord,' answered his chief clerk.

'Never heard of it!' exclaimed Sir Samuel. 'Mind that I never take my seat here again without that book by my side.'[38]

* * *

It was in April 1869 that Benjamin appeared before Vice-Chancellor James in another interesting and significant case resulting from the Civil War—*United States* v. *McRae*. A bill was filed in England by the United States Government for the purpose of obtaining an account of all the money and goods that came into the hands of the defendant as agent or otherwise on behalf of 'the pretended Confederate government during the late insurrection'; and for payment by him of the money and goods received while he retained this account. There was an imposing array of counsel: Sir Roundell Palmer, Q. C., soon to be counsel for Great Britain in the *Alabama* case and created Lord Chancellor, and also Mr. Wickens, for the plaintiff; Mr. Kay, Mr. Martin, and Mr. Benjamin for the defendant.

Because of Benjamin's special knowledge of the case, his role was particularly important. With his associates he contended that the relief sought by the bill was limited (1) to money and goods originally the public property of the United States, or (2) to money and goods contributed by persons owing allegiance to the United States, or (3) to money and goods seized by the Confederate Government in exercise of their usurped authority. It did not include money raised by loan from persons in a foreign country owing no allegiance to the United States; the agency of the defendant was entirely confined to the Confederate loan that he was employed to raise by subscription from persons in England and Paris.

When the case came on appeal to the Vice-Chancellor, it appeared that the court was about to direct a private inquiry by the judges. But suddenly Benjamin arose from his seat. To the astonishment of every one present he began to speak in a stentorian voice: 'Notwithstanding the somewhat offhand and supercilious manner in which this case has been dealt with by my learned friend, Sir Roundell Palmer, and to some extent acquiesced in by my learned leader, Mr. Kay, if you will only listen to me—if you will only listen to me . . . [repeating the same words three times in a crescendo]— I pledge myself you will dismiss the suit with costs.'

Vice-Chancellor James, Sir Roundell Palmer, and the entire court stared at Benjamin in amazement. Yet he continued calmly without intermission for 'an hour or two.' And as he did so, the room became crowded, for it was soon noised about that something singular was occurring in the unusually quiet court of the Vice-Chancellor.

Largely as a result of Benjamin's argument, the suit was dismissed, the court holding that there was 'not a tittle of evidence' to show that 'any money or goods of the plaintiffs in their own right as distinguished from their right as successors *de facto* of the suppressed government ever reached the hands of the defendant.'

Incidentally, it will be noted that Vice-Chancellor James, who delivered this opinion, referred to the United States as a plural word —thus blandly overlooking the result of Appomattox.[39]

*   *   *

Since Benjamin never returned to the South after the war and became absorbed with his English practice, it might be assumed that he retained little interest in American affairs. But such was not the case. His letters show not only his usual loving solicitude for his family in the South but continued affection for all that was once dear to him there.

At the same time, however, his view of American politics appeared to be that of one who was increasingly remote and, if possible, increasingly determined to erase bitterness from his mind. Benjamin was never one to live in the past. In fact, he was so successful in removing the harsh memories of his earlier life that a hostile critic might offer the fact as another proof of his lack of deep feeling.

In a letter of 11 April 1867 to Mrs. Kruttschnitt, Benjamin commented with his usual interest on family matters: with Victorian sentimentality he said that he had 'fallen desperately in love with your little blossom Alma, whom I have never seen, but I can imagine from the photograph what a darling cherub she must be'; he inquired about various members of the Kruttschnitt household, and wanted his sister to send some articles by Mr. Kruttschnitt on microscopy, 'for I like to read everything, although I know little or nothing about the microscope.' [40]

In other family letters during the next few years we find him acknowledging a remittance to his nephew, Lionel Levy; busy as he was, securing some rare stamps for his little nephews and nieces in New Orleans, and commenting on the education of his young nephews:

[They] must be made to take an education, not be allowed to fancy a profession or business yet, for boys are really incapable of forming judgments of such things, and only long to get into business in order to seem grown up; let it be a good education first; if you will, let them come to me; after they are fitly educated, then business or a profession, what you will. [41]

Of the members of the Confederate cabinet at the end of the Civil War, only Benjamin and Breckinridge had escaped capture and imprisonment by the United States Government. The desire of the Northern radicals for revenge against Jefferson Davis and the other Southern leaders was whetted not only by the death of Abraham Lincoln, but by stories given further circulation in the early post-war period of alleged atrocities committed on Northern prisoners, and by a general desire to fix individual responsibility for the suffering and horrors of the long civil struggle.

Thus after his capture in Georgia the former Confederate President was made a scapegoat for many things for which he should never have been held responsible. He was confined in a damp casement at Fortress Monroe; for some weeks he was never removed from the prying eyes of a sentinel, and was even kept in heavy irons. And as the months passed without any prospect of his being allowed to stand trial and answer his accusers, his health, already none too good, failed badly, so that it seemed quite possible that he would be killed by his infamous treatment.

It was in the effort to influence public sentiment in favor of Davis and other 'honorable men, who less fortunate than myself are now held in close confinement by their enemies, and are unable to utter an indignant word in self defense' that Benjamin wrote in September 1865 a long letter to the London *Times*.[42] He did not attempt to examine in detail the question whether the Northern or Southern authorities were responsible for 'interrupting the exchange of prisoners, and thus producing a mass of human misery and anguish of which few examples can be found in history,' but he did give considerable evidence to show that the Northern authorities were responsible for the obstacles to the exchange. The sense of duty which impelled him to write the letter would be 'imperfectly satisfied' were he to withhold the testimony which none could offer so well as himself in relation to the charge of inhumanity made against Jefferson Davis.

During the four years Benjamin had been 'one of his most trusted advisers, the recipient of his confidence and the sharer to the best of his abilities' in Davis's labors and responsibilities, he had learned to know Davis 'better, perhaps, than he is known by any other living man,' and he offered this strong tribute to the Confederate President:

Neither in private conversation nor in Cabinet council have I ever heard him utter one unworthy thought, one ungenerous sentiment. On repeated occasions, when the savage atrocities of such men as Butler, Turchin, McNeil and others were the subject of anxious consideration, and when it was urged upon Jefferson Davis, not only by friends in private letters, but by members of his Cabinet in council, that it was his duty to the people and to the army to endeavor to repress such outrages by retaliation, he was immovable in his resistance to such counsels, insisting that it was repugnant to every sentiment of justice and humanity that the innocent should be made victims for the crime of such monsters.

Benjamin's letter, which also dealt with such explosive subjects as the Dahlgren Raid on Richmond, was reprinted in the *New York Times*,[43] along with a reply, full of sharp counter-charges, from Captain Henry Augustus Wise, U.S.N., which may have been an early cause for Benjamin's aversion to engage in public controversy regarding the war. At any rate, his communication received considerable attention and must have been sweet reading for his imprisoned chief once he could see it.

About the same time Jefferson Davis, in a frank discussion with his prison doctor on the members of his original cabinet, accorded superlative praise only to Benjamin, 'the ablest and most faithful member of his advisory council; a man who realized that industry is the mistress of success, and who had no personal aspirations, no wishes that were not subordinate to the prosperity of the cause.'[44]

While Davis was suffering—and retrospecting—in his prison cell, President Johnson was attempting to restore the Southern states to their place in the Union, following, though none too tactfully, the plan that Lincoln had outlined. But looming like a dark cloud in the sky was the determination of the Northern Radicals to prevent such a moderate policy. In a letter to Thomas F. Bayard, on 11 November 1865, Benjamin, referring to the grave Negro problem which had remained after the emancipation of the slaves, said

if the Southern States are allowed without interference to regulate the transition of the negro from his former state to that of a freed man they will eventually work out the problem successfully, though with great difficulty and trouble, and I doubt not that the recuperative energy of the people will restore a large share of their former material prosperity much sooner than is generally believed.

Yet he added this warning:

but if they are obstructed and thwarted by the fanatics, and if external influences are brought to bear on the negro and influence his ignorant fancy with wild dreams of social and political equality, I shudder for the bitter future which is in store for my unhappy country.[45]

A year afterwards, in late October 1866, Jefferson Davis was being treated much more humanely, but Benjamin wrote Mason that he greatly feared 'an additional rigorous season, passed in confinement should prove fatal.' And he added bitterly,

It is the most shameful outrage that such a thing should be even possible, but I have ceased to hope anything that justice or humanity demands from the men who seem now to have uncontrolled power over public affairs in the United States. I believe Johnson would willingly release Mr. Davis, but he is apparently cowed by the overbearing violence of the Radicals and dare not act in accordance with his judgment.[46]

Benjamin also sent Mason news of McRae, MacFarland, Slidell, and other friends. And since 'it may be very long, if ever, before I can hope to press your hand,' forwarded his 'counterfeit presentment' in wig and gown to remind Mason of his 'truly attached friend, J. P. Benjamin,' likewise praying him to send a photograph of himself if he had any.[47] The following May he informed Mason that their friend, McRae, who was preparing to leave for Honduras, 'is the "last of the Romans" and I shall be left all alone.'[48]

Actually, another prominent ex-Confederate, former Senator Wigfall, was in London, but Benjamin—speaking with unusual severity—said that he had never seen him. Wigfall 'called on everybody but me when he arrived, and it has been very agreeable to me not to meet him.'[49]

The antipathy was mutual, for in a letter to Clement Clay late in 1866 Wigfall had, after alluding to his business plans, delivered himself of a broadside against Benjamin. That Wigfall, a bitter opponent of Benjamin during the last period of the Confederacy, had not softened his opinion, was now made very clear:

As to Benjamin he turned out to be an Englishman & as he has plenty of money & can attend the clubs, entertain friends & extend his acquaintance he found no difficulty in being admitted after six months at the Inns. I have not seen him but saw his name in the list of Stock holders of Overand, Gurney & Co. after their bankruptcy for a good round sum of pounds sterling. He had managed somehow or other to accumulate about two hundred bales of cotton at Liverpool & drew his salary after getting here. He also drew from the Confederate agent on the Islands between 3 & 4 hundred pounds on his way here. On his arrival here he reported himself authorized by the President to take charge of financial matters & my own belief is that he and the agents have divided among themselves all that was left of Confederate funds. But enough of this disgusting subject.[50]

This is not the only story that has been repeated to the effect that Benjamin pocketed some of the Confederate funds in Europe.[51] If he did divide the money with the other agents, he certainly did not get very much. Nor is it likely that he felt he was doing anything unethical, in view of the fact that the Confederacy was now defunct and he had sacrificed so heavily in its behalf.

* * *

When writing Mason in May 1867, Benjamin had also asked him to forward a letter to 'our dear friend [Jefferson Davis] whose release from captivity is a source of so much joy among us here.' Early that month a Federal grand jury in Richmond had with much legal fanfare found that Jefferson Davis 'did at Richmond . . . on the twenty-fifth day of May, in the year one thousand eight hundred and sixty-one, conspire and unite with Robert E. Lee, Judah P. Benjamin, John C. Breckinridge, William Mahone,' H. A. Wise et al. to levy war against the United States.[52] So far as Benjamin was concerned, the indictment probably furnished him with a subject for some grim humor. They would have to catch him first! The charges were of a piece with the resolution introduced in the packed Louisiana legislature near the end of the war, ordering the state attorney-general and district attorneys, under penalty of loss of office, to institute criminal proceedings for perjury and treason 'or either' against him and certain other prominent Confederates.[53]

But by 1867 public opinion in the United States did not favor such extreme measures. The Federal indictment was quashed and it was clear that there would be no further criminal proceedings against the Confederate leaders. So in his letter Benjamin asked Mason, then in Canada, if he would find it 'consistent with self respect' to return to Virginia. 'There cannot be the least risk of persecution now, and of course no one could expect you to ask for "*pardon*"*!* God save the mark!' [54]

Returning now to the United States, Benjamin might himself quickly secure a large practice in New Orleans, despite the difficulties with the Carpetbag regime. Or he might establish himself in some metropolis, such as New York. But he preferred to remain in England.

While concentrating on his legal work, Benjamin had little time or inclination for society. His old friend Dick Taylor was 'rather put out' on a visit to England when Benjamin declined an opportunity to meet the Prince of Wales.[55] He dined out at times, however, with friends, and particularly enjoyed the company of Southerners or Southern sympathizers in England, as, for example, George Campbell of Liverpool and his Virginia wife, who elegantly entertained him one evening in 1868.

A young girl from Warrenton, North Carolina, the daughter of a noted Confederate blockade-runner, felt honored to leave the party in the same cab with Benjamin, and noted in her diary:

He is a funny little man, I don't think he can be taller than me—and so fat—with the brightest black eyes—he is very lively and they shut right up when he laughs. He is a most entertaining man—nearly as old as Father, I should suppose.

And this about his irregular domestic relations:

His wife and grown daughter (the only child) are in Paris. He says he can't have them with him in London because he cannot afford to keep them in the style they should be.[56]

Among the numerous Southerners who came to England during this period was Jefferson Davis. His sufferings had not curbed his die-hard courage, and late in 1868 he was about to take up his cudgels against the author of a book making some unfair charges against him and, as he believed, the state of Mississippi. But Benjamin, whose advice he sought, dissuaded him for a number of reasons based on 'that close observation of men and things in England which has been indispensable to one who is driven to seek a livelihood in a new land.'

If you publish the statement you will find it impossible to remain silent under the replies, and your existence here will be empoisoned by the necessity of engaging in a newspaper warfare at every disadvantage against hosts of unscrupulous enemies. The book you notice, I never heard mentioned, and it will drop still-born into oblivion, unless advertised by your notice of it.[57]

On this occasion Davis accepted Benjamin's wise advice, but after his return to America he was not always so prudent.

Meantime, in the South, the Carpetbag regime was still indulging in an orgy of corruption and misgovernment. Late in 1870, Benjamin was moved to comment to Bradford:

Poor Finney! I don't wonder that he writes gloomily. For myself nothing strikes me with more amazement and fills me with more disgust than the almost total wreck of morals and principles that have followed the war. The absence of anything like common honesty and fair dealing has become the rule instead of the exception, and the high standard of honor and integrity of which we used to boast, (and I think with reason) as characteristic of the Bench and Bar have become so much as a thing of the past that the few exceptional instances which are still to be found are rather ridiculed for their quixotism than respected for their virtues. But I must stop, for I feel that I must be getting quite an old 'guache'[?] to be thus exhibiting myself as a *laudator temporis acti!* . . .[58]

XIX. *A Leader of the British Bar*

WITH the early eighteen-seventies Benjamin entered upon the last decade of his law practice in England. Again he had to face years of grim, back-breaking toil, toil from which he now richly deserved relief. But at any rate the labor would be sweetened by notable—and highly profitable—professional recognition and a number of lesser compensations. Although he continued his quasi-bachelor existence, which, paradoxically, had been his lot since his early married life, he could again make it comfortable, even quietly elegant. Never ostentatious like Disraeli, he still wanted clothes of the finest quality, in good but not extravagant style; good wine, good food, good society. And these he could now enjoy, as well as an increasing number of brief but pleasant vacations with his family. Although Natalie would not live in London, she was somewhat less difficult than in her younger years, and Ninette would be happily married to a French army officer.

The year after Benjamin's arrival in England the great Prussian military machine had overrun Austria, and in August 1870 it was turned loose on France, finding her little better prepared than she would be for the blitzkrieg of 1940. Even less militaristic than he had been in the 'sixties, Benjamin referred in a letter to Bradford to 'this dreadful war . . . God knows when it will end.'[1] And later he said that he was as sick of the cold weather as of the war, adding, 'I can say nothing stronger than that.' He would be heartily glad when the struggle was over, since it was a hopeless one for France; and he felt that she had better make the best peace she could.[2]

Did Benjamin sound a prophetic note when he wrote a friend that France should 'gird up her loins, and learn from the stern lesson she has received that her people must be educated and manly virtues instilled into them instead of the blistering vanity and idle pleasure-seeking which have emasculated the present generation'?[3]

By the summer of 1871 the war was over and also the bloody insurrection of the Communards. After finishing his work on Circuit, Benjamin was in late August again off for Paris, where he had a long vacation of over seven weeks. A large part of his visit, however, was spoiled by an attack of neuralgia or rheumatism, which kept him in almost constant pain for several weeks. Natalie also suffered from a similar complaint, only much more severe, and was in bed for two months. She recovered, however, by the same treatment of hot sulphurous baths that was given Benjamin, and when he left his family to return to London they were all in excellent health and spirits.[4]

Meantime, difficulties had arisen between England and the United States over the extravagant claims by the latter for damages resulting from the raids on her commerce by the Confederate cruiser, *Alabama*, built in a British port. The issue was submitted in 1871 to arbitration by an international commission but, pending its decision, there was much ill-feeling between the two countries. On 7 March 1871 Benjamin commented on this and other matters relating to America in a letter from Manchester to James A. Bayard:

Your letter of the 19th ulto. has followed me here on circuit, and as I already owe a letter to the Hon. T. F. I shall answer both together. I am really very glad to see how hopeful the prospect is at last for some check to the career of the Republicans, but I quite share your opinion that stable government by the people is absolutely impossible in countries where the urban population have a preponderance in political influence, and I cannot doubt that democratic institutions will still linger in Western America long after in the more populous East they will have been replaced by some other form of government as the sole refuge from absolute anarchy. As to the English Commission, the Times of today already shows how completely the first hopes entertained of it have been succeeded by indignation at the extravagant pretentions seriously put forward on the other side. I have long been of opinion that war is inevitable between the countries, and that our main cause of the calamity will be the inexplicable and inconceivable folly of the English in supposing that it is to be averted by concessions and indications of dread of results, instead of by a firmness of attitude and a manifestation of resolution to repel aggression.

But the Manchester Cotton School with Bright as their leader have so misled popular opinion that I regard the future with dismay, knowing as I do that if you once touch the spirit of this people with the conviction that their honor is assailed, they will flame into a fury that may render peace impossible, while the sincere desire they now manifest to obtain peace by concession will inevitably be mistaken on the other side for cowardice & weakness—I suppose it is as it always has been, as a man gets old he becomes querulous and dissatisfied with all that he sees around him, but none can imagine how ardently I long with the poet for that shade, where 'rumors of oppression and deceit, of unsuccessful or successful war may never reach me more'—I am *so* sick of the endless wrongs that men commit without scruple and without even apparent adequate motive . . .[5]

By now it was clear what form of English legal practice was best fitted to Benjamin's taste and ability. As in America, he appears to have been less effective in handling witnesses and juries than in straight arguments before judges. Nevertheless, he made several masterly addresses before juries and was sometimes adroit enough to obtain favorable verdicts. His friend Charles Pollock credited him with the ability to make effective cross-examination. When an opponent would tell the jury that Benjamin had not proved his case, his favorite stratagem was as follows: 'My learned friend says I have not proved this. Why should I, when all of you gentlemen of the jury know perfectly well from experience in the trade that it must be so?' [6]

Once in a Liverpool case, the plaintiff sued for damages to cotton allegedly sustained through collapse of the walls of a store in which it was housed. An expert testifying for the defendant attempted to demonstrate that the owner of the store was free from liability, and Benjamin cross-examined him somewhat in this fashion:

'I think, sir, you said you had great experience in the building of warehouses?'

'Yes.'

'And you have carefully considered the causes which lead to their weakness?'

'Certainly.'

'And you have applied those considerations to the present case?'

'I have done so.'

'Then will you kindly answer me one more question. Why did that warehouse fall?'

Caught unawares, the expert paused and Benjamin sat down with such a humorous twinkle in his eye that everyone in court laughed heartily at the witness's discomposure. Although he recovered and gave a reasonable reply, it was of no avail.

'Thank you,' said Benjamin, slowly and calmly. 'I have no more questions with which to trouble you.'

No effort on the part of the defendant's counsel could restore his influence. Benjamin got his verdict.[7]

* * *

As early as 1868 Benjamin had been encouraged to hope for professional promotion—appointment as a Queen's Counsel. On 12 November 1868 he wrote Reverdy Johnson, now the American minister to England, that he was sending him a dozen letters from members of the Northern Circuit to whom he had given customary notice of application for the position. 'Several of the gentlemen who warmly express their wish for my success, are themselves applicants for silk . . . You may observe that Gainsford Bruce writes that "there is not a man on Circuit who will not rejoice to see [me] promoted." '[8]

By early 1870 Benjamin had been made Queen's Counsel for Lancashire County only, which was very important for Liverpool business, and he hoped within twelve months to have the same promotion for all England.[9] Moreover, in December he proudly wrote Bradford that he had just received a retainer for his first case in the House of Lords.[10] As he wrote Mason, soon afterwards, he was doing better than he had dared to hope. At last he was making an income sufficient to support his family and to put something aside for them 'when I am no longer able to work, in the place of what our Northern friends confiscated for me.'[11]

Benjamin was not made a Queen's Counsel.[12] But in 1872 he was given a patent of precedence, the first ever presented to a former American lawyer. It was awarded him after his notable appearance at the House of Lords in *Potter* v. *Rankin*, later regarded as a leading case on the law of abandonment in marine insurance. Benjamin led for the appellant citing American text writers and decisions and, although the Lords decided against him, his argument moved Lord Chancellor Hatherley to recommend to the Queen that he be given the patent of precedence. He now had rank above all future Queen's Counsel and all Sergeants at Law (except a few who already held such patents).[18] Writing his family in New Orleans, he sent them the most encouraging news of himself since he had left America:

I received it [the patent of precedence] in person from the Lord Chancellor at his own house, and he gave it to me with some very flattering expressions. I need hardly say that as the law journals and the *Times* have contained some articles on the subject it will be of immense value to me in my profession in various ways, both in increased income and in greater facility of labor; for you must know that a 'leader' who has a patent of precedence has not half as hard work as a 'junior,' because it is the business of the junior to do all the work connected with the pleadings and preparation of a cause, and the leader does nothing but argue and try the causes after they have been completely prepared for him.

As the ladies always want to know all details of ceremonies, I will say for the gratification of the feminine mind that my patent of precedence is engrossed on parchment, and to it is annexed the great seal which is an enormous lump of wax as large and thick as a muffin, enclosed in a tin box, and the whole together contained in a red morocco box highly ornamented. As nothing of this kind is ever done under a monarchy without an endless series of charges, etc., it costs me about £80, or $400, to pay for stamps, fees, presents to servitors, etc., etc.

Then he told the ladies about his new legal regalia:

I have now to wear a full bottomed wig, with wings falling down on my shoulders, and knee breeches and black silk stockings and shoes with buckles, and in this ridiculous array, in my silk gown, to present myself at the next levee of Her Majesty to return thanks for her gracious kindness. In the same dress I am also to be present at the grand breakfast which the Lord Chancellor gives to Her Majesty's Judges and to the leaders of the bar every year in October (at the end of the month), when the Michaelmas Term begins. Fortunately, I have three months for bracing up my nerves to the trial of making myself such an object, and as it is usual to have photographs made of one's self on these occasions I will send some to enable you all to laugh at 'how like a monkey brother looks in that hideous wig.'

Before I forget it, I must just mention that I don't want anything of this sort that I write for the family to get into the papers, for if it were repeated here, it would be known that such details must have originated with me, and I should be suspected, to my great mortification, of writing puffs of myself, than which nothing is deservedly regarded with more contempt. Of course, the *fact* of my promotion being announced could do no harm, but none of the details which can come *only* from *me* must get into the papers.[14]

Benjamin did not mention the praise and congratulation that were showered upon him by newspapers and legal magazines both in England and America.[15] After only six years in England and five as a member of the English bar, he had definitely arrived, and the future looked even brighter.

But along with a further increase in his cases, the patent of precedence brought added labor. Benjamin's holiday for Christmas 1871 was cut short by a client who offered him a hundred guineas for three days' work.[16] Moreover, not long afterwards he delayed writing his sisters because he could not risk the eye strain from further effort by gaslight;[17] on 13 June 1872 he said that he was leaving in the evening for Liverpool where he had a bankruptcy case the next day and had to be on the train half the following night in order to return to London in time for a special jury case fixed for Saturday;[18] and two months later he was with his 'brethren' at Liverpool 'straining every nerve to get through the work this coming week, so as to be free by Saturday the 24th' in order to make a trip to Paris.[19]

In November 1872 Benjamin was back in Paris again, this time on a sad errand: to attend the funeral of E. A. Bradford. He took Bradford's nine-year-old son, Sidney, then in school in England, with him to Paris for the funeral,[20] and apparently in December again carried the lad over to France to see his mother.[21] There are many other instances of his kindness to the fatherless boy, and also to his older brother, Willie.[22] In one letter we find Benjamin sending his love to Willie and adding, 'Tell him that this is the time of his life to which he will look back in after years with the greatest pleasure, if he only takes good care to mix a *quantum suff* of work with his amusements—*Carpe diem* shd be his motto now.'[23] Later Willie studied in Benjamin's law office.[24]

From 1873 through 1877 Benjamin's home address was 15 Ryder Street, and from then until 1883, 29 Duke Street, St. James's; both addresses were in the fashionable section near Buckingham Palace.[25] He was also made a member of the Junior Athaeneum Club and seems to have frequently dropped by there after leaving the Temple;[26] with no regular home ties, he needed the fellowship of the club members, just as he had in New Orleans. Of his social life at this time we get a further glimpse in some of his personal letters. Aside from his trips to France, he would sometimes plan little excursions for the week end—excursions that were often interrupted by his legal cases.

During the summer of 1873 Dick Taylor was in Europe and Benjamin wrote another American friend at Cambridge not to be surprised if he and Dick made 'an excursion "with drums, trumpets, and alarums" as Shakespeare says, on Saturday evening—Our present project is to leave at 5 p.m. and come in to dine with you when you least expect us, say at seven p.m.'[27] Again, in another letter he wrote that he had planned a visit to Brighton the previous Sunday but on Saturday a heavy brief had been brought to his Chambers and he 'spent eleven hours on Sunday in mastering it, so as to make my argument yesterday—The attorneys are terrible in this respect, giving us no time to get up heavy cases, but thrusting them on us at the last moment.'[28]

Benjamin was now restricting himself more and more to practice in London, and he was refusing except under special retainer of a hundred guineas to appear anywhere but the House of Lords and the Privy Council.[29] On one occasion when a client was particularly anxious to have a consultation at Benjamin's private residence instead of his Chambers, his clerk arranged a meeting at a purposely prohibitive fee of three hundred guineas.[30] It is not surprising that his favorite tribunal was the Privy Council, where the judges heard appeal cases from various parts of the Empire. His varied experience and comprehensive knowledge of foreign laws and customs probably made him more at home with such litigation than any other British lawyer. Still particularly effective in pure argument and, above all, in stating his case, a brother barrister said that 'he makes you see the very bale of cotton that he is describing as it lies upon the wharf at New Orleans.' [31]

Another of his strong points was his linguistic ability. He not only had an easy command of English and French and considerable knowledge of Latin, but he could also read, if not speak, Spanish. And yet Benjamin was never a pedant. In his cases he used only simple language, and Charles Pollock declared that he was punctilious in avoiding 'false' or figurative expressions. [32]

However desperate his case, Benjamin habitually addressed the court as if it were impossible for him to lose. In one instance when he was arguing an apparently hopeless appeal, his leader stated to the Bench that he would permit his learned friend Mr. Benjamin, 'to open the case, as he did not agree with his view in regard to the soundness of the appeal.' Benjamin did so and the court decided in his favor. [33] On another occasion during a case before the House of Lords when the reply was called for, the same leader rose and said that he did not favor appeal but would make way for Benjamin, who did. Again Benjamin opened for his side and won the case. [34]

In arguing his cases Benjamin would usually speak as briefly as practicable, a habit that was largely the result of his incisive mind. It may also, however, have been a result of his training in the United States, where the Federal Courts had limited each lawyer to two hours in which to state his case. [35] This was a rule which would probably have been welcomed by many British judges. Yet its successful operation would have depended upon their co-operation, for they often interrupted the barristers with unnecessary questions. Once Benjamin ended a string of questions from the Bench by commenting that the case in hand was very puzzling but that if he were to answer all the puzzling questions put to him it would become more puzzling than the facts themselves. [36]

Under the stern regime of work to which Benjamin forced himself, how could he get much happiness out of life? Although he was modest in expressing his feelings in this regard, it was obvious that he derived deep satisfaction from his success at the English bar, the more so since he was greatly interested in the law and enjoyed the associations he obtained thereby. No other member of the Confederate cabinet could boast of such an achievement, and only too many of his other American colleagues lived in the past, absorbed with unhappy memories.

Benjamin retained the ability to throw off trouble, which had helped carry him through the hectic Confederate days. He still managed to find some time each day in which he could completely relax and forget his work. As he wrote early in 1873, 'I make it a rule that I *will not* work after dinner, so that after wine in the evening I do as I please; it is only in the day-time that I am a "nigger" . . .[37] Until his labors at the bar 'exceeded all ordinary bounds he was a very social being,' his friend John George Witt, K.C., added.

[He] had a good appetite for his dinner, drank his wine, smoked his cigar, and took life like a philosopher. His conversation was very bright, full of humour, and not too full of anecdote, and for years he managed to end his day of toil before the dining hour. In after years he was compelled to work late in the evening, and that was a necessity against which his whole soul revolted. But his determination to make money not for himself, for he cared little for money, but for those he loved conquered his aversion.[38]

* * *

After the publication in 1873 of the second edition of *Benjamin on Sales*, he concentrated entirely on his legal practice. His fee book showed that his legal earnings, which were £2100.17s. in 1871 and £5623.7s.4d. in 1872, increased to £8934.3s.11d. in 1873—more than fourfold within two years.[39] Nor did the figure for the latter year—some $44,000—include the income from his book and investments, of which we get a hint as early as 1871 when he mentions buying $10,000 worth of New Jersey Central Railroad (stock?).[40] Despite his heavy expenses he was now able to lay aside a large sum each year and was looking forward to retirement. He wrote his friend at Cambridge,

I quite envy yr pleasant life. I am sure that at my age I could dream away the remainder of life there in quiet content, but my battle with the world is not yet *quite* ended, though I hope in two or three years at most to feel satisfied that I can withdraw from active work without disquietude as to means of living in the modest way that best suits my tastes . . .[41]

Not long afterwards, in August 1873, he was very hard at work at Liverpool, where he was attending court. It met at 9:30 in the morning and did not adjourn until 6:00 in the evening, so that the barristers, with their briefs to read after dinner, were at their wits' end to find time to study their cases before entering court in the morning. But Benjamin wrote that the regime was to last only another fortnight and then he would be off for the Pyrenees.[42] More and more he seemed to look forward to the periods when he could get away from his work and enjoy relaxation with his family and friends. The next February, after another siege of what was now becoming a real drudgery, he declared, 'I am now over the heaviest of my work & feel like a school-boy who has just got his holiday.'[43]

In volume five of the Privy Council appeal cases, for 1873-4, we find Benjamin listed in a considerable number of his now customary appeals, including several from outlying parts of the Empire. During his legal career he had appeared in a remarkable variety of cases. In the United States there had been land and mercantile litigation over the old French and Spanish and the American law of Louisiana; occasional criminal cases; *United States* v. *Castillero* with its intricate and romantic background in California; numerous appeals before the Louisiana and United States Supreme Court; and the legal issues on which he had to give opinions while a Confederate cabinet minister. And now in England there came to his desk a variety of civil suits, springing from many of the lands in the Empire as well as foreign countries.

Considering the number and variety of the briefs that were pouring into Benjamin's office, it is small wonder that his fees in 1874 reached £9861.1s.4d., an increase of nearly a thousand over the previous year.[44] With the earnings from his profession and investments, he had accumulated within eight years after becoming an English barrister an ample estate with which to support himself and his family. He was now sixty-four years old. Surely he had worked hard enough, had won honors enough to deserve a rest from his strenuous labors, and to live with his family from whom he had been separated, except at occasional intervals, for so many years. But again something intervened to prevent his retirement.

* * *

On 7 September 1874, Ninette Benjamin was married in Paris to Captain Henri de Bousignac of the French Army. The wedding was celebrated at the church of St. Pierre de Chaillot in Paris and the bridegroom's uncle, Abbé de Rolleau, performed the Catholic ceremony. As for further facts about the grand occasion, we only know that Benjamin gave an account 'almost feminine' in detail to Mrs. Kruttschnitt, though not attempting to describe the 'toilettes.' But from another of his letters shortly before we do learn why he gave up his hopes for early retirement.

With Ninette now past thirty, it was high time for him and Natalie to get their daughter securely settled in matrimony. And Benjamin—was he influenced by thoughts of his own unfortunate marriage?—did as much 'as human foresight can predict' to assure that 'the match will prove happy.'

Benjamin proudly wrote Mrs. Kruttschnitt,

Captain de Bousignac is represented on all sides as one of the most promising officers of the French army. At the age of thirty-two he has acquired a distinguished position on the general staff from his merits both as an artillery and engineer officer; he is of excellent family, irreproachable habits, beloved by all around him for his frank, gay and amiable character, and I know no better test of a man than his possession of the affection of those most intimate with him.[45]

Settling on Ninette a dowry of \$3,000 a year, Benjamin felt that she was now secure against want. But it had been at the price of giving up all his savings and postponing his own richly deserved retirement. He had to make provision for the old age of himself and his wife, a difficult task that he optimistically declared he would undertake with courage. They would not require a great deal, and his practice was so much more lucrative than before that in two or three years he would see the end of 'necessary labor' and be able to work 'as little or as much as I please.'[46]

Captain de Bousignac, who had been stationed at Versailles, was transferred to Orleans, and Ninette spent most of the winter with her mother. However, in the spring the young couple opened an establishment of their own at Orleans.[47] Perhaps it was just as well for them to get away from Natalie during that period of the marriage, even though Captain de Bousignac's amiability seemed proof even against her jealous absorption in her daughter.

At any rate, Benjamin, happy in the knowledge that the marriage was off to a good start, could concentrate again on his English practice. In March 1875 he wrote that his new son-in-law was 'all that I could desire.' [48]

Despite the large settlement he had made on Ninette, he sent a thousand dollars as a wedding present to one of his nieces.[49] That was on 17 March 1875, and Benjamin had just finished the trial of a case lasting eight days; on Sunday he had gone to his desk after breakfast and remained there until two hours after midnight with an interval of only a half hour for 'some light food, as one cannot *dine* when so deeply absorbed.' [50] On another Sunday two months later, however, he was enjoying a 'free holiday' with no work on hand and was 'as gay as a bird' because there was no court the next week. Instead of remaining in his 'dull lodging' he strolled into the park and enjoyed the spring day 'with a sky as blue as my memory paints the Californian sky to have been some fifteen years ago.' [51]

Benjamin felt all the more happy because he had recently had another great legal honor conferred upon him: he had been elected a Bencher of Lincoln's Inn. A vacancy had occurred upon the death of Lord Saint Leonard, one of the most distinguished of the contemporary English lawyers. And Benjamin could not but wonder at his 'marvellous good fortune in becoming after so short a probation a "bencher" that is one of the Governing Committee who control the whole bar, admit to its ranks, and on occasion expel an unworthy member . . .' [52]

* * *

In the cases in which Benjamin appeared during the next few years he was obviously more concerned with making money than in establishing a record for the number of suits which he won. For example, of the seven cases in which he is listed in a volume of the *Law Reports Appeal Cases* for 1875-6, he won three and lost four.

Somewhat typical was *Thorn* v. *Mayor and Commonalty of London*, a case involving an implied warranty in building a bridge at Blackfriars for the city of London, in which Benjamin appeared before the House of Lords. Lord Chancellor Cairns said in his opinion that 'nothing could be more ingenious and able than the two arguments which your Lordships have heard from Mr. Benjamin and Mr. Bompas in support of the case of the appellant,' but they lost the suit and the judgment of the Court of Exchequer was affirmed with costs.

In June 1876 Benjamin appeared before the Supreme Court in *Queen* v. *Keyn*. A leading case in international law and also involving an important principle in criminal law, it was the most significant cause which he ever pleaded in England. Not only for this reason but because of the prominence given the trial, it was a highlight in his entire legal career, comparable to his American appearances in *Murdoch* v. *McDonogh* or *United States* v. *Castillero*.

Ferdinand Keyn was the captain of a German vessel that ran down an English steamer in the Channel within three miles of Dover, sinking the ship and causing the death of a passenger. Tried in the Old Bailey, Keyn was found guilty of manslaughter, but Charles (now Baron) Pollock, who presided at the trial, was not convinced that the court had jurisdiction. There was an appeal, and after a delay of some five years the case was tried in 1876 before a special court of fourteen judges.

Presiding was Chief Justice Cockburn, the eminent judge who had represented Great Britain at the *Alabama* arbitration in Geneva, and among the other judges were Baron Kelly, the Chief Baron of the Exchequer and the former Attorney-General, Chief-Justice Coleridge, Sir P. Phillimore, and Baron Pollock. On the part of the counsel for the Crown, the case was considered of great importance and prepared with corresponding labor and research, since it was felt that the lives of English subjects and the security of the English coast were affected. Indeed, according to the London *Times*, it in reality involved the question whether foreign seamen guilty of an offense similar to Keyn's were 'liable to criminal jurisdiction at all, as it is not likely that the relatives of those of our subjects whose deaths are thus caused will undertake the task of following the foreigners into their own country, with their witnesses, and prosecuting them there.'

Veteran though he was of many hard-fought legal battles, Benjamin was put on his mettle by several days of sharp jousting with Sir Hardinge-Giffard, the Solicitor-General, and other keen legal minds. The leader for the defense, he had to face the severe quizzing not only of the opposing lawyers but the judges. It was a 'talking court' such as he had encountered many years before in Louisiana as well as in England, and it tried his patience, to say nothing of the usual weapons of his legal armory. In the copious reports in *The Times* there were whole columns devoted chiefly to the tilts between Benjamin and the judges—tilts in which he proved that he could hold his own with the best of them. Thus in the report for 16 June 1876:

During his argument on that day Benjamin had cited a long array of cases, domestic and foreign, textbook writers and other authorities, in the face of interruptions from the judges. He had just quoted Keltenborn and Heffter, two German writers on international law, with the usual quizzing from the Bench, and also Bluntschli, another German, when, to quote from the *Times:*

The Lord Justice observed that he did not think the opinions of these writers of much authority on the question.

Mr. Benjamin said he had nothing else to offer except the opinion of the jurists. There were no judicial decisions, except, indeed, so far as he had cited them in his favour; but there was no direct decision. He was compelled, therefore, to cite the opinions of jurists.

Sir R. Phillimore observed that the opinions of jurists were cited by Blackstone.

The Lord Chief Baron said there were no decisions, and there was, he believed, no instance in which in any country, criminal jurisdiction had been exercised over foreigners for acts in the high seas in a ship not of that country. No such instance, he believed, was to be found in the history of the world.

Mr. Benjamin said that was so; and, in the absence of judicial authority, he could only cite the opinions of jurists. He urged that this was not a question of municipal law, as the fact occurred at sea, and was the act of a foreigner. It was a question, properly, of the maritime laws; whereas, in this case municipal law, the law as to manslaughter, was applied to the foreigner. By the ordinances of

Wisbev, a collection of marine law, the case of collision was provided for by the payment of damages.

The authority of Chief Justice Cockburn 'great and undisputed as it was' was insufficient 'to restrain the copious and often irrelevant interruptions of the argument by some of his judicial associates,' wrote Herbert Asquith, the future Prime Minister, who was present at the trial. Once Asquith heard Benjamin say to Sir Hardinge-Giffard in a loud voice, 'If this goes on much longer, Solicitor, I propose that we should agree to withdraw a judge.'

Finally, after Benjamin had continued through the interruptions for several days one of the judges, Baron Bramwell, asked him how much more time he expected to require. Benjamin replied that he hoped to finish the middle of the next day; it largely depended upon the discussion on the Bench. To this pointed comment Baron Bramwell answered good-naturedly, 'You might pertinently, perhaps, ask us the questions,' a remark which brought laughter in the court room and even from the judges.

The trial was finally concluded and, after a further delay of three months, the judges by a 7 to 6 vote freed Keyn on the ground that the English courts lacked jurisdiction in the case—the principle contention made by Benjamin. Not long afterwards Parliament passed the *Territorial Waters Act*, which provided adequate legislation to deal with such cases.[53]

At the time that Benjamin appeared in the *Franconia* case a considerable transformation was being made in the English legal procedure through the Judicature Acts of 1873 and 1875, adopted for the purpose of increasing the efficiency of the cumbersome British courts. Chiefly the work of Lord Chancellors Selborne and Cairns, the acts were influenced in some particulars by Benjamin's work on *Sales*. The ideal of Lords Selborne and Cairns was 'the fusion of law and equity' and the laws provided for the abolition of the old Chancellory and Common Law Courts and the substitution of a single Supreme Court of Judicature consisting of a Court of Appeal and a High Court of Justice. As Baron Pollock wrote in one of his Swinburnian verses commemorating the event,

> The courts, that were manifold, dwindle
> To divers Divisions of One.[54]

Despite their new features, the acts did not accomplish all that their learned authors hoped for, as Benjamin foresaw in a letter of 13 July 1875. Writing an American correspondent, Conway Robinson, to thank him for the gift of a law book which Robinson had written, Benjamin said that he felt the new Judicature Bill would in some respects prove 'eminently beneficial,' but the fusion of law and equity would turn out to be a delusion. He was sure that

there are certain divisions inherent in their very nature in judicial enquiries, and in so crowded a community as this, subdivision of labor becomes as much a necessity in law as in any other business or profession that deals with the multifarious affairs of men . . . when we come to practical details, in spite of theory, separate Courts will be found necessary for dealing with successions and estates, with bankruptcy, with admiralty, with the settlement of partnerships and with family settlements; and in the end what are termed law-suits will separate themselves from judicial *administrative* matters, and the latter again become the subjects of what we now call Chancery. We are to begin 'spick and span new' in Nov. and 'nous verrons' as father Ritchie used to say when I was a boy.[55]

*　*　*

As the years passed Benjamin's letters contained fewer and fewer references to American politics, though he appeared as much interested as ever in his relatives across the water. Early in 1875 he noted that Pinchbeck, a Negro, had been registered by the United States Senate as the Senator-elect from Louisiana but observed that the Republican party was rapidly declining into a decided minority and as soon as that occurred there would be a 'speedy and radical change' in the condition of affairs in Louisiana and the entire South. 'A few months will see "the beginning of the end," & we must possess our souls in patience in the internal [eternal?] . . . "Man is Man, & master of his fate" as my poet Tennyson says.'[56]

About the same time he delivered himself at length on American affairs to a group of Southern admirers then at Liverpool. Among other things, he told them he left the United States because he knew the 'ravenous' nature of the Abolitionist class of politicians of the North who really urged the War between the States. The war should have been averted and would have been, if these rabid Abolitionists had been at all reasonable, fair, and honest; Benjamin knew that they would bring hardships and impositions 'on my people,' which he would have been powerless to prevent. He also warned the Americans against foreign entanglements and against amending their Constitution, which he compared to the rudder of a ship.

It is significant to note that he commented favorably on the sincerity and honesty of purpose of Abraham Lincoln, who, he said, was influenced by rabid and unscrupulous men.[57] Benjamin is never known to have spoken unkindly of Lincoln, while Lincoln called him 'the smartest' of the Confederate civil leaders.[58]

Late in 1875 Benjamin was saddened by the death of Jules St. Martin, which removed one more tie with his old Richmond and New Orleans years.[59] Solomon Benjamin also had died not long after the end of the Civil War, but Judah does not appear to have been very close to his older brother. As for Joseph Benjamin, he had left the United States at the end of the war and gone to Mexico, thence to Spanish Honduras. And here after various vicissitudes, this cultured graduate of the University of North Carolina operated a store and plantation near Puerto Cortes.

Asked by a New Orleanian who met him at his adopted home why he had left America, Joseph answered, 'I wouldn't take the oath of allegiance to the United States.' He read to this friend a letter from Judah, inviting him to come to England and live with him; in case he did not have the necessary money, Judah wrote that he would send him all that he needed. But Joseph, although he was very fond of his brother and corresponded with him frequently, did not now wish to leave his family and property in Honduras. He left a number of children; their descendants, still living in the country, are among Judah's nearest surviving relatives.[60]

Just about the time of Benjamin's appearance in the *Franconia* case, Moncure Conway, in his London letter to the *Cincinnati Commercial*, stated that he 'must be regarded as the most famous advocate at the English Bar at the present moment.' Conway had heard Benjamin speak in the Senate before the war and said that he had greatly improved since his residence in London 'in manner as well as power'; he was 'very eagerly sought for in all great cases, especially those which involved questions of foreign and international law.' Conway thought that Benjamin was being selected as 'the best defender of forlorn hopes.'

He did not know whether Benjamin's Confederate experiences had had anything to do with this reputation, but certainly he had 'been appearing in some desperate cases.' [61]

Presently, so Conway asserted, Benjamin would have to consider whether or not it would be a greater advantage for him to be famous for defending the indefensible or to run the risk of a reaction by losing so many cases of that kind as must be lost when the judges are as learned and experienced as those in England. Only two days before, Benjamin had received 'three severe falls . . . of which two at least were such as one would have supposed so clever a gentleman must have foreknown.' One of these cases was in the House of Lords, the others in the Supreme Court of Judicature. Moreover, in one of these cases Benjamin received rebukes from the Court that led Conway to suggest that Benjamin may have been in danger of suffering from a reaction among the legal and judicial minds that had shown him such exceptional favor.[62]

But Benjamin's reputation and the size of his practice continued to increase until he received more work than he could possibly handle; in Volume Three of the *Appeal Cases* for 1877-8 alone he is listed in 30 of the 65 cases. They included a suit over the infringement of a patent for 'a new or improved expander of boiler tubes'; [63] an appeal from the Supreme Court at Shanghai on a question of fraudulent misrepresentation by an agent; [64] and another from the Supreme Court of South Australia in which Herbert Asquith, the future Prime Minister, was associated with him among counsel for the appellants.[65] There were also two appeals from Canada,[66] one from the British Supreme Consular Court of Constantinople,[67] and a shipping case, *Inglis* v. *Buttery*, involving a London and a Glasgow firm in which, although Benjamin's side was defeated, Lord Hatherley referred to him as having pressed a certain point upon the judges 'with very great power and vigour' and said that his interpretation of certain words in the agreement was very ingenious.[68]

Early in 1877 Benjamin was able to write Mrs. Kruttschnitt that he was no longer working so hard. 'I very seldom have to work after seven in the evening, and from ten in the morning to seven in the evening is no excess of labor!'[69] Nevertheless, he was still making money hand over fist. His fees, which in 1876 had amounted to £13,812.9s.4d., increased in 1877 to £14,741.3s.7d. and in 1878 to £15,742.6s.[70] By this time he was longing to retire, but he still did not do so.[71]

And why? One explanation was the large amount of money that Benjamin gave the extravagant Natalie and various other relatives. During 1877 he casually mentioned that his brother Joseph lost £5,000 ($25,000!) for him,[72] and at Christmas he sent $500 to his family in the South.[73] Moreover, he is known to have helped at various times a number of ex-Confederates and others who needed assistance.[74]

A more important reason for his not retiring was that he had built a large mansion or 'hotel' in Paris. Located in a fashionable section, at 41 Avenue d'Iéna, it was a large stone house built in the grand manner: three stories connected by a marble stairway and with furnishings that could only be afforded by a very rich man. The mansion took a great deal of Benjamin's time before it was finished as he desired; there were labor troubles and other complications and at the end it cost him $80,000. Mrs. Benjamin and Madame de Bousignac devoted themselves to choosing wallpaper and colors for the decorations of the rooms and furniture in the French style, and by September 1879 the mansion was ready except for Benjamin's study which he wanted to take his time in furnishing to suit his tastes.[75]

With such a fine mansion—it was later owned by one of the Rothschilds—Mrs. Benjamin must have outdone herself in giving soirées and entertainments of all kinds. Such things meant much to her, and Ninette seems to have taken more after her mother in this way than her father.

Benjamin also liked social life but not the kind in which Mrs. Benjamin indulged herself. He had by now allowed himself to go out in society, which he had resolutely avoided when he first came to England. He was much in demand and on easy terms with a number of English celebrities. Genial, simple, utterly unaffected in his manner, it was impossible for him not to make friends. At congenial parties he was ready to entertain his friends with a wealth of stories from his own varied and exciting experiences; and his gift for repartee had not suffered with the years.[76]

It was at a dinner in Paris that Benjamin first met Gambetta. During the course of the conversation he remarked, perhaps a little acidly: 'Monsieurs les journalistes anglais sont les rois de la terre.' To which Benjamin replied: 'Parfaitment, et ils ne sont jamais détrônés.' [77]

On another occasion, during the 70's, Benjamin and General Robert Schenck, the American Minister, met at the house of a mutual friend. In the early part of the evening they did not speak to each other. Whatever his personal inclinations, the official representative of the United States could not afford to be cordial 'with a proclaimed traitor' and leader of the late rebellion.

But after dinner a game of poker was started. With a number of other guests, the two Americans stood looking on, then drifted together.

'I recollect very well, General Schenck, when we last met over a game of poker,' said Benjamin, speaking first.

'So do I,' promptly replied the Minister, 'For I remember well what you won from me,' mentioning an amount quite large enough to be won or lost at a sitting.

'Well, sir, if I did,' Benjamin answered, 'You have had your revenge, for since then I have lost and you have won a bigger stake than that.' [78]

XX. *Full of Years and Honors*

'RARELY have I met a smile so genial as that which welcomed me from the little gentleman whom Abraham Lincoln considered the "smartest" of all the Richmond Revolutionary Junta,' wrote a correspondent of the *New York Times* who interviewed Benjamin about 1 January 1879. 'Mr. Benjamin's physique is eminently Southern, of that jolly, well-fed Southern type which so nearly resembles the traditional John Bull . . .'

'Nobody will call you a Yankee, anyway,' the correspondent remarked, upon which Benjamin laughed and said he was born what he now was—an Englishman.

The fact that he had come from America had not hindered him at the British bar, Benjamin added, 'except that I should have been made a Queen's Counsel several years earlier if some of the powers that be had not imagined that to honor me might not be regarded as friendly by the government at Washington.'

But fourteen years after the Civil War the people of the United States were losing some of their old sectional hatreds. As the *Times* correspondent remarked, 'Americans of every part of the united world rejoice to see you elevated to the judicial Bench.'

'That will never be,' Benjamin answered.

'And why not?'

'I couldn't afford to be a judge. I couldn't sacrifice my income at the Bar for the comparatively small salary of a seat on the Bench!'

The *Times* representative added that Benjamin was making at least $150,000 a year (including income from his book and investments), whereas his salary as a judge would have been only $25,000.

The correspondent, who interviewed Benjamin at his chambers in the Temple (never had he seen any there 'as cosy and pleasant'), was also struck by Benjamin's youthful appearance. 'Very seldom,

366

indeed, does one meet a man who, having almost attained the scriptural three score years and ten, looks and acts like a man of forty. Mr. Benjamin is the best preserved man I have ever seen with the exception of the late Lord Palmerston.'[1]

With such publicity for Benjamin, we are not surprised to find the New Orleans *Democrat*[2] writing of him in superlative terms. In a feature article that must have delighted friends and relatives in his home city, the *Democrat* went so far as to assert that the fugitive from the South had fourteen years afterwards become 'the recognized head of an institution . . . the most exclusive and difficult in which to attain prominence and success—the bar of England.' The writer put Benjamin's yearly income from his practice at some $120,000—actually it was about $75,000; and added that the briefs he declined would double his income.

Always accustomed to do well and completely everything he undertook, he had been forced to reduce the amount of his labor within the compass of his wonderful capacity and industry. We doubt if these have ever been equaled by any other aspirant for distinction and success at the English or American bar.[3]

In several respects his record had not been equalled. Indeed, he himself felt that the simple facts were 'almost a miracle' when compared with his condition when he arrived in England. It was enough to turn the head of almost any man. Yet he wrote Finney, his old law partner, 'I sometimes feel ashamed of my own success, when I see others quite as deserving still forced to continue the battle against fortune.'[4]

* * *

Among Benjamin's clients in September 1878 was Cyrus McCormick of Chicago, who consulted him in Paris about some matters relating to European sales of the McCormick reaper. Later Benjamin wrote him from the Temple that he went entirely beyond his usual sphere in advising and counseling McCormick in Paris, 'but in London where I now resume my professional duties, I could not possibly devote the time required to your business, even if the rules to my profession permitted it.' And in a postscript he added that he was returning McCormick's original letter since he would have to give it to his solicitor. Upon authorization from McCormick, Benjamin engaged Clark, Rawlings, and Clark as his solicitors, assuring him that he could place 'the most implicit confidence' in their ability and integrity and urging him to give them all the contracts, memoranda, correspondence, and other information relating to the matter. After being employed by McCormick, the solicitors consulted Benjamin, and on 21 December 1878 he drew up an opinion in the case.[5]

It is curious to note the extra trouble to which the Chicagoan had to put himself in order to continue his business relations with Benjamin; it would have been so much simpler if he could have continued his direct dealings with him instead of making the contact through a solicitor. Benjamin is on record as stating that he felt the separation of the English legal profession into barristers and solicitors was 'a real public mischief.'[6] And among Englishmen who agreed with him were Sir Edward Clarke, K.C., and Baron Bramwell, a distinguished judge with a clear and independent mind.[7]

In January 1880, one of his friends, evidently not yet recovered from the shock of her husband's death, wrote Benjamin a despondent letter and in replying he strongly advised her to give herself an occupation. To Benjamin the greatest remedy for despondency and brooding over adverse circumstances was to keep busy, and that he had always done. He also admitted that he was of a temperament that always looked on the bright side of things, though he agreed with the lady about the gloomy London fogs in winter. He did not find them actually depressing, but he frequently complained of them and could not accustom himself to the damp cold temperature of the city.[8] It was too much to expect of one who had spent over fifty years of his life in the warm Southern climate of the United States.

But Benjamin did say that he would 'always be tempted to spend May and June in London.' He was planning upon his retirement to live in Paris with his family, but the French capital never seemed to interest him greatly aside from his associations with his people there. He much preferred London in which 'there is so much that is congenial to my taste and interesting to my mind.'[9]

In May 1880, Benjamin received a letter from his niece, Eugenia Kruttschnitt,[10] which took him back many years to the time when he was absorbed with something very different from legal appeal cases. The letter affected him so much that he stayed later than usual at his chambers in order to answer it that evening. Eugenia wanted to marry a certain suitor and when her family objected to the match turned to her beloved uncle for advice and consolation.

Benjamin urged his 'own sweet darling,' not to take any hasty action. 'Don't imagine I am going to read you a moral lesson, for I hate them whether as giver or receiver,' and he said that he was not writing as an old man who had forgotten he was once young. Could Benjamin have been thinking of his own hasty marriage and all the unhappiness it had caused him when he added, 'I *don't* forget this, and I feel for you just as I felt for myself over fifty years ago . . . What I want to warn you against is the impatience and rashness which are so natural at your age and which may prove fatal to your happiness.'

With his family in Louisiana Benjamin's ties still seemed to be almost as close as ever, though antipathy to the Carpetbag regime, the pressure of his legal work, and other causes had prevented him from ever visiting them there. But his public career in America, particularly during the tragic Confederate years, was now a fading memory, a memory which he was loath to revive. When L. Q. Washington saw him in London Benjamin barely mentioned the subject of the Confederacy.[11] And Jefferson Davis, who wrote him about an old war-time controversy, found from the reply that Benjamin preferred to let the matter be buried:

I have thus given you my dear friend the recollections which you ask for. So far as the use of my name is concerned, I freely confess that it is not agreeable to mix in any way in controversies of the past which for me are buried forever. If at any time your character or motives should be assailed and my testimony needed, I should be indeed an arrant coward to permit this feeling to interfere with my prompt advance to your side to repel the calumny. But in any other case, I long only for repose. I seek rest and quiet after the exhausting labours of 68 years of a somewhat turbulent or rather adventurous life.[12]

Later in May 1881, however, Benjamin wrote Lawley to inquire whether Jefferson Davis's book on the Confederacy had appeared 'on this side,' and if so, where it could be secured; [13] and in a letter to S. L. M. Barlow the following November he labelled as false the current rumors that large sums of money belonging to the late Confederacy were still in Europe.[14]

It was the last letter of any significance that Benjamin is known to have written regarding Confederate affairs. Suppose he had prepared a full account of his American experiences. What extraordinary facts would have been revealed, what deep secrets uncovered! But unlike many surviving Confederates who devoted a large part of their time to writing their reminiscences and observations on the war and earlier events of American history, he never prepared so much as a magazine article about his career.

Benjamin's legal practice was to include only a few more cases of particular interest. In March 1881, he appeared in the House of Lords in the then well-known Tichborne case, or *Castro* v. *the Queen*. Castro had perjured himself by swearing that he was Roger Tichborne in the effort to recover the Tichborne estates and had been sentenced to fourteen years of penal servitude. The question raised by the writ of error in the court below was not concerned with Castro's guilt, but with the validity on technical grounds of the sentence imposed upon him. Now on appeal to the House of Lords, Mr. Benjamin, Mr. Atherly-Jones, Mr. Hedderwick, and Mr. Russell Spratt appeared for the appellant; the Attorney-General, the Solicitor-General, Mr. Poland, and Mr. A. L. Smith for the Crown. The report of the case, which filled more than two columns in the *Times*, showed clearly that this was another of Benjamin's desperate cases. After the arguments of the counsel had continued for two days, the appeal was dismissed, Lord Watson even saying in his opinion that 'after hearing the very able and ingenious arguments for the appellant,' he had come to the conclusion that no ground whatever had been shown for setting aside this judgment.[15]

In April 1882, however, Benjamin was on the winning side at the House of Lords in the *Earl of Zetland* v. *Hislop and Others*, a suit which became a leading case in Scotch feudal law.[16] During his last decade of practice Benjamin had appeared in a number of Scotch appeals. As early as 1874 he was associated with Lord Advocate Young in a Scotch shipping case,[17] and after 1876 there was considerable increase in his Scotch briefs. He was among the counsel for the liquidators of the City of Glasgow Bank in all the appeals made from the judgment of the First Division,[18] and he represented the Caledonian Railway Company, the Clyde Navigation trustees, and other important Scotch companies.[19] In 1881 he made a record for a foreign-born barrister when he appeared in eight of the fifteen cases listed in the *Session Reports*.[20]

Moreover, these Scotch appeals often dealt with matters with which the average English lawyer was unfamiliar—as, for example, cases like the *Earl of Zetland* v. *Hislop*, relating to the Scotch feudal system.[21] Benjamin was associated with a number of the leading lawyers of the Scotch bar, and a member later wrote that 'the exceptional grasp of highly technical law which he exhibited was marvellous.'[22]

One large business transaction about which Benjamin was consulted related to a Scotch company that was constructing several hundred miles of railroad in Oregon. After this company, of which Lord Airley was president, had completed the railroad they leased it to Henry Villard, who had acquired all the railroads entering Portland, Oregon. J. B. Montgomery, who had built the railroad for the Scotch company and was a large stockholder in it, was selected to go to Scotland to arrange for the leasing of the road. After the lease was signed, Montgomery took it to London for examination by Benjamin, 'who was esteemed the greatest international lawyer living.' Benjamin kept the lease for several days; when Montgomery and his wife called upon him he proudly stated, 'If it does not stand it is impossible for the ingenuity of man to construct a lasting document.'[23]

By this time Benjamin's most cherished hope was that he would have a grandchild to play with in his old age, but although he wrote Lawley late in 1882 that 'I still live in hopes' his fond desire was never realized.[24] Now seventy-one years old, he was feeling his years, and his health was very bad. Heart trouble, a lingering result of a serious tramway accident in Paris the previous year, was added to a chronic diabetic condition.[25] He still hoped to enjoy a few years of tranquil life, but it would be at the price of taking no liberties with himself—'of avoiding steep stairs and *all* excitement, and doing my best to guard against catching cold, which the doctors warn me might easily prove fatal.'[26]

Incidentally, in view of Benjamin's political career in America it might be thought that he would be keenly interested in the significant political events in England. But such was not the case; he was interested, but only as an outsider. A conservative in England as well as in America, he was surprised and disappointed at the result of the spring elections in 1880 when the Disraeli ministry was overthrown and the Liberals returned to power. Commenting on the election Benjamin wrote, 'Nothing is so abhorrent to me as the Radicalism which seeks to elevate the populace into the governing class.' The election results, however, were not altogether unpleasant to him, for he added, 'But I am much consoled by the success of a number of personal friends who have succeeded in contests which seemed almost desperate.' [27]

The last American known to have called upon him was a Cincinnati Jew, Gustavus Wald. Arriving with a letter of introduction from Senator Jonas of Louisiana, he was cordially received by Benjamin. He took Wald to hear him argue a case before the Privy Council, 'the court above all others in Christendom in which one can practice law like a gentleman.'

This court, so Wald learned, had the widest jurisdiction of any in the world, for it was the final court of appeal of the entire British Empire except for Great Britain and Ireland. And yet it presented the 'singular anomaly of not having the authority to pronounce any judgments whatsoever.' In theory, the judges merely advised the queen, and carrying out this fiction 'the judges sit at a large table; they wear neither robes nor wigs and there were no tip-staves or usual court functionaries but only liveried servants.'

The case on trial was an appeal from the court of last resort in Canada, on the question of the constitutionality of a law passed by the Dominion Parliament. 'In a discussion of this kind Mr. Benjamin, of course, had English lawyers at a great disadvantage, and his argument was more than anything else like an authoritative statement to the judges of the law applicable to the case. The court did in the end decide the case in his favor.' Wald continued:

English lawyers are much less emphatic and vehement in argument before a court than are American lawyers. But no lawyer whom I heard in England was so absolutely impersonal as Benjamin.

On both occasions that I heard him he seemed not to represent his client, but abstract justice, the law . . . Never raising his voice above the conversational tone, making no gestures, apparently having no personal interest in the event of the matter in hand, he stated his views upon the subject under discussion so easily and so quietly that no one not interested in it would have been moved to pay any attention. But anyone following him while he spoke would be ready at once to declare that the traditional belief that the law is difficult, obscure, or uncertain is false. As he spoke all uncertainty seemed to vanish; there appeared to be but one view which could in reason be accepted, and that view was presented so simply and clearly that it seemed that any boy of ten could not fail to grasp it.

Shortly before noon the judges retired, and Wald had lunch with Benjamin and the other counsel in another room across the hall: Mr. Bethume, a Canadian lawyer; Sir John Holker, and Sir Farral Herschel, the Solicitor-General. Beer and wine were served and while the men were smoking and chatting word was brought to them that the judges were ready to resume the case; the arguments were then concluded. Benjamin said to Wald, as they drove back to the Temple,

I suppose that the lawyers in America think that we make much less money here than they do, because you don't hear often of large single fees in cases here as you do on the other side, but I have done quite well. Now I practice only in three courts, the Court of Appeals, the Privy Council, and the House of Lords; I take no brief accompanied by less than fifty guineas and generally none marked less than one hundred guineas. As I try no case at nisi prius, and so, of course, get my cases on a record made up, I have simply to prepare the law applicable to a fixed state of facts, and that I can do in most cases over night.

From the time each case of mine is called, until the argument in it is concluded, I receive in it a refresher of ten guineas a day. As I can be in only one court at a time, while I am engaged in a case in one of the courts my refreshers in a case or cases in one or both the other courts are running on. And what is the most delightful thing about a practice here is that I never have to talk to, or even see, a client. My terms are known and solicitors either choose to employ me on them or they don't; of course, there is no such thing as bargaining about fees.[28]

On 19 May 1881 Benjamin opened in the House of Lords for the appellants in *London and County Banking Company* v. *Ratcliff*, a case which, because of an incident that occurred during the hearing, was one of the most spectacular in which he ever appeared in England. Beginning his argument, Benjamin expounded at somewhat more than the usual length upon the facts as stated in the case, with the purpose of making the Lords familiar with the difficult and involved facts before the House was informed of the legal consequences to be derived from them. Sir H. Jackson, the leader for the appellants in the hearing at the lower court, had fully concurred in Benjamin's action, remarking that never before in the course of his practice had his mind been so exercised by the difficulties of a case.

The Lords began to show a little impatience, however, at what they deemed unnecessary protraction of the case and from time to time requested Benjamin to state the propositions of law on which he relied. After ignoring the requests for a while, Benjamin was so strongly importuned that he stated one or two propositions that were at once challenged by the Lords.

When he restated one of these propositions in a slightly different form, Lord Chancellor Selborne, an able judge but of a very different disposition from Benjamin, commented, 'Nonsense!' The comment was made *sotto voce* and not intended to be heard, but it did reach Benjamin's ear.

Disturbed by such a remark from the Lord Chancellor and in the supreme tribunal of the realm, he began with 'heightened color' to tie up his papers. This done, he bowed gravely to the members of the House and after saying, 'That is my case, my Lord,' he turned and left the House.

'You would not stand that, would you?' he remarked to one of the counsel as he passed him.

It was then only about midday and the second counsel for the appellant being absent, their junior counsel had to continue the argument as best he could. The next day when the case was resumed, Benjamin being still absent, Davey, the second counsel, rose to argue for the appellants. When he did so the Lord Chancellor remarked, in substance, 'Mr. Davey, it is unusual for the House to hear three counsel for the same party, and we have already heard Mr. Benjamin and Mr. Russell Roberts. I notice Mr. Benjamin's absence, however, and I fear that it may be attributable to his having taken umbrage at an unfortunate remark which fell from me during his argument; and in which I referred to a proposition he stated as "nonsense." I certainly was not justified in applying such a term to anything that fell from Mr. Benjamin, and I wish you to convey to him my regret that I should have used such an expression.'

Whereupon Davey informed Benjamin what Lord Selborne had said and induced him to write a note to the Lord Chancellor acknowledging the apology and, so Davey thought, expressing regret that the incident had occurred. Thus it had ended happily for all concerned.[29]

* * *

Benjamin was definitely planning to retire in August 1883 and was arranging his affairs to that end.[30] He wanted to spend his last years in Paris with his family. Although he still would have preferred to live in England, the elegant mansion on the Avenue d'Iéna afforded him every comfort and was so arranged that Ninette and her husband could live there with him and Natalie. Benjamin, the cosmopolitan, adjusted himself to a French ménage with the French language spoken in the family; indeed, Natalie and Ninette had lived so long in Paris that they had almost forgotten how to speak English.[31]

On 24 and 25 July 1882 Benjamin appeared before the House of Lords in what was destined to be his last case before that august body. The 'noble and learned Lords' present that morning, according to the *Times,* were the Lord Chancellor, Lord O'Hagan, Lord Blackburn, and Lord Watson; the case before them *Neill and Another* v. *the Duke of Devonshire,* carried up from the Irish Court of Appeal. The counsel included Mr. Serjeant Hemphill and Mr. R. Lane for the appellants; Mr. Benjamin, Mr. S. Walker, Q.C., Mr. J. Atkinson, Q.C., and Mr. Bewley, Q.C., for the defendant.

The appeal, somewhat analogous to one of Benjamin's Scotch cases, resulted from litigation about certain fishing rights in Ireland belonging to the Duke of Devonshire, who based his title upon Crown grants and rights, some dating from before Magna Charta. The Duke had brought actions for trespass to vindicate his right as against the general public to the valuable salmon fisheries in the lower part of the Blackwater River in Ireland; the appellants, who were fishermen, alleged that the public had from time immemorial exercised the right of salmon fishing in the *locus in quo*. Since the case had first been tried in 1869, it had been submitted to seven special juries, and there had been two verdicts for the appellants, two for the defendant, and in three the juries had disagreed.

Now the Lord Chancellor held in his opinion that the practice of 'cot fishing' on the Blackwater had been by sufferance rather than by right; the fishing did not displace a prescriptive right supported by written titles and evidence of long possession. 'It is the wise policy of the law,' he quoted Mr. Justice Heath as saying in the celebrated gleaning case of *Steel* v. *Houghton*, 'not to construe acts of charity, though continued and repeated for ever so many years, in such a manner as to make them the foundation of legal obligation.' The Lord Chancellor was, therefore, of the opinion that the appeal should be dismissed with costs.[32]

Thus Benjamin was on the winning side in his last case before the House of Lords. He had planned to leave for Paris in December and to return to London again in the middle of February for its next meeting, 'as almost all my work is confined to that tribunal.' He was looking forward keenly to his final retirement from the bar the following August and for a time surrendered to one of his rare fits of despondency.

I am tired of work and need repose—I suppose that this feeling overcomes me by reason of the shock given to my whole system in May 1880, from which it seems impossible for me to recover radically—I am always ailing in some way, and I 'give up'— . . . Such weather as we have here! fog, fog, fog! I am most impatient to [go] *somewhere* where I can breathe.[33]

At Christmas Benjamin had a severe heart attack and was forced to have absolute rest and to retire completely from his professional work. He had fondly hoped ' "to spend, to lend and to give" when once I shuffle off my wig and gown,' but could now live only the unhappy life of an invalid.[34] He formally announced his retirement and returned the briefs in his office along with the money that had been advanced him for retainers ($100,000, it was reported).[35] He remained in Paris where he was kept in absolute repose and he despondently wrote a friend, 'whether I shall die in a few months or continue to live as a confirmed invalid for some years, I neither know nor much care.' [36]

Yet there was much to cheer and encourage him, as he fully realized when his health took a temporary turn for the better. The announcement of his retirement brought forth a series of ovations such as have been accorded few lawyers in the history of the legal profession. There were laudatory articles and editorials in the newspapers and legal magazines,[37] a shower of personal letters from friends and associates,[38] and, to cap it all, a dinner given in his honor by the bar of England.

After regretfully announcing Benjamin's retirement from practice, the *Times* said that he had been for many years 'almost the leader of the English Bar in all heavy appeal cases,' and 'in the widest sense of the term, an international lawyer,' and expressed its disappointment that he had not been made an English judge 'whatever the apparent inconveniences in the way of his elevation.' Exception might be taken to the assertion by the *Times* that Benjamin employed no 'sophistries' and his argument was 'as judicial a statement as could have been the weightiest summing up from the bench.' Yet there would be few to dispute its statement that in mercantile law Benjamin had 'equal authority with a standard textbook'; for many years he had been 'more like an assessor of the Supreme Courts of Appeal than a simple practitioner . . . When circumstances deny to exceptional talents their proper native sphere, it is for the benefit of the common stock of human intelligence that its products should not be lost for want of hospitality elsewhere.' [39]

And the *Telegraph* was even more laudatory: 'The history of the English bar will hereafter have no prouder story to tell, than that of the marvellous advance of Mr. Benjamin from the humble position he occupied as a junior in 1866 to the front rank of his profession in 1883.' [40]

* * *

The neo-Gothic hall of the Inner Temple, with its fine panelling, its succession of coats of arms, its noble paintings and statuary, was filled for the banquet that evening with a splendid company. In the chair sat the Attorney-General, Sir Henry James. On his right was Benjamin, on his left the Lord Chancellor, the Earl of Selborne, while the guests comprised some two hundred other members of the legal profession including not only 'all the higher and more distinguished ornaments,' such as the Lord Chief Justice, the Solicitor-General, the Lord Advocate for Scotland, and the Attorney-General for Ireland, but a long list of judges, Queen's Counsel, and other lawyers.

Upon Benjamin's retirement, the Attorney-General on behalf of the Bar of England had invited him to a farewell dinner in his honor. Delayed because of his feeble health, it was given on Saturday evening, 30 June 1883. No American lawyer had ever before been given such recognition by this bar.

After the toast to the Queen was drunk with the usual warmth, the Attorney-General rose to propose the toast of the evening, 'The Health of Mr. Benjamin,' which 'was received with great enthusiasm.'

The Attorney-General made a few references to the American Civil War which had left Benjamin with 'little save honour, reputation, and great gifts.' Then quoting the lines from Virgil on Dido's reception of Aeneas, *Ejectum littore egentem accepimus*, the speaker declared that Benjamin had found a place in the 'foremost rank of the English bar but it had not begrudged him the leadership he had so easily gained.' For the bar was

ever generous even in its rivalry towards success that is based on merit. And the merit must have been here, for who is the man save this one of whom it can be said that he held conspicuous leadership at the bars of two countries . . . The years are few since Mr. Benjamin was a stranger to us all, and in those few years he had accomplished more than most can ever hope in a life time to achieve.

Expressing the strong friendship felt for Benjamin by the members of the bar, the Attorney-General called on all the lawyers present from the Lord Chancellor to the 'veriest junior among us' to show their guest that 'as in past times our welcome to him was earnest and true, so now our hopes for his future life come with like sincerity from our hearts.'

Benjamin was deeply touched by the words of the Attorney-

General and by the fact that he was bidding a final farewell to most of his legal friends. In a few sincere words he expressed his appreciation for his kind reception from the time he was first admitted to the English bar 'down to this magnificent testimonial, the recollection of which will never fade from my memory, and on which I shall always love to dwell.' [41]

The rest could be only anti-climax. Returning to France, he stayed for some time with his family in the country near Le Mans, which did his health 'a great deal of good,' so he thought, and he wrote a long and cheerful letter to Thomas F. Bayard.[42] His life with Natalie now appears to have been harmonious enough. When she had to undergo a painful operation, he held her hand throughout the ordeal.[43] Despite the winter season and the recurrence of his own illness, he still tried to look on the bright side of things but there was now an underlying note of pessimism. Thus he wrote to Lawley late in the following April,[44]

I have been very ill (but I believe I have turned the corner this time), otherwise I could not have left unanswered your sympathetic and affectionate letter; but I have been quite unable to write. For more than two months, I have alternated between my bed and my armchair; but if we can only get rid of this glacial temperature and dry East wind, I shall get some strength. What I require is warmth—will it never come?

For Benjamin, it came too late. After a relapse, he died on 6 May 1884 at his house in Paris. He was buried at the cemetery of Père-lachaise in a tomb that for many years after his death bore inscriptions only for the families of St. Martin and de Bousignac.[45] But in 1938 [46] the Paris chapter of the Daughters of the Confederacy put a marker on the grave of the man whose life, despite its share of human weaknesses, offers one of the most remarkable examples in modern history of successful struggle against adversity.

Notes

CHAPTER I

1. In conversation with the late James W. Dinkins, who repeated it to the writer at his (Dinkins's) home in New Orleans, 26 Dec. 1936.
2. Ibid.
3. *The Times*, 9 May 1884.
4. There is a dispute about how many of Disraeli's ancestors are Sephardic Jews. See Monypenny, *Disraeli*, I, chap. I. At any rate, some of his forebears were Sephardim and he was generally regarded as a Spanish Jew.
5. For interesting data on the Sephardim in Europe and America see *World's Work*, Dec. 1922 and Jan. 1923, articles by Burton Hendrick.
6. *Jewish Encyclopedia*, v, pp. 363-4.
7. Data from Moses D. Sasso, reader of the Hebrew congregation, Saint Thomas, Virgin Islands.
8. Thus Judah P. Benjamin would be only remotely connected with the Mendes who escaped from Spain to any country other than Portugal. For the Portuguese Mendes, the reference here is to the *Jewish Encyclopedia*, VIII, p. 485, which adds that King John II of Portugal assigned the city of Oporto as their residence.
9. From original memorandum of Lieut. Governor Henry M. Hyams Sr. of Louisiana, written in a family Bible about 1860. Copy through courtesy of Hyams's granddaughter, Mrs. Judith Hyams Douglas of New Orleans. In the memorandum, Hyams, a descendant of Eleazar Levy of Holland, a brother of Eva Levy, says that Eleazar 'was a man of good education and highly instructed in the Hebrew Language and Literature.' And as for Eva, she was said to have 'been of great beauty' and to have become 'the wife of a very opulent Spanish Jewish merchant [De Mendez] . . . This marriage between the Portugee and the Tedaesqua [from which issued the mother of Judah P. Benjamin] was the first of any note in Europe as . . . the educated rich and proud . . . De Mendez, exiled as he was, held in all the capitals of Europe, a social position high above the Native Jew and especially in Holland and Germany.'
10. The cemetery record for the Hebrew Cemetery, Canal and N. Anthony Sts., New Orleans, as transcribed by the W.P.A. survey, shows that Rebecca Mendez (De Mendes) Benjamin died 2 Oct. 1847, aged 58. She was born, therefore, presumably in late 1789 or before 2 Oct. 1790. Solomon de Mendes is first listed in the London directories in 1790, but Rebecca was born presumably before the arrival of her parents there, for her baptism is not recorded at Bevis Marks, as is that of two younger sisters.

11. Contemporary London city directories in British Museum and personal interview with Albert M. Hyamson, author of *A History of the Jews in England*, London, 1928.
12. Their first child, Rebecca Benjamin (Levy), was born in 1809. Obituary in New Orleans *Picayune*, 17 Nov. 1884. See also Virgin Islands records (in Danish) at National Archives. The description of Philip Benjamin is from the New York *Tribune*, 9 Apr. 1884, and data given by the late Rabbi Barnett Elzas of Charleston, S. C. Philip's naturalization record in the Postoffice Building, Charleston, shows that he was a native of Nevis and 44 years old when admitted to citizenship on 26 Oct. 1825.
13. Lawley MSS., chap. 1.
14. Personal visit to Bevis Marks.
15. 'Matriculs' or lists of taxpayers for Saint Croix in National Archives. Translation from the Danish by Harold Larson of the National Archives.
16. Data from Moses D. Sasso, Saint Thomas, Virgin Islands.
17. *The Virgin Islands of the United States, Report by the Governor*, pamphlet, Washington, D. C., 1928; and other information supplied by U. S. Department of Interior officials in Washington and the Virgin Islands. Also see Gertrude Atherton, *The Conqueror*, New York, 1902.
18. Data from Moses D. Sasso. The date and place of Benjamin's birth are sometimes confused with those of his cousin, Judah Benjamin, son of Emmanuel and Esther Benjamin, born at Saint Thomas, 30 Nov. 1811. See also Butler, *Benjamin*, p. 367.
19. Information from Moses D. Sasso and Harry E. Taylor, U. S. Administrator for Saint Croix.
20. Benjamin to his sister, Mrs. John (Peninah) Kruttschnitt, 29 Sept. 1865. Copy in Pierce Butler papers.
21. Contemporary records of Jacob Levy in courthouse, Wilmington; *Publications of American Jewish Historical Society*, No. 19, p. 75. Philip Benjamin in 1813 was a member of St. Tammany Lodge, No. 30, of Wilmington.
22. *Cape Fear Recorder*, 9 Sept. 1816.
23. Ibid.
24. Record Book Q, p. 183, 16 Aug. 1817. Wilmington Courthouse.
25. Ibid. p. 20, 28 Mar. 1817.
26. *Recorder*, op. cit.
27. Contemporary records in Cumberland County Courthouse, Fayetteville, N. C.; advertisement in North Carolina *Observer*, 4 Mar. 1819.
28. Lawley MSS., chap. 1, letter from Benjamin's schoolmate, R. C. Belden.
29. *War Days in Fayetteville, North Carolina*, compiled by the J. E. B. Stuart Chapter, United Daughters of Confederacy, Fayetteville (pamphlet); G. G. Johnson, *Antebellum North Carolina*, Chapel Hill, 1937, various citations.
30. Data from Charles G. Rose, Fayetteville.
31. James C. MacRae, 'The Highland-Scotch Settlement in North Carolina,' in *The North Carolina Booklet*, IV, Feb. 1905, No. 10, p. 20.
32. Courthouse records. Belden letter, Lawley MSS.
33. North Carolina *Observer*, 4 Mar. 1819.
34. Belden letter, Lawley MSS.
35. Data from Henry Levy, Fayetteville.
36. Lawley MSS. Another Belden letter, of 30 Oct. 1897.

37. *War Days in Fayetteville*, op. cit.
38. *Cape Fear Recorder*, 2 Feb. 1822; Lawley MSS. with Benjamin's statement to Lawley about the Academy.
39. Johnson, *Antebellum North Carolina*, pp. 309-10.
40. Belden letter, Lawley MSS.
41. Cumberland Courthouse records.
42. Ibid.
43. Belden letter, 12 Jan. 1898. Lawley MSS.
44. Charleston *Courier*, 8 May 1822.
45. The facts about this slave conspiracy are given in *An Account of the Late Intended Insurrection*, pamphlet (published by authority of city of Charleston, 1822); Wallace, *History of South Carolina*, II, pp. 416-18; Benjamin Brawley, *A Social History of the American Negro*, New York, 1921, pp. 132-40; contemporary issues of the Charleston *Courier;* John B. Adger, *My Life and Times*, Richmond, 1899 (out of print), pp. 52-3.
46. Articles on Petigru and Memminger in *Dictionary of American Biography*.
47. *Writings of Hugh Legaré*, Charleston, 1846, I, p. 207.
48. *Courier*, 27 Mar. 1822.
49. Ibid. 17 Aug.
50. Ibid. 12 Aug. *et al.*
51. Wallace, *South Carolina*, II, esp. chap. 74.
52. Elzas, *The Jews of South Carolina*, esp. chap. VIII; 'Charleston' in *Jewish Encyclopedia.*
53. Elzas, pp. 185-7.
54. Office of Register of Means and Conveyance, Charleston, Book M9, pp. 231-2.
55. Ibid. R9, pp. 271-3, and T9, pp. 486-9.
56. See note 12.
57. In Ripley's 'Believe It or Not' syndicated newspaper feature.
58. Contemporary Charleston city directories.
59. For this data on the Jewish reform movement in Charleston and Philip's connection therewith see Robert Mills, *Statistics of South Carolina*, Charleston, 1826, pp. 416-18; Elzas, *The Jews of South Carolina*, p. 163 *et al.* and *Leaves From My Historical Scrapbook*, 2nd Ser., No. 6; personal data from the late Rabbi Elzas; 'Charleston' in *Jewish Encyclopedia.*
60. Letter from Simeon North, Benjamin's tutor at Yale to 'Mr. Brayton,' 30 Jan. 1827, in Library of Congress.
61. This information on Mrs. Benjamin is from Elzas, *Scrapbook*, 2nd Ser., No. 6; Butler, *Benjamin*, pp. 24, 32; contemporary Charleston directories; letter of 29 Dec. 1937 from Miss Mabel Runnette, Librarian, Beaufort Township Library.
62. Personal interview with Mrs. G. G. Myrover, Fayetteville. Her mother-in-law was Mrs. H. G. Myrover, née Urbana du Hadway of Charleston.
63. William P. Trent, *William Gilmore Simms*, Boston, 1892, p. 5.
64. The facts about Benjamin's education in Charleston were secured from these sources: Charleston *Courier*, 4 Jan. 1898; Elzas, *The Jews of South Carolina*, pp. 185-7; and personal data from the author; data from Thomas T. Southworth, New York City.

CHAPTER II

1. Letter from Porter in Lawley MSS., chap. 1; data from Rabbi Elzas, Charleston; Butler, pp. 26-7. Benjamin's student accounts for 1826-7 show two notations which are evidently scholarship credits. Letter from George P. Day, Treasurer, Yale University, 21 July 1933 with information from H. J. Ostrander, cashier. See also letters from Simeon North to 'Mr. Brayton,' and Benjamin to President Day, cited later in this chapter.
2. Stokes, *Eminent Yale Men*, II, pp. 196-7.
3. Porter letter, op. cit.
4. Yale catalogue, Nov. 1825.
5. *Matriculation Book* in Yale records.
6. Catalogue, Nov. 1825.
7. Bagg, *Four Years at Yale*, pp. 519-20; *The Laws of Yale College*, 1795-1843.
8. *Matriculation Book*, op. cit.
9. Stokes, *Eminent Yale Men*, I, pp. 247-9.
10. See North letter, op. cit.; *New York Times*, 27 Feb. 1883, quoting reminiscences of Simeon North in Utica *Observer*, 24 Feb. 1883.
11. Catalogue, Nov. 1825.
12. Kingsley, *Yale*, I, p. 277.
13. Contemporary Yale catalogues.
14. North reminiscences, op. cit.
15. Ibid.
16. Kingsley, *Yale*, p. 304.
17. Bagg, *Yale*, pp. 319-20.
18. Philencratian Society records, Yale University.
19. Brothers in Unity Records, Yale University.
20. Calliopean Society Records, Yale University. Stokes, op. cit.
21. See Burton Hendrick, *Statesmen of the Lost Cause*, Boston, 1939, pp. 158-64, and book reviews thereof.
22. New Haven *Daily Morning Journal and Courier*, 5 Feb. 1861; F. Moore, *Rebellion Record*, I, 'Poetry and Incidents,' p. 20; *Independent*, 31 Jan. 1861.
23. Hendrick, op. cit. and data from Anson P. Stokes, author of *Eminent Yale Men*.
24. *Delta*, 2 Mar 1861.
25. See copies in Pierce Butler Papers.
26. Lawley MSS., chap. 1.
27. See note 1 above.
28. Calliopean Society Records. See meeting No. 294 in Minute Book, Dec. 1827 and Register of the Society.
29. In MS. Division, Library of Congress.
30. North to 'Mr. Brayton,' 30 Jan. 1827, in Library of Congress.
31. At Yale University.
32. Stokes, *Eminent Yale Men*, II, p. 263.
33. This information was given the writer by a former Yale official, who based it on a statement made to him by a Yale historian of the past century.

CHAPTER III

1. 'Henry M. Hyams,' in *Jewish Encyclopedia*, VI, p. 512.
2. William P. Trent, *William Gilmore Simms*, Boston, 1892, p. 4.
3. See files of the *Argus* for early 1828.
4. For valuable data on New Orleans of this period see the histories of New Orleans by King, Rightor, and Kendall; Asbury, *The French Quarter* and Atkinson's *Philadelphia Saturday Bulletin*, 25 May 1833.
5. Butler, op. cit. p. 32.
6. Lawley MSS., chap. 1, and quoted letter from Benjamin's friend, Capt. J. R. Hamilton, in Charleston *News and Courier*, 11 Jan. 1898. Butler, *Benjamin*, pp. 32-4.
7. Benjamin to James A. Bayard, 19 Mar. 1861, in Pierce Butler Papers; Butler, op. cit. p. 33.
8. For details of this epidemic see Asbury, *The French Quarter*, p. 292; King, *New Orleans*, pp. 283-6; William Allen, *Life of John McDonogh*, Baltimore, 1886, p. 54.
9. *Picayune*, 2 Feb. 1843.
10. King, *New Orleans*, p. 283.
11. Benjamin was admitted to the bar on 16 Dec. 1832, and married about 12 Feb. 1833. Max Kohler, *Publications of American Jewish Historical Society*, No. 12. Donation Book. No. 3, p. 321, in Civil District Courthouse Building, New Orleans. Lawley MSS., chap. 3.
12. Contemporary New Orleans city directories and Butler, op. cit. p. 34.
13. Elzas, *Leaves From My Historical Scrapbook*, 2nd Ser., No. 1, quoting Papers of Gabriel Manigault.
14. Natalie's obituary record in Palace of Justice, Paris, France and contemporary New Orleans directories.
15. Letter from Mrs. Jefferson Davis in Lawley MSS. Natalie's obituary record, op. cit.
16. Contemporary city directories; Ripley, *Social Life in Old New Orleans*, New York, 1912, p. 90. Records of St. Martin house, Civil District Courthouse, New Orleans, courtesy of Miss Mary Evelyn Kay, New Orleans. Mrs. Andrew Maggio, wife of the owner of the Condé (Chartres) Street house, told Miss Kay in August 1938 that the second story was added by her (Mrs. Maggio's) father about thirty-five years before.
17. Stanley Arthur, *Old New Orleans, a History of the Vieux Carré*, pp. 216-17; contemporary city directories; data from Miss Kay. St. Martin apparently built this house. See Arthur, op. cit. and record of sale of the lot to St. Martin on 28 July 1835 in Civil District Courthouse.
18. Butler, op. cit. pp. 35-6, 228 *et al.*; letter from Mrs. Jefferson Davis in Lawley MSS.
19. Obituary record of Ninette Benjamin de Bousignac, in Palace of Justice, Paris.
20. Butler, op. cit. p. 35. Benjamin's life also offers abundant evidence of this fact.
21. Contemporary New Orleans city directories.
22. Contemporary city directories; record of sale of St. Martin house in Civil District Courthouse (Auguste St. Martin to William A. Gasquet, 23 Nov. 1853).

23. Butler, op. cit. pp. 37-8.
24. *Miller's Louisiana Reports, Eastern District*, v, 1832-1833, pp. 280-81.
25. *Louisiana Reports*, VII, pp. 483-4 and VIII, pp. 221-3.
26. For Benjamin's office address see contemporary city directories. Later from 1838 to about 1855 it was in Exchange Place. J. P. Benjamin and T. Slidell, *Digest of the Reported Decisions of the Superior Court of the Late Territory of Orleans and the Supreme Court of the State of Louisiana*, New Orleans, 1834. See also revised edition, 1840; Butler, op. cit. pp. 37-8; and W. D. Lewis, *Great American Lawyers*, VI, pp. 263-4.
27. Thomas D. Clark, *A Pioneer Southern Railroad*, p. 39.
28. Contemporary *Louisiana Reports;* letters from Benjamin to John McDonogh, 9 Sept. 1836 and 7 Aug. 1838 in Howard Library, New Orleans and MS. Room, Duke University Library, respectively.
29. For available data about these and other contemporary New Orleans lawyers see the books on New Orleans history cited in note 4 above, the *Dictionary of American Biography*, and Appleton's *Cyclopoedia*. The difficult case in which Benjamin is mentioned as defeating Janin was *Guinault v. Le Carpentier*, 14 *Louisiana Reports*, pp. 113-16.
30. 14 *Louisiana Reports*, pp. 164-6.
31. 17 *Louisiana Reports*, pp. 120-21.
32. 14 *Louisiana Reports*, pp. 113-16.
33. See contemporary volumes of the *Louisiana Reports;* Butler, op. cit. pp. 38-40. Senator William Cabell Bruce of Baltimore wrote this author that he heard Gen. Joseph R. Anderson of Richmond say he had served on juries addressed by Benjamin 'and that a more finished and persuasive advocate it would be hard to conceive' (letter from Bruce, 8 Apr. 1931).
34. *McCargo* v. *New Orleans Insurance Company* covers over 130 pp. in *Robinson's Reports*, I. James G. Blaine later asserted that Benjamin was the author of the doctrine that the Federal Government must protect slave property. Blaine, *Twenty Years in Congress*, Norwich, Conn., 1884-6, I, p. 160. Louis Gruss, 'Judah P. Benjamin,' in *Louisiana Historical Quarterly*, Oct. 1936, pp. 1023-6. Brief for defendants in *Lockett* v. *Merchants Insurance Company* in Howard Library, New Orleans. John Bassett Moore, *A Digest of International Law*, Washington, 1906, II, p. 352. George Richards, *Law of Insurance*, 4th ed., New York, 1932, p. 764. 43 *American Decisions*, pp. 180-98.
35. Butler, op. cit. p. 47.
36. There is valuable data on the Gullahs and their environment in D. C. Heyward, *Seed from Madagascar*, Chapel Hill, 1937.
37. Lawley MSS., chap. 1; William Elliott, *Carolina Sports*, Columbia, S. C., 1918, chap. 1.
38. John Whitaker, *Sketches of Life in Louisiana*, New Orleans, 1847, pp. 27-30.

CHAPTER IV

1. See Monypenny, *Disraeli*.
2. For a discussion of this and other questions relating to contemporary Louisiana see Kendall, *New Orleans*, I, esp. pp. 206-9, and Shugg, *Class Struggle in Louisiana*, pp. 1-156.
3. See letter to editors of *Picayune*, 27 Mar. 1841 from 'Many Wellwishers':

'In view of the questions of vast importance to this municipality which are now in agitation, and the successful solution of which requires the exercise of great unanimity of action, and much talent, zeal and judgment on the part of the members of the Council,' Benjamin and three other men were offered as suitable candidates for aldermen, First Ward, First Municipality. But Benjamin was defeated (*Picayune*, 6 Apr. 1841). For further details about his first political efforts see New Orleans *Bee*, 4, 20 Apr.; 4, 25 June; 1, 4, 5 July 1842; *True Delta*, 14 July 1853; and Butler, op. cit. pp. 64-8.

4. *Picayune*, 31 Jan. 1843; 'Alexander Mouton' in *Dictionary of American Biography*.

5. For greater facility in the liquidation of the property of banks chartered by the state. *Picayune*, 4 Feb. 1843.

6. Ibid. 5 Apr. 1843.

7. Ibid. 6 Apr. 1843. The report was adopted.

8. Ibid. 21 Feb. 1843. The Whigs had been defeated in the local election the previous April. *Bee*, 4, 5, 20 Apr. 1842.

9. *Picayune*, 14 Mar. 1843.

10. For other references to Benjamin's work at this legislative session see *Picayune*, 3, 6, 10, 11, 12, 20, 21 Jan.; 2 Feb. 1843, *et al*. On 9 January Benjamin nominated Charles M. Conrad for United States Senator but the vote in the Legislature was Alexander Porter, 45; C. M. Conrad, 22; and John Slidell, 5 (*Picayune*, 10 Jan. 1843). For further data on fencing and duelling in New Orleans, see Lyle Saxon, *New Orleans*, pp. 187-201.

11. *The Occident and American Jewish Advocate*, 1, 1844, pp. 216-353; *The Israelites of Louisiana*, W. E. Myers, publisher (no author or date given), pp. 40-41.

12. Mrs. Myrover, *ante*, chap. 1, note 62, quoted her mother-in-law as saying that Benjamin inquired complainingly of his own mother why she named him Judah.

William Cabell Bruce (letter to author, 8 Apr. 1931) gave the following story which was repeated to him by John K. Cowen, for many years General Counsel for the Baltimore and Ohio Railroad: 'On one occasion, Benjamin, when in Baltimore, went before a Justice of the Peace to make affidavit to a paper. A blank had been left in the certificate of affidavit for the insertion of the name of the affiant, and, when Benjamin handed the paper to the Justice, he asked him to fill in the blank. Instead of inserting the name Judah, the Justice inadvertently inserted the name Judas; whereupon, Benjamin reclaimed possession of the paper and dashed it down with great force on the desk of the Justice, exclaiming, as he did so: 'My God, man, is not Judah Jew enough?'

13. For this data on the Convention of 1844-5 and related events see Butler, op. cit. pp. 72-95; New Orleans *Tropic*, 25 June, 30 Sept., and 14 Nov. 1844, and *Courier*, 19, 20, 23 Nov.; *Picayune*, 24 Jan. 1845; *Proceedings and Debates of the Convention of Louisiana*, New Orleans, 1845, pp. 89, 131-4, 142, 156-7, 187-9, 220-25, 382, 906-11, *et al*. Kendall, *New Orleans*, 1, pp. 204-9; *Louisiana Historical Quarterly*, xii, No. 3, July 1929, pp. 406-7 (from article by James K. Greer).

14. *De Bow's Review*, 1, p. 83.

15. Robert Barnwell, ed., *The New Orleans Book,* New Orleans, 1851; *World's Best Orations,* x, pp. 99-110.
16. Whitaker, *Sketches,* op. cit.
17. Elzas, *Scrapbook,* op. cit.; article on Bellechasse by John P. Coleman, courtesy of Yale Alumni Office; Butler, op. cit. pp. 36, 57-8.
18. Butler, op. cit. p. 36.
19. See letter from one of Benjamin's law clerks, in Lawley MSS.
20. Personal visit to Bellechasse; data from Mrs. Judith Hyams Douglas and General Allison Owen, Judah P. Benjamin Memorial Association, New Orleans; *Congressional Globe, 2nd Session, 35th Congress,* 2 Mar. 1859, p. 1573. *Picayune,* 12 May 1925 and 6 May 1934, and numerous other references chiefly in 1923-7; William P. Spratling, *Old Plantation Houses in Louisiana,* New York, 1927, pp. 157-8.
21. Butler, op. cit. pp. 58-9, 62, and tombstone data (see chap. 1, Note 10).
22. For this account of Benjamin's work as a sugar planter, see contemporary volumes of *De Bow's Review,* especially II, pp. 332-45, Nov. 1846; v, pp. 44-57, Jan. 1848, and pp. 357-64, Apr. 1848; Rightor, *New Orleans,* pp. 669, 679, *et al.;* Butler, op. cit. pp. 48-60; Herbert Kellar, ed., *Selected Writings of Solon Robinson, Pioneer and Agriculturist,* Indianapolis, 1936, II, 1846-51, pp. 178-85; Solon Robinson, ed., *Facts for Farmers,* New York, 1865, II, p. 947; *Annual Report of the Commissioner of Patents for* 1848; House of Representatives, 2nd Session, 30th Congress, Executive Document No. 59, pp. 278-336.
23. *Lockett* v. *Merchants Insurance Company,* brief for defendant. In Howard Library, New Orleans.
24. *Picayune,* 19 June 1848.
25. *New Orleans City Guide,* Federal Writers Project, 1938, pp. 64-5.
26. Butler, op. cit. p. 82.

CHAPTER V

1. *De Bow's Review,* I, pp. 498-502, June 1846.
2. *The Israelites of Louisiana,* Myers, W. E., publisher, p. 26; London *Times,* 9 May 1884.
3. Butler, op. cit. p. 95; *The Diary of James K. Polk,* Chicago, 1910, IV, pp. 357-9.
4. Ben. Perley Poore, *Perley's Reminiscences,* Philadelphia, 1886, I, p. 409.
5. Data in letter of 29 Mar. 1938 from Micou's grandson, the late Reverend Paul Micou, Charles Town, W. Va.; *William and Mary Quarterly,* 1st Ser., VI, p. 93; Butler, op. cit. p. 141; New Orleans *Crescent,* 24 Mar. 1854.
6. *Shultz and Hadden* v. *J. W. Payne, Louisiana Annual Reports,* VII, pp. 222-4.
7. *Rugely, Blair and Company* v. *Sun Mutual Insurance Company, Louisiana Reports,* VII, pp. 279-83; *St. Victor Barret* v. *New Orleans Insurance Company, Louisiana Reports,* VIII, pp. 3-4.
8. *Louisiana Reports,* VII, pp. 229-31.
9. For these facts about the filibuster trials, see Butler, op. cit. pp. 179-84; New Orleans *Delta,* 3, 10, 11, 14, 18, 22, 23 Jan. 1851; *True Delta,* 14 July 1853; 'John A. Quitman' and 'John Henderson' in *Dictionary of American Biography;* correspondence U. S. Department of Interior, 1850-51, courtesy of National Archives.

10. For the McDonogh case see *McDonogh* v. *Murdoch*, 15 *Howard*, pp. 367-415; Benjamin to McDonogh, 7 Aug. 1838, at Duke University; 'John McDonogh' in *Dictionary of American Biography*; 'Judah Philip Benjamin' by Louis Gruss in *Louisiana Historical Quarterly*, Oct. 1936, esp. pp. 989-92; W. D. Lewis, *Great American Lawyers*, IV, esp. p. 424; Rightor, *New Orleans*, p. 415; William Allen, *Life of John McDonogh*, pp. 51, 59, 79-80; Edgar M. Cahn, 'A Lawyer's Tale of Two Cities' in *The Tulanian*, Apr. 1939.

11. This account of Benjamin's railroad activities is derived from T. D. Clark, *A Pioneer Southern Railroad*, Chapel Hill, 1936, pp. 55-82; *Picayune*, 9 Aug. 1851 and 7 Jan. 1852; *Delta*, 7, 8 Jan.; 10, 17 Apr.; 8 June 1852, 15 *et al* July 1853; Butler, op. cit. pp. 119-36, a detailed and painstaking account; 'Judah Philip Benjamin' (author not given) in *Illinois Central Magazine*, Nov. 1913, courtesy of R. E. Collons, Assistant in Public Relations, Illinois Central System; Rightor, *New Orleans*, p. 302; *Congressional Globe*, XXIII, pt. I, 7, 12 Dec. 1853; 27 Feb. 1854; *True Delta*, 14 July 1853, editorial on Benjamin and the common council; W. E. Dodd, 'The Fight For The Northwest' in *American Historical Review*, XVI, No. 4, July 1911; Kendall, *New Orleans*, I, pp. 188-90.

12. Coleman article, op. cit.; Butler, op. cit. pp. 58-60; Lawley MSS., chap. 3, letters to Lawley of 13 Aug. 1897 and 27 Sept. 1898 from Benjamin's nephew, Ernest Kruttschnitt.

13. Butler, op. cit. pp. 97-8; *True Delta*, 28 Oct. 1851; *Orleanian*, 17 Oct., 7 Nov., and *Delta*, 9, 10, 14 Oct.

14. *Delta*, 10 Oct. 1851.

15. 'Duncan Kenner' in *Dictionary of American Biography;* data supplied by Kenner's son, Duncan Kenner of Nashville, Tenn.

16. *Delta*, 7 Feb. 1852, Washington correspondence, 28 Jan. 1852.

17. For the connection between Benjamin and Slidell and the effort to contest Benjamin's senatorial election, see Butler, pp. 116-18; *True Delta*, 6 Nov. 1852; 6, 22 Jan.; 1 Feb.; 11 June 1853; 28 June 1854; *Picayune*, 25, 27 Jan. and 13 Feb. 1853.

18. The Whig candidates in New Orleans for the convention were Benjamin, Christian Roselius, L. Matthews, and Cyprien Dufour. The *Delta* 21 May 1851 criticizes Benjamin as a prominent member of the constitutional convention of 1845 who was conspicuous for his 'maintenance of those very restrictions which have exerted the hostility of the Constitution that has lead to the present movement to change it.' *Delta*, 8, 15 May; 13, 15 June; Butler, op. cit. p. 104, quoting *Delta*, 2 July, 19 Sept.

19. For this data on the convention see *Journal, Louisiana Constitutional Convention of 1852*; Butler, op. cit. pp. 104-12; Shugg, *Class Struggle*, pp. 134-53, *True Delta*, 9, 11, 12, 19, 23, 26, 28 Sept.; 3, 20, 31 Oct.

20. See Stuart O. Landry, *History of the Boston Club*, New Orleans, 1938, esp. pp. 11, 13, 79, 203, 307, for this material relating to Benjamin's club life.

21. Butler, op. cit. pp. 136-7.

22. For an account of this banquet see Landry, pp. 50-55; *Picayune*, 23 Nov. 1853; and Butler, op. cit. pp. 138-9.

23. See Charles Warren, *Supreme Court in United States History*, II, pp. 516-

19; data from Micou's grandson, Reverend Paul Micou, Charles Town, W. Va.; and Butler, op. cit. pp. 118-19.

CHAPTER VI

1. This account of Pierce's inauguration and Benjamin's induction into office is based on *Appendix, Congressional Globe*, xxvii, pp. 243-5 and Washington *National Intelligencer*, 5 Mar. 1853.
2. See Frederick Bancroft, *Life of William H. Seward*, New York, 1900, i, pp. 333-4.
3. For an interesting reference by Benjamin to his 'nightmare' of '*Black* republicanism,' see his letter to James A. Bayard, 19 Mar. 1861. Copy in Pierce Butler Papers.
4. In Howard Library, New Orleans.
5. Mrs. Chesnut, *Diary From Dixie*, p. 55.
6. Mrs. Davis to Lawley, 8 June 1898.
7. Pierce Butler Papers.
8. Mortality records and contemporary city directories, Charleston; Lawley MSS., chap. 3, Ernest Kruttschnitt to Lawley, 27 Sept. 1898.
9. For this data on Bellechasse and related subjects see Solon Robinson, editor, *Facts for Farmers*, ii, p. 947; Herbert Kellar, editor, *Solon Robinson Selected Writings*, ii, pp. 178-85; *Report of Commissioner of Patents for 1848, Appendix*. Lawley MSS., chap. 3; Coleman article on Bellechasse, op. cit.; Butler, op. cit. pp. 60-61; Frederick Bancroft, *Slaveholding in the Old South*, Baltimore, 1931, pp. 325-6.
10. Data from Reverend Paul Micou, op. cit., and from Bradford's daughter-in-law, Mrs. Sidney Bradford, Avery Island, La. Butler, op. cit. pp. 141-2.
11. *True Delta*, 20 Mar. 1853; William H. Russell, *My Diary North and South*, p. 252.
12. See originals preserved in Federal Archives Building, Washington, D. C., and contemporary issues of the *Congressional Globe*.
13. *Congressional Globe*, xxviii, pt. 1, p. 361.
14. Ibid. pt. 2, p. 1199.
15. *Intelligencer*, 18 May 1854.
16. *Congressional Globe*, 1st Session, 33rd Congress, p. 1298; Rhodes, *History of United States*, New York, 1893, ii, p. 27.
17. *Congressional Globe*, 1st Session, 33rd Congress, Appendix, pp. 766-8.
18. Ibid. xxviii, pt. iii, pp. 1789-90.
19. For interesting data on Sumner, see Mrs. Davis, *Jefferson Davis*, i, pp. 557-8.
20. Rhodes, op. cit. i, chap. v.
21. 26 May 1854.
22. On 11 June 1854. Copy through courtesy of Raymond Wilkin, Boston.
23. For important MS. material relating to this episode, see the State Department archives for the period in Federal Archives Building. See esp. Philo White to Secretary of State Marcy, State Department Dispatches, 30 Sept., 2, 18 Oct., 2, 21, 22 Nov. 1854 and 17 Jan., 14 Feb., 31 Mar., 16 May 1855. See also the valuable treatment, based chiefly on MS. sources, in Curtis Wilgus, editor, *Modern Hispanic America*, i, 1938, Washington, 1938,

chap. 20, written by Roy F. Nichols; Butler, op. cit. pp. 142-4. *Delta*, 3 Jan. 1855; *True Delta*, 6, 7 Jan. 1855.

Benjamin made a contract with the Ecuador Government whereby one-fifth of all the guano was to go to the discoverers in proportion of one-third of one-fifth to De Brissot and two-thirds of one-fifth to Villamil. President Urbina of Ecuador was now willing to sign a treaty with White by which the United States was to lend Ecuador $3,000,000 to be paid from the proceeds of guano sales, and in return was to be permitted to buy guano at one dollar a ton less than the price paid by other nations, the lower price remaining in effect until the loan was repaid.

24. Petersburg *South-Side Democrat*, 4, 5, 7 Apr. 1856 and *Daily Express*, 7 Apr. 1856. Data through courtesy of Edward Wyatt, editor of the present Petersburg *Progress-Index*.

25. On 11 Jan. 1855. *Congressional Globe*, xxx, p. 236.

26. On 10 Jan. 1856. *Congressional Globe*, 2nd Session, 34th Congress, p. 207.

27. Ibid. p. 203, 10 Jan. 1856. See also pp. 388, 400-404.

28. For these arguments for economy see *Congressional Globe*, 1st and 2nd Session, 34th Congress, pp. 746, 787-8.

29. This speech with accompanying debate is in *ibid*. 1st Session, 34th Congress, pp. 1092-8. See also *Intelligencer*, 3 May 1856; Benjamin to Bayard, 3 May 1858, in Pierce Butler Papers; *Courier*, 11 May 1856.

30. These facts about Buchanan's nomination are derived from L. M. Sears, 'Slidell and Buchanan' in *American Historical Review*, xxvii, p. 724; G. F. Milton, *The Eve of Conflict*, Boston, 1934, pp. 224-7; and Sears, *Slidell*, pp. 122-4.

31. There is an excellent account of this speech in the Portland *Argus*, 9 Aug. 1856. See also *Congressional Globe*, 3rd Session, 34th Congress, 4 Dec. 1856, p. 36.

CHAPTER VII

1. For Benjamin's card playing see William H. Russell, *My Diary North and South*, i, p. 252; A. J. L. Fremantle, *Three Months in the Southern States*, New York, 1864, p. 210; Notes by T. F. Bayard in Pierce Butler Papers.

2. *Congressional Directory*, 3rd Session, 34th Congress, Dec. 1856 and subsequent years. The Directory for 1860 lists Benjamin as living at Jackson Place, Corner H and 16½ Sts. (the Decatur House), and as being the third-ranking member of the Judiciary Committee as well as chairman of the Committee on Private Land Claims. Mrs. Clement Clay, *A Belle of the Fifties*, pp. 42-3.

3. The sources of information for these two paragraphs are: data from Mason family through courtesy of the late Herbert Ezekiel, Richmond, Va.; Mrs. Clay, op. cit. p. 92; T. F. Bayard Notes, op. cit.; 'David L. Yulee' in *Dictionary of American Biography*, and data from Yulee family.

4. Records of Library of Congress. Of course these books merely supplemented those in his private library. Among the books that Benjamin borrowed during 1853-61, it is particularly interesting to note the last entries, taken from the Library on 28 Jan. 1861 and returned on 6 Feb., after his farewell speech in Congress. They included Kingsley's *Alton Locke*; Crowley's *Marston*, 3 vols.; *Amadis of Gaul*, 4 vols.; *British Novelists*,

vol. 22; and *Standard Novels,* vol. 80. Evidently Benjamin was seeking relaxation during this hectic period.

5. Data from Horace's *Works,* courtesy of Professor Herbert Lipscomb, Lynchburg, Va.

6. *Ure* v. *Coffman et al.,* 19 *Howard,* pp. 56-63.

7. *Coiron et al.* v. *Millaudon et al.,* pp. 113-15; *Shaffer* v. *Scudday,* pp. 16-21, in 19 *Howard.* Various citations in 20 *Howard.*

8. *Mussina et al.* v. *Cavazos et al.,* 20 *Howard,* pp. 280-90.

9. *Commercial Bank of Manchester* v. *Buckner,* 20 *Howard,* pp. 108-25.

10. *Belcher et al.* v. *Lawrason,* 21 *Howard,* pp. 251-7.

11. *Commissioners of Knox County, Indiana* v. *Aspinwall et al.,* 21 *Howard,* pp. 539-46; 'Samuel Judah' in *Dictionary of American Biography.*

12. George G. Vest, 'A Senator of Two Republics: Judah P. Benjamin,' in *Saturday Evening Post,* 3 Oct. 1903.

13. *Congressional Globe,* 3rd Session, 34th Congress, 4 Dec. 1856, p. 36.

14. Sears, *Slidell,* p. 152; Willson, *Slidell,* pp. 18-19. A year later Slidell wished to have the post in order to reconcile Napoleon III to the purchase of Cuba, but Buchanan had appointed John Y. Mason of Virginia and unless his 'dear friend' Slidell insisted he felt reluctant to recall him. Slidell was already beginning to feel coldly toward Buchanan. Willson, op. cit.

15. Courtesy of Maine Historical Society.

16. The *True Delta* was being sarcastic; Benjamin had not become a colonel.

17. Butler, op. cit. p. 165; *True Delta,* 2 Feb. 1858.

18. Sears, op. cit. p. 152.

19. Pickett Private Papers, Library of Congress. This is one of the letters which seem to have been left in Benjamin's trunks when he escaped from the South in 1865.

20. *Allgemeine Zeitung des Judenthums,* XXII, p. 553.

21. *Congressional Globe,* 1st Session, 35th Congress, p. 616.

22. Ibid. Pt. II, pp. 1065-72, and 1114; 'Roger Taney' in *Dictionary of American Biography.*

23. For this near-duel with Davis see *Congressional Globe,* 1st Session, 35th Congress, pp. 2775-82; Notes from Thomas F. Bayard in Pierce Butler Papers; *Intelligencer,* 9 June 1858; Butler, pp. 177-9. Butler says that the report in the *Congressional Globe* was 'probably toned down.' Also see letter of Gen. R. S. Ripley to Lawley, quoting an account of the affair by Senator Louis Wigfall. Lawley MSS.

24. Mrs. Davis to Lawley, 4 Apr. 1897. Lawley MSS.

25. *True Delta,* 15 and 26 Jan. 1859.

26. For an account of the Houmas affair, see *True Delta,* 21 Jan., 8, 13 Mar. 1859; Report of Congressional Committee, No. 150, 23 May 1860, Archives Building; *Congressional Globe,* 1859-61, esp. 4, 26 Jan., 23 Mar., and 29 May 1860; Butler, op. cit. pp. 166-70; Sears, *Slidell,* pp. 157, 164-7.

27. For this election see *Picayune, Delta,* and *True Delta,* all for 26 Jan. 1859.

28. *Congressional Globe,* 2nd Session, 35th Congress, p. 1553.

29. H. W. Conner to his son James, New Orleans, 13 Apr. 1859. Copy of letter through courtesy of Miss Caroline Conner, Charleston, S. C.

30. Lawley MSS., chap. 3, copy of letter to Lawley from E. B. Kruttschnitt, 13 Aug. 1897. The nephews were Henry and Coleman Sessions and Lionel

Levy. Kemp P. Battle, *History of the University of North Carolina*, Raleigh, 1907, I, pp. 493, 507, 634, 671, 800, 801, 813; Butler, op. cit. p. 61.

31. The black box belonging to Benjamin was seized by Gen. B. F. Butler when the Federal commander in New Orleans. After a lengthy and apparently hopeless search, the writer, who was materially assisted by Senator Bailey of North Carolina, learned that the box was at the U. S. State Department. It has since been removed to the Archives Building. For other references to Benjamin's Tehuantepec activities during this period see Butler, pp. 185-90; Instructions Nos. 27 and 28, Dispatches Nos. 48, 52, 57, and letter from John Forsyth to Lewis Cass of 14 Jan. 1858 *et al.* in State Department records, National Archives; *True Delta*, 2 May, 30 July, and 3 Aug. 1859; *Congressional Globe*, 3 May 1859, p. 1615; *Picayune*, 26 Jan., 10, 11 Mar. 1859; Benjamin to Buchanan, 10 Apr. 1859, at Historical Society of Pennsylvania, Philadelphia.

32. These facts about Natalie's misadventures and related events were derived from the following sources: Mrs. Clement Clay, *A Belle of the Fifties*, pp. 52-4; data from Mrs. Wallace Neff and Mrs. Sherman Miles, Washington, D. C., daughter and granddaughter respectively of Yulee; and personal inspection of the former Benjamin articles which they then owned; 'Decatur House and Lafayette Square,' monograph by Dr. Alvin Stauffer, historian, National Park Service; *Congressional Directory*, 1860.

33. Conversation of the writer with Benjamin's niece, Miss Alma Kruttschnitt of New York City, who died on 13 Oct. 1942.

34. For these general facts about the case see *United States* v. *Castillero*, in U. S. District Court, Northern District of California, No. 420. *New Almaden*, Transcript of the record, 4 vols., San Francisco, 1859-61. Also see Hubert H. Bancroft, *History of California*, San Francisco, 1888, VI, pp. 531-47; Abraham Glasser, data for doctoral thesis, Princeton University; and Oscar T. Shuck, *History of the Bench and Bar of California*, San Francisco, 1889, pp. 452-4.

35. Papers of John Jordan Crittenden, XXI, 1858-9. Letter to Benjamin, Crittenden, and Johnson (also Rockwell) written from New York, 10 Mar. 1859. In Library of Congress.

36. Shuck, *History of the Bench and Bar of California*, pp. 441, 452-4; Richmond *Examiner*, 10 Oct. 1861; 'Edmund Randolph' and 'Edward M. Stanton' in *Dictionary of American Biography*.

37. Letter from P. Della Torre, U. S. Attorney at San Francisco, to Jeremiah Black, 5 May 1858, in Attorney-General Files, National Archives.

38. John B. Williams, U. S. Attorney's Office, San Francisco, to Jeremiah Black, 23 Jan. 1860. Attorney-General Files, National Archives.

39. *New York Times*, 10 Nov. 1860, quoting *San Francisco Sun*, 14 Oct. 1860; also *Times*, 12 Nov. 1860, San Francisco correspondence.

40. *Times*, 12 Nov. 1860.

41. Transcript of *U. S.* v. *Castillero*, and *Times*, 14 Nov. 1860.

42. *Times*, 10, 12, 14 Nov. 1860.

43. Transcript of *U. S.* v. *Castillero*. A few changes have been made in the paragraphing.

44. *Times*, 28 Nov. 1860.

45. Letter of 9 Nov. 1860 to 'Mr. Dear Judge' in National Archives. The un-

identified author is given as a government counsel in Cummings and McFarland, *Federal Justice*, pp. 140-41.

46. James D. Richardson, *Messages and Papers of the Presidents*, Washington, 1897, v, p. 653.

47. *Times*, 28 Nov. 1860. See also the valuable article by Leonard Ascher, 'Lincoln's Administration and the New Almaden Scandal,' in *Pacific Historical Review*, v, pp. 38-42.

48. 2 *Black* (Supreme Court Reports), pp. 17-371; Butler, op. cit. pp. 201-2, and 'Edmund Randolph' in *Dictionary of American Biography*. For further data on the case, see Glasser thesis and Jeremiah Black Papers, Library of Congress.

49. *Intelligencer*, 15, 21, 23 May 1860. See also Mrs. Pryor, *Reminiscences*, pp. 62-5.

50. Mrs. Pryor, op. cit. pp. 101-2 and *Intelligencer*, 21 May 1860.

51. *Congressional Globe*, 1st Session, 36th Congress, pt. 3, p. 1967-8.

52. Butler, op. cit. pp. 193-4.

53. *Congressional Globe*, 1st Session, 36th Congress, pp. 2239-41. There is a copy of the pamphlet in the Library of Congress. See also Milton, *Eve of Conflict*, pp. 363-5; and *Intelligencer*, 23 May 1860, which refers to Benjamin's 'elaborate and earnest speech' about Douglas.

54. *Congressional Globe*, 1st Session, 36th Congress, p. 2309.

55. Ibid. 2nd Session, 33rd Congress, pp. 825-6.

56. Ibid. 1st Session, 36th Congress, pp. 800-806. For further data on Benjamin's senatorial career, see the valuable study by Louis Gruss in *Louisiana Historical Quarterly*, Oct. 1936.

CHAPTER VIII

1. Lawley MSS.
2. Pierce Butler Papers.
3. *New York Times*, 1 Sept. 1860, quoting 'Advices' from San Francisco to 18 Aug.
4. Thurlow Weed Barnes, *Memoir of Thurlow Weed*, Boston, 1884, II, pp. 313-14.
5. *New York Tribune*, 25 May 1884.
6. San Francisco *Weekly Herald*, 11 Oct. 1860.
7. Pamphlet copy of this speech in New York Public Library. For critical comment, see California news in *New York Times*, 28 Nov. 1860.
8. *Times*, ibid.
9. See note 7 above.
10. For some excellent material on this subject with copious references to the contemporary Louisiana newspapers and other primary sources, see Edwin J. Putzell Jr., *Cui Bono*, an unpublished MS. written in connection with his work at Tulane University, and W. M. Caskey, *Secession and Restoration of Louisiana*.
11. Putzell, op. cit. pp. 35-8; *Bee*, 9 Jan.
12. The total vote for senatorial and representative delegates to the Louisiana state convention showed them to be presumably committed as follows: for secession, 80; for co-operation, 44; doubtful, 6. In New Orleans Parish the vote was 4,300 for secession and 3,900 for co-operation. See *Delta*, 18 Jan.

1861. The Co-operationists were in favor of delaying or ending the Secession Movement.

After the meeting of the convention on 23 January it was obvious that the opposition to secession had crumbled. The vote in the convention for the Ordinance of Secession was 113 to 17. For a detailed treatment see Caskey, op. cit. p. 33.

13. Putzell, op. cit. pp. 5-6; *Delta*, 8 Nov., Caskey, pp. 1-15. In the presidential election Orleans Parish polled 2,645 votes for Breckinridge, 5,219 for Bell, and 2,998 for Douglas. Putzell, appendix, Table III.

14. The article is unsigned.

15. Putzell, op. cit. pp. 17-18, 81-3; *Picayune*, 2 Dec. 1860.

16. *Picayune*, 16 Dec. 1860; Putzell, p. 48.

17. Putzell, op. cit. pp. 89-97, who also lists the Reverends W. T. Leacock and J. J. Henderson among the chief pulpit influences for secession in Louisiana. See likewise 'B. M. Palmer' in *Dictionary of American Biography* and Putzell, pp. 101-3, quoting a letter from Professor S. E. Morison of Harvard and the Baton Rouge *Gazette*, 17 Nov. 1860, which wrote, 'The press seems to have let go. Even the conservatism which seemed a month ago to view the coming storm with calmness now gives way to consternation. The excitement spreads like an evil contagion.' See also Caskey, pp. 19-20.

18. Putzell, op. cit. p. 93, and *Delta*, 4 Dec. 1860.

19. Putzell, op. cit. pp. 79-87, quoting a letter from John S. Summerlin to Moore, 5 Dec. 1860. MS. in possession of Mrs. S. B. Staples, Alexandria, La.

20. *Memoirs of General W. T. Sherman*, 2nd ed., New York, 1886, I, pp. 177-8. 'Because at the time all men in Louisiana were dreadfully excited on questions affecting their slaves, who constituted the bulk of their wealth, and without whom they honestly believed that sugar, cotton, and rice, could not possibly be cultivated.'

21. Lloyd Lewis, *Sherman—Fighting Prophet*, New York, 1932, p. 129.

22. Putzell, op. cit. pp. 61-2.

23. *Delta*, 23 Dec. 1860.

24. Randall, *Civil War and Reconstruction*, pp. 200-201.

25. *Picayune*, 16 Dec. 1860.

26. *Congressional Globe*, 2nd Session, 36th Congress, pp. 212-17.

27. Ibid.

28. Quoted in Butler, op. cit. pp. 212-13.

29. *Times*, 1 Jan. 1861.

30. *Commercial*, 10 Jan. 1861.

31. *Delta*, 16 Jan. 1861.

32. Putzell, op. cit. pp. 101-3; Rhodes, *History of United States*, III, p. 276, quoting Charleston *Mercury*, 17 Jan. 1861.

33. *Congressional Globe*, 2nd Session, 36th Congress, p. 226.

34. 'The Diary of a Public Man' in *North American Review*, v. 129 (1879), pp. 133-4. There is some dispute concerning the authenticity of this diary. Information from Professor James G. Randall, University of Illinois.

35. Robert W. Winston, *Andrew Johnson, Plebeian and Patriot*, New York, 1928, p. 177; unpublished diary of Thomas Bragg, courtesy of his descendants, Robert and H. B. Gilliam and Mrs. William Prizer, Petersburg, Va.; John A. Logan, *The Great Conspiracy*, New York, 1886, pp. 157-60;

Congressional Globe, 2nd Session, 36th Congress, p. 408. For a defense of Benjamin's conduct, see Butler, op. cit. pp. 213-16.

36. *Congressional Globe*, 2nd Session, 36th Congress pp. 727 *et seq.*
37. Bragg diary, 4 Feb.
38. Butler, op. cit. p. 211; Edwin A. Alderman and Armistead Gordon, *J. L. M. Curry*, New York, 1911, p. 401.
39. E. D. Keyes, *Fifty Years' Observation of Men and Events*, New York, 1884, p. 49.
40. *Congressional Globe*, op. cit. p. 744.
41. Whitaker, *Sketches*, op. cit. See chap. 3, note 38.
42. Henry G. Connor, *John Archibald Campbell*, Boston, 1920, p. 83. 'Of the attorneys practicing in the Court, Reverdy Johnson, of Maryland, and Judah P. Benjamin, of Louisiana, had the largest number of appearances.'
43. Selections from Benjamin's speeches are included in *Library of Southern Literature*, Atlanta, 1907, I, pp. 303-22, and Mr. Justice Brewer's *The World's Best Orations*, St. Louis, 1899, I, pp. 398-407.
44. Alderman and Gordon, *J. L. M. Curry*, pp. 402-3.
45. Vest article in *Saturday Evening Post*, 3 Oct. 1903.
46. *Congressional Globe*, op. cit. p. 429, 17 Jan. 1861.
47. See Benjamin's correspondence regarding these lands, at University of Texas.
48. Copy through courtesy of U. S. Signal Corps.

CHAPTER IX

1. For an account of the Washington's Birthday celebration see *Delta*, 24 Feb., William M. Owen, *The Washington Artillery of New Orleans*, Boston, 1885, p. 6. Extracts from Benjamin's speech are given in the *Richmond Dispatch*, 1 Mar. 1861 and *Charleston Mercury*, 4 Mar.
2. *Delta*, 21 Feb.
3. Under the terms of the Confederate constitution Benjamin was eligible for the vice-presidency. See Article II, Sect. 1 of the constitution in appendix of Davis, *Rise and Fall of the Confederate Government*, I.
4. Butler, op. cit. pp. 227-8.
5. *Journal of Confederate Congress*, I, p. 85. There was a report, quoted in the *Dispatch* for 20 Feb., that John A. Elmore of Alabama would probably be appointed Attorney-General but if the place was given to Benjamin 'John Forsyth [of Alabama] will go into the War Department.'
6. In a letter to his wife, dated from Montgomery 20 Feb. 1861, Howell Cobb of Georgia wrote, 'The cabinet is not yet appointed, and no one knows who will be, as Davis consults no one out of his own State, as far as I have heard. I have positively refused to go into the cabinet.' *American Historical Association Reports*, 1911, II, p. 544.
7. Mrs. Davis, *Jefferson Davis*, II, pp. 37-8.
8. Davis, *Rise and Fall of the Confederate Government*, I, p. 242.
9. Montgomery correspondence, 23 Feb. of *Mercury*, 26 Feb.
10. T. C. DeLeon, *Four Years in Rebel Capitals*, p. 34.
11. *Journal*, 21 Feb.
12. Data from Peter A. Brannon, Department of Archives and History, State of Alabama. Mrs. Cleveland's boarding house was on the southwest corner

of Montgomery and Catoma Streets, two squares west of the Exchange
Hotel. I am also indebted to Mr. Brannon for copies of some contemporary
writings relating to Benjamin's career at this period.

13. Montgomery correspondence, 18 Feb. of *Mercury*, 22 Feb.
14. Mrs. Chesnut, *Diary*, pp. 14-15.
15. For their diplomatic correspondence, see Pickett Papers, Library of Congress.
16. See chapter on Benjamin at Yale.
17. Copy in Pierce Butler Papers.
18. For example, James A. and T. F. Bayard and S. M. Barlow, as is indicated
    by later correspondence in this volume and Benjamin's correspondence with
    Barlow in *War of Rebellion, Official Records*.
19. Data from Will R. Gregg of New York City, member of the Union Club.
20. Text of constitution in Davis, *Confederate Government*, I, appendix.
21. Benjamin to Bayard, op. cit.
22. Butler, op. cit. p. 234.
23. Davis, *Short History of the Confederate States*, p. 77; Eckenrode, *Davis*,
    p. 120; Mrs. Chesnut, *Diary*, p. 53.
24. Robert Barnwell Rhett, 'The Confederate Government at Montgomery,'
    Battles and Leaders of the Civil War, I, p. 108.
25. P. A. Stovall, *Robert Toombs*, New York, 1892, p. 226; McElroy, *Jefferson
    Davis*, I, p. 289.
26. Richmond *Examiner*, 25 Apr. 1861.
27. *Confederate Military History*, III, p. 913.
28. Letter from Benjamin of 14 Apr. 1861 to W. L. Coleman, University of
    Georgia. Copy through courtesy of Professor E. M. Coulter. See also his
    College Life in the Old South, New York, 1928, p. 313.
29. Special correspondence from Montgomery, 9 Apr. in Richmond *Dispatch*,
    13 Apr.
30. Mrs. Clement Clay, *A Belle of the Fifties*, p. 158.
31. Cummings and McFarland, *Federal Justice*, p. 225.
32. *Journal of Southern History*, II, pp. 464-5; William M. Robinson Jr.,
    Justice in Grey, pp. 27-38.
33. Richardson, *Compilation of the Messages and Papers of the Confederacy*, I,
    p. 78; *Journal of Southern History*, II, pp. 464-5; Robinson, *Justice in Grey*,
    various references.
34. *Journal of Southern History*, II, pp. 461-5; Robinson, op. cit. Some records
    of the Confederate Department of Justice may be found in the Pickett
    Papers, Library of Congress.
35. Letter from Benjamin to Memminger, 1 Apr. 1861. Opinion Book of the
    Confederate Attorney-General in N. Y. Public Library.
36. Letter from Benjamin to Memminger, 8 July 1861. Opinion Book.
37. Montgomery correspondence, 5 Apr., of *Mercury*, 9 Apr.
38. Montgomery correspondence of 6 Mar., in *Courier*, 9 Mar.
39. Mrs. Chesnut, *Diary*, pp. 55 et al.
40. William H. Russell, *Pictures of Southern Life*, New York, 1861, pp. 16-18.
41. Russell, *My Diary North and South*, pp. 249-57; data from Peter A.
    Brannon, op. cit.
42. *North American Review*, Mar. 1898, p. 373.
43. J. M. Morgan, *Recollections of a Rebel Reefer*, Boston, 1917, p. 36.

44. Jones, *Diary of a Rebel War Clerk*, I, p. 38.
45. 'John Beauchamp Jones' in *Dictionary of American Biography; Diary*, I, p. 29 *et al.*
46. 'The ordinance, which was prepared by Judah P. Benjamin, was brought to Raleigh from Montgomery by James Hines, a North Carolinian, and delivered to Gov. Ellis, who asked Burton Craige, the member from his county, to introduce it.' J. G. de R. Hamilton, *Reconstruction in North Carolina*, New York, 1914, p. 29.
47. Jones, *Diary*, I, p. 35.
48. Article by Henry D. Capers, a former official of the Confederate Treasury, in a Southern newspaper clipping (no place or date given) loaned by the late Rabbi Barnett Elzas of Charleston. In the article Capers quotes from a letter received from Benjamin in England.
49. M. F. Steele, *American Campaigns*, p. 533. 'Richmond, chosen as the capital only as a sop to Virginia, of course, was always the point of greatest weakness in the Southern Confederacy. The choice really was the worst thing that could have been imposed upon Virginia, for it subjected her soil to four years of steady campaign. Strategically considered, Chattanooga should have been made the seat of the Confederate government. It is possible, however, that a newly established government, which has to fight for its existence, would get along better with no fixed capital, or with one easily shifted, like that of our forefathers of the Revolution.'
50. For the references in this paragraph see contemporary issues of the *Examiner*.
51. De Leon, *Belles, Beaux and Brains of the 60's*, pp. 91-3.
52. For this and the remaining references to Jones in this chapter see *Diary*, pp. 63-79.

CHAPTER X

1. For Benjamin's ironic reference to the 'bed of *roses*' left him by L. P. Walker, see Benjamin to Walker, 9 Nov. 1861, Confederate War Department *Letterbook*, National Archives.
2. These dates of Benjamin's tenure are in *Journal of Confederate Congress*, I, p. 474, and *War of Rebellion, Official Records, Army* (hereafter cited as *O. R.*), Ser. IV, vol. I, p. 1176.
3. Richmond correspondence, 21 Sept. in *Courier*, 25 Sept.
4. *Examiner*, 19 Sept. 1861.
5. Ibid. 18 Sept. Editorial.
6. Basso, *Beauregard*, pp. 92-3.
7. Alexander Hunter, *Johnny Reb and Billy Yank*, New York, 1905, p. 566.
8. *O. R.*, I, v, p. 920.
9. See article on Northrop by this writer in *Dictionary of American Biography* with references in *O. R.*; Northrop Papers in New York Public Library, *et al.*
10. For an authoritative treatment of Lee's work here, see Freeman, *Lee*, I, pp. 510-40.
11. Jones, *Diary*, I, p. 68.
12. For a memorandum dated 31 Jan. 1862 containing the recollections of the three generals about the interview, see *O. R.*, I, v, pp. 884-7, and Alfred Roman Papers, Library of Congress. There is a good treatment of Mc-

Clellan's organizing efforts in John C. Ropes, *The Story of the Civil War*, New York, 1894, I, pp. 161-86.

13. *Mercury*, 25 Sept.
14. In Huntington Library, San Marino, Calif.
15. See note 1.
16. For the letters to General Walker and Gardner, see War Department *Letterbook;* for the Myers letter and the espionage data see O. R., I, v, pp. 871 and 928-9.
17. Chiefly in the National Archives and those at the capitals of former Confederate states.
18. O. R., I, IV, p. 661.
19. O. R., I, v, pp. 230-31.
20. O. R., IV, I, pp. 790-97 and 955-62.
21. Ibid. p. 541.
22. Ibid. p. 958.
23. Ibid. p. 555.
24. Ibid. p. 557.
25. Ibid. p. 599.
26. Ibid. p. 1176; Jones, *Diary*, various references; 'Albert Bledsoe' in *Dictionary of American Biography*.
27. Data from Gorgas family through courtesy of his daughter, Miss Mary Gorgas, Tuscaloosa, Ala., and Professor Keener Frazer, Chapel Hill, N. C. This material includes extracts from the unpublished Gorgas diary. See also *A Sketch of the Life of General Josiah Gorgas* (author not given) in *Southern Historical Papers*, XIII, pp. 216-28; and Josiah Gorgas, *Notes on the Ordnance Department*, in *Southern Historical Papers*, XII, pp. 67-94. For praise of Gorgas by Joseph E. Johnston, see *Confederate Military History*, I, p. 623.
28. For a list of these bureau chiefs see O. R., IV, I, p. 1176; also consult articles on certain of them in *Dictionary of American Biography* and *Confederate Military History*.
29. Benjamin to Gen. Walker, 2 Oct. 1861. War Department *Letterbook*.
30. For details regarding this house and Benjamin's residence, see Richmond *Times-Dispatch*, 26 May 1912; letters from Mrs. Davis to Lawley in Lawley MSS., and *post*, chap. on 'Life in Richmond.'
31. For frank data on this subject, see the various books on the Civil War by Edward Pollard of the *Examiner*.
32. *Examiner*, 27 Jan. 1862.
33. 1 Nov. 1862. Courtesy of Raymond Wilkins, Boston.
34. 28 Oct. 1861. War Department *Letterbook*, National Archives.
35. Ibid. 10 Dec. 1861. To Gen. Gatlin.
36. War Department *Letterbook*.
37. Ibid.; Richard Taylor, *Destruction and Reconstruction*, New York, 1879, p. 23.
38. O. R., IV, I, p. 594.
39. Ibid. pp. 614-15.
40. See various references in O. R., IV, I, *et al.*
41. O. R., IV, I, p. 616.
42. *Diary*, I, pp. 84-5.
43. Mrs. Davis to Lawley, 4 Apr. 1897. In Lawley MSS.

44. Ibid.
45. *O. R.*, I, v, pp. 928-9.
46. John Lewis Peyton, *The American Crisis*, London, 1867, II, p. 145-6.
47. F. L. Owsley, *States Rights in the Confederacy*, p. 1.
48. *O. R.*, IV, I, pp. 634, 646-7, 666.
49. For Benjamin's quarrel with Gov. Letcher of Virginia regarding the re-
    tention of some of the state ordnance by the Confederate Government, see
    Virginia Executive Papers, Sept. 1861-Feb. 1862, State Library, Richmond.
    Defending the War Department, an employee wrote that of its '1,000 Em-
    ployees, Clerks, Mechanics, and Laborers at least nine-tenths are Virginians.
    . . . Is it reasonable to suppose that a command thus constituted would
    wrong Virginia?'
50. *O. R.*, I, vi, pp. 284-5.
51. Ibid. pp. 315, 318.
52. *O. R.*, I, iv, pp. 660-62.
53. 25 Oct. 1861. Ibid. p. 690.
54. Ibid. p. 697.
55. *O. R.*, I, iii, pp. 739, 742.
56. *O. R.*, IV, I, pp. 695-6.
57. Ibid. p. 696.
58. *Diary*, I, pp. 81 *et al.; Examiner*, 30 Sept., 11 Oct.
59. For an interesting discussion of Johnston's personality see Gamaliel Brad-
    ford, *Confederate Portraits*, Boston, 1914, pp. 3-31.
60. *O. R.*, IV, I, pp. 605-8.
61. Ibid. p. 611.
62. *O. R.*, I, v, pp. 882-3.
63. Ibid. p. 926. For an excellent resumé of the difficulties between Benjamin
    and Johnston, see Freeman, *Lee's Lieutenants*, I, pp. 111-36.
64. Jones, *Diary*, I, p. 71.
65. Ibid. p. 89. See also the valuable treatment in Freeman, op. cit. I, pp. 99-110.
66. Roman, *Beauregard*, I, p. 158.
67. For these two letters, see *O. R.*, I, v, p. 920; Basso, *Beauregard*, p. 154.
68. Ibid. p. 904.
69. Ibid. p. 945.
70. Ibid. esp. p. 1048, and Freeman, op. cit. pp. 104-11.
71. *O. R.*, IV, I, pp. 624-25.
72. Ibid. I, v, pp. 148-9 *et al.;* 'Henry A. Wise' by this writer in *Dictionary of
    American Biography*.

CHAPTER XI

1. *O. R.*, II, I, pp. 824-33; Clifton R. Hall, *Andrew Johnson, Military Governor of Tennessee*, Princeton, 1916, p. 14.
2. *O. R.*, I, iv, p. 231. The Unionists were emboldened by the belief that the
   Federal troops were about to enter Tennessee.
3. *O. R.*, I, iv, pp. 234-43.
4. Ibid. p. 238.
5. Ibid. pp. 250-51.
6. *O. R.*, I, vii, p. 701.
7. Oliver P. Temple, *East Tennessee and the Civil War*, pp. 397-411.

8. Oliver P. Temple, *Notable Men of Tennessee*, p. 308; W. G. Brownlow, *Sketches of the Rise, Progress, and Decline of Secession*, various citations.
9. Oliver P. Temple, op. cit. p. 310.
10. Ibid. pp. 310-16; *O. R.*, I, VII, p. 785.
11. *O. R.*, I, IV, p. 565.
12. *O. R.*, I, IV, pp. 707-8.
13. For a treatment of this subject see Steele, *American Campaigns*, I, pp. 142-9.
14. *O. R.*, IV, I, pp. 763-4, 794-6.
15. J. H. Claiborne, *Seventy-Five Years In Old Virginia*, New York, 1904, p. 198.
16. Benjamin's diary and *O. R.*, I, V, esp. p. 1011.
17. Ibid. p. 1011.
18. Ibid. pp. 1006-7.
19. *Whig*, 1 Jan. 1862, and *O. R.*, I, IV, p. 249.
20. *Examiner*, 2 Jan. 1862.
21. P. S. Flippin, *Herschel V. Johnson*, Richmond, 1931, p. 211.
22. Henderson, *Stonewall Jackson*, I, chaps. VI and VII.
23. *O. R.*, I, V, pp. 909, 913-22, 937-9.
24. W. B. Wood and J. E. Edmonds, *The Civil War in the United States*, London, 1905, pp. 81-2; Henderson, *Jackson*, I, pp. 225-8; *O. R.*, I, V, pp. 937-9 *et al.*
25. Wood and Edmonds, op. cit. pp. 82-3; Frederick Morton, *The Story of Winchester*, Strasburg, Va., 1925, pp. 152-3; *Battles and Leaders of the Civil War*, II, pp. 282-3. Jackson's official report of this campaign is in *O. R.*, I, V, pp. 389-95.
26. *Battles and Leaders*, II, p. 283; Wood and Edmonds, p. 83; Henderson, I, chap. VII; Jackson's Report, op. cit.
27. *O. R.*, I, V, pp. 1046-8. Personal papers of Jackson, courtesy of his grandson, Gen. T. J. J. Christian, U. S. A.
28. *O. R.*, I, V, pp. 1040-2; Henderson, op. cit., and Christian Papers.
29. *O. R.*, V, pp. 1043-4, 1049.
30. Ibid. pp. 1051-3, and Christian Papers.
31. *O. R.*, I, V, p. 1056.
32. Ibid. p. 1059.
33. The letters from Johnston, Letcher, Bennett, and McFarland are all in the Christian Papers.
34. *O. R.*, I, V, pp. 1057-8.
35. Ibid. pp. 1071-2.
36. Ibid. and pp. 882-3; also Benjamin to Johnston, 9 Dec. 1861, in Huntington Library.
37. *O. R.*, I, IV, pp. 657 *et seq.*; John W. Porter, *A Record of Events in Norfolk County, Virginia*, Portsmouth, Va., 1892, pp. 233-5; *Confederate Military History*, V, pp. 403-4.
38. *Papers of Military Historical Society of Massachusetts*, IX, article by Lt.-Col. Thomas F. Edmonds, esp. p. 65.
39. *O. R.*, I, IV, pp. 711-12.
40. Ibid. p. 715 and IX, pp. 183-4; *Confederate Military History*, IV, p. 34; 'Henry A. Wise' by this writer in *Dictionary of American Biography*.
41. *O. R.*, I, IX, pp. 126, 133.

42. Ibid. p. 114. Huger did add, however, that 'if men can help you, you shall have them, if we have boats here to take them.'
43. Ibid. pp. 114-15.
44. Ibid. pp. 132, 135-6.
45. Ibid. p. 184.
46. John S. Wise, *The End of an Era*, p. 182; *O. R.*, I, ix, pp. 147-8 *et al.*
47. Wise, op. cit. p. 178.
48. Ibid.
49. Ibid.; *O. R.*, I, ix, pp. 420-27, and Gen. Wise's Official Report, *O. R.*, ix, esp. pp. 138-9.
50. *O. R.*, I, ix, pp. 140-45.
51. This was a Negro servant loaned Mrs. Davis by Miss Elizabeth Van Lew, a Richmond lady of Northern birth who served as a Union spy. Miss Van Lew lived on Church Hill, near historic St. John's Church. For valuable data about her, see the clipping file in the Valentine Museum, Richmond.
52. *Massachusetts Military Historical Society Papers, Edmonds article*, op. cit.
53. Charles Coffin, *Drum-beat of the Nation*, New York, 1888, pp. 174-5; Gen. A. E. Burnside, 'The Burnside Expedition' in *Battles and Leaders*, i, p. 667.
54. For this account of the battle see *O. R.*, I, ix, pp. 72-190; *Massachusetts Historical Society Papers*, op. cit.; Wise, *The End of an Era*, pp. 174-90. The figures for the Confederate troops engaged are exclusive of several hundred in the northern part of the island who failed to arrive at the battlefield.
55. Richmond *Dispatch*, 15, 17 Feb., and *Examiner*, 17 Feb. 1862.
56. *O. R.*, I, ix, pp. 118-21.
57. Letter to the writer from Henry A. Wise Jr., Kiptopeke, Va.
58. *Standard*, 5 Mar. 1862.
59. In Bryan Grimes Papers, State Library, Raleigh.
60. *Register*, 19 Feb. and *Mercury*, 14 Feb.
61. *O. R.*, I, ix, pp. 183-91.
62. Bragg's Diary.
63. Ibid.
64. Personal interviews in Richmond with Edward Willis, who fought in the battle with the Blues, and Andrew Krouse, another of the Blues, who was then at near-by Nags Head. John S. Wise, *The End of an Era*, p. 188.
65. Extract from speech through courtesy of the late Herbert Ezekiel, Richmond.
66. For further data on Webster, see clipping file in the Valentine Museum, Richmond.
67. *Southern Historical Society Papers*, New Series, No. vi (whole no. xliv), p. 22.

CHAPTER XII

1. In Manuscript Division, Library of Congress.
2. For an account of this inauguration see *Journal of Confederate Congress*, 22 Feb. 1862, in *Southern Historical Society Papers, New Series*, No. vi (whole no. xiv), pp. 38-9; Mrs. Davis, *Jefferson Davis*, ii, pp. 182-3.
3. *O. R.*, I, vii, p. 908. Pillow to Benjamin, 26 Feb. 1862.
4. Bragg, *Diary*, 25 Feb. 1862.
5. *Journal of Confederate Congress*, v, p. 57.

6. Foote, *War of the Rebellion*, pp. 355-6; *Journal of Confederate Congress*, various references, Feb.-Mar. 1862.
7. Foote, op. cit. pp. 355-7; J. W. Draper, *History of the American Civil War*, New York, 1867-70, III, p. 290; Jones, *Diary*, II, p. 116; personal interview with Robert Hughes of Norfolk, great-nephew of Gen. Johnston, who repeated information given him by the general.
8. Foote, op. cit. p. 357; *Journal Confederate Congress*, III, pp. 73-4.
9. 'G. W. Randolph' and 'James A. Seddon' by the writer and also 'J. C. Breckinridge' by E. M. Coulter in *Dictionary of American Biography*.
10. *O. R.*, IV, I, pp. 955-62; also see pp. 626-31, 962-4 *et al.*
11. Ibid. pp. 955-62.
12. Mrs. Davis to Lawley, 4 Apr. 1897, Lawley MSS.
13. Memo. from Clifton Rodes Breckinridge, Wendover, Ky., 17 June 1932.
14. Craven, *Prison Life of Jefferson Davis*, pp. 177-8.
15. *Dispatch*, 19 Mar.
16. Ibid. 21 Mar.
17. For the data in this paragraph, see contemporary Richmond newspapers, esp. the *Whig*.
18. Although now almost forgotten, 'The Bonnie Blue Flag' was, next to 'Dixie,' the most popular of the Confederate war songs. In a later and more familiar version the line 'Fighting for the property we gained . . .' was replaced by 'Fighting for our liberty with treasure, blood, and toil.'

CHAPTER XIII

1. Henry D. Capers, *Life of C. G. Memminger*, Richmond, 1893, p. 532.
2. L. Q. Washington, 'The Confederate State Department,' in *Independent*, Sept. 1901.
3. Edmund Kirke [J. R. Gilmore], 'Our Visit to Richmond,' *Atlantic Monthly*, Sept. 1864.
4. Pickett Papers, Library of Congress; *Confederate Military History*, I, pp. 628-9.
5. Dunbar Rowland, ed., *Jefferson Davis, Constitutionalist*, VIII, p. 345, letter of 8 Feb. 1879.
6. Confederate State Department records in Pickett Papers, Library of Congress, and in National Archives.
7. *Official Records of the Union and Confederate Navies in the War of the Rebellion* (hereafter cited as *O. R. Navy*), II, III, pp. 373-8.
8. *O. R. Navy*, II, III, p. 379, letter of 8 Apr. 1862.
9. Memorandum by L. Q. Washington in Lawley MSS.
10. For the dates of receipt of these dispatches to Slidell see *O. R. Navy*, II, III, pp. 479, 481, 603, 634, 705, 707 *et al.* Also see p. 579.
11. The dates of receipt of these dispatches are given in *O. R. Navy*, II, III, pp. 490, 537, 581, 646, 728, 772, 773 *et al.*
12. Pickett Papers.
13. *O. R. Navy*, op. cit. p. 931. The writer is indebted to Mr. V. L. Eaton of the MS. Division, Library of Congress, for explaining the working of this cipher.
14. Mrs. Davis to Benjamin, Lawley MSS.
15. *O. R. Navy*, II, III, p. 762 *et seq.*

16. *Jefferson Davis, Constitutionalist,* v, pp. 217-19.
17. Jones, *Diary,* I, pp. 120, 123-4.
18. Ibid. pp. 165-6.
19. Pickett Papers.
20. *O. R. Navy,* II, III, p. 387.
21. Ibid. p. 463.
22. Richmond *Whig,* 30 May 1862; Owsley, *King Cotton Diplomacy,* p. 326 *et seq.*
23. *O. R. Navy,* II, III, p. 462.
24. Ibid. p. 461.
25. Ibid. pp. 484-6.
26. Ibid. pp. 574-8.

CHAPTER XIV

1. Benjamin's Diary.
2. Ibid.
3. Ibid.
4. See Benjamin's dispatches during this period in *O. R. Navy,* II, III; also Benjamin's diary, 6 Jan. 1863.
5. *O. R. Navy,* II, III, p. 344.
6. Ibid. pp. 379-82.
7. L. Q. Washington Memo. Lawley MSS.
8. *O. R. Navy,* op. cit. pp. 446, 503-4.
9. Ibid. pp. 537-43.
10. For illuminating discussions of this subject based on the documentary evidence see Owsley, *King Cotton Diplomacy,* pp. 361-83, and E. D. Adams, *Great Britain and the American Civil War,* II, esp. pp. 63-5.
11. *O. R. Navy,* op. cit. pp. 214-16.
12. *O. R. Army,* IV, II, p. 101. For an account of the dismissal of De Leon after he had read some of Benjamin's confidential dispatches, see Owsley, op. cit. pp. 175-82.
13. This information was repeated by Kenner a few years before his death to William Wirt Henry, who in turn gave it to Professor J. M. Callahan of Johns Hopkins University. See *William and Mary Quarterly,* July 1916, pp. 9-12.
14. Pickett Papers.
15. Ibid.
16. *O. R. Navy,* II, III, various citations, and Wesley, *Collapse of the Confederacy,* pp. 126-7.
17. *O. R. Navy,* op. cit. p. 567.
18. Pickett Papers.
19. *Enquirer,* 7 May 1863.
20. *O. R. Navy,* op. cit. pp. 651-3.
21. Extracts through courtesy of his daughter, the Marquise de Courtivron.
22. *O. R. Navy,* op. cit. p. 665.
23. Polignac Diary, op. cit.
24. *O. R. Navy,* op. cit. pp. 764, 770, 775.
25. *American Historical Review,* vol. XLVI, pp. 78 *et al.*
26. For these details about the Erlanger contract see *O. R. Navy,* op. cit. pp. 569-72, 649-50, and Owsley, op. cit. pp. 393-406.

27. *O. R. Navy*, op. cit. pp. 668-9.
28. Sir Arthur Fremantle, *Three Months in the Southern States: April-June, 1863*, New York, 1864, pp. 206-11.

CHAPTER XV

1. Mrs. Burton Harrison, *Recollections, Grave and Gay*, pp. 79-80.
2. Jones, *Diary*, I, pp. 123, 126.
3. Mrs. Harrison, op. cit. p. 80.
4. *Memoirs of John H. Reagan*, New York, 1906, p. 139.
5. This information was given to Pierce Butler by Mrs. Popham. See Butler, *Benjamin*, pp. 336-8.
6. Information secured by the writer in the course of his search for the box. Also see *Autobiography of George Dewey*, New York, 1913, p. 79 and *O. R.*, III, II, p. 39.
7. *Memoirs of John H. Reagan*, pp. 150-53.
8. *Jefferson Davis, Constitutionalist*, VIII, pp. 355-7.
9. Dr. Hoge was a noted Presbyterian Minister of Richmond. His statement was given the writer by the late Herbert Ezekiel of Richmond.
10. L. Q. Washington Memo. Lawley MSS.
11. Mrs. Davis to Lawley, 4 Apr. 1897. Lawley MSS.
12. John S. Wise, *The End of an Era*, p. 177.
13. Mrs. Davis to Lawley, op. cit.
14. Ibid.
15. Personal conversation with Harvie's niece, the late Mrs. Martha Harvie of Danville, Va. The late Mrs. Wm. B. Lightfoot (née Emmeline Crump) of Richmond also told the writer that she remembered seeing Benjamin at her father's home there.
16. Mrs. Harrison, op. cit. p. 129.
17. Ibid. p. 160, and De Leon, *Belles, Beaux and Brains*, pp. 198-9.
18. Mrs. Davis to Lawley, op. cit.
19. Now preserved at the Confederate Museum in Richmond.
20. Henry D. Capers, *Memories of Men and Events* in Rabbi Elzas clipping file, op. cit. Also see H. D. Capers, *Recollections of the Civil Service of the Confederate Government*, clipping from a Georgia newspaper, not entirely identifiable, at Confederate Memorial Hall, New Orleans.
21. See Rhodes, *History of the Civil War*, New York, 1917, p. 395. Another story of corruption on Benjamin's part, repeated to the writer by the late Harry Harwood of Richmond, could not be definitely substantiated.
22. In Pickett Private Papers, Library of Congress.
23. Ibid.
24. In Pickett (Public) Papers, Library of Congress.
25. War Department *Letterbook*.
26. Jones, *Diary*, I, p. 277.
27. For this account of the Richmond bread riot see Jones, op. cit. pp. 284-7. Virginia State Executive Papers for May 1863 (pardon for Minerva Meredith) in State Library, Richmond; *Examiner*, 3, 6, 13, 24 Apr.; *Whig*, 6 Apr.
28. Jones, op. cit. p. 294.
29. *Enquirer*, 21 May 1863.
30. Jones, op. cit. II, pp. 17, 36; 16 Aug. and 6 Sept. 1863.

31. It was this Lawley who wrote the uncompleted biography of Benjamin so often cited in this volume.
32. Richmond correspondence of 7 June in London *Times*, 18 July 1864.
33. Butler, op. cit. p. 47; Herbert T. Ezekiel and Gaston Lichtenstein, *The Jews of Richmond*, Richmond, 1917, p. 170, and conversation with the authors. They wrote that it was a Richmond Jew, Ellis Bottingheimer, who remembered seeing Benjamin being 'called up' at the synagogue.
34. Ezekiel and Lichtenstein, op. cit. pp. 163-4 *et al.*
35. London *Times*, 4 Aug. 1864.
36. Mrs. Davis to Lawley, op. cit.
37. Dr. Moses Hoge to Lawley. Lawley MSS.
38. *Dispatch*, 26 May 1912, article by Alice M. Tyler. The *Dispatch* erroneously dates the note as 5 Nov. 1863 instead of 5 Nov. 1864.

CHAPTER XVI

1. *O. R.*, IV, II, p. 674.
2. *Enquirer*, 17 Sept. 1863; Jones, *Diary*, II, pp. 46-7. See also the Richmond *Sentinel*, 18 Sept. 1863 for an answer to Benjamin's attack.
3. Benjamin to William T. Dortch, Goldsboro, N. C., 11 Aug. 1863. Pickett Papers.
4. Benjamin to Benjamin H. Micou, Tallassee, Ala., 18 Aug. 1863, in Pickett Papers. Data from Micou's relative, Richard Micou Daniel, Philadelphia.
5. This correspondence between Benjamin and Spence is in the Pickett Papers. See also Owsley, *King Cotton Diplomacy*, esp. pp. 407-8.
6. Reagan, *Memoirs*, p. 148 and *O. R.*, I, LII, pt. 2, pp. 586-94.
7. See esp. Edward Pollard, *Secret History of the Confederacy*, pp. 407, 445.
8. *O. R.*, IV, II, p. 824; Owsley, op. cit. pp. 408-10.
9. *O. R. Navy*, II, III, p. 852.
10. Paris dispatch from 'The Regular Correspondent' in *Tribune*, 25 May 1884.
11. Benjamin to A. Fullerton, 8 Oct. 1863, courtesy of Raymond Wilkins, Boston; *O. R. Navy*, op. cit. pp. 928-36; Owsley, pp. 513-14.
12. *O. R. Navy*, op. cit. pp. 853-4.
13. Ibid. pp. 99, 202-8 *et al.*; Owsley, op. cit. pp. 88-97.
14. Ibid., various citations and Owsley, esp. the valuable treatment in chap. IV.
15. For this later phase of Benjamin's Mexican relations, see *O. R. Navy*, op. cit. pp. 988-90 and 1062-3.
16. Benjamin to Capston, 3 July 1863, in Valentine Museum, Richmond. See also *O. R. Navy*, op. cit. pp. 828-9.
17. Ibid. pp. 893-5; Owsley, op. cit. p. 517.
18. *O. R. Navy*, op. cit. pp. 954-5; Owsley, op. cit. pp. 517-26.
19. *O. R. Army*, I, XLVIII, pt. II, pp. 194-7; and II, VIII, p. 516.
20. L. E. Orris to Benjamin in Pickett Papers. See also the account of Benjamin's relations with Clement Clay and Jacob Thompson later in this chapter.
21. Duncan Kenner to Benjamin. Courtesy of Raymond Wilkins, Boston.
22. The Conrad letter with enclosure is in the MS. Room, Duke University. See also Freeman, *Lee's Lieutenants*, vol. I, p. 84, and De Leon, *Belles, Beaux and Brains*, p. 451.
23. *O. R. Army*, III, III, p. 1008.

24. A. F. Robertson, *Alexander Hugh Holmes Stuart*, Richmond, 1925, pp. 205-8.
25. B. Pitman, editor, *The Trials for Treason at Indianapolis*, Report from J. Holt, Judge Advocate General to the Secretary of War, Cincinnati, 1865, pp. 323-39; *O. R. Army*, I, XLIII, pp. 930-36; Randall, *Civil War*, pp. 618-21.
26. *O. R. Navy*, II, III, p. 174.
27. Ibid. pp. 1105-6.
28. L. Q. Washington Memo. Lawley MSS.
29. John W. Headley, *Confederate Operations in Canada and New York*, pp. 210-11.
30. For this data about the activities of Clay and Thompson and connected events, see Thompson's report in *O. R. Army*, I, XLIII, pt. 2, pp. 930-36.
31. Ibid.
32. Ibid., Rhodes, *History of United States*, v, pp. 332-5.
33. J. B. McMaster, *The History of the People of the United States during Lincoln's Administration*, 534-6.
34. *Sentinel*, 27 Oct. 1864.
35. For example, see Headley, op. cit. pp. 280-81. Benjamin was now nothing if not a determined revolutionist, and there may be strong reason for feeling that he, like Headley, was willing to resort to some extreme measures of retaliation.
36. Thompson's report, op. cit.
37. Headley, op. cit. pp. 264-83; Rhodes, op. cit. pp. 339-40.
38. There are some copies of these Personals in the Clement Clay Papers, Duke University.
39. *O. R. Army*, I, XLIII, pt. 2, p. 935.
40. Thompson's report, op. cit.
41. 'One could most earnestly wish . . . that the first tentatives towards a foreign policy . . . were entrusted to some uncircumcised Christian man' (*Examiner*, 2 Mar. 1864). '. . . they say that gentlemen of independence and pride of character are somewhat shy of accepting Secretaryships in this Government' (ibid. 18 Mar.). See also *Examiner*, 26 Aug. 1864, 6 Jan. 1865; J. B. Jones, *Diary*, II, various references; and *O. R. Army*, IV, III, pp. 5-6.
42. G. G. Vest in *Saturday Evening Post*, 3 Oct. 1903; *Journal of Confederate Congress*, 1864-65, various citations.
43. Jones, *Diary*, II, p. 132; *Journal of Confederate Senate*, IV, various references, Dec. 1863-Feb. 1864.
44. *O. R. Army*, IV, III, pp. 797-9.
45. Wesley, *Collapse of the Confederacy*, pp. 157-60.
46. Benjamin to Porcher, 21 Dec. 1864 in Pickett Papers.
47. For an account of the Hampton Roads Conference see Rhodes, *History of the Civil War*, pp. 417-21.
48. There is no literal report of this speech. See *New York Times*, 13 Feb. 1865, quoting Richmond *Sentinel*, 10 Feb.; also *Examiner*, 10 Feb.
49. Dodd, *Jefferson Davis*, Philadelphia, 1907, pp. 347-8.
50. *Journal of Confederate Senate*, IV, pp. 550, 552, 553.
51. Courtesy of Raymond Wilkins, Boston.
52. Jones, op. cit., II, p. 451.
53. *O. R. Navy*, II, III, pp. 1253-6, 1272-3.

CHAPTER XVII

1. *Times-Dispatch*, 26 May 1912.
2. Ibid.
3. In MS. Room, Duke University.
4. In Pickett Private Papers, Library of Congress. Contrary to the opinion here expressed that Benjamin may have been preparing for flight from the South, John H. Reagan wrote, 'I think I am entirely safe in saying that neither Mr. Davis nor any member of his Cabinet contemplated leaving the country when we left Richmond.' *Annals of the War*, published by the Philadelphia *Times*, Philadelphia, 1879, p. 151.
5. Douglas Freeman, *Lee's Dispatches*, New York, 1915, pp. 358-60.
6. Hanna, *Flight Into Oblivion*, p. 4. This book contains an interesting and authoritative account of the flight of the Confederate cabinet.
7. *Times-Dispatch*, 26 May 1912.
8. *McClure's Magazine*, Dec. 1900.
9. Conversation of this writer with the late Joseph B. Anderson and Danville *Register*, 14 Jan. 1934. Further information on the Davis party in Danville was secured by personal interviews with the late Miss Jennie Grasty and the late Miss Nannie Wiseman, both residents of Danville, who were living there when it was the Confederate capital. See likewise article by Harry C. Ficklen in *Register*, 24 Mar. 1935 and Jefferson Davis, *Rise and Fall*, II, pp. 677-8.
10. Dr. Hoge to Lawley, 14 Aug. 1897 in Lawley MSS., and conversation with Howard Lanier of Danville, a nephew of Mrs. Johnston.
11. Conversation in Lynchburg, Virginia, on 13 July 1938 with Langhorne Dabney Lewis, a nephew by marriage of Major Hutter.
12. According to Howard Lanier, op. cit. Benjamin was reading from Tennyson's poems to his aunt, Miss Martha Lanier (a sister of Mrs. Johnston) when he was informed of Lee's surrender. See also *Register*, 24 Mar. 1935.
13. Hanna, *Flight Into Oblivion*, p. 26; *McClure's Magazine*, Dec. 1900.
14. These facts regarding the Davis party in Greensboro are derived from the following sources: personal interview on 14 Sept. 1936 with the late Robert M. Hughes of Norfolk, Va., a great-nephew of Gen. Johnston; Joseph E. Johnston, *Narrative*, pp. 396-400; S. R. Mallory in *McClure's Magazine*, Dec. 1900 and Jan. 1901; Hanna, op. cit. pp. 25-39; Roman, *Beauregard*, II, pp. 394-5; W. H. Parker, *Recollections of a Naval Officer*, New York, 1883, pp. 354-5; Joseph Addison, *Cato: A Tragedy*, II. i; Burton Harrison, 'The Capture of Jefferson Davis' in *Century*, Nov. 1883.
15. Burton Harrison, ibid. Further data on this stage of the flight was derived from conversation with the late Dr. Paul Barringer of Charlottesville, Va., who was staying at the home of his uncle, Victor Barringer, in Concord, N. C., when members of the Davis party stopped there. See also Hanna, op. cit. pp. 38-45; J. W. Headley, *Confederate Operations in Canada and New York*, p. 428, describing his meeting with Benjamin in Salisbury, N. C.; and Pupils of Sixth Grade, Corbin Street School, Concord, N. C., *A Short History of Cabarrus County and Concord*, pamphlet, 1933, pp. 38-9, containing a letter from Mrs. Victor Barringer of 7 Feb. 1901 with an account of the visit of the Davis party to her home.

16. Headley, op. cit.; Hanna, op. cit. pp. 45-6.
17. Data from Mrs. Julius Cone of Proximity, Greensboro, N. C., with information from her aunt, Caroline Weill (Mrs. N. L. Mayer), who was present at the time of Benjamin's visit to their home. Burton Harrison, op. cit.
18. Mrs. J. A. Yarborough in *Charlotte Observer*, 1 Nov. 1842.
19. Benjamin to Davis, 22 Apr. 1865. Copy in Edward M. Stanton Papers, Library of Congress.
20. J. Davis to Mrs. Davis, 23 Apr. 1865. Copy in Rowland, *Jefferson Davis, Constitutionalist*, VI, pp. 559-62.
21. Gen. Basil W. Duke, 'Last Days of the Confederacy,' in *Battles and Leaders*, IV, pp. 762-7; John K. Aull in Columbia, S. C., *State*, 27 Sept. 1931.
22. *Battles and Leaders*, op. cit.; Parker, *Recollections*, p. 366.
23. Butler, op. cit. p. 362; *Memoirs of John H. Reagan*, p. 211.
24. Burton Harrison, op. cit. p. 134.
25. Jefferson Davis, *Rise and Fall*, II, p. 694; Benjamin to Mrs. Kruttschnitt, 2 July 1865, copy in Pierce Butler Papers.
26. *Memoirs*, p. 211.
27. John Taylor Wood, *Famous Adventures and Prison Escapes of the Civil War*, New York, 1893, p. 298; Louis Gruss in *Louisiana Historical Quarterly*, XIX, p. 965.
28. Benjamin to Mrs. Kruttschnitt, op. cit.
29. Wood, op. cit.
30. Reagan, *Memoirs*, p. 211.
31. Benjamin to Mrs. Kruttschnitt, op. cit.
32. Letter in Lawley MSS. of 18 Oct. 1889 from William H. Gregory, a former governor of Ceylon. Benjamin told him the story after a dinner at the Garrick, in London, given by Napier Stuart. At the time of the adventure, Benjamin was in Florida and 'approaching the sea.'
33. Lillie G. McDuffee, *The Lures of Manatee*, Nashville, 1933, pp. 157-62. Hanna, op. cit. pp. 197-200. The historic Gamble mansion was purchased in 1924 by the Judah P. Benjamin Chapter of the United Daughters of the Confederacy and deeded to the state of Florida. The state legislature has since made two appropriations for its restoration and maintenance. Hanna, p. 270.
34. For details of Benjamin's flight from the time he left the Gamble mansion until he reached Knight's Key, see Benjamin to James A. Bayard, 20 Oct. 1865, copy in Pierce Butler Papers; Benjamin to Mrs. Kruttschnitt, op. cit.; McDuffee, op. cit. pp. 162-71; Hanna, op. cit. pp. 200-203; and interview with H. A. McLeod in Galveston *Daily News*, 27 May 1894.

On 22 January 1942, a marker was unveiled, with appropriate exercises, at Sarasota, Fla. to mark the spot in that vicinity where Benjamin set sail for foreign shores. Data through courtesy of Mrs. Mary P. Brownell, chairman of the committee on arrangements.
35. The details of the trip from Knight's Key to Nassau are derived from Benjamin to Mrs. Kruttschnitt, op. cit.; McDuffee, op. cit. pp. 162-71; Galveston *News*, 27 May 1894; and Hanna, pp. 203-6.
36. Benjamin to Mrs. Kruttschnitt, 20 Sept. 1865, copy in Pierce Butler Papers.

CHAPTER XVIII

1. Letter from Benjamin to Mrs. Kruttschnitt. Butler, op. cit. pp. 370-72.
2. Ibid.
3. Ibid.
4. Benjamin to Bayard. Copy in Pierce Butler Papers.
5. Benjamin to Bradford, 21 Feb. 1866. From original loaned by Paxton Blair of New York, a great-nephew of Benjamin.
6. From copy in Pierce Butler Papers.
7. Butler, op. cit. pp. 377-8.
8. Ibid. p. 377.
9. Benjamin to Bradford, op. cit.; also London *Daily Telegraph*, 10 Feb. 1883.
10. Butler, op. cit. p. 378.
11. Ibid.
12. In Bradford Papers at Avery Island, La. Letter of 25 Jan. 1880.
13. Benjamin to Bradford, op. cit.; articles on Brougham, St. Leonards, Palmer, and Cairns in *Dictionary of National Biography*.
14. London *Times*, 9 May 1884.
15. Edward Jones, *American Members of the Inns of Court*, London, 1924, p. xiii.
16. Information from Treasurer's Office, Lincoln's Inn. Also see note 5.
17. See note 5 and 'Charles Pollock' in *Dictionary of National Biography*.
18. Charles Pollock, 'Reminiscences of Judah Philip Benjamin' in *The Green Bag*, vol. I, No. 9, Sept. 1889.
19. Ibid.
20. Mason to his wife, 18 Jan. 1866. In Virginia Mason, *The Public Life and Diplomatic Correspondence of James M. Mason*, pp. 578-9.
21. Ibid.
22. Ibid.
23. Pollock article in Boston *Transcript*, 7 May 1898; Butler, op. cit. pp. 381-2.
24. Ibid.; Butler, op. cit. p. 382.
25. London *Times*, 9 May 1884, and information from Treasurer's Office, Lincoln's Inn; also see *The Law Journal*, Nov. 1932.
26. *The Law Journal*, Nov. 1932.
27. Charles Pollock, 'Reminiscences of Judah Philip Benjamin' in *Fortnightly Review*, vol. LXIX, pp. 354-61, Mar. 1898, and *The Green Bag*, vol. I, No. 9, Sept. 1889.
28. Benjamin to Mason, 25 Oct. 1866. In Library of Congress.
29. Recollections of Lord James of Hereford. In Lawley MSS.
30. *The Green Bag*, op. cit.
31. *American Law Review*, I, 1866-7, p. 220.
32. London *Times*, 2 July 1883.
33. *Law Reports Equity Cases*, III, pp. 724-36, 27 Feb. and 6 Mar. 1867; *Law Reports Chancery Appeal Cases*, II, 1866-7, pp. 582-95; London *Times*, 30 May, 3, 18 June 1867.
34. Benjamin to Mrs. Kruttschnitt, 11 Apr. 1867, in Butler, op. cit. pp. 388-9.
35. Data from Benjamin's fee book in Lawley MSS.
36. Butler, op. cit. p. 391-2.
37. Ibid. and preface to *Benjamin on Sales*.
38. London *Daily Telegraph*, 10 Feb. 1883.

39. *Law Reports Equity Cases*, VIII, pp. 69-77, and *Law Times*, 10 June 1939, p. 391.
40. Butler, op. cit. pp. 388-9.
41. Ibid. pp. 390-92. Letters from Benjamin to his sisters, 5, 18 June and 22 Feb. 1868.
42. Quoted in *Southern Historical Society Papers*, VI, pp. 183-7.
43. *New York Times*, 27 Sept. 1865.
44. John J. Craven, *The Prison Life of Jefferson Davis*, New York, 1866, pp. 155-6.
45. Benjamin to Bayard, 11 Nov. 1865, op. cit.
46. Benjamin to Mason, 25 Oct. 1866. In Library of Congress.
47. Ibid.
48. Benjamin to Mason, 29 May 1867. In Library of Congress.
49. Ibid.
50. L. T. Wigfall to Clement Clay, 7 Oct. 1866. Courtesy MS. Division, Duke University Library.
51. Among several stories of this type that have reached the writer was one told him by the late Charles Moore of the Library of Congress, who had it from an unidentified ex-Confederate.
52. Rowland, *Jefferson Davis, Constitutionalist*, VII, p. 182.
53. Alcée Fortier, *A History of Louisiana*, New York, 1904, IV, p. 56.
54. Benjamin to Mason, 29 May 1867. In Library of Congress.
55. Butler, op. cit. p. 391.
56. From diary of Mrs. Mary White Beckwith, Petersburg, Va., daughter of John White of Warrenton, N. C.
57. Rowland, op. cit. VII, pp. 246-51, and Robert McElroy, *Jefferson Davis*, New York, 1937, II, pp. 612-13.
58. Letter of 4 Nov. 1870 in Bradford Papers.

CHAPTER XIX

1. Benjamin to Bradford, 26 Aug. 1870.
2. Bradford Papers, letter of 30 Jan. 1871.
3. Ibid.
4. Benjamin to his sister, 15 Oct. 1871, in Butler, pp. 396-7.
5. Lawley MSS. Benjamin to Bayard, 7 Mar. 1871.
6. Baron Pollock in *The Green Bag*, op. cit., and *Fortnightly Review*, op. cit. Some changes have been made in the paragraphing. G. W. Wilton, *Judah Philip Benjamin*, Edinburgh, n.d., pamphlet.
7. Ibid.
8. Benjamin to Reverdy Johnson, 12 Nov. 1868.
9. Benjamin to Mrs. Levy, 8 Feb. 1870, in Butler, op. cit. pp. 394-5.
10. Benjamin to Bradford, 24 Dec. 1870.
11. Benjamin to Mason, 8 Feb. 1871. In MS. Division, Library of Congress.
12. *The Law Times*. 10 June 1939, p. 391.
13. Ibid.; also Benjamin to his sisters, 10 Aug. 1872, in Butler, op. cit. pp. 398-400.
14. Butler, op. cit. pp. 398-9. Letter to Benjamin's sisters, 10 Aug. 1872.
15. For example, the *London Law Review*, VII, 3 Aug. 1872, p. 387. See also Butler, op. cit. p. 400.

16. Benjamin to Miss Harriet Benjamin, 21 Feb. 1872, in Butler, op. cit. pp. 397-8.
17. Ibid.
18. Bradford Papers. Letter of 13 June 1872.
19. Ibid. Letter of 17 Aug. 1872.
20. Information from Mrs. Sidney Bradford, Avery Island, La.
21. Bradford Papers. Letter of 11 Dec. 1872.
22. Information from Mrs. Sidney Bradford; Bradford Papers; Butler, op. cit. p. 435.
23. Bradford Papers. Letter of 6 Aug. 1873.
24. Information from Mrs. Sidney Bradford.
25. Contemporary London Directories.
26. Numerous letters to friends written from the Junior Athenaeum Club. Also see Lawley MSS. Memo. by Benjamin's friend, J. G. Witt.
27. Bradford Papers. Letter of 23 July 1873.
28. Ibid. Letter of 22 Apr. 1873.
29. London *Times*, 9 May 1884; Wilton, *Judah Philip Benjamin*, op. cit.
30. Ibid.
31. *Daily Telegraph*, 10 Feb. 1883.
32. See Wilton, op. cit. for an anecdote about his knowledge of Spanish; also *Green Bag*, op. cit.
33. Ibid.
34. Ibid.
35. Ibid.
36. Ibid.
37. Bradford Papers. Letter of 22 Apr. 1873.
38. Witt Memo. Lawley MS.
39. Data from Benjamin's Fee Book. Lawley MSS.
40. Bradford Papers. Letter of 25 Feb. 1871.
41. Ibid. Letter of 6 Aug. 1873.
42. Ibid. Letter of 18 Aug. 1873.
43. Ibid. Letter of 24 Feb. 1874.
44. Benjamin's Fee Book, op. cit.
45. Benjamin to Mrs. Kruttschnitt, 9 Aug. and 24 Oct. 1874, in Butler, op. cit. p. 406.
46. Ibid.
47. Ibid.
48. Benjamin to a member of his family, 17 Mar. 1875, in Butler, op. cit. p. 407.
49. Ibid.
50. Ibid.
51. Bradford Papers. Letter of 16 May 1875.
52. Ibid.
53. For *Queen* v. *Keyn*, see contemporary issues of the London *Times*, esp. as cited in the text; Louis Gruss in *Louisiana Historical Quarterly*, Oct. 1936, pp. 1059-60; The Earl of Oxford and Asquith, *Memories and Reflections*, I, pp. 72-9.
54. Asquith, op. cit.
55. Benjamin to Conway Robinson, 13 July 1875. Courtesy Virginia Historical Society.
56. Benjamin to Mrs. Bradford, 21 Feb. 1875.

57. Interview by the writer of R. D. Bowen, Paris, Tex.
58. See article on Benjamin in London *Times*, 2 Jan. 1879.
59. Bradford Papers. Letter of 6 Sept. 1875 and another undated but during same period.
60. Interview by the writer of O. A. Duvernet, New Orleans, a friend of Joseph Benjamin. Also Lawley MSS., chap. 3, and data from Myron H. Schraud, American Vice Consul, Puerto Cortes, Honduras.
61. *Cincinnati Commercial*, 18 June 1876.
62. Ibid.
63. *Law Reports Appeal Cases*, vol. III, pt. I, 1877-8, pp. 34-57.
64. Ibid. pp. 106-14.
65. Ibid. pp. 133-48.
66. Ibid. pp. 148-58, and pp. 605-14.
67. Ibid. pp. 880-888.
68. Ibid. pp. 552-81.
69. Benjamin to Mrs. Kruttschnitt, 18 Mar. 1877, in Butler, op. cit. p. 408.
70. Fee Book, op. cit.
71. Benjamin to John Finney, 12 Mar. 1878. Courtesy of Robert Moore and Allison Owen, both of New Orleans.
72. Bradford Papers.
73. Letter of 14 Dec. 1877 in Butler, op. cit. pp. 436-7.
74. Butler, op. cit. p. 425. See also Benjamin to 'Walter,' 4 Nov. 1881 in Yale Library.
75. The data on this phase of the Benjamin's life in Paris is derived from Butler, op. cit. pp. 408-409 and 430-32 and a personal visit to the mansion 41 avenue d'Iéna.
76. Butler, op. cit. pp. 408 and 434-5, and various contemporary Benjamin letters in the Bradford Papers.
77. Memo. by Sir Campbell Clarke in Lawley MSS.
78. Memo. by Lord James of Hereford in Lawley MSS. Incidentally, Gen. Schenck was an authority on draw poker and published a book on the subject. See 'Robert Schenck' in *Dictionary of American Biography*.

CHAPTER XX

1. Quoted in Lynchburg *Virginian*, 30 Jan. 1879.
2. New Orleans *Democrat*, 10 Aug. 1879.
3. *Democrat*, op. cit.
4. Benjamin to Finney, 12 Mar. 1878.
5. See the correspondence between Benjamin and McCormick in Cyrus McCormick Papers at Chicago. Courtesy of Herbert Kellar and W. T. Hutchinson, both of Chicago.
6. Sir Edward George Clarke, *The Story of My Life*, New York, 1919, p. 271.
7. Ibid.
8. Bradford Papers. Letter of 5 Apr. 1880.
9. Ibid.
10. Photostat through courtesy of Paxton Blair, New York City.
11. L. Q. Washington in *Independent*, Sept. 1901.
12. Rowland, *Jefferson Davis, Constitutionalist*, VIII, pp. 356-7.
13. Lawley MSS.

14. *New York Tribune,* 20 Jan. 1882.
15. *Law Reports Appeal Cases,* VI, pp. 229-50. London *Times,* 11 Mar. 1881.
16. *Law Reports Appeal Cases,* VII, pp. 427-62.
17. Wilton, *Benjamin,* op. cit.
18. Ibid.
19. Ibid.
20. Ibid.
21. *Law Reports Appeal Cases,* VII, op. cit.
22. Wilton, *Benjamin,* op. cit.
23. Letter from Mrs. Mary Phelps Montgomery, Portland, Oregon, to the writer, 25 Feb. 1937.
24. Bradford Papers.
25. Butler, op. cit. p. 410.
26. Bradford Papers.
27. Ibid.
28. Gustavus Henry Wald, *Miscellany,* Cincinnati, 1906, pamphlet, pp. 35-44.
29. Memoranda by E. Russell Roberts and Richard Horton Smith in Lawley MSS. Also *Law Reports Appeal Cases,* VI, pp. 722-39.
30. Bradford Papers. Letter of 15 Dec. 1882.
31. Ibid.
32. *Law Reports Appeal Cases,* VIII, pp. 135-94.
33. Bradford Papers. Letter of 15 Dec. 1882.
34. Ibid.
35. *Democrat,* op. cit.
36. Bradford Papers. Letter of 22 Feb. 1883.
37. For example London *Times,* 9 and 10 Feb. 1883; *Telegraph,* 10 Feb. 1883; and *The Law Journal,* 24 Feb. 1883, p. 109. See also Butler, op. cit. pp. 412-13, letter to Mrs. Kruttschnitt of 12 Feb. 1883.
38. Butler, op. cit.
39. London *Times,* 9 and 10 Feb.
40. *Telegraph,* 10 Feb.
41. London *Times,* 2 June 1883; also see *The Law Journal,* 10 Mar. 1883 p. 148.
42. From 41 avenue d'Iéna, Paris, 2 Aug. 1883.
43. Butler, op. cit. p. 417.
44. 23 Apr. 1884. Lawley MSS.
45. Personal visit to the tomb in 1936. Photograph through courtesy of Mrs Judith Hyams Douglas, New Orleans.
46. Data from Judah P. Benjamin Memorial Association, New Orleans, which wrote the inscription for the marker. Benjamin's will, which disposed of an estate of some £60,000 personalty and the Paris mansion, is preserved at Somerset House, London. Dated 30 April 1883, the will left £10,000 to his American relatives and virtually all the remaining estate to his wife and daughter.

Select Bibliography

THIS IS NOT intended as a comprehensive Benjamin bibliography but only as a partial list of useful printed sources. For further references with bibliographical data, see Notes.

Contemporary law reports for Louisiana, the United States Supreme Court, and the English appellate courts.

Contemporary newspapers in New Orleans, Washington, Richmond, and London.

Adams, Ephraim Douglass, *Great Britain and the American Civil War*, New York, 1925.
American Historical Review.
Arthur, Stanley C., *Old New Orleans, a History of the Vieux Carré*, New Orleans, 1936.
Asbury, Herbert, *The French Quarter*, New York, 1936.
Bagg, Lyman H., *Four Years at Yale*, New Haven, 1871.
Basso, Hamilton, *Beauregard*, New York, 1933.
Brownlow, W. G., *Sketches of the Rise, Progress, and Decline of Secession*, Philadelphia, 1862.
Butler, Pierce, *Judah P. Benjamin*, Philadelphia, 1906.
Callahan, James Morton, *Diplomatic History of the Southern Confederacy*, Baltimore, 1901.
Caskey, W. M., *Secession and Restoration of Louisiana*, Baton Rouge, 1938.
Chesnut, Mrs. Mary Boykin, *A Diary from Dixie*, New York, 1905.
Clark, Thos. D., *A Pioneer Southern Railroad from New Orleans to Cairo*, Chapel Hill, 1936.
Clay-Clopton, Mrs. Virginia (Mrs. Clement Clay), *A Belle of the Fifties*, New York, 1905.
Craven, John J., *Prison Life of Jefferson Davis*, New York, 1866.
Cummings, Homer S. and McFarland, Carl, *Federal Justice*, New York, 1937.
Davis, Jefferson, *Rise and Fall of the Confederate Government*, New York, 1881.
——*Short History of the Confederate States*, New York, 1890.
Davis, Mrs. Varina, *Jefferson Davis*, New York, 1890.
De Leon, Thomas C., *Belles, Beaux and Brains of the 60's*, New York, 1909.
——*Four Years in Rebel Capitals*, Mobile, 1890.
Eckenrode, Hamilton J., *Jefferson Davis*, New York, 1923.
Evans, C. A., ed., *Confederate Military History*, 12 vols. Atlanta, 1899.
Foote, Henry S., *War of the Rebellion*, New York, 1866.

Freeman, Douglas S., *Lee's Lieutenants*, New York, 1942–.
— *R. E. Lee*, New York, 1934-1935.
Gayarré, Charles E. A., *History of Louisiana*, New Orleans, 1903.
Hanna, Alfred J., *Flight into Oblivion*, Richmond, 1938.
Harrison, Mrs. Burton, *Recollections, Grave and Gay*, New York, 1912.
Headley, John W., *Confederate Operations in Canada and New York*, New York, 1906.
Henderson, George F. R., *Stonewall Jackson and the American Civil War*, London, 1900.
Jones, J. B., *A Rebel War Clerk's Diary*, Philadelphia, 1866.
Johnson, R. U. and Buel, C. C., *Battles and Leaders of the Civil War*, New York, 1887-1888.
Johnston, Joseph E., *Narrative of Military Operations Directed During the Late War Between the States*, New York, 1874.
Journal of Southern History.
Kendall, John Smith, *History of New Orleans*, 3 vols., Chicago, 1922.
King, Grace E., *New Orleans*, New York, 1895.
Kingsley, William L., ed., *Yale College*, New York, 1879.
Lewis, W. D., ed., *Great American Lawyers*, Philadelphia, 1909.
Louisiana Historical Quarterly, esp. Oct. 1936, 'Judah P. Benjamin' by Louis Gruss.
McElroy, Robert, *Jefferson Davis*, New York, 1937.
Mason, Virginia, *The Public Life and Diplomatic Correspondence of James M. Mason*, New York, 1906.
Monypenny, William Flavelle, *The Life of Benjamin Disraeli*, New York, 1910-1920.
Moore, Frank, *The Rebellion Record*, 11 vols., New York, 1861-1868.
Official Records of the Union and Confederate Navies in the War of the Rebellion, 31 vols., Washington, 1894-1927.
Owsley, Frank L., *King Cotton Diplomacy*, Chicago, 1931.
— *States Rights in the Confederacy*, Chicago, 1925.
Pryor, Sara Agnes (Rice), *Reminiscences of Peace and War*, New York, 1905.
Publications of the American Jewish Historical Society.
Putzell, Edwin J., Jr., *Cui Bono*, unpublished manuscript for Tulane University.
Randall, James G., *The Civil War and Reconstruction*, Boston, 1937.
Reagan, John H., *Memoirs*, New York, 1906.
Rhodes, James Ford, *History of the Civil War*, New York, 1917.
— *History of the United States from the Compromise of 1850*, New York, 1896-1920.
Rightor, Edward, ed., *Standard History of New Orleans*, Chicago, 1900.
Robinson, William Morrison, Jr., *Justice in Grey*, Cambridge, Mass., 1941.
Roman, Alfred, *Military Operations of Gen. Beauregard in the War Between the States*, New York, 1884.
Rowland, Dunbar, ed., *Jefferson Davis, Constitutionalist*, 10 vols., Jackson, Miss., 1923.
Russell, William H., *My Diary North and South*, London, 1863.
Saxon, Lyle, *Fabulous New Orleans*, New York, 1928.
Sears, Louis Martin, *John Slidell*, Durham, N. C., 1925.
Shugg, Roger W., *Origin of Class Struggle in Louisiana*, University, La., 1939.
Southern Historical Papers.

Steele, Matthew F., *American Campaigns*, Washington, 1909.

Stokes, Anson Phelps, *Memorials of Eminent Yale Men*, New Haven, 1914.

Temple, Oliver P., *East Tennessee and the Civil War*, Cincinnati, 1899.

—— *Notable Men of Tennessee*, New York, 1912

Wallace, David Duncan, *The History of South Carolina*, New York, 1934.

War of the Rebellion, Official Records of the Union and Confederate Armies, 128 vols., Washington, 1880-1901.

Warren, Charles, *The Supreme Court in United States History*, Boston, 1922.

Wesley, Charles H., *The Collapse of the Confederacy*, Washington, 1937.

Willson, Beccles, *John Slidell and the Confederates in Paris*, New York, 1932.

Wise, John S., *The End of an Era*, Boston, 1927.

Index

Abbeville, S. C., 317, 318
Abolitionists, 14, 55, 102, 103, 148, 361-2
Adams, John Quincy, 101, 123
Addison, Joseph, 315
Address of Certain Southern Members of Congress to Our Constituents, 145-6
African slave trade, 266
Airley, Lord, 371
Alabama Case, the, 337, 347, 358
Alabama Secession Convention, 250
Albemarle Island, 97
American Conflict, by Greeley, 245
American Law Review, the, 335
American Union, the, by Spence, 265
Anderson, Joseph B., 313
Anderson, Major Robert J., 174
Antelope Case, the, 101
Antietam, battle of, 254
Arce, Mr., 130, 131
Argyll, Duke of, 141
Arista, President of Mexico, 74
Army of the Cumberland, 193
Ascamot, the, 17
Ashby's Harbor, 225
Asquith, Herbert, 360, 363
Atherton, C. G., 86
Atkinson, J., 375
Atlantic Monthly, 245
Autores Espagnoles, by Quevedo, 109

Bacon, Lord, 330
Bacon, D. Francis, 25
Badger, George E., 84
Baker, E. D., 150
Baker, James B., 246
Baker, Newton D., 180
Ball, Dyer, 20, 25, 26, 27
Ball's Bluff, 207

Baltimore, Md., 68, 69, 71
Baltimore Convention, 136
Banks, General N. P., 215, 267
Bannon, John, 296
Barings, the, 122
Barlow, S. L. M., 25, 26, 105, 370
Barron, James, 123
Barron, Forbes and Company 127
Bastrop Weekly Dispatch, the, 160
Bayard, James A., 25, 27, 108, 111, 164, 165, 327, 347
Bayard, Mrs. James A., 108, 116
Bayard, Thomas F., 25, 26, 101, 108, 139, 341, 379
Beaufort, S. C., 42, 43
Beauregard, General P. G. T., 88; at cabinet meeting, 315; fires on Sumpter, 167; quarrel with Benjamin, 200, 203-6, 276; received at Richmond, 174; rupture with Davis, 177, 180, 181, 184
Beecher, Henry Ward, 25
Belden, R. C., 10, 11
Bell, Senator John, 65, 108, 143
Bellechasse, 57, 58-9, 60, 61, 63, 89, 90, 120
Belmont, August, 113
Benjamin, Hannah, 10, 11
Benjamin, Harriet, 120, 273, 328
Benjamin, Jacob Levy, 11
Benjamin, Joseph, 120, 328, 362, 364
Benjamin, Judah P., ability as cross-examiner, 348-9; acting Secretary of War of Confederacy, 178-207; admitted to bar, 33; advocates economy in government, 99; ancestry, 3-4; as an administrator, 187, 200; as lawyer, 39-42, 44, 46, 189-90; as an orator, 54, 56-7, 93-5, 98, 100-104, 146-54, 157; as railroad pro-

Benjamin, Judah P. (Cont.)
moter, 38, 66, 71-5, 121-3; as state senator, 77; as sugar planter, 57, 59, 60, 61; as U. S. Senator, 78-155; Attorney-General of Confederacy, 161-78; birth, 6; builds Paris mansion, 364; called to English bar, 332; capacity for work, 276, 286-7; charges of corruption refuted, 279-81; childhood, 7 ff.; contemporary descriptions of, 3, 88-9, 117, 162, 170-72, 175, 176, 179-80, 187, 276, 331, 341, 344, 362-3; counsel to California land commissioner, 64; and Jefferson Davis, 115-17, 177, 195-6, 201, 238-9, 251, 294, 315, 340-41; death, 379; debates with Sumner, 93-5; declines nomination to Supreme Court, 84-5; declines post of Minister to Spain, 113-14; defends captured Negroes, 137-8; defends Taney, 114; Digest published, 37; dispatches to agents in Europe and foreign recognition of Confederacy, 247-50, 251-8, 293; earnings from law practice, 91, 354-5, 364, 367; education, early, 10-11, 18-19, at Yale, 20-30, 164; efforts to curb Irish volunteers, 296, 297; elected Bencher of Lincoln's Inn, 357; elected to Louisiana legislature, 46, 48; enters Lincoln's Inn, 330; enters politics as Whig, 43; failing health, 371, 376, 377; farewell speech in Senate, 152-4; flight from South, 318-23; and Franco-Prussian War, 346; guano concession, 96-8; Kansas question debate with Seward, 100-104; laments moral breakdown after war, 345; in London, 326 ff.; Louisiana Constitutional Convention of 1844-5, 50-55, of 1852, 80; love of literature, 109, 313-14; marriage, 33-6, 57-8, 123-6; on the Judicature Acts, 360-61; proposes seal for Confederacy, 270-71; on public education, 55-6; relations with Mexico, 295-6; religious attitude, 285; reorganizes Confederate financial setup in Europe, 292; retirement, 376; on secession, 139, 141-51; secret

service operations, 297-8, 299-305; Secretary of State of Confederacy, 235, 241; Secretary of War of Confederacy, 207-40; and slavery, 12-14, 62, 63, 92, 101-103, 156, 266, 306-308, 309-10, 328; speech at Petersburg, Va., 98; on temperance in army, 193, 231-2, 233
Benjamin, Judith, 11
Benjamin, Natalie, 34-36, 48, 57, 58, 60, 66, 77, 123, 124, 125, 126, 155, 212, 280, 326, 346, 347, 356, 357, 364, 375, 379
Benjamin, Ninette, 35, 58, 60, 77, 126, 212, 326, 346, 356, 357, 364, 375
Benjamin, Philip, 4, 5, 6, 7, 9, 10, 11, 12, 16, 17, 18, 89
Benjamin, Rebecca, see Levy, Mrs. Rebecca Benjamin
Benjamin, Rebecca de Mendes (Mrs. Philip Benjamin), 4, 5, 6, 7, 11, 12, 17, 18, 58-9
Benjamin, Solomon, 6, 10, 11, 362
Benjamin and Micou, firm of, 66
Benjamin on Sales, 337, 360
Benlissas, the, 5
Bennett, J. M., 217, 218
Bennett, James Gordon, 83
Berreyesa, 127
Beth Ahabah Synagogue, 285
Beth Elohim Synagogue, 17
Bevis Marks Synagogue, 5, 17
B. F. Butler in New Orleans, 245
Bimini Islands, 322, 323, 325
Bishopgate Within, 4
Black, Jeremiah, 111, 112, 126, 128, 131, 132, 133, 156
Black Republicans, 102, 108, 137, 165
Blackburn, Lord, 375
Blackburn on Sales, 337
Blackwater River, Ireland, 376
Bledsoe, Colonel A. T., 190
Blockade, The Law of, see Law of Blockade
Blockade of Confederacy, 185, 200, 259
Blonde, the, 322
Boardman, John D., 30
'Bonnie Blue Flag,' 243, 245
Boston Club, 82, 83, 107
Boswell, James, 109, 330

Bracebridge Hall, 15
Bradford, Edward A., 82, 84, 85, 91, 345, 346, 349, 351
Bradford, Willie, 351-2
Bragg, General Braxton, 184, 209, 254, 288, 292, 294
Bragg, Thomas, 152, 154, 207, 228, 231, 234
Bramwell, Baron, 360, 368
Bread riot in Richmond, 282-3
Breckinridge, General John C., 137, 141, 143, 235, 239, 317, 339, 343
Bright, Senator J. D., 105
British Essayists, 109
Brockenbrough residence, 177
Brodhead (Broadhead), Senator J. O., 108
Bromwell, William J., 246, 311
Brooks, W. M., 250
Brothers in Unity, 23
Brougham, Lord, 329
Brown, Senator A. G., 306
Brown, John, 135
Brown, Governor Joseph E., 197-8, 306
Browne, William M., 246
Brownlow, 'Parson' William G., 208, 210
Bruce, Gainsford, 349
Buchanan, James, 105, 112, 113, 120-22, 123, 130, 133, 151, 301
Bull Run, battle of, 176 (*see also* Manassas, battles of)
Bulwer-Lytton's novels, 109
Burnett, Senator, 235
Burnside, General Ambrose E., 225, 228
Butler, Senator Andrew Pickens, 91, 92, 107, 108
Butler, General B. F., 122, 274-5, 341
Butler, Pierce, 165
Byrd, William, II, 330

'Cab votes,' 47-8, 50
Cabildo, the, 44
Cairns, Sir Hugh, 329, 358, 360
Calhoun, John C., 20, 87
'Callan,' 186
Calliopean Society at Yale, 24, 28
Campbell, Lord, 326
Campbell, George, 344

Campbell, Judge John A., 163, 278, 288, 306
Campbell's *Negro Mania*, 109
Canby, General, 299
Canning, George, 330
Castro v. *the Queen*, 370
Cape Fear Recorder, 8
Cape Fear River, 7-9
Cape Hatteras, capture of, 198, 219, 220, 221
Capers, Henry, 279
Capston, Lieutenant J. L., 296
Caroline, Queen of England, 329
Carpetbag regime, 344, 345
Carroll, General W. H., 209
Cass, Lewis, 65, 86, 104, 121
Castillero, Captain Andres, 127, 129, 133
Catron, John, 65
Centreville, Va., 184
Chancellorsville, battle of, 214, 268
Charleston, S. C., 11, 12, 15, 16, 17, 18, 20, 27, 31, 89, 135
Charleston, Convention of 1860, 135
Charleston Courier, the, 15, 179, 187
Charleston Mercury, the, 150, 162, 163, 169, 184, 227, 288, 306
Charles Town, W. Va., 135
Charlotte, N. C., 174, 311, 316, 317
Chesnut, Mrs., *Diary*, 163-4
Chickamauga, Confederate victory at, 288
Christiansted, 5, 6
Churchill, Benjamin P., 303
Cincinnati, 105
Cincinnati Commercial, 149, 362
City of Glasgow Bank, 371
Claiborne, John Herbert, 212
Clara Bell, the, 182
Clark, Confederate Senator, 235
Clark, Senator from New Hampshire, 152
Clark, Rawlings, and Clark, 368
Clark, Governor Henry T., 198-9, 220, 221
Clarke, Sir Edward, 368
Clay, Clement C., 95, 115, 124, 298, 301, 302, 304, 342
Clay, Mrs. Clement C., 107, 124
Clay, Henry, 46, 51, 52, 87, 123
Clayton, J. M., 92

Cleveland, Mrs., 163
Clingman, Senator T. L., 135
Cobb, Howell, 123, 306
Cockburn, Chief Justice, 358, 360
Cocke, General W. H., 174
Coleridge, Chief Justice, 358
Commissary Department, 181-2, 190
Compromise of 1850, 87, 93
Confederacy, the, 161-7
Confederate Congress, 183, 188, 234-5, 308-9
Confederate Constitution, 164-5, 261
Congress, U. S., 33rd, 89, 92, 98; 34th, 98; 36th, 135
Congress of Paris, 170
Conner, H. W., 120
Conrad, Charles M., 50, 51, 191
Conrad, F. D., 40
Conrow of Arkansas, Representative, 232
Constitution of the United States, 93, 94, 95, 100, 142, 147, 150, 151, 173
Constitutional, the, 257
Contempt proceedings against Andrew Jackson, 68
Conway, Moncure, 362
Cooper, S. C., 205, 316
Cooper's Justinian, 102
Cooperationists, 142, 144
Corcoran, W. W., 105
Corresponding Society of Israelites, 17
'Cosmos,' 118
Cotton subsidy proposal, 253-6
Crawford, G. M., 293
Creole, the, 40-42, 62, 63
Crittenden, Colonel, 67
Crittenden, General G. B., 210
Crittenden, John J., 127, 134, 152
Crittenden Compromise, 152
Cuban filibuster trials, 66-7
Cuban question, the, 92, 93
Curry, Captain John, 320
Curry, J. L. M., 157

Dabney, Benjamin F., 24
Da Costas, the, 5
Dahlgren Raid, 341
Daily Telegraph, the London, 247, 328
Dallas, George M., 52, 123

Dallas, Mrs. George M., 65
Daniel, John M., 225
Danville, Va., 312-14
Danville Register, 313
Darwin, Charles, 97
Daughters of the Confederacy, 379
Davenport, Griffin, 191, 287
Davenport House, 191, 287
Davey, Mr., 374, 375
Davis, George, 8, 316, 317
Davis, Jefferson, advised by Benjamin, 344-5, 369; appoints Benjamin acting Secretary of War, 178, 179; appoints Benjamin Attorney-General, 161, 162; cabinet meetings, 166, 167, 170, 172; capture, 318; censured after loss of Roanoke Island, 227, 228; conference with Joe Johnston, Smith and Beauregard, 184; criticism of, 288, 305; dependence on Benjamin, 175, 195, 238-9, 244; determination to continue fighting, 315; determines course of war, 180, 181; difficulties with Joe Johnston, 201-6; and English attitude to blockade, 258, 259; estimate of Benjamin, 3, 44, 48, 134, 136, 138; estrangement of Beauregard, 204-6; feared serious war, 166; Gladstone's remarks on, 261; grants reprieve, 209, 210, 213; imprisoned at Fortress Monroe, 340-43; inaugurated President of 'permanent' government, 233; indicted by Federal grand jury, 343; makes emancipation offer to Europe, 309-10; near duel with Benjamin, 115-17, 139, 150, 155; opposes sending Lee into Pennsylvania, 275; plan to re-establish Confederacy west of Mississippi, 317; promotes Benjamin to Secretary of State, 235, 238; recommends arming of slaves and future emancipation, 306; reported rupture with Beauregard, 177; responsible for quarrel of Benjamin and Jackson, 216, 217, 220, 221; secret service operations, 297, 301, 305
Davis, Joseph, 233
Davis, Varina Howell (Mrs. Jefferson Davis), 88-9, 117, 125, 161-2, 169,

176, 195-6, 233, 234, 238, 249, 276, 277, 278, 285-6

Day, the Rev. Jeremiah, 21, 22, 29, 30

Debates in the Federal Convention, 146

De Bousignac, Captain Henri, 356-7

De Bow's Review, 61, 64, 109

de Castros, the, 5

Decatur, Stephen, 123

Decatur House, 123, 124

Defoe's *History of the Union*, 109

De Leon, Edwin, 263

De Leon, T. C., 162, 175

Della Torre, P., 128

Delta, the, 75, 78, 79, 119, 144, 145, 150, 160

de Marigny, Bernard, 51

de Mendes, Eva Levy (Mrs. Solomon de Mendes), 4

de Mendes, Rebecca, *see* Benjamin, Mrs. Rebecca de Mendes

de Mendes, Solomon, 4

Democrat, the New Orleans, 367

Democratic National Committee, 137

Democratic National Convention of 1856, 105

Democratic Party, 47, 51, 52, 55, 79, 96, 98, 99, 103, 104, 112, 136, 137, 141; Northern, 136, 300, 302; Southern, 137, 155, 300

de Morny, Duke, 293

Department of Justice, 168

de Polignac, Prince and Confederate general, 267, 268

de Rolleau, Abbé, 356

Desertion among Confederate troops, 288

Devil fishing, 43

Devonshire, Duke of, 375

Diary, Mrs. Chesnut's, 163-4

Diary, J. B. Jones's, 172, 175, 176, 177, 178

Digest of the Reported Decisions of the Superior Court, 37, 336

Disraeli, Benjamin, 3, 46, 88, 155, 258, 326, 331, 346, 372

Disraeli, Isaac, 17

Dortch, Senator, 235

Douglas, Stephen A., 86, 93, 105, 136, 137, 143, 151

Dowdell, Congressman, 108

Downs, General Solomon, 53, 54, 78

Dred Scott Decision, 101, 114, 136, 137

Dubose, Theodore, 24

Duelling, 49

Duncan, Blanton, 193, 251, 281

Duncan, Garnett, 84

Duncan, Stephen, 83

Duties of Human Life, 109

Dwight, the Rev. Timothy, 21

'Dykeland,' Amelia County, Va., 278

Earl of Zetland v. *Hislop and Others*, 370, 371

East Tennessee, 208-10

Ecuador, 97

Edinburgh Review, 15

Edward, Prince of Wales, 344

Emancipation, Benjamin on, 263-4; Confederate agent Spence and, 265, 266; immediate effect on Negroes, 328; meetings in England on, 265; problems arising from, 341-2

Emancipation Proclamation, 257, 265

Episcopal Church of the Advent, 141

Erie Canal, 72

Erlanger and Company, 269-70

Eustis, George, 83

Examiner, the Richmond, *see* *Richmond Examiner*

Exchange Alley, 47, 49

Exchange Hotel, 163, 166, 167

Exploration de l'Oregon by Mopras, 109

Ezra, Ibn, 3

Fallon, Bernard, 74

Fayetteville, N. C., 9, 10, 11, 12

Federal basis of representation, 80

Ferdinand of Aragon, 4

Ferguson, Sir James, 326

Fillmore, Millard, 65, 84, 85

Finality Period, 87

Finney, John, 91, 345

Fish, Senator Hamilton, 138

Fitch, Senator, 136

Fitzpatrick, Benjamin, 108

Fleischmann, Charles, 89

Foote, Henry S., 235, 305

Forsyth, John, 121

Fort Donelson, 229, 234

Fort Henry, 229, 234

Fort Sumter, 165, 167, 180
Fortress Monroe, 225, 306, 340
Fossat, 127, 128
Franconia Case, see Queen v. *Keyn*
Fraser and Company of Charleston, 195, 248
Fraser, Trenholm, and Company of Liverpool, 280, 336
Frazor, Edward, 297-8
Fredericksburg, battle of, 268
Fremantle, Lieutenant-Colonel, 271
Freeport Debate, 136
Free-Soilers, 100, 108
Frémont, John C., 106, 129

Gaines, General E. P., 115
Gaither, B. S., 227
Galapagos Islands, 97
Gambetta, 365
Gamble, Major Robert, 320
Garay grant, 75
Gardner, E., 186
Garnett, Brevet-Colonel, U.S.A., 65
Gasparilla Island, 321
Gayarré, Charles, 52
Georgina, H.R.M., 324
Gettysburg, battle of, 250, 264, 271, 275, 288, 292
Gibbes, William Hasell, 15
Giffard, Lord Justice, 332
Gipsy, the, 110
Gladstone, W. E., and Newcastle speech, 261, 327, 331
Glasgow, Ellen, 191
Goode, Representative, 107, 108
Goodman's Fields, 4
Gordon, John B., 278
Gordon, Martin, 268
Gorgas, Josiah, 190
Grafton, W. Va., 215
Grant, General U. S., 275, 284, 311
Gray, General Henry, 119
Greeley's *American Conflict*, 245
Green, Philip, 246
Greenhow, Mrs. Rose, 186
Grimes, General Bryan, 227
Grymes, John Randolph, 39, 52, 84
Guadeloupe Hidalgo, treaty of, 75

Hale, Senator J. P., 104
Hall, Judge, 68

Halleck, Mr., 133
Halmans, the, 5
Halyburton, Judge, 233
Hamilton, Alexander, 7
Hamilton College, 21
Hampton, General Wade, 278
Harding, Sir John, 293
Hardinge-Giffard, Sir, 359, 360
Hargous, P. A., 74, 121
Hargous Brothers, 122
Hartford, Conn., 20
Harpers Ferry, 216
Harrison, Burton, 316
Harrison, Constance Cary (Mrs. Burton Harrison), 278
Harvie, Lewis, 278
Hatherley, Lord (Page Wood), 332, 336, 350, 363
Hawley, Sir Joseph, 327
Haynes, Senator, 235
Headley, Lieutenant John W., 301, 303
Headley's *History*, 245
Heath, Justice, 376
Hebrew Orphan Society, 19
Hemphill, Senator, 152
Hemphill, Sergeant, 375
Henderson, Archibald, 24
Henderson, Senator John, 67
Hereford, Lord James, 334
Herschel, Sir Farral, 373
Hill, Colonel B. H., 299
Hines, Captain T. Henry, 303
Hodge, Colonel, 65
Hoge, Dr. Moses, 276, 279, 313, 314
Hoge, Mrs. Moses, 287
Holker, Sir John, 373
Hood's Division, 281-2
Horace, 109, 110, 313
Hotze, Henry, 245, 248, 260, 264-5
Houmas Indians, 118
Houmas land claims, 118
Houston, Sam, 86, 115
Hubard, R. O., 292
Huger, General Benjamin, 220-29
Hunt, Randall, 70, 78, 82, 119
Hunter, R. M. T., 86, 87, 115, 195, 231, 245, 246, 247, 306
Huntington, Walter, 82, 120
Huntington, Washington, 82, 120

Huse, Caleb, 189, 195
Hyams, Henry M., 31

Inglis v. *Buttery*, 363
Insurrection, attempted at Charleston, 12, 13
Intelligencer, see National Intelligencer
Irving, Washington, 15
Isabella of Castille, 4
Isthmus of Tehuantepec, 66, 73, 74, 121, 122
Iverson, Senator Alfred, 152
Izard, Captain, 34

Jackson, Andrew, 68
Jackson, Sir H., 374
Jackson, Mrs. Mary, 283
Jackson, General T. J. ('Stonewall'), 184, 213-218
Jackson, Louisiana, 50, 51
Jackson, Mississippi, 66, 71, 72
James, Sir Henry, 338, 378
James, G. P. R., 42
James River, 174, 273
Janin, Louis, 38-9
Japanese, first delegation of, 134-5
Jeane (Jeune) *Pierre*, the, 31
Jefferson, Thomas, 15, 68, 242
Jewish Advocate, 50
Jews, in Charleston, 15; in New Orleans, 49-50; in South Carolina, 162
Johnson, Senator, 152
Johnson, Andrew, 154-5, 208, 209, 341
Johnson, Ben, 330
Johnson, Henry, 52
Johnson, Herschel V., 214
Johnson, Reverdy, 70, 111, 126, 127, 132, 133, 134, 156, 158, 349
Johnson's Island, 299
Johnston, General Albert Sidney, 184, 211, 234
Johnston, J. M., 313, 314
Johnston, General Joseph E., 177, 184, 185, 190, 200, 201-2, 203-6, 212-13, 216-19, 235, 273, 276, 299, 315, 317
Johnston, William Preston, 246
Jonas, Senator, 372
Jones, J. B., 172, 175, 176, 177, 178, 183, 195, 200, 204, 250, 251, 282, 284

Jordan, Thomas, 196
Josephine, Empress, 7
Journal, the Wilmington, 162
Juarez, Benito, President of Mexico, 122, 255
Judah, Samuel, 111
Judicature Acts of 1873 and 1875, 360, 361
Judiciary Committee of Senate, 123
Justinian, 102

Kansas-Nebraska Bill, the, 93, 95, 96, 98-104
Kay, M., 338
Kelly, Baron, 358
Kelly, General, 215
Kelly, Sir Fitzroy, 332
Kenner, Duncan F., 78, 82, 191, 264, 298, 309
Kent, Chancellor, 50
Keyes, General E. D., 154
Keyes, Wade, 169, 179
Keyn, Ferdinand, 358, 360
King Cotton theory, 253
King Street, 12, 13, 14, 16
Knights of the Golden Circle, 300
Know-Nothing Party, 103, 119, 296
Kruttschnitt, Alma, 339
Kruttschnitt, Eugenia, 368-369
Kruttschnitt, John, 339
Kruttschnitt, Penina Benjamin (Mrs. John Kruttschnitt), 325, 339, 356, 363

La Grange, Ga., 274, 318
Lamar, L. Q. C., 174
Lambs Building, Middle Temple, 335
Landor's *Imaginary Conversations*, 109; *Pericles and Aspasia*, 109
Lane, R., 375
Lanneau, John, 24
Lanzas, Castillo, 130, 131
La Sère, Emile, 121
Latham, Senator, 128
Latrobe, Benjamin H., 123
Law of Blockade, the, 64, 259
Law of Sale of Personal Property, 337
Law Reports, Louisiana, 39
Law Reports Appeal Cases, 357, 363
Lawley, Francis, 271, 284, 285, 379

Lawton, General A. R., 207

Leavitt, Charles, designs plan for submarine, 199, 200

Lee, General Robert Edward, 183, 214, 229, 254, 273, 284, 285, 299, 305, 306, 311, 312, 314, 343

Lee, Stephen, 299

Lee, William Henry Fitzhugh ('Rooney'), 174

Legaré, Hugh, 15

'Legislature of a Thousand Drinks,' the, 128

Lesley, Major John, 320

Letcher, U. S. Minister to Mexico, 75

Letcher, Governor John, 217-18

Levy, Eva, see de Mendes, Mrs. Eva Levy

Levy, Jacob, 7, 8, 9, 10, 11

Levy, Leah, 76

Levy, Lionel, 120, 339

Levy, Mrs. Rebecca Benjamin, 6, 11, 12, 58, 120, 273, 274, 322, 328

Levy and Gomez, 7, 8

Lewis, Northern spy, 230

Lewis, Sir George Cornewall, 154

Library of Congress, 109

Lincoln Abraham, 35, 112, 136, 137, 141, 143, 165, 167, 265, 299, 300, 302, 305, 317, 340, 341

Lincoln's Inn, 327, 330, 336, 357

Linonian Society at Yale, 24

Livingston, Edward, 68, 123

London, 4, 5, 247, 258, 260, 326-78

London and County Banking Company v. Ratcliff, 374

London Daily News, the, 293

London Times, 3, 169, 247, 330, 340-41, 358, 359, 370, 375, 377

Long, Huey, 82

Lopez, Moses, 19, 20

Lopez, Narcisco, 66-7

Loring, General, 215, 216

Lossing's Pictorial History, 245

'Lost Colony,' the, 219

Louis Philippe, the, 57

Louisiana Constitutional Convention of 1844-5, 50

Louisiana Courier, 104

Louisiana Law Reports, 39

Louisiana railroads, 38

Louisiana Tehuantepec Company, see Tehuantepec Company

Lubbock, Colonel, 315

Lynch, Commander, 222, 223, 224

Lyons, Lord, 259

Macarthy, Harry, 242

Macaulay, Lord, 157, 330

Macdonald, Flora, 11

MacFarland, J. E., 342

Madison's Debates in the Federal Convention, 146

Magazine of Botany, by Paxton, 109

Magruder, General John B., 211

Mahone, William, 343

Mallory, Ruby, 278

Mallory, Stephen R., 92, 138, 161, 174, 231, 233, 240, 278, 288, 312, 315, 318

Mallory, Mrs. Stephen R., 278

Manassas, battles of, 183, 204, 214, 254, 261

Manatee River, Fla., 320

Manigault, Gabriel, 58

Mann, A. Dudley, 164, 263, 268, 297

Marshall, Colonel Charles, 229

Marshall, John, Chief Justice, 50, 98, 101

Marshall's Washington, 109

Marshfield, Mass., 75

Martin, Mr., 338

Martin, Colonel Robert, 301, 303, 304

Martin, Baron Samuel, 337

Martinique, island of, 63

Mason, James H., 107, 108, 115, 138, 241; Confederate diplomatic representative in England, 245, 247, 248, 257; efforts to secure English recognition, 258, 260; recalled, 293; unsuccessful interview with Palmerston, 310; 331, 333, 342, 343, 344, 349

Matriculs, 6

Maximilian, Emperor of Mexico, 295-6

Mayo, Mayor of Richmond, 283

Mazureau, Etienne, 38

McAllister, Judge, 129, 133

McCaleb, Theodore, 70

McCargo v. New Orleans Insurance Company, 40-42

McClellan, General George B., 183, 254, 272, 273, 302

McCormick, Dr., 65
McCormick, Cyrus, 367-8
McDonogh, John, 68, 69, 70
McFarland, Francis, 217, 218
McIver, the Reverend, Colin, 11
McKinley, John, 84
McLane, Minister to Mexico, 122
McLeod, H. A., 321, 323, 325
McNeil, Captain Archibald, 320
McRae, Colin J., 292, 342
Mechanics Institute, 191
Memminger, C. G., 15, 161, 169, 174, 231, 233, 240, 244
Mendes, see de Mendes
Mercier, Count Henri, 254
Mercury, the Charleston, see Charleston Mercury
Meredith, Minerva, 283
Metropolitan Hall, Richmond, 230, 243
Metternich, Prince, 14
Mexican archives, 129
Mexican War, 64, 88
Mexico City, 121, 130
Michigan, the, 303
Micou, B. H., 289
Micou, William C., 66, 85, 91
Missouri Compromise, 14, 24, 114
Mobile, Ala., 299
Moise, E. Warren, 298
Moltke, General H. von, 180
Monroe Doctrine, 296
Montgomery, J. B., 371
Montgomery, Ala., 161, 163, 167, 169-70, 173
Monticello, Miss., 72
Morgan, James Morris, 172
Mopras, Exploration de l'Oregon, 109
Moore, Governor, 144, 145
Moore, Frank, Rebellion Records, 245
Morny, see de Morny
Mouton, Governor Alexander, 48, 52
Murdoch et al. v. Executors of McDonogh et al., 68-71, 358
Murphy, Dennis, 157
Myers, Quartermaster-General A. C., 186, 281, 288

Nags Head, 220, 224
Napoleon I, 182, 214

Napoleon III, 77, 252, 255-7, 293, 296
Nashville, Tenn., 73, 234, 297
Nassau, 325
National Archives, 122
National Intelligencer, the, 92, 95, 100, 134
Native American Party, 103
Naval Board, 99
Navy, the U. S., 99
Nebraska Bill, see Kansas-Nebraska Bill
Negro Mania, by Campbell, 109
Negro soldiers, 266-7, 306
Negroes, 137-8; arming of, 289-90, 291, 305, 306; problem after emancipation, 341-2; slave auction in Montgomery, 169-70
Neill and Another v. the Duke of Devonshire, 375
Nelson, George E. W., 169
Nevis, island of, 4
New Almaden mining case, see United States v. Castillero
New Almaden quicksilver mine, 126, 127
Newbern Progress, the, 227
New Haven, Conn., 20, 23, 28, 30
New Haven Journal, 25
New Jersey Central, 354
New Orleans, 30-40, 42-4, 46, 47, 49, 51, 64, 66, 67, 69, 71, 72, 73, 76, 81, 83, 84, 88, 89, 91, 96, 97, 118, 119, 120, 121, 143, 159, 160, 234, 241, 272, 274, 339
New Orleans Argus, 31
New Orleans Bee, 142
New Orleans Delta, 25
New Orleans, Jackson, and Great Northern Railroad Company, 72, 73
New Orleans Whig Convention of 1851, 77
New York City, 304
New York Herald, 83
New York Independent, the, 25
New York News, the, 304
New York Times, the, 129, 133, 149, 341, 366-7
New York Tribune, the, 293
Nixon, J. W., 112

Norfolk, Va., 40, 220, 223, 224, 229
North, Simeon, 21, 22, 29
Northern anti-war Democrats, 299, 302
Northern Radicals, 339, 341, 342
Northern Whigs, 96
Northrop, Lucius B., 182, 184, 190, 288

O'Connor, Charles J., 25, 26, 134
'Ode on the Duke of Wellington,' 316
O'Hagan, Lord, 375
Ohio River shipping, 72
O'Neale, Peggy, 66, 124
Ordinance of Secession, the, 142
Ordnance Department, 190, 191
Orr, James, 108, 235
Orris, L. E., 298
Ostend Manifesto, 92
Overend, Gurney, and Company, 328, 343

Packwood, Samuel, 90
Packwood, Theodore, 57, 59, 60, 61
Palmer, the Rev. B. M., 143-4, 155
Palmer, Sir Roundell, 329, 337, 338
Palmerston, Lord, 310, 331, 367
Paloma of Toledo, 4
Panic of 1837, 38, 80
Paris, 326, 347, 368, 376-7, 379
Parliamentary Debates, 245
Parliamentary Papers, 109
Parrott, John, 133
Parton, B. F., *Butler in New Orleans*, 245
Patrie, the Paris, 257
Patterson, Judge, 209
Paul, George W., 246
Paxton's *Magazine of Botany*, 109
Peachy, Archibald, 126, 128, 129, 131
Pendleton, George H., 152
Peoria, Ill., 302
Perry, Commodore, 134
Perryville, 254
Petersburg, Virginia, 98
Petigru, James L., 15
Peyton, John L., 196
Philadelphia, the, 122, 134
Philadelphia Bulletin, 149
Philadelphia Convention of Know-Nothings, 103

Philencratian Society at Yale, 23
Phillimore, Sir P., 358, 359
Pictorial History, by Lossing, 245
Picayune, the, 48, 49, 63, 87, 119, 143, 146
Pickens, Colonel, 209
Pickett, John T., 295
Pierce, Senator, 65
Pierce, Franklin, 86, 87, 88, 105
Pigott, Edward, 293
Pillow, General Gideon, 234
Pitt, William, 330
Pius IX, Pope, 297
Placquemines Frauds, 51, 52
Platt, Senator, 107
Polk, James K., 51, 52, 55, 65, 123
Polk, Mrs. James K., 65
Pollock, Baron Charles, 330, 331, 332, 333, 348, 353, 358, 360
Pollock, Sir Frederick, 330, 331, 332
Pontalba, Madame de, 326
Popham, Mrs. Leah, 273, 274
Porcher, Frederick, 24, 306
Port Hudson, 267
Port Royal, S. C., 207
Porter, Samuel, 20, 27, 28
Porterfield, John, 303
Portland, Maine, 106
Potter, T. B., 293
Potter v. *Rankin*, 349
Presidential election of 1844, 51, 52
Preston, Senator William, 235, 295, 296
Pritchard, Jack, 13
Private Land Claims Committee, 115, 119, 123
Pugh, Senator George E., 108

Quarterly Review, London, 265
Quartermaster's Department, 186, 190
Queen v. *Keyn*, 358-60, 362
Quevedo's *Autores Espagnoles*, 109
Quin, James, 284
Quitman, General John A., 67, 68

Railroad development, 71
Raleigh, Sir Walter, 219
Raleigh Register, 227
Raleigh Standard, the, 227
Ramsey, J. C., 210

Randolph, Edmund, 126, 128, 129, 130, 131, 132, 134
Randolph, George Wythe, 235, 240, 242, 251
Randolph, John, 177
Reagan, John F., 161, 231, 233, 240, 275, 317, 318
Rebellion Records, edited by Frank Moore, 245
Rector, Governor H. M., 199
Red Republicans, 165
Reformed Society of Israelites, 17
Republican Party, 98, 100, 101, 103, 114, 152, 361
Rhett, Robert Barnwell, 150, 155
Rhett, Major Thomas G., 216
Rhode Island Case, 146
Rhodes, James Ford, 280
Richard the Third, 243
Richmond, Va., 136, 173, 174, 183, 191-2, 226, 230, 231, 244, 279, 281-5
Richmond and Danville Railroad, 278
Richmond Dispatch, the, 167, 230, 242
Richmond Enquirer, the, 266, 289, 292
Richmond Examiner, the, 174, 180, 181-2, 192, 200, 229, 231, 262, 279, 283
Richmond Sentinel, the, 292, 303-4, 305
Richmond Whig, the, 213, 243, 283
Rillieux, Norbert, 60-61
Rillieux process, the, of refining sugar, 60
Ritchie, 'Father,' 65
Roanoke Island, N. C., 219-29, 234
Robb, James, 71, 73, 77, 81, 84
Roberts, Russell, 374
Robinson, Conway, 361
Robinson, Solon, 90
Rochester, New York, 29
Roman, Governor A. B., 52
Romney, (W.) Va., 215, 217
Roon, Albrecht von, 180
Roselius, Christian, 39
Rosecrans, General W. S., 215
Rost, Pierre, 66, 164
Rothschilds, the, 113
Russell, Earl, 257, 258, 262, 293
Russell, William, 330
Russell, William H., 107, 169-70
Rutledge, Nicholas, 24

Saint Albans, Vermont, 303
Saint Cecilia Society, 15
Saint Croix, island of, 5, 6, 7, 109
Saint Joseph, the, 7
Saint Leonards, Lord, 329, 357
Saint Louis Hotel, 52
Saint Martin, Auguste Barthelmy, 34, 76
Saint Martin, Françoise Peire, 34
Saint Martin, Jules, 57-8, 169, 171, 191, 212, 272-3, 278, 286, 316, 362
Saint Thomas, island of, 5, 6, 7, 109, 325
San Francisco, 128, 130, 132, 133, 141
San Francisco Sun, 129
Sanders, Major, 248
Sandidge, J. W., 108, 113, 119
Santo Domingo, 12, 14, 63, 76, 92
Sassos, the, 5
Satterthwaite, F. B., 227
Schenck, General Robert, 365
Scotch emigrants at Fayetteville, 9, 10
Scott, General Winfield, 80
Scully, Northern spy, 230
Secession Movement, the, 139, 142-3, 144, 150, 152
Seddon, James A., 235, 288, 301, 308
Selborne, Lord Chancellor, 360, 374-5, 378
Semmes, Senator, 235, 278
Sempronius's speech, quoted, 315
Senate Judiciary Committee, 114
Sephardic Jews, 3, 4, 5, 7, 49, 87
Session Reports, the, 371
Sessions, Mrs., 120
Sessions, Coleman, 120
Seven Days' Battle, 254, 260, 261, 273
Seven Pines, battle of, 273
Seward, William H., 41, 100, 101, 102, 104, 241, 242, 295, 306
Sharpe's rifles, 101
Shelby, D. M., 165
Sheridan, General Philip H., 304
Sherman, General William Tecumseh, 144-5, 304, 305, 311, 317
Shorter, Mr., 108
Silliman, Benjamin, 21
Simms, William Gilmore, 18, 31
Slidell, John, 51, 52, 79, 83, 105, 106, 108, 112, 113, 117, 118, 119, 120, 122, 136, 145, 152, 154, 242, 245, 248, 249,

Slidell, John (Cont.)
253, 254, 255, 256-7, 269-70, 301, 310, 326, 342
Slidell, Rosine, 249
Slidell, Thomas, 37, 40
Smith, A. L., 370
Smith, General G. W., 184
Smith, General Kirby, 298-9
Smith, William, 232, 306
Societé Française de Bienfaisance, 34
Solomon, E. J., 49-50
Sonora, the, 142
'Sons of Liberty,' 300, 302
Soulé, Pierre, 52, 79, 82, 117-18, 278
Southern Whigs, 96
Southwestern Railroad Convention in New Orleans, 72, 73
Southworth, Rufus, 19
Spanish consulate in New Orleans, 67
Spanish Government, in Cuba, 66-7, 68
Spence, James, 265, 266, 289, 291
Spence, James, *The American Union*, 265
Spinoza, Baruch, 3
Spoils system, 99
Spottswood Hotel, 174, 176, 191
Spratt, Russell, 370
Stanard, Mrs. Robert C., 278
Stanton, Edward, 156
State Department, Confederate, 245, 246, 247, 249, 281, 292
States' Rights, 100, 150-51, 197
Steel v. *Houghton*, 376
Stephens, Alexander H., 214, 278, 306
Stewart, H. A., 186
Stone, Samuel, 28
Stoneman's Cavalry, 315, 316
Story of Disunion, by Jones, 172
Stowe, Harriet Beecher, 87
Stringer, Greenbury R., 33
Stuart, Captain, 324
Stuart, A. H. H., 95, 299-300
Submarine gunboat, 199, 200
Suffrage and office-holding, in La., 47, 48
Suffrage requirements, 80
Sugar industry, the, in La., 59, 60, 61
Sugden, Richard, 329
Sumner, Charles, 93-5, 107

Supreme Court, U. S., *see* United States Supreme Court
Tammany methods, 51
Taney, Roger B., 114
Taylor, Congressman, 108
Taylor, General Richard, 82, 186, 194, 202, 344, 352
Taylor, Zachary, 65, 82
Tehuantepec, Isthmus of, *see* Isthmus of Tehuantepec
Tehuantepec Company, 75, 79, 84, 121, 122
Tehuantepec Railroad, 113, 158
Telegraph, the London, 377
Tennyson, Alfred Lord, 313, 316, 327, 361
Territorial Waters Act, 360
Texas, 47, 55
Texas, the, 121
Thackeray, W. M., 330
Thompson, Jacob, 298, 301, 302, 303, 304
Thomson, Senator, 108
Thorn v. *Mayor and Commonalty of London,* 358
Tichborne case, the, *see Castro* v. *the Queen*
Times, the *New York, see New York Times*
Toombs, Robert, 115, 138, 155, 160, 161, 295
Total population basis of representation, 80, 81
Toucey, Isaac, 112
Transylvania College, 24
Treaty of Ghent, 31
Trenholm, George A., 315, 317
Trent Affair, the, 332
Tresca, Captain Fred, 320, 321, 322, 325
Tresca, Mrs. Fred, 321
True Delta, 113, 118, 119, 121
Truxtun Beale residence, *see* Decatur House
Turner, Lord Justice, 332
Tuyl, Baron, 123
Tybee, Island, Ga., 207
Tyler, John, 109

Uncle Tom's Cabin, 87, 102
Union Club of New York, 82, 164

Union League Club, 164
United States Commissioner of Patents, 89
United States Circuit Court of the Eastern District of Louisiana, 69
United States Land Commission, 127
United States Senate, 86
United States Supreme Court, 68, 70, 91, 101, 110, 111, 112, 114, 126, 134, 136, 156
United States v. *Castillero,* 65, 126-34, 139, 141, 358
United States v. *McRae,* 337
United States v. *Wagner,* 336
University of Georgia, 167
University of North Carolina, 120, 362
Urbina, President of Ecuador, 98

Vallandigham, Clement L., 302
Valley Campaign, 214-15
Van Buren, Martin, 123, 124
Vance, Zebulon, Governor of N. C., 198
Vaughn, Sir Charles, 123
Vesey, Denmark or Télémaque, leader of attempted slave insurrection, 12, 13, 14, 19
Vest, G. G., Senator, 157
Vicksburg, battle of, 250, 269, 271, 275
Villamil, General José, 97
Villard, Henry, 371
Vinton, Mr., associated in case with Benjamin, 111
Virgin Islands, *see* St. Croix and St. Thomas
Virginia Military Institute, 216
Volkman, C. W., 311

Wald, Gustavus, 372-3
Walker, Governor of La., 74, 77
Walker, L. P., 161, 165-6, 174, 175, 176, 177, 178, 179, 185, 186, 189, 190, 195
Walker, S., 375
Walker, Thomas, 293
War Department, Confederate, 161, 178-9, 191, 218, 222, 226, 230, 231, 245, 289
Ward, Maria, 177

Washington, George, 159
Washington, Lucius Quinton, 246, 260, 276, 301
Washington, D.C., 65, 86, 92, 98, 107, 108, 114, 115, 118, 120, 121, 123, 124, 125
Washington, by J. Marshall, 109
Washington Artillery, of New Orleans, 159, 160
Washington Union, 65, 104
Watson, Lord, 370, 375
Watts, F. H., Judge, 241
W. D. Brewer and Company, 280
Webster, Daniel, 39, 46, 75, 87, 96, 146, 156, 176
Webster, Timothy, 230
Weed, Thurlow, 140, 293
Weill, Abram, 316
Weller, Senator, 108
Wellington, Duke of, 331
Wenlock, Lord, 284
Westminster (Review), 109
Whig, the Knoxville, 210
Whig Convention of 1851, *see* New Orleans Whig Convention of 1851
Whig Party, 43, 46, 47, 48, 49, 50, 51, 52, 77, 78, 79, 80, 81, 82, 98, 101, 103, 104
White, Governor of La., 52
White, Philo, 97
Wickens, Mr., 337
Wickliffe, 'Duke,' 109
Wigfall, Senator L. T., 152, 174, 203, 306, 342
Will of John McDonogh, 68-70
Wilmington, N. C., 7, 8, 12
Wilmot Proviso, 114
Winchester, Judge, 65
Winchester, Va., 215, 216
Winder, General, 251
Wise, Henry A., 105, 157-8, 174, 207, 220-29, 343
Wise, Captain Henry Augustus, 341
Wise, John S., 223
Wise, Captain O. Jennings, 225, 226, 229
Witt, John George, 354
Wood, Colonel John Taylor, 318
Wood, Page, *see* Hatherley, Lord
Wood, Colonel W. B., 209

World's End, islands, 97
Worsham's faro bank, 279
Wright, Mrs. Harriet, 9

Yale College, 20-30
Yancey, William L., 150, 155, 164, 263

Yellow fever epidemics, 33
Yorktown, Siege of, 272
Young, Lord Advocate, 370
Yulee, David Levy, 87, 108, 109, 125, 162
Yulee, Mrs. David Levy, 109, 125